Land Records of Sussex County Delaware

1789-1792

Judith K. Ardine

Colonial Roots
Lewes, Delaware
2011

Colonial Roots
17296 Coastal Highway
Lewes, Delaware 19958
1-800-576-8608

Reprinted 2011

Printed in the United States of America

CONTENTS

INTRODUCTION

Few records of the Swedish Colony (1638-1655) have survived. From 1655 to 1664 and from 1673 to 1674, the Dutch West India Company and the City of Amsterdam were proprietors of the land which became Delaware (ignoring claims by the Calverts of Maryland). The surviving records are held by the Archives of New York at Albany.

The Duke of York was proprietor from 1664 to 1673 and from 1674 to 1682. These land records are also held at Albany. *Original Land Titles in Delaware, commonly known as The Duke of York Records, 1646-1679*, was printed by order of the General Assembly of the State of Delaware (1899), reprinted by Family Line Publications in 1989 and later by Colonial Roots.

The southern most portions of Sussex County were once treated as part of Somerset County, Maryland. Somerset County was created in 1666 with the Atlantic Ocean and Chesapeake Bay its eastern and western boundaries, and its northern boundary - which today lies well inside Sussex County, Delaware - the Nanticoke River. Worcester County, Maryland, was formed out of Somerset in 1742; at that time the northern boundary of Worcester was set at "Broad Creek Bridge," the present location of the town of Laurel, Delaware. In 1769 the new line, established by Charles Mason and Jeremiah Dixon, was officially accepted. Prior to 1769 all records of the resident of land south of the Nanticoke and Indian Rivers should be sought in Maryland record books. When in doubt check records in both states.

The records abstracted in this book are found in Liber (Book) O-14 and cover the period, 1789-1792. At the beginning of each entry in parentheses is the Liber followed by the original page number.

F. Edward Wright
Lewes, Delaware
2002

ABBREVIATIONS

ack - acknowledged
Admin - Administration or Administrator
Adm'x - Administratrix (female administrator)
afsd - aforesaid
apptd - appointed
Apr - April
Atty - Attorney
Aug - August
cnty - county
ct - court
d - died or day
Dec - December
dec'd - deceased
dtd - dated
dtr(s) - daughter(s)
e - east
Esq - Esquire
et al - and others
Exec(s) Executor(s)
Exec'x - Executrix (female executor)
Feb - February
ft - feet
Jan - January
JP - Justice of the Peace
Jul - July
Jun - June
m - month
Mar - March
md - married
mthr - mother
n - north
Nov - November
Oct - October
p - pence
Proth'y - Prothonotary (The title given (in this case Delaware) to an officer who officiates as principal clerk of the court.
Rec - recorded
rec'd - received
Reg - Register
s - shilling(s) or south
sd - said
Sep - September
w - west
wit - Witnesses
w/ - with
w/o - without

Standard Postal Abbreviations

SUSSEX COUNTY, DELAWARE LAND RECORDS

Liber O-14
1789 - 1792

NOTE: Pages 1 and 2 are missing.

O-14:1. (From the Grantee Index). Thos WHARTON, Administrator for dec'd, to Richard BLOXOM

O-14:2-3. Incomplete document. John JESSOPS was indebted to Francis JOHNSON & sd JOHNSON obtained a judgement against sd JESSOPS. Thomas EVANS, present Sheriff of Sussex cnty, DE for the sum of £5 paid to Peter Fretwell WRIGHT, then Sheriff, by sd Francis JOHNSON hath sold unto sd JOHNSON the 2 parcels of land, he being the highest bidder. Signed: Thomas EVANS, Sheriff. Wit: John INGRAM, Nathaniel HICKMAN. Ack: 04 Feb 1789. Nath'l MITCHELL, Proth'y.

O-14:4. Deed of Gift. This Indenture made 19 Jan 1789 between Mary TURNER of Sussex cnty, DE, widow, of the one part & John TAM & Joseph TAM of sd cnty & state, yeomen, of the other part. Mary TURNER had surveyed about 28 Mar 1754 (by William SHANKLAND, the Surveyor for sd cnty) 200 acres of land in Broadkill forest, cnty afsd. Sd survey afterward confirmed to her by a Proprietary Warrant, she being seized of sd surveyed tract. Mary TURNER in consideration of the natural love & affection she hath for John TAM & Joseph TAM her nephews & for the sum of 5s current money of DE to her paid by sd John & Joseph grants to sd John TAM & Joseph TAM, their heirs et al the 200 acres of land & premises in two equal parts to be divided between them, except, the use thereof of Mary TURNER during her natural life. Sd 200 acres is bounded by lands of George DUTTON, Thomas REYNOLDS, Manlove VIRDAN, Daniel JESTER & Zachariah REED. Mary TURNER authorizes John CLOWES, Esq. to acknowledge this Deed in open Court for her. Signed: Mary TURNER (mark). Wit: Pettijohn DODD, Rhoads SHOCKLEY. Executed -4 Feb 1789 by oath of Rhoads SHOCKLEY & Acknowledged by John CLOWES, Esq, Atty. Rec: 12 Feb 1789 Nath'l MITCHELL, Proth'y.

O-14:5. Deed. 02 Feb 1789 William BLACK of Kent cnty, DE. blacksmith, & Sarah his wife of the one part for the sum of £125 lawful money of DE paid by Nathaniel STOCKLEY of Cedar Creek & Slaughter Neck Hundred, Sussex cnty, DE, blacksmith, of the other part have sold to sd STOCKLEY, his heirs, et al; all that messuage, plantation & tract of land situate in Slaughter Neck containing 100 & 1/2 acres more or less being part of a tract of land of 357 acres formerly possessed by John BOWMAN in his lifetime who d: & Sheriff of the cnty at the Suit of Benjamin CHERO, Esq against Mary BOWMAN as Exec of John BOWMAN & sold to Mary BOWMAN by sd Sheriff by Indenture. Mary BOWMAN on 06 Sep 1763 sold to Richard SHOCKLEY 150 acres by Deed. Richard SHOCKLEY sold sd 150 acres to Mitchell BLACK. Mitchell BLACK, father of William BLACK, afterwards d: intestate leaving sundry children to whom the sd land w/his other lands descended 31 Mar 1786 Orphans Court ordered 5 Freeholders to make division who did same & allotted the above 100 & ½ acres to William BLACK as his full part. William BLACK & Sarah, his wife, grant sd messuage, plantation & land to Nathaniel STOCKLEY, his heirs, et al. William BLACK & Sarah, his wife, appoint John CLOWES of Sussex cnty, Esq to be their Attorney to deliver this Indenture in Open Court. Signed: William BLACK (mark), Sarah BLACK (mark). Wit: Mills RICKARDS, Mary CLOWES. Rec'd of Nathaniel STOCKLEY the sum of £125 above mentioned. John CLOWES certifies he examined Sarah CLARK being of full age separate from her husband, she saying the above Deed was of her own free will w/o compulsion. Signed: 02 Feb 1789 John CLOWES. Rec: 19 Feb 1789 Nath'l MITCHELL, Proth'y.

O-14:6. Deed. This Indenture made 24 Nov 1788 between Reece WOOLF Jr of Monongohale cnty, VA, bricklayer, & Sarah, his wife, of the one part & John WOOLF of Lewes & Rehoboth Hundred in Sussex cnty, DE, cordwainer, of the other part. There is a parcel of land containing lotts of one acre being 1/4 part of a four acre lott situate in Lewes town bounded on the NW by Shipscarpenter Street, on the SE by Mulberry street originally granted by the Court 06 Sep 1693 to Capt Thomas PEMBERTON who d: seized thereof Intestate leaving 2 dtrs, Elizabeth & Mary, to whom the 4 acres descended. Elizabeth afterwards md: Daniel BROWN & Mary md: Thomas CARLISLE. Sd Daniel & Elizabeth BROWN & Thomas & Mary CARLISLE by Robert SHANKLAND, their Attorney, by Deed of Sale conveyed sd lotts to Jonathan HENRY who afterwards d: seized thereof Intestate leaving issue, William, his only son, & 2 dtrs, Sarah & Elizabeth to whom the 4 lotts descended. Sarah afterwards md: Benjamin STOCKLEY who by Deed conveyed their right (being the ¼ part thereof) to William HENRY whereupon sd William & Elizabeth became seized of the whole., William of 3/4 part & Elizabeth of 1/4 part. Elizabeth md: John MAXWELL of Sussex cnty, barber whom she survived. Elizabeth MAXWELL & William HENRY by their Deed of Release dtd 25 Apr 1768 conveyed sd lotts to Daniel NUNEZ Jr of Lewes town, Sussex cnty, DE bounded on the NW side of Mulberry street, on the NE side the property of Daniel HOUSEMAN, on the SE side of Shipscarpenter Street & on the SW side of

William HENRY's part. Jonathan HENRY d: seized. Daniel NUNEZ Jr seized of the one acre made his last will & testament dtd 09 May 1772 wherein he devised to Sarah PRETTYMAN, dtr of William & Comfort PRETTYMAN after the death of his wife the house & lott whereon Charles ELBERT now lives. Sarah PRETTYMAN md: Reece WOOLF Jr, both parties hereto. Hannah NUNEZ, late wife of sd Daniel by her Deed of Release dtd 15 Feb 1785 granted her right to the lott to Reece WOOLF Jr & Sarah his wife, in right to sd Sarah. Reece WOOLF Jr & Sarah his wife by their Deed of Sale dtd 09 Feb 1788 sold the sd 4 lotts or one acre of land. There is some doubt since the making of the sd Deed whether Sarah at time of executing same was of age 21 years. Wherefore it is thought expedient Reece & Sarah make another Deed to John WOOLF, Sarah now having attained to full age. Reece WOOLF Jr & Sarah his wife, for the sum of £70 lawful money of DE paid by John WOOLF sold sd WOOLF all 4 lotts or one acre of land as above. Signed: Reece WOOLF Jr, Sarah WOOLF. Wit: Sam'l HANAWAY, Robert HOOD, Benjamin JENNINGS. On 34 Mar 1788 Reece WOLF Jr & Sarah his wife before JP of Monongalia cnty, Commonwealth of VA acknowledged above instrument to be their act. Signed: Sam'l HANAWAY. I certify Samuel HANWAY was & is an acting JP in sd cnty. 24 Nov 1788. Signed: John EVANS, Clk of Monongalia Cnty Court. Ack: 04 Feb 1789 Nath'l MITCHELL, Proth'y.

O-14:8. Deed. This Indenture made 13 Dec 1788 between Joshua FISHER & wife of Sussex cnty, DE, yeoman, of the one part & John WOOLF of same cnty, cordwinder, of the other part. There is a tract of land situate in Lewes & Rehoboth Hundred in Sussex cnty being part of a larger tract whereon Joshua FISHER now lives bounded by land John WOOLF bought of Thomas FISHER Jr, the 112 acre tract sd Joshua FISHER, line of Samuel ROWLAND containing 8 acres of land. Joshua FISHER for the sum of £24 to him paid by John WOOLF hath sold sd 8 acres to sd WOOLF. Signed: Joshua FISHER, Nancy FISHER. Wit: Jno WILTBANK, Jno WHITE Jr. Nancy FISHER, wife of Joshua, being of full age did acknowledge she became a party to sd Deed of her own free will. 13 Dec 1788. Signed: Jno WILTBANK. Ack: 04 Feb 1789 Nath'l MITCHEL, Proth'y.

O-14:9. Deed. 22 Mar 1788 Jonathan CALLAWAY of the one part, planter of Henry cnty, VA for the sum of £80 lawful money of DE sold to Samuel HEARN, son of Benjamin, of Sussex cnty, DE of the other part a tract of land called Buck Ridge containing 50 acres. Jonathan CALLAWAY appoints Isaac HENRY & Elijah CANNON his lawful Attorney to acknowledge this Deed. Signed: Jonathan CALLAWAY (mark). Wit: Samuel HALL, James CANNON. Ack 04 Feb 1789 Nath'l MITCHELL, Proth'y.

O-14:10. Deed. 11 Jul 1788 John McGEE Sr of Sussex cnty, DE of the one part for the sum of £50 sold to William LON Sr of the same place of the other part two tracts of land called Stepny & Parish which Thomas WALLER Deeded to his son John WALLER dtd 10 Jan 1763 & also the same land John WALLER Deeded to Robert PITT in 1768 containing 52 acres. John McGEE appoints Isaac HENRY & Elijah CANNON Sr my Attorney to acknowledge this Deed for me. Signed: John McGEE. Wit: Caleb BALDING, Sam'l HEARN. Ack: 04 Feb 1789 Nath'l MITCHELL, Proth'y.

O-14:11. Deed of Mortgage. Joseph HALL for use of Lydia HALL from Stephen COSTON. This Indenture made 06 Feb 1789 Stephen COSTON of Broadkiln Hundred in Sussex cnty, yeoman, of the one part & Joseph HALL of Lewes town, Sussex cnty, practioner of physics, of the other. Stephen COSTON is seized of 1/3 part in three parts to be divided of a tract of land situate in Broadkiln Hundred, cnty afsd, bounded by land formerly belonging to Jacob PHILLIPS, dec'd, & the original tract of land called Finch Hall containing 275 acres & a tract of land situate in the Hundred afsd containing 81 & 1/2 acres purchased by Stephen COSTON from Nehemiah REED. Stephen COSTON stands bound to Joseph HALL for the sum of £176 15s conditioned for payment of £88 7s 6p on or before 06 Feb 1791 w/interest for same. Stephen COSTON to secure repayment of sd sum & interest to Joseph HALL & for further sum of 5s by Joseph HALL to Stephen COSTON sd COSTON doth grant to Joseph HALL the sd tracts of land & premises called Finch Hall & the other. If sd COSTON pay sd HALL the sum of £88 7s 6p on 06 Feb 1791 w/interest shall become void. Signed: Stephen COSTON. Wit: Robert SHANKLAND, D HALL. Ack: 06 Feb 1789 Nath'l MITCHELL, Proth'y.

O-14:12 Deed. This Indenture made 06 Feb 1789 between Henry NEILL, Esq & Mary his wife of Lewes town, Sussex cnty, DE of the one part & Walter HUDSON of afsd cnty & state, of the other part. Josiah MARTIN of cnty afsd by Deed dtd 15 Oct 1765 sold to John LITTLE of sd cnty, merchant, a tract of land in Sussex cnty. Joseph HAZZARD of Sussex cnty by Deed dtd 10 Jan 1769 sold to John LITTLE of sd cnty a tract of land in sd cnty. Nicholas LITTLE, son & Exec of afsd John LITTLE, dec'd, & Hester his wife, of Sussex cnty by Deed dtd 10 Feb 1785 sold to Walter HUDSON of sd cnty, blacksmith, a parcel of land, part of the two first cited Deeds, situate in Angola Hundred, sd cnty, beginning at a corner of Jonathan STEPHENSON's land, bounded by the County road, land belonging to heirs of William ALLEN, Bundox's Bridge, containing sixty two acres. Henry NIELL obtained judgement against Nicholas LITTLE, Exec of last will & testament of John LITTLE, dec'd for the sum of £487 & half penny. Peter Fretwell WRIGHT, Esq, High Sheriff of Sussex cnty executed sd judgement by taking the tract of land situate on the S side of Bundox Branch together w/as much land on the N side of Bundox Branch as made up 550 acres & sold same to Henry NIELL for £620 for which sd Sheriff made Deed to Henry NIELL dtd 05 Sep 1787 as rec: in Sussex cnty Rolls Office Lib N 13, Folio 441. Henry NIELL & Hester his wife by their Deed of Sale to Walter HUDSON rec: in Lib N 13, Folio 116 sold a tract, part of the land situate on the S side of Bundox Branch bounded by land of Jonathan STEPHENSON, the County Road, land belonging to heirs of William ALLEN, dec'd, & Bundox Bridge containing 62 acres. Signed: Henry NIELL, Mary NEILL. Wit: Peter F WRIGHT, Sam'l PAYNTER Jr. Mary NIELL, wife of Henry NIELL came before me, one of the JPs of Ct of Common Pleas, & was privately apart from her husband examined & she declared she was a party to the above Deed of her own free will. 06 Feb 1789 Signed: Peter F WRIGHT. Ack: 12 Feb 1789 Nath'l MITCHELL, Proth'y.

O-14:13. Deed. Eunice JESSOP of Sussex cnty, DE, widow of John JESSOP, late of sd cnty states her sd husband was seized in his lifetime of lands & tenements in Northwest Fork Hundred of sd cnty & d: Intestate 31 Oct 1785. Admin of the estate was granted to sd Eunice JESSOP 05 Jan 1786. 08 Feb 1787 Eunice JESSOP preferred a Petition stating the personal estate of sd John JESSOP was insufficient to discharge his just debts & asked the Ct to empower her to sell as much real estate as needed to discharge sd estate debts. Such order was granted. 05 Mar last part of a tract of land situate in Northwest Fork Hundred called Bridge Branch which sd land Patrick BRAUGHAM by his Deed dtd 30 Aug 1779 conveyed to afsd John JESSOP & Eleanor his wife found by a late survey to contain 5 & 1/4 acre & a piece of joining land being part of a tract called Jessop's Meadow containing 2 & 3/4 acres, sd 2 pieces containing 8 acres more or less, were sold at public sale to Daniel POLK, Esq for the sum of £116, he being the highest bidder. Eunice JESSOP appoints trusty friends John RODNEY & Phillips KOLLOCK of Lewes town, gentlemen, 15 Feb 1788. Signed: Eunice JESSOP (mark). Wit: John LAWS, Gillis HITCH, Tristen S POLK. Ack: 03 Mar 1789 Tristen Saul POLK, Phillips KOLLOCK, Esq. Rec: 09 Feb 1789 Nath'l MITCHELL, Proth'y.

O-14:15. Deed. 25 Dec 1788 Isaac WILLIAMS of Caroline cnty, MD, gent, of the one part & Daniel POLK of Sussex cnty, DE, Esq, of the other part. For the sum of £100 money of DE to Isaac WILLIAMS paid by Daniel POLK sd WILLIAMS sold to sd POLK a tract of land called Brotherly Love containing 10 acres more or less, also part of a tract called Biter Bitt situate in Sussex cnty, DE in Northwest Fork Hundred running w/the Patten Round containing 109 acres. Isaac WILLIAMS appoints John RODNEY, Phillips KOLLOCK & William HARRISON of Lewes as his lawful Attorney to deliver this Deed. Signed: Isaac WILLIAMS. Wit: Tristen

Saul POLK, Mary POLK. Ack: Phillips KOLLOCK, Esq. Rec: 09 Mar 1789 Nath'l MITCHELL, Proth'y.

O-14:16. Deed. This Indenture made 04 Mar 1789 between Thomas EVANS, Esq, High Sheriff of Sussex cnty, DE of the one part & Daniel POLK of same place, farmer, of the other part. Willington HITCH of same place was seized of lands situate in Northwest Fork Hundred in afsd cnty & being considerably indebted to sundry persons by writ of the Ct of Common Pleas at Lewes town of Sussex cnty dtd 07 May 1787 directed to Peter Fretwell WRIGHT, Sheriff, ordered the goods, chattels, lands & tenements of Willenton HITCH & a debt of £58 16s 6p which Daniel ROGERS lately in our cnty Ct of Common Pleas before our JPs recovered against him, also 44s 7p which Daniel ROGERS in sd Ct was adjudged for his damages as well as by the detention of that debt for his costs & charges expended by him on that behalf whereof afsd Whittenton HITCH is convicted & you shall have that money before our Justices at Lewes Ct of Common Pleas on Wednesday after 1st Monday in Aug unto sd Daniel ROGERS in satisfaction for his debt & damages afsd. For want of goods & chattels sufficient belonging to sd Defendant he had seized in Execution all the tracts of land belonging to sd Defendant situate in Northwest Fork Hundred in cnty afsd called Davises Illusage & Davises Delight both containing 50 acres more or less which sd lands he had appraised by 2 judicious & substantial Freeholders of his Bailiwick who found the rents, issues & profits w/the premises & appurtenances thereunto was of a clear yearly value sufficient w/in 7 years to satisfy the debts & damages. By a writ issued 07 Nov 1787 directed to Peter Fretwell WRIGHT by which he was seized (?) of the goods, chattels & lands of sd HITCH. He should cause to be levied a debt of £400 continental money which John LAWS Sr recovered against him, also 44s 7p sd John LAWS Sr was adjudged for damages whereof Willenton HITCH is convicted on the Wednesday after the 1st Monday of February st which day sd Peter Fretwell WRIGHT did return 2 tracts of land situate afsd called by names afsd containing 50 acres were not sufficient to satisfy afsd debts & damages & that same remains in his hand for want of buyers. By writ of V E issued 07 May 1788 to sd Peter Fretwell WRIGHT was commanded & taken by him in Execution remaining unsold he should put to sale & have the money to the Ct the 1st Wednesday after the 1st Monday in Aug next. He so did. Same were purchased by afsd Daniel ROGERS for the use of above named Daniel POLK, Esq 27 Jun past for the sum of £55 6s, he being the highest bidder. Whereas sd Peter Fretwell WRIGHT was removed from office before he made a Deed. Thomas EVANS, Sheriff, for the sum of £55 6s pd to afsd Peter F WRIGHT by sd Daniel POLK doth discharge sd Daniel POLK, his heirs, et al & have granted unto sd Daniel POLK the lands & premises afsd containing 50 acres more or less & containing 20 acres more or less & also all the right, title, interest, etc. of sd Willenton HITCH. Signed: Thomas EVANS, Sheriff. Wit: Mark DAVIS, William HINDS. Ack: 04 Mar 1789. Rec: 09 Mar 1789. Nath'l MITCHELL, Proth'y.

O-14:18. Deed. This Indenture made 25 February 1789 between Nathan SPENCER of Sussex cnty, DE, yeoman, of the one part & William BLOXOM of sd cnty & state, yeoman, of the other part. A tract of land in Broadkiln Hundred in Sussex cnty containing 199 acres was by Proprietor's Warrant dtd at Philadelphia 16 Apr 1748 granted to John FLEETWOOD was surveyed 14 Feb 1749 by William SHANKLAND, Deputy Surveyor, & sd John FLEETWOOD by Deed dtd 07 Feb 1756 conveyed to Ezreal SPENCER. Sd Ezreal SPENCER by his Deed dtd 05 Aug 1760 conveyed same land to Nathan SPENCER party these presents. Sd Nathan SPENCER for £50 species paid to him by William BLOCKSOM sold sd BLOCKSOM sd 50 acres of land together w/house, orchards, etc. Sd Nathan SPENCER appoints John CLOWES, Esq as his Attorney. Signed: Nathan SPENCER (mark). Wit: George MESSICK, John RILEY. Rec: 09 Mar 1789 Nath'l MITCHELL, Proth'y.

O-14:19. Deed. Sarah JOHNSON, widow, surviving Exec of the estate of her late husband Purnal JOHNSON, late of Broadkiln Hundred, Sussex cnty, DE, yeoman, dec'd. Whereas Purnal JOHNSON in his lifetime was seized of a tract of land & marsh situate in hund & cnty afsd bounded by Peter's Pattent, land late of Robert SHANKLAND, dec'd, now in the tenure of Simon KOLLOCK, Esq, Cornelius JOHNSON's creek, marsh late the property of John PILES, dec'd, containing 405 acres by Deed from Joseph PILES to William BUSTON dtd 07 Nov 1721 rec: Rolls Office of sd cnty in Liber E 4, folio 161. Purnal JOHNSON made his last will & testament dtd 20 Nov 1778 wherein ordered his Exec as soon as his son David attain 21 years of age, or if he should d: under that age, as soon as his son Burton attained that age, sell his plantation & appurtenances after giving legal & Public Notice to the highest bidder for the highest & best price to be had for same & appointed his wife, afsd Sarah Exec & David TRAIN Exec of his estate. Sd Sarah hath survived David TRAIN & sd David JOHNSON, son of sd Purnal JOHNSON, hath attained 21 years. Sarah JOHNSON has sold by public venue the above lands & premises dtd 12 Jul 1788 to Peter Fretwell WRIGHT, Esq for the sum of £780, he being the highest bidder (excepting 80 sq ft for a burial ground). 18 Feb 1789 Signed: Sarah JOHNSON. Wit: Hap HAZZARD, Jacob HAZZARD. Sarah JOHNSON appointed John RUSSEL & Daniel RODNEY as her Attorney. Rec: 09 Mar 1789 Nath'l MITCHELL, Proth'y.

O-14:21. Deed. This Indenture made 25 February 1789 between Nathan

SPENCER of Sussex cnty, DE, yeoman, of the one part & John RYLEY of sd cnty & state, yeoman, of the other part. A tract of land in Broadkiln Hundred, Sussex cnty, DE containing 199 acres was by Proprietor's Warrant dtd Philadelphia 16 Sep 1748 granted to John FLEETWOOD for whom sd land was surveyed by William SHANKLAND, Deputy Surveyor, 14 Feb 1749. John FLEETWOOD by his Deed dtd 07 Feb 1756 sold same to Ezael SPENCER & sd Ezael SPENCER by his Deed dtd 05 Aug 1760 conveyed same to Nathan SPENCER, party to these presents. Sd tract of land is called Oliver's Folly or Fleetwood Choice, bounded by land of George PURKINS, David SMITH's land, INGRAM's line, & also 35 acres of land adjoining the sd 199 acres, part of a larger tract granted to David SMITH of cnty afsd by a Proprietor's Warrant dtd at Philadelphia 24 Apr 1742 & surveyed for 200 acres more or less, which sd 35 acres by sundry conveyances became the property of William BLOXOM of VA. William BLOXOM empowered William BLOXOM of Sussex cnty, DE to sell sd 35 acres which sd BLOXOM did by Deed dtd 09 Feb 1769 to Nathan SPENCER party to these presents, rec: in Liber L 11, folio 7. Nathan SPENCER for £120 sold to John RYLEY the 199 acres & the above described 35 acres containing in the whole 184 acres (excepting as above) & reserving to sd Nathan SPENCER during his natural life the full use & rents of same). Nathan SPENCER appoints John CLOWES, Esq, as his Attorney. Signed: Nathan SPENCER (mark). Wit: George MESSICK, William BLOXTON (mark). Ack: 04 Mar 1789. Rec: 09 Mar 1789 Nath'l MITCHELL, Proth'y.

O-14:23. Deed. This Indenture made 19 Jun 1788 between Peter Fretwell WRIGHT of Lewes, Sussex cnty, DE, tanner, of the first part & Jacob HAZZARD of same place, blacksmith, of the other part. Joseph ELDRIDGE & Mary ELDRIDGE late of cnty afsd devised by their last will & testament to their 2 grandsons, Thomas MOORE & Obediah ELDRIDGE a certain messuage, tan yard, orchard & tract of land situate in Hund & cnty afsd near the town of Lewes. At a Ct of Common held at Lewes, Sussex cnty, DE in May term 1778 Thomas MOORE by Jacob MOORE, Esq, his Attorney, & Obediah ELDRIDGE by Jabez FISHER, gent, his Guardian, caused an amicable action of Partition between them to be entered. With consent of the Ct & parties Messires Reece WOOLF, Anderson PARKER & Samuel PAYNTER were appointed to make partition of the land & premises. On motion of sd Thomas MOORE by Jacob MOORE his Attorney it was ruled by the Ct to set aside the partition advised by sd WOOLF, PARKER & PAYNTER. Whereupon by consent of the parties the Ct apptd John RUSSELL, Rhoads SHANKLAND & Percy PRETTYMAN to make partition, which they did. The Ct thereupon approved & accepted the partition. That part of the lands & premises allotted to Thomas MOORE as his full share land bounded by land now in the tenure of Thomas FISHER, containing 7 acres. Thomas MOORE by Indenture dtd 05 Nov 1778 sold to

Peter Fretwell WRIGHT, rec: in Liber M 12, folio 225. Peter Fretwell WRIGHT for £200 gold & silver coin sold sd 7 acres to Jacob HAZZARD. Signed: Peter F WRIGHT. Wit: J RUSSELL, John HAZZARD. Ack: 04 Mar 1789. Rec: 09 Mar 1789 Nath'l MITCHELL, Proth'y.

O-14:24. Deed. William ARNELL of Sussex cnty, DE, house carpenter & joyner. Samuel ARNELL late of town & cnty afsd, pilot, dec'd, in his lifetime was seized of sundry lotts & parcels of land & marsh situate on the Bank of Silver Creek & lower end of Pilot town. He made his last will & testament whereof he appointed Joseph BAILY & William ARNALL, both late of town & cnty afsd, pilots, dec'd, his Execs wherein he directed his Execs afsd to sell afsd lands to the advantage of the estate. Sd Joseph BAILY & William ARNELL having will duly proven & registered & had fully administered the personal estate of sd Samuel ARNELL d: Intestate before they had sold sd lands or any part of. Whereby the unadministered estate of sd Samuel ARNELL were in due form of law committed by Phillips KOLLOCK, Esq, apptd Reg for Probate of Wills granted Letters of Administration for the cnty afsd to William ARNALL, party to these presents. Whereas the personal estate of sd Samuel ARNELL was insufficient to discharge his debts & support & educate his small children. William ARNELL, Admin, obtained an order of Orphans Ct of sd cnty for the sale of sd lands. Having given due public notice of sale, on 04 Mar 1789 the lands (when all the moiety or half of that parcel of upland divided lengthwise joining the lands belonging to the heirs of Jacob ART, dec'd, on the SE; & land late of Ann BAILY on the NW, also one moiety of the marsh divided crossway by a NW line) were purchased by Brinkley EWING of sd town & cnty, yeoman, for the sum of £40, he being the highest bidder. 05 Mary 1789 Signed: William ARNEL. Wit: John STAFFORD, Sam'l PAYNTER Jr. Ack: 05 Mar 1789. Rec: 09 Mar 1789 Nath'l MITCHELL, Proth'y.

O-14:26. Deed. William ARNELL of Sussex cnty, DE, house carpenter & joyner. Samuel ARNELL late of town & cnty afsd, pilot, dec'd, in his lifetime was seized of sundry lotts & parcels of land & marsh situate on the Bank of Silver Creek & lower end of Pilot town. He made his last will & testament whereof he appointed Joseph BAILY & William ARNALL, both late of town & cnty afsd, pilots, dec'd, his Execs wherein he directed his Execs afsd to sell afsd lands to the advantage of the estate. Sd Joseph BAILY & William ARNELL having will duly proven & registered & had fully administered the personal estate of sd Samuel ARNELL d: Intestate before they had sold sd lands or any part of. Whereby the unadministered estate of sd Samuel ARNELL were in due form of law committed by Phillips KOLLOCK, Esq, apptd Reg for Probate of Wills granted Letters of Administration for the cnty afsd to William ARNALL, party to these presents.

Whereas the personal estate of sd Samuel ARNELL was insufficient to discharge his debts & support & educate his small children. William ARNELL, Admin, obtained an order of Orphans Ct of sd cnty for the sale of sd lands. Having given due public notice of sale, on 04 Mar 1789 one part of the lands afsd bounded on the SE by lands late of Joseph BAILEY, dec'd, on the NW by land of the heirs of Jacob ART, dec'd, on the NE by the Bank of Lewes Creek 60 ft in breadth & in length 200 ft, were purchased by William HARRIS of town & cnty, house carpenter & joyner, for the sum of £18, he being the highest bidder. 05 Mar 1789 William ARNEL, Admin. Wit: Jno RUSSELL, Woodman STOCKLEY. Rec: 09 Mar 1789 Nath'l MITCHELL, Proth'y.

O-14:27. Deed. 10 Oct 1788 Edward ROBERTS & William ROBERTS each of Sussex cnty, DE of the one part for the sum of £41 10s sold to Alex'r LAWS, Esq, of cnty & state afsd of the other part 53 & 1/8 acres of land situate in Northwest Fork Hundred, Sussex cnty, DE as follows: part of a tract called David Hope containing 367 & 1/2 acres in the whole & part of one other tract called Adventure containing in the whole 85 & 1/2 acres & part of one other tract called Prevention containing 78 & 3/4 acres in the whole; containing in the whole 531 & 3/4 acres, the above lands patented to David POLK the elder, dec'd, willed by him to his grandson William POLK, ediot; then to his 4 dtrs Elizabeth ROBERTS, Marah DUELL, Lovey COLLINS & Emilah LAWS & their heirs. Sd grandson, Wm POLK d: w/o such heir & the sd lands now in the possession of the heirs & legal representatives of the 4 dtrs afsd & the sd Edward & Wm ROBERTS do dispose of being the heirs of Elizabeth ROBERTS & do sell the 53 & 1/8 acres to Alex'r LAWS. Signed: Edward ROBERTS, William ROBERTS. Wit: Charles POLK, James COULTER. Ack: John RODNEY, Atty for the Grantors. Rec: 10 May 1789 Nath'l MITCHELL, Proth'y.

O-14:28. Deed. 25 Mar 1789 Thomas PULLET & Nancy PULLET his wife of Sussex cnty, DE of the one part for the sum of £21 10s sold to Alex'r LAWS, Esq, of the cnty & state afsd, of the other part 26 & 1/2 acres & 1/16 of an acre of land situate in Northwest Fork Hundred, it being their full parts of 3 different tracts of land to wit: part of a tract called David's Hope containing 367 & 1/2 acres in the whole & part of a tract of land called Adventure containing in the whole 85 & 1/2 acres & part of one other tract called Prevention containing in the whole 78 & 3/4 acres, the 3 tracts containing in the whole 531 & 3/4 acres; the above lands patented to David POLK the elder, dec'd, & willed to his grandson, Wm POLK, ediot & his lawful heir, & if he should have no such heir, his will was that the above lands should then go to his 4 dtrs to wit: Elizabeth ROBERTS, Mary JEWETT, Lovey COLLINGS & Emeliah LAWS & their heirs, et al. Sd Wm POLK since d: w/o such heir & above mentioned lands fell to sd dtrs & their legal representatives. Sd Thomas PULLET & Nancy his wife do depose as being the heirs & legal representatives of Elizabeth ROBERTS. Thomas PULLET & Nancy his wife do appoint their friends John RODNEY & Phillips KOLLOCK of the town of Lewes as their Attorney. Signed: Thomas POLLITT, Nancy POLLITT. Wit: John CLOWES, Thomas W,HAM. Ack: 06 May 1789. Rec: 16 May 1789 Nath'l MITCHELL, Proth'y. 25 Mar 1789 John CLOWES JP of Ct of Common Pleas, Sussex cnty, DE examined Nancy PULLITT wife of Thomas PULLETT, being of full age was examined & she did declare she became a party to above Deed of her own free will w/o compulsion from her husband or others. Signed: John CLOWES.

O-14:29. Deed. Daniel ROGERS of Sussex cnty, DE, gent, lately in Ct of Common Please at Lewes at August term 1786 before the Justices of sd Ct recovered against Isaac INGRAM of cnty afsd a certain debt of £212 & 24s 7p damages now to be levied against the goods, chattels, lands & tenements of sd Isaac INGRAM. By writ of Fieri Facias issued by the Ct of Common Pleas at Lewes 09 May 1787 directed Peter Fretwell WRIGHT, High Sheriff of sd cnty to seize sd goods, lands, etc. of sd INGRAM. Sd WRIGHT took in Execution a tract of land situate in Nanticoke Hundred in sd cnty containing 250 acres w/all improvements which he had appraised by 2 Freeholds of his Bailiwick who by their solemn oath said the rent, issue & profits of the sd land premises are not of a clear yearly value sufficient to satisfy the debt & damages w/in the space of 7 years & same remained in his hands for want of Buyers. By writ of Venditioni Exponas issued 04 Nov 1788 directed sd Peter Fretwell WRIGHT to sell w/due public notice sd lands, etc. Same was purchased 10 Jan 1789 by John COLLINGS of Sussex cnty afsd for the sum of £130 5s, he being the highest bidder. Peter Fretwell WRIGHT afterwards was removed from office of Sheriff before he executed a conveyance to the sd John COLLINS for the land & premises. Thomas EVANS for the sum of 130 5s to sd Peter Fretwell WRIGHT, my predecessor, by the sd John COLLINS, have granted to the sd John COLLINS all that before mentioned tract of land, premises, etc. containing 250 acres adjoining lands belonging to the heirs of Barnet VANKIRK & John LANE on the NW, lands of Job SMITH on the W, Collings Mill Pond on the SE & lands of the above named John COLLINGS on the S. 06 May in the 13th year of American Independence & 1789. Signed: Thomas EVANS, Sheriff. Wit: Jno WILTBANK, Phillips KOLLOCK. Ack: 06 May 1789 Peter Fretwell WRIGHT. Rec: 16 May 1789 Nath'l MITCHELL, Proth'y.

O-14:31. Deed. 05 Mar 1789 William MORRIS of Worcester cnty, MD of the one part for the sum of £100 current money of MD sold to Jesse GRAY of the cnty & state afsd of the other part a tract of land & cypress swamp called Truman's Neglect situate in Sussex cnty, DE, heretofore conveyed by

Capt John MORRIS, fthr of sd William, to his fthr John MORRIS, that part of sd tract which his fthr John MORRIS sold to John MASSEY in sd cnty & gave a bond of conveyance but was not conveyed & sd bond conveyed over to sd Jesse GRAY, the whole of sd parts to sd land to contain 98 acres more or less left which has not been conveyed by the sd John MORRIS. To better effect conveyance of sd land & premises to the afsd GRAY William MORRIS does appoint William PEERY & John Wise BAKON of Sussex cnty my lawful Attorneys to complete this conveyance. Signed: William MORRIS. Wit: John POSTLY, Joseph ROGERS. Rec: 16 May 1789 Nath'l MITCHELL, Proth'y.

O-14:32. Deed. 20 Apr 1784 Isaac BRONN of Sussex cnty, DE, planter, & Ann, his wife, of the one part for the sum of £5 sold to Ezekiel SMITH of same place, planter, of the other part part of a tract of land called Poplar Ridge situate in Northwest Fork Hundred, Sussex cnty, DE containing 4 acres. Isaac BRONN & Ann BRONN his wife appoint John RODNEY & John LAWS of Sussex cnty their Attorneys. Signed: Isaac BRONN, Ann BRONN (her mark). Wit: Daniel POLK, William RICHARDS. 20 Apr 1784 came before me, one of the JPs of Sussex cnty, DE Ann BRONN who being separately examined apart from her husband she became a party to the above Deed of her own voluntary & free will. Signed: Daniel POLK. Rec: 16 May 1789 Nath'l MITCHELL, Proth'y.

O-14:33. Deed. 28 Jan 1789 James CANNON Jr & Priscilla his wife & Mary his mother of Sussex cnty, DE of the one part for the sum of £141 sold to John TENNENT of same cnty & state of the other part a tract of land called Cannon's Meadow situate in cnty afsd bounded by a tract of land called Friendship containing 50 acres more or less & likewise sold to John TENNENT part of a tract of land called Mushroom Hill laid off for James CANNON Jr on a division made between him & his father containing 66 acres situate on the W side of the tract called Cannon's Meadow. James CANNON Jr, Priscilla his wife & Mary his mother appoint well beloved friends William PEERY or Rhoads SHANKLAND our Attorney. Signed: James CANNON Jr (mark), Priscilla CANNON (mark), Mary CANNON (mark). Wit: Joshua OBIER, Wm NOBEL. This is to certify that Priscilla CANNON wife of James CANNON Jr, yeoman, & Mary CANNON wife of James CANNON Sr, yeoman, were examined in private & acknowledged they signed the within Deed of Sale of their own free will & consent & are well satisfied same may be acknowledged by their Attorney. Signed: Alex'r LAWS, JP Sussex cnty, DE. Rec: 16 May 1789 Nath'l MITCHELL, Proth'y.

O-14:34. Deed. This Indenture made 24 May 1788 between John CANNON of

Sussex cnty, DE, planter, of the one part & Jules Agustus JACKSON of same place, doctor, of the other part. John CANNON for the sum of £300 sold all parts of tracts hereafter mentioned: 1st part of a tract called Sallamander & part of a tract called Cannon's Increase & part of a tract called Noble Quarter & all that part of a tract called Sallamander that lyes on the S side of County Road that leads to Creatiher's Ferry containing 67 & 1/2 acres & also that part of Canonn's Increase that lyeth on the S side of the afsd road containing 20 & 3/4 acres & all that part of Noble Quarter in manner & form following: beginning at a corner post standing between sd JACKSON's plantation & Clement BAYLEY's plantation, originally a corner of Henry CANNON's land, now the corner of Joshua OBEAR's land to the division line between land of John CANNON & land of Henry CANNON containing for this part 19 & 1/4 acres. John CANNON appoints John RODNEY & Phillips KOLLOCK of Lewes town, Sussex cnty, DE his Attorney. Signed: John CANNON Sr (mark). Wit: John CANNON Jr, Willington CANNON, Noble TULL (mark). Rec: 16 May 1789 Nath'l MITCHELL, Proth'y.

O-14:35. Deed. This Indenture made 18 Apr 1789 between John DUTTON & James DUTTON of Sussex cnty, DE, yeomen, of the one part & Edmond DICKERSON of same cnty, yeoman, of the other part. The Proprietaries of Pennsylvania Province & the cntys on DE 27 Oct 1757 by Warrant granted to James STEVENSON of the cnty afsd a survey for 200 acres adjoining his other lands called White Oak Swamp & on the S side of John PETTYJOHN's land contiguous to surveys already made. John DUTTON by marrying w/one of the dtrs of James STEVENSON & by having children born to him of her body became entitled to a life estate in all lands & tenements of his sd wife. The sd James DUTTON being a son of John DUTTON by the marriage afsd, also being entitled by inheritance to a part of the sd land contained in the Warrant afsd. John DUTTON & James DUTTON for the sum of £50 sold a tract of land bounded by Rhoads SHANKLAND's land containing 140 acres & being the same which was devised by the last will of James STEVENSON to his 2 dtrs together w/all improvements, etc. Signed: John DUTTON, James DUTTON. Wit: Jos MILLER, D HALL. Rec: 16 May 1789 Nath'l MITCHELL, Proth'y.

O-14:36. Deed. This Indenture made 24 Apr 1789 between Josiah HUET of Sussex cnty, DE of the one part & Joshua POLK of the same place of the other part. Joshua HURT by his bond of conveyance sold to Edward POLK, which bond is assigned to John JACOBS & from John JACOBS to Joshua POLK afsd dtd 1784 for 130 acres of land receiving out of the sd land 1/2 acre of land to be laid off so as to include the Burying Ground, & Josiah HURT hereby sold the land & tenements that was left to him by his fthr William HUET by his last will

& testament left to sd Josiah HURT his son & agreeable to the bond sd Joshua HURT hath for the sum of £100 sold to Joshua POLK all the afsd land that was left to him by his fthr's will of a tract of land called Stalomn's Slt & Betty's Fancy situate in Sussex cnty containing 100 acres. Josiah HUET appoints Rob't Henry NEIL of Lewes & Rob't David HALL my Attorneys. Signed: Josiah HUET. Wit: Robert OWENS, Joshua POLK Jr. Rec: 16 May 1789 Nath'l MITCHELL, Proth'y.

O-14:37. Deed. 19 Apr 89 Joseph DAWSON & Elizabeth his wife of Sussex cnty, DE, yeoman, of the one part for the sum of £82 19s 4p sold to John LANGRELL of sd cnty & state, carpenter, of the other part. a tract of land situate in Northwest Fork Hundred, Sussex cnty containing 73 & 3/4 acres being part of three tracts of land called Second Addition to Canaan, Canaan & Addition to Canaan; 42 & 3/4 acres in Second Addition to Canaan, 27 & 1/2 acres in Canaan & 3 & 1/2 acres in Addition to Canaan, containing 73 & 3/4 acres afsd. Joseph DAWSON & Elizabeth his wife appoint well beloved friends William PEERY & Rhoads SHANKLAND our Attorneys. Signed: Joseph DAWSON, Elizabeth DAWSON. Wit: Alex'r LAWS Hunphries BROWN. This is to certify as one of the Judges of the Ct I examined Elizabeth DAWSON, wife of Joseph DAWSON, apart from her husband & acknowledged she signed the w/in Deed to John LANGRELL of sd cnty, ship carpenter, of her own voluntary will. 09 Apr 1789 Signed: Alex'r LAWS. Rec: 16 May 1789 Nath'l MITCHELL, Proth'y.

O-14:38. Deed. This Indenture made 14 Apr 1789 between Jacob ADDISON & Jonathan ADDISON of Sussex cnty, DE, yeomen, of the one part & Bevins MORRIS of sd cnty, yeoman, of the other part. Halminus WILTBANK by virtue of a Warrant from Court dtd 10 Mar 1681/2 had surveyed unto him on 12 Feb following by Cornelius VERHOOF then Surveyor a tract of land called Newtown situate on the W side of Delaware Bay & S side of Primehook Creek in Sussex cnty containing 580 acres. By order of Sussex cnty Orphans Ct the above tract of land was on 22 Mar 1755 by 5 men apptd w/William SHANKLAND, Surveyor) divided amongst surviving heirs of Halminous WILTBANK: John WILTBANK, Abraham WILTBANK, pilot, Isaac WILTBANK Jr, hatter & Abraham WILTBANK the elder in his lifetime were part of the heirs of the above sd Helminous WILTBANK. Abraham WILTBANK the elder in his lifetime on 16 Aug 1755 by a writing obligation under the penalty of £210 (jointly & severally w/the above named John WILTBANK & Abraham WILTBANK Jr) did obligate himself, his heirs, Exec, etc to convey to Jacob ADDISON part of the above mentioned tract of land, that is to say 320 acres thereof. Neomy WILTBANK, Exec of the last will & testament of Abraham WILTBANK the elder dec'd & John WILTBANK, Abraham WILTBANK pilot, Isaac WILTBANK Jr & Naomy WILTBANK Exec afsd for the sum of £105 current money of PA paid to them by

Jacob ADDISON the elder (now dec'd) did by their Deed duly perfected dtd 1764 did convey the sd 320 of land. Jacob ADDISON the elder d: Intestate leaving 3 sons viz: John, Jacob & Jonathan ADDISON who by their mutual agreement divided the 320 acres dtd 10 Mar 1783. Jacob ADDISON & Jonathan ADDISON for the sum of £75 current money of DE sold to Bevin MORRIS part of the afsd 320, that is to say 68 acres bounded by land of Morris & John HAZZARD , Cord HAZZARD's land. Jacob ADDISON & Jonathan ADDISON appoint Thomas EVANS Esq & Jonathan HEAVERLO, yeoman, of Sussex cnty to be their Attorney. Signed: Jacob ADDISON, Jonathan ADDISON. Wit: John HAZZARD, Caleb CIRWITHIN. Rec: 16 May 1789 Nath'l MITCHELL, Proth'y.

O-14:40. Deed. 17 Feb 1789 James CANNON Sr, & Mary his wife of Sussex cnty, DE, yeoman, of the one part for the sum of £47 sold to William NOBLE of Dorchester cnty, MD of the other part, part of 2 tracts of land one called Friendship & the other Mushroom Hill both situate in Northwest Fork Hundred, Sussex cnty, DE containing 19 acres & 31 acres of the tract called Mushroom Hill. James CANNON Sr & Mary his wife appoint William PEERY Esq or Rhoads SHANKLAND as their Attorney. Signed: James CANNON (mark), Mary CANNON (mark). Wit: John TENNENT, Joshua OBEIR. Mary CANNON wife of James CANNON, was examined in private by me, one of the Judges of Ct of Common Pleas & acknowledge that she signed & delivered sd Deed to William NOBLE of her own voluntary will & is well satisfied same may be acknowledged in Ct by her Attorney. 26 Mar 1789. Signed: Alex'r LAWS. Rec: 16 May 1789 Nath'l MITCHELL, Proth'y.

O-14:41. Deed. Thomas EVANS Esq, High Sheriff of Sussex cnty, DE. A tract of land situate in Paine Hook in Cedar Creek Hundred, Sussex cnty, DE containing 280 acres which was granted by Pattent dtd 17 May 1688 to John WATTSON & Samuel WATTSON which by sundry conveyances became the property of another John WATTSON, namely by Deed of Sale from William CRAMMER of Kent cnty, DE dtd 04 Jan 1721. Sd John WATTSON by his last will & testament dtd 03 Jan 1729 did devise to his 3 sons James WATTSON, Hezekiah WATTSON & Luke WATTSON the above mentioned tract containing 280 acres. Sd Hezekiah afterwards d: Intestate seized of an undivided 1/3 part of the afsd tract whereby the same descended to his son, Thomas WATTSON which sd Thomas WATTSON together w/the above Luke WATTSON by their Deed dtd 01 Feb 1776 conveyed to John WATTSON late of Sussex cnty, cordwainer, dec'd 1/6 part of the sd tract of 280 acres. John WATTSON, cordwainer, by Indenture dtd 04 Feb 1778 between sd John WATTSON of the one part & John RODNEY

Esq, trustee of the General Loan Office for sd cnty of the other part. John WATTSON for the sum of £31 10s did convey to John RODNEY & trustees for the time being 1/6 part of the above mentioned tract. In sd Indenture provision was made if sd John WATTSON paid the £31 10s plus interest in a timely manner sd Indenture would become void. Sd John WATTSON afterwards & before he had satisfied the Indenture died Intestate whereof Admin of his estate was committed to Isaac WATTSON of cnty afsd, joiner. Joseph HALL, Trustee of the GLO, at Aug term 1788 obtained judgement 07 May year afsd gained judgement against Isaac WATTSON, Admin of afsd John WATTSON & sd Indenture of Mortgage. A writ dtd 06 Aug in the year last directed Peter Fretwell WRIGHT Esq, High Sheriff he should expose to public sale the sd land of the Indenture & to have the money to the Ct at Lewes on Wednesday 05 Nov next to render to the sd Joseph HALL, Trustee. Sd WRIGHT did so & sold sd land 05 Nov afsd to George RICKARDS for the sum of £30, he being the highest bidder. Whereas sd Peter Fretwell WRIGHT was discharged from his office before he executed a Deed to sd RICKARDS. Thomas EVANS Esq for the sum of £30 pd to Peter Fretwell WRIGHT his predecessor hath conveyed to sd George RICHARDS all the above mentioned land being 1/6 part of 280 acres. Signed: Thomas EVANS, Sheriff. Wit: Jno WILTBANK, Phillips KOLLOCK. Ack of receipt of £30 from George RICKARDS. 06 May 1789 Signed: Peter F WRIGHT. Rec: 16 May 1789 Nath'l MITCHELL, Proth'y.

O-14:43. Deed. This Indenture made 28 Apr 1788 between Rhoads SHANKLAND Esq of Lewes & Rehoboth Hundred, Sussex cnty, DE of the one part & William PRETTYMAN of same cnty & Hund of the other part. A tract of land situate in the hund & cnty afsd bounded by land of the heir of Percy PRETTYMAN, dec'd, & land of John WILTBANK Esq containing 1 acre & 10 sq perches of land. Rhoads SHANKLAND for the sum of £10 sold to William PRETTYMAN. Signed: Rhoads SHANKLAND. Wit: Abr'm HARGUS, Polly JESSOP. Ack: 06 May 1789. Rec: 16 May 1789 Nath'l MITCHELL, Proth'y.

O-14:44. Deed. 06 May 1789 Matthias JONES of Sussex cnty, DE, yeoman of the one part for the sum of £200 sold to Thomas MARVEL Jr of cnty afsd, yeoman, of the other part a parcel of land in Nanticoke Hundred, sd cnty, being part of a larger tract called Good Will bounded by land of Abram ADAMS containing 84 acres & another small parcel being part of a larger tract granted to the afsd Abram ADAMS adjoining the 84 acres of land afsd bounded by Elias JOHNSON's land & Good Will containing 116 acres containing in the whole 200 acres of land. Mathias JONES by his writing obligatory dtd 01 Mar 1786 to convey sd 200 acres which he did 03 May 1786 but sd Deed of Sale was not satisfactory. This Indenture in due form of law replaces sd Deed. Signed: Matthias M JONES (mark).

Wit: Chas MOORE, Thos GRAY. Rec: 16 May 1789 Nath'l MITCHELL, Proth'y.

O-14:45. Deed. There is a parcel of land situate in Sussex cnty in the forrest of Indian River Hundred being part of a larger tract containing 210 acres surveyed for Robert WEST in 1717 by Robert SHANKLAND then Surveyor of Sussex cnty which sd parcel of land is part of the sd larger tract & containing 115 acres. William Brittingham ENNES for the sum of 5s & other considerations me unto there moving sold to Thomas BURBAGE the above sd parcel of land. 06 May 1789 Signed: William Brittingham ENNES. Wit: Joseph DYER, Rhoads SHANKLAND. Rec: 16 May 1789.

O-14:46. Deed. There is a parcel of land situate in Sussex cnty in the forrest of Indian River Hundred being part of a larger tract containing 210 acres surveyed for Robert WEST in 1717 by Robert SHANKLAND then Surveyor of Sussex cnty which sd parcel of land is part of the sd larger tract & containing 100 acres. Thomas BURBAGE for the sum of 5s & other considerations & me unto there moving hath sold to William Brittingham ENNES the afsd 100 acres. 06 May 1789 Signed: Thomas T BURBAGE (mark). Wit: Joseph DYER, Rhoads SHANKLAND. Rec: 16 May 1789 Nath'l MITCHELL, Proth'y.

O-14:47. Deed. This Indenture made 22 Sep 1787 between James BROWN Sr of Sussex cnty, DE, planter, of the one part & Henry SMITH of the afsd cnty & province, planter, of the other part. James BROWN for the sum of £50 sold to Henry SMITH all that part of a tract of land called Canaan Improved bounded by the road leading from William CANNON's & containing 109 acres. Signed: Jas BROWN Sr. Wit: White BROWN, Charles TEVYFORD, Alex'r LAWS. James BROWN of Sussex cnty afsd appoint Messrs John LAWS & John CLOWES Esqs my Attorney. 22 Sep 1787. Signed: Jas BROWN Sr. Rec: 16 May 1789 Nath'l MITCHELL, Proth'y.

O-14:48. Deed of Mortgage. This Indenture is made 17 Nov 1788 between George CONWELL of Sussex cnty, DE & Eunice CONWELL his wife of the one part & Baptist LAY, John CONWELL & Nehemiah REED, all of the cnty afsd of the other part. Whereas there is a certain tract of land situate in Broadkiln Hundred in cnty afsd containing 147 acres being part of a larger tract granted by patent dtd 29 d 2nd m 1686 to James GRAY for the quantity of 1000 acres of land commonly called Millford, which sd 147 acres by sundry more conveyances became the property of the above named George CONWELL & Eunice CONWELL his wife, & is bounded by land of John ROWLAND. George CONWELL is indebted to Samuel PAINTER of cnty afsd in the sum of £182 the payment thereof the sd Baptist LAY, John CONWELL & Nehemiah REED by their Obligation together w/the sd George CONWELL dtd 08 Aug 1788 have firmly bound themselves. By this Indenture the sd George CONWELL & Eunice CONWELL his wife in consideration of the afsd £182 by the sd Baptis LAY, John CONWELL & Nehemiah REED to be paid to sd Samuel PAINTER for the debt of the afsd George CONWELL, sd George & Eunice CONWELL have granted & sold to sd Baptis, John & Nehemiah all their right & title to the above sd 147 acres & improvements, as tenants in common & not as joint tenants. Provided nevertheless that if sd George CONWELL shall pay to Samuel PAINTER the above named sum of £182 at the time above cited Obligation specified together w/interest thereon until the whole is fully paid & also pay all court costs & damages that may arise by reason of any suit that may be commenced against the afsd LAY, CONWELL & REED for the recovery of the afsd sum then this Indenture shall be null & void. Signed: George CONWELL (mark), Eunice CONWELL. Wit: William PEERY, Gerhardus CONWILL. John CLOWSE, one of the Judges of Ct of Com Pleas for Sussex cnty, DE certify that Eunice CONWELL being of full age, was examined apart from her husband & did say that she signed sd Deed as her on voluntary act & as deed was made purely for security & indemnification of the persons therein she became a part of her own free will. Signed: John CLOWES. Rec: 16 May 1789 Nath'l MITCHELL, Proth'y.

O-14:49. Deed. This Indenture made 16 December 1788 between Phebe VINING (late Phebe WYNKOOP) & Benjamin WYNKOOP, Exec of the last will & testament of Abraham WYNKOOP late of Sussex cnty, DE, Esq, dec'd, of the one part & Matthew COVERDALE of the Forrest of Cedar Creek Hundred in cnty afsd, yeoman, of the other part. Abraham WYNKOOP was in his lifetime seized of a tract of land situate in the head of the great neck on the SE side of Gum branch in the forrest of Cedar Creek Hundred called Hammond Bold Adventure 223 & 1/2 acres & did for valuable consideration sd land & appurtenances to Thomas PASWATER but no actual Deed was conveyed. Whereas the sd Abraham WYNKOOP afterward d: having made his last will & testament dtd 15 Nov 1753 wherein after sundry bequests he directs that all his lands & tenements lying w/in the cntys of Kent & Sussex be sold & monies arising therefrom to be paid in discharge of the several legacies he bequested & apptd his wife Mary, his dtr Phebe & his sons Thomas & Benjamin Execs. Sd Mary & Thomas being since dec'd Admin of the estate of Abraham WYNKOOP devolved to sd Phebe VINING & Benjamin WYNKOOP. Sd Phebe VINING & Benjamin WYNKOOP in consideration of monies already paid & the further sum of 5s have granted all the above described tract to sd Matthew COVERDALE. Sd Phebe VINING & Benjamin WYNKOOP appoint Rhoads SHANKLAND & Charles POLK Esqs their lawful Attorneys. Signed: Benjamin WYNKOOP, Phebe VINING. Wit: Joseph WYNKOOP, William ROBINSON, Dan'l Chas HEATH. Rec: 16 May 1789 Nath'l MITCHELL, Proth'y.

O-14:51. Deed. This Indenture made 07 May 1789 between John METCALF of Sussex cnty, DE, gentleman, of the one part & Thomas DAVIS & Elias TOWNSEND of cnty & state afsd of the other part. Thomas DAVIS & Elias TOWNSEND for the sum of £95 sold to John METCALF a tract of land & marsh situate in Slaughter Neck, Sussex cnty bounded by the Delaware Bay, land of Elias TOWNSEND containing 95 acres of marsh & land, being part of a pattent known as Good Luck & being part of a pattent granted by Sir Edward ANDROP Governor of NY to Thomas DAVIS dtd 29 Sep 1677 for 300 acres laid off for John MECALF out of the sd pattent by the afsd Elias TOWNSEND & Thomas DAVIS together all & singular. Signed: Thomas DAVIS, Elias TOWNSEND. Wit: Avery DRAPER, Wm DAVIS. Rec: 16 May 1789 Nath'l MITCHELL, Proth'y.

O-14:52. Deed. This Indenture made 07 May 1789 between Thomas DAVIS of Sussex cnty, DE, yeoman & Elias TOWNSEND of the same of the other part. Thomas DAVIS for the sum of £47 10s sold to Elias TOWNSEND a tract of land & marsh known as Good Look, it being part of a pattent granted by Sir Edmond ANDROP Governor of NY to Thomas DAVIS dtd 29 Sep 1677 for 300 acres of land & marsh situate in Slaughter Neck, cnty afsd, being part of afsd patent & bounded by land of Edward FURLONG's pattent, containing 47 & 1/2 acres of land & marsh. Signed: Thomas DAVIS. Wit: Avery DRAPER, Wm DAVIS. Rec: 16 May 1789 Nath'l MITCHELL, Proth'y.

O-14:53. Deed. This Indenture made 07 May 1789 between Elias TOWNSEND of Sussex cnty, DE, yeoman, of the one part & Thomas DAVIS of Sussex cnty of the other part. Elias TOWNSEND for the sum of £47 10s sold to Thomas DAVIS a tract of marsh known as Good Look being part of a pattent granted by Sir Edmon ANDROP Governor of NY to Thomas DAVIS dtd 29 Sep 1677 for 300 acres of land & marsh situate in Slaughter Neck, cnty afsd bounded by Edward FURLONG'S pattent Elias TOWNSEND's marsh, laid out for 47 & 1/2 acres. Signed: Elias TOWNSEND. Wit: Avery DRAPER, Wm DAVIS. Rec: 16 May 1789 Nath'l MITCHELL, Proth'y.

O-14:54. Deed. This Indenture made 07 May 1789 between Walter HUDSON of Indian River Hundred, Sussex cnty, DE, blacksmith, & Mary his wife, of the one part & Benjamin McILVAIN of hund & cnty afsd, taylor, of the other part. Walter HUDSON & Mary his wife for the sum of £71 to Benjamin McILVAIN all that piece of land situate in the hund & cnty afsd being part of two parcels of land whereof John LITTLE d: seized. The first sd John LITTLE purchased of Josiah MARTIN by Deed dtd 15 Oct 1765, the other parcel sd John LITTLE purchased of Joseph HAZZARD by deed dtd 10 Jan 1769. Henry NEILL of Lewes, merchant, obtained a judgement against Nicholas LITTLE, Exec of the estate of John LITTLE for the sum of £487 & 1/2 penny for nonperformance of promise to the afsd Henry by the afsd John LITTLE. Peter Fretwell WRIGHT Esq, High Sheriff of Sussex cnty, took in execution the above cited two parcels of land together w/as much other lands of sd John LITTLE situate on the N side of Dover or Bundocks Branch as would make up the quantity of 500 & 50 acres which sd lands were purchased by Henry NEILL for the sum of £620, he being the highest bidder by Deed of sd Sheriff dtd 05 Sep 1787. Henry NEILL, being so seized of sd land, & his wife, by Deed dtd 06 Feb 1789 sold to Walter HUDSON 62 acres of land part thereof, situate in Angola & Indian River Hundred on the S side & adjoining sd Doves or Bundock Branch afsd bounded by Jonathan STEVENSON's land laid out for 31 & 1/2 acres of land. Signed: Walter HUDSON, Mary HUDSON. Wit: John WOLFE, Shepard PRETTYMAN. Being one of the Judges of the Ct of Com Pleas personally examined the above named Mary HUDSON separate from her husband, she being of full age, acknowledged she was a party to the above Indenture of her own free will. Signed: Peter F WRIGHT. Rec: 16 May 1789 Nath'l MITCHELL, Proth'y.

O-14:56. Deed. This Indenture made 08 Dec 1788 between Samuel BASSETT & Sarah his wife of Sussex cnty, DE, yeoman, & Belitha LAWS of the same place, yeoman, of the other part. Samuel BASSETT & Sarah his wife for the sum of £300 sold to Belitha LAWS a tract of land in the Forrest of Cedar Creek in Sussex cnty containing 96 acres & 36 sq perches of land being part of a larger tract called Freeland's Adventure (which by several conveyances appears to have been legally transferred to the above Belitha LAWS who afterwards by Deed conveyed same to above sd Samuel BASSETT as made by Deed made 1780 & recorded in the cnty in Liber M 12, folio 343). Samuel BASSETT & Sarah his wife appoint Messrs Phillips KOLLOCK & William HARRISON as the Attorney. Signed: Samuel BASSETT, Sarah BASSETT (mark). Wit: William JOHNSON Jr, Nehemiah CAREY, Robert HOUSTON. 08 Sep 1788 before me, Judges of the Ct of Comm Pleas, came Sara the wife of Samuel BASSETT, she being of full age, & being examined apart from her husband acknowledged she became a part to the above of her own free will. Signed: Alex'r LAWS. Rec: 08 Jun 1789 Nath'l MITCHELL, Proth'y.

O-14:57. Deed of Mortgage. This Indenture made 20 Jul 1788 between Uriah HAZZARD of the town of Lewes, Sussex cnty, DE, yeoman, & Sarah his wife of the one part & Rhoads SHANKLAND of Sussex cnty afsd Esq of the other part. Uriah HAZZARD & his wife for the sum of £65 11s gold & silver coin sold to sd Rhoads SHANKLAND a parcel of land situate near the town of Lewes containing 12 & 1/2 acres being the same land Uriah HAZZARD purchased of Phillips KOLLOCK, notwithstanding if sd Uriah HAZZARD shall pay unto the sd Rhoads SHANKLAND the afsd sum of £65 11s on or before 29 Aug next then above Deed & every matter therein contained to be void. Sd Uriah HAZZARD & Sarah his wife agrees they will pay the afsd sum of £65 11s on or before 29 Aug next with lawful interest from date hereof & further if sd sum not be paid on or before date sd then it shall be lawful for sd Rhoads SHANKLAND to take possession of sd land, goods & chattels. Signed: Uriah HAZARD, Sarah HAZARD. Wit: Jno RUSSEL, Elizabeth RUSSEL. There personally appeared before me, one of the Judges of the Ct of Comm Pleas, Sarah HAZARD, wife of Uriah, she being of full age, & by me examined separate from her husband declared she became a part to above Deed of her own free will. 21 Jul 1788. Signed: Jno WILTBANK. Rec: 14 Jul 1789. Jno RUSSELL, Recd'r 11 Feb 1791 Rhoads SHANKLAND Esq Mortgagee of this recorded Deed certified he had rec'd full satisfaction from the Mortgagers in this Deed & therefore released & quit claimed the land & premises therein mentioned. Jno RUSSELL, Recd'r.

O-14:58. John WITTBANCK Esq, Trustee, Inc for St Peters Church, Sussex cnty, DE. In pursuance of directions of Act of General Assembly of DE state & agreeably to advertisements dtd 08 July 1789 giving notice to the congregation of St Peters Episcopal Church at Lewes, in Lewes & Rehoboth Hundred, to meet Sat, 18 July instant at sd church to elect any number of the congregation not exceeding 7 nor less than 3, to be Trustees of the same. Sd Trustees & their Successors in office are hereby constituted a body Politic, & Corporate in Deed, Tract, name & in Law" agreeably to the above recited Act of Assembly & provided -

The Congregation met accordingly or so many of them as thought fit to give their attendance, & by plurality of voice did then & then elect the following persons: Messrs John WILTBANK Esq, Anderson PARKER, Reece WOOLF, John RUSSELL, Phillips KOLLOCK, Hap HAZZARD & George PARKER to be Trustees which we do hereby certify this 18 Jul 1789. Signed: Jno WILTBANK, Anderson PARKER, Reece WOOLF, Jno RUSSELL, Phillips KOLLOCK, Hap HAZZARD, George PARKER. Wit: Henry FISHER, John WOOLF, David HAZZARD, William BURETON, George HAZZARD.

O-14:59. Deed. This Indenture made 15 Jul 1789 between Joseph DERRICKSON of Sussex cnty, DE of the one part & George MITCHELL of same place of the other part. Joseph DERRICKSON for the sum of £5 & in consideration of sd George MITCHELL becoming liable for payment of £60 w/interest which sd Joseph DERRICKSON has taken out of the Loan Office of Sussex cnty, hath sold to George MITCHELL all that parcel of land called Herman's Addition in cnty afsd on Vine's Branch between County Rd & Sea Side Rd it being a resurvey made by Herman WHARTON the younger on a tract of land containing 75 acres called Daniel's Luck & patented by an assignment on the Warrant in the name of Joseph DERRICKSON the sd Herman's Addition containing 210 acres w/all improvements excepting a saw mill whereon erected & now belonging to Samuel LOCKWOOD & Amwell LONG & one acre of land to be laid off afsd tract on side of sd tract next to sd mill. Joseph DERRICKSON appoints John W BATSON & Phillips KOLLOCK Esq his lawful Attorney. Signed: Jos DERRICKSON. Wit: John W BATSON, William TRUMAN. Rec: 15 Aug 1789 Nath'l MITCHELL, Proth'y.

O-14:60. Deed. This Indenture made 05 Aug 1789 between John LITTLE of Sussex cnty, DE, yeoman, & Sarah his wife of the one part & Robert BURTON of cnty afsd, Merchant, of the other part. There is a tract of land situate in Indian River Hundred in cnty afsd on SW side of Bracy's Branch adjoining lands formerly belonging to Isaac FLEMING supposed to contain 230 acres, originally surveyed for Thomas BEATES & by sundry conveyances became the property of James THOMPSON of cnty afsd. There is another parcel lying on the North sid of the above recited land containing 18 acres surveyed by virtue of a warrant dtd 18 Apr 1754 for Margaret LITTLE, widow. Whereas sd James THOMPSON & Margaret his wife, for a valuable consideration to them paid by John LITTLE did by Deed of Release dtd 03 May 1780 sold to sd John LITTLE all right & claim to sd two parcels of land. Sd John LITTLE & Sarah his wife for the sum of £130 sold to Robert BURTON all that part of the afsd lands bounded by land of Benjamin MCILVAIN & herein described containing & now laid out for 133 acres. Signed: John LITTLE, Sarah LITTLE (mark). Wit: Phillips KOLLOCK, W HARRISON. 05 Aug 1789 before me, one of the Justices of the Ct of Comm Pleas of Sussex cnty personally appeared Sarah LITTLE wife of above named John LITTLE, who being examined separate from her husband declared she became a part thereto of her own free will. Signed: Peter F WRIGHT. Rec: 15 Aug 1789 Nath'l MITCHELL, Proth'y.

O-14:61. Deed. This Indenture made 18 Mar 1789 between Benjamin WYNKOOP of city of Philadelphia, gent, & Sarah his wife, of the first part, Thomas FISHER, Samuel Rowland FISHER & Meirs FISHER of same city, merchants, of the 2nd part & John WALTON of Sussex cnty, De, yeoman, of the other part. Benjamin WYNKOOP & Sarah FISHER late of same cnty, spinster, by force of divers conveyances in law stood seized by equal moieties of a tract of land situate in Cedar Creek Hundred in Sussex cnty being parcels of a larger tract called Farmer's Delight & thereof being seized Sarah FISHER by Indenture tri partite dtd 25 Jan 1785 w/ consent & approval of Abijah DAVES to whom she was about to be md: testified by his becoming a party to that Indenture conveyed her moiety of sd tract of land w/improvement to Thomas, Samuel & Meirs FISHER but in trust for certain purposes in sd Indenture excepted. Afterwards sd marriage took effect & sd Sarah is since dead leaving issue two sons, Samuel Fisher DAWES & Edward DAWES infants of tender age. Sd Trustees conceive it for the Benefit of the sd children to convert sd moiety of sd lands into money to be placed at interest for their use during their minority. Sd Benjamin WYNKOOP & sd Trustees have agree to sell to sd John WALTON 300 acres, part of sd tract of land, at 40s per acre. Benjamin WYNKOOP & Sarah his wife for the sum of £300 for his moiety, and sd Thomas, Samuel & Meirs FISHER in consideration of the further sum of £300 for their moiety, sold to John WALTON all that tract of land, part of the sd tract called Farmers Delight situate as afsd bounded by land now or late of Thomas CAREY Jr, part of original tract belonging to heirs of Benja'm RILEY, dec'd, intended to contain 300 acres of land strict measure. Benjamin WYNKOOP, Thomas, Samuel & Meirs FISHER appoint Nicholas RIDGELY & Joseph MILLER Esqs their Attorney. Signed: Benj' WYNKOOP, Sarah WYNKOOP, Thomas FISHER, Samuel R FISHER, Miers FISHER. Wit: Joseph WALTON, Edward STAPLEFORD. Before the subscriber, one of the Justices of the Ct of Com Pleas for cnty of Philadelphia, personally came Benjamin WYNKOOP, Sarah, his wife, & Thomas, Samuel & Miers FISHER & acknowledged the above Indenture as their act & deed & Sarah being first separately examined declared she consented to above w/o compulsion . 19 Mar 1789. Signed: Wm POLLARD, Philadelphia cnty JP. James BIDDLE Esq, Proth'y of Ct of Comm Pleas for Philadelphia cnty certify William POLLARD Esq is one of the Justices of the Ct of Com Pleas for sd cnty. 25 Mar 1789 Signed: James BIDDLE, Proth'y. Rec: 15 Aug 1789 Nath'l MITCHELL, Proth'y, Sussex cnty, DE.

O-14:63. Deed. This Indenture made 26 Oct 1787 between Elijah COOPER of Washington cnty, NC of the one part & Isaac COOPER of Sussex cnty, DE of the other part. For the sum of £80 paid to him by afsd Isaac COOPER, Elijah COOPER sold a tract of land called Hound's Ditch which part was conveyed unto Elijah COOPER by James COOPER & Jane his wife as will appear on records of Worcester cnty bounded near where Thomas HUGG did live, land where James JONES did live containing 120 acres of land, excepting the right of Jane COOPER during her natural life. Elijah COOPER appoints Phillips KOLLOCK or Peter F WRIGHT of the town of Lewes, Sussex cnty, DE as his Attorney. Signed: Elijah COOPER. Wit: Barkley TOWNSEND, James TULLEY. Rec: 15 Aug 1789 Nath'l MITCHELL, Proth'y.

O-14:63. Deed. This Indenture made 31 Mar 1789 between William WALTON of Sussex cnty, DE & Sarah WALTON his wife, of the one part & Thomas SHERMAN of Sussex cnty of the other part. There are two tracts of land situate in Indian River Hundred in Sussex cnty about 2 miles from Indiana River & near Warwick, part of a larger quantity sd to have been surveyed to Francis POPE on 19 Apr 1722 & afterwards allotted to his dtr Ann POPE who md: John HOMES. Sd John HOMES afterward by virtue of a Warrant of resurvey from Honorable Thomas PENN, Proprietary, dtd 22 Feb 1739 had part of one of the above sd dividends of land surveyed to him by William SHANKLAND then Deputy Surveyor of cnty afsd 12 Jan 1741/2 & the other dividend was surveyed to sd John HOLMES by the sd Warrant of resurvey on 14 Jan 174/2 (or on 09 Apr 1755) by sd William SHANKLAND, Deputy Surveyor of sd cnty. John HOMES & Ann HOMES his wife by their Deed dtd 05 Feb 1756 conveyed 200 acres, part of the above two surveys to Jonathan JACOBS. Jonathan JACOBS by Deed dtd 30 Nov 1757 sold afsd 200 acres to William COLLINS. William COLLINS by his last will & testament dtd 03 Mar 1775 amongst other things did devise his land purchased of Jonathan JACOBS & others between his son Matthias COLLINS & his dtr Sarah COLLINS. Sarah COLLINS md. above named William WALTON parties to this Indenture. Sd dividends are bounded by land Matthias COLLINS did convey some part of Samuel WAPLES; land John HOMES laid off for Joel WOODBRIDGE but afterwards conveyed same to Margaret WAPLES, plantation where John RIGS dwells, land formerly surveyed to Robert PRETTYMAN & now held by Burton PRETTYMAN. William COLLINS purchased 10 acres of land from William WAPLES, son of sd Margaret WAPLES, which is part of land John HOMES conveyed to Margaret (and remaining part now held by Capt Joseph WAPLES saving only 2 acres). Sd 10 acres was laid off to William COLLINS in their lifetime which sd William COLLINS in his lifetime & since his death his sd dtr Sarah & her husband William WALTON have ever since peaceably held, occupied & enjoyed which sd three several dividends or parcels of land contain 88 acres more or less. This Indenture further witnesseth William WALTON & Sarah WALTON for the sum of £60 in gold & silver coin hath sold to Thomas SHERMAN all their rights, title, etc to the above described dividends & parcels of land. William WALTON & Sarah WALTON appoint Col Henry NEILL & Col David HALL, Mjr William PEERY & Dr Joseph HALL of Sussex cnty, DE as their lawful Attorneys. Signed: William WALTON, Sarah WALTON. Wit: James WILKINS, N WAPLES. Sarah WALTON, being of full age, examined apart from her husband declared the above Indenture to be of her own free will. 07 Apr 1789 Signed: John CLOWES. Rec: 15 Aug 1789 Nath'l MITCHELL, Proth'y.

O-14:66. A plat of the land William COLLINS willed to his dtr Sarah who md: William WALTON & by them sold to Thomas SHERMAN, surveyed at the request of the parties by William PRETTYMAN 30 Mary 1789.

O-14:66. Deed. This Indenture is made 05 Aug 1789 between Andrew SIMPLER of Broadkiln Hundred, Sussex cnty, DE, farmer, of the one part and William Brittingham ENNES of Indian River Hundred in sd cnty, farmer, of the other part. Andrew SIMPLER for the sum of £300 sold all that parcel of land being part of a large tract situate in Indian River & Angola Hundred in sd cnty formerly granted to Cord HAZZARD & called Sockerocket bounded by land formerly surveyed for Thomas WALKER, laid out for 150 acres to William Brittingham ENNES. Signed: Andrew SIMPLER. Wit: Robert HECK, William YOUNG, Rhoads SHANKLAND. Rec: 15 Aug 1789 Nath'l MITCHELL, Proth'y.

O-14:67. Deed. This Indenture made 14 May 1789 between Ephraim VAUGHAN of Sussex cnty, DE, planter, of the one part & Thomas MOORE of same of the other part. William VAUGHAN and Seven VAUGHAN late of the cnty afsd were in their lifetime seized of two several parcels of land situate in Little Creek Hundred, Sussex cnty, DE; one tract containing 158 acres being a resurvey on a pattent called Coxes Discovery per Warrant & certificate thereof, the other tract containing 150 acres, 100 acres of which last mentioned tract was purchased by the Grantor's father from Thomas KENNERLY by Deed & the other 50 acres was devised by William EVANS to Matthias JONES who devised same to his son, William JONES, which sd William by his deed conveyed sd 50 acres of land to Ephraim VAUGHAN, father of the present Grantor which sd William VAUGHAN & Sevin VAUGHAN being so seized of sd land, viz: 158 acres being resurvey & the other 150 acres, 100 of which was purchased of sd Thomas KINNERLY & the remaining 50 acres being purchased of William JONES, the whole amounted to 308 acres of land, afterwards d: intestate, unmarried & w/o issue, whereby sd lands & premises descended to his brother & sisters. Whereas at an Orphans Ct held in Lewes, Sussex cnty, DE in the present year 1789 sd Ct appointed 5 Freeholds to make division of the intestate lands amongst the heirs of the sd William & Sevin whereupon the Ct apptd Messrs Robert HOUSTON, James BRATTEN, Barclay TOWNSEND, William MOORE & Shiles MOORE to make divisions which sd Freeholders on their solemn Oath did report sd lands & premises would not admit of partition amongst the sd heirs of sd dead w/o marring & spoiling the whole. Whereupon sd Orphan Ct at the prayer of Ephraim VAUGHAN did on 08 Mar in year afsd appoint sd James BRATTEN, Barcley TOWNSEND & William MOORE to a value on the lands afsd who on 06 Apr last past did report they valued the lands at 12s 6p per acre. Whereupon the sd lands & premises on the day last afsd were by the sd Orphans Ct adjudges to the sd Ephraim VAUGHAN & his assigns at the valuation set. Sd Ephraim VAUGHAN for the sum of £200 sold to sd Thomas MOORE all those lands above described containing in the whole 308 acres. Signed: Ephraim VAUGHAN. Wit: Chas MOORE, John MITCHELL. Ephraim VAUGHAN apptd David HALL or Joseph MILLER Esqs to be his Attorney. Signed: Ephraim VAUGHAN. Wit: Chas MOORE, John MITCHELL. Rec: 15 Aug 1789 Nath'l MITCHELL, Proth'y.

O-14:69. Deed. This Indenture made 02 Mar 1789 between John Wilson DEAN & Mary DEAN his wife of Sussex of the one part & Benjamin JOHNSON, house carpenter, of the other part. John W DEAN & Mary his wife for the sum of £150 to Benjamin JOHNSON a parcel of land situate in Broadkiln Hundred within Sussex cnty bounded by a tract called Talberts containing 111 acres being part of a large tract of land called Carlisles Mill which sd 111 acres was by Deed of Gift from Charles PEERY in his lifetime granted to his dtr Marget CALE the wife of Thomas CALE which sd Marget together w/her husband Thomas mortgaged to the Trustees of the GLO & the sd Trustees caused same to be extended & by the High Sheriff of sd cnty sold to John CLOWES Esq he being the highest bidder. Sd John CLOWES by his Deed of Sale conveyed sd land to Richard BLOXOM & Richard BLOXOM by Deed dtd 13 May 1763 conveyed same to Baptis NEWCOMB. Sd Baptis NEWCOMB by his Deed dtd 02 Nov 1764 conveyed sd land to John CLOWES, sd John CLOWES by Deed dtd 05 May 1773 conveyed same to John W DEAN. John W DEAN & Mary his wife appoint John CLOWES or Phillips KOLLOCK Esqs their Attorney. Signed: John W DEAN, Mary DEAN. Wit: Stephen REDDEN, Hugh PATTERSON. John CLOWES certifies that Mary DEAN being of full age was examined separate from her husband and declared the executed sd Deed of her own free will. Rec: 15 Aug 1789 Nath'l MITCHELL, Proth'y.

O-14:70. Deed. This Indenture made 02 May 1789 between William WAPLES & Zadock VEAZEY of Sussex cnty, DE, yeomen, of the one part & Paul WAPLES Sr & Peter WAPLES of same place of the other part. William Naples & Zadock VEAZEY of Sussex cnty, DE for the sum of £200 (and in consequence of a Bond given by William WAPLES for the conveyance of a parcel of land called Aydelotts Meadow dtd 23 Mar 1767) sold to Paul WAPLES Sr & Peter WAPLES all the parcels of land being part of three tracts viz: Aydelotts Meadow, Luck & Narrow Chance between Old & New River Landings containing & now laid out for 117 acres. Wm WAPLES & Zadock VEAZEY appoint Woolsey BURTON, Jacob BURTON, Jon WINGATE, Solomon WILLEY & John Wise BATSON Esqs as their Attorney. Signed: William WAPLES, Zadock VEZEY. Wit: Wm TINGLE Sr,

Edw DINGLE. Rec: 15 May 1789 Nath'l MITCHELL, Proth'y.

O-14:71. Deed. This Indenture made 13 Oct 1788 between Allen SHORT of Sussex cnty, DE, yeoman, of the one part w/Rachel his wife & Winder CROCKET of same place, yeoman, of the other part. Allen SHORT late of Sussex cnty d: & by his last will & testament dtd 1788 did devise unto son Allen SHORT above 1 tract of land containing 100 acres called Shorts Chance on SE side of Nanticoke River in a neck of land called Carr's Neck bounded by land of Thomas JONES containing 100 acres. Allen Short & Rachel his wife for the sum of £41 2s 4p paid 01 Jan 1784 sold to Winder CROCKET all that land sd Abraham SHORT dec'd devised to sd Allen SHORT. Allen SHORT & Rachel his wife appoint Mr Phillips KOLLOCK of Lewes & Mr William HARRISON of same their Attorney. Signed: Allen SHORT (mark), Rachel O SHORT (mark). Wit: Caleb EVANS, Elizabeth CHRISTOPHER (mark). 22 Jul 1789 before me, one of the Justices of the Ct of Comm Pleas, appeared Rachel SHORT, wife of Allen SHORT, who being examined by me separately from her husband did declare she became a party to the above of her own free will. Signed: Alex'r LAWS. Rec: 15 Aug 1789 Nath'l MITCHELL, Proth'y.

O-14:73. Deed. This Indenture made 12 Jan 1788 between Jedediah TINGLE of Sussex cnty, DE, of the one part, planter, & Richard Holland LOCKWOOD of same place, shipwright, of the other part. Jedediah TINGLE for the sum of £100 sold to Richard Holland LOCKWOOD a parcel of land called Tingles Choice (it being a grant from the Governor to Littleton TINGLE, grandfather of Jedediah TINGLE & Samuel TINGLE, sons of the sd Littleton TINGLE, aft his father's death being heir to the afsd land & for a consideration conveyed to Daniel BARNS which sd Barns signed over to John LOCKWOOD which he bequeathed to his son the afsd Richard Holland LOCKWOOD) containing 100 acres. Jedediah TINGLE appoints William BAUINGTON, John Wise BATSON Esq, Phillips KOLLOCK his Attorney. Signed: Jedediah TINGLE. Wit: John AYDELOTT, Benjamin HOLLAND. Rec: 15 Aug 1789 Nath'l MITCHELL, Proth'y.

O-14:73. Deed. Indenture made 05 Aug 1789 between Charles POLK of Sussex cnty, DE, of one part & James POLK of same cnty of the other part. Charles POLK for the sum of £40 sold to James POLK all that parcel of land situate in Sussex cnty & Nanticoke Hundred in a neck called Jones Neck being part of a tract of land first patented to George LAYFIELD since Deeded by Isaac LAYFIELD to the afsd Charles POLK bounded by land called Fruitfull Plain, land of John NEWBOLD & James POLK containing 77 & 1/2 acres. Signed: Charles POLK. Wit: Phillips KOLLOCK, W HARRISON. Rec: 15 Aug 1789 Nath'l MITCHELL, Proth'y.

O-14:74. Deed. This Indenture made 05 Jun 1789 between Clement JACKSON & Polly JACKSON his wife of Sussex cnty, DE, of the one part & Stephen REDDEN of sd cnty, carpenter, of the other part. There is a certain tract of land in cnty afsd in Broadkiln Hundred known as Gaults Swamp which was granted to Andrew COLLING (grndfthr to afsd Polly JACKSON) by a Proprietors Warrant & by virtue thereof surveyed for him in 1756. The sd Andrew COLLINGS by his last will & testament, amongst other things, did devise the afsd tract to his son, Andrew COLLINGS (fthr of afsd Polly JACKSON) & sd Andrew COLLINGS the younger d: Intestate leaving issue 2 dtrs, the afsd Polly, party to these presents, and Elizabeth to whom his lands descended; and by division of sd Intestate land made agreeable to law afsd Goults Swamp, to sd Polly JACKSON. Afsd Clement & Polly JACKSON for the sum of £52 10s sold to Stephen REDDEN all that part of sd tract called Gaults Swamp lying on the NW side of the main road that leads from John CLOWES' to John COLLINGS containing 75 acres of land & swamp. Clement & Polly JACKSON appoint John WILTBANK or Peter WRIGHT Esqs as their Attorney. Signed: Clement JACKSON, Polly JACKSON. Wit: John CLOWES, Joseph MORRIS. Polly JACKSON, being of full age, being separate from her husband was examined & declared she became a party to the above Deed of her own free will 08 Jun 1789. Signed: John CLOWES. Rec: 15 Aug 1789 Nath'l MITCHELL, Proth'y.

O-14:76. Deed. This Indenture made 19 Apr 1789 between Thomas DAVIS & Mary his wife of Sussex cnty, DE of the one part & Joshua BENNETT of same place of the other part. There is a piece of land situate in Slaughter Neck in cnty afsd being part of a tract which formerly belonged to Thomas DAVIS Esq, dec'd, containing 10 acres of land laid off & surveyed 21 Mar 1789 by Thomas PULLETT at the request of the above sd Thomas DAVIS bounded by land formerly belonging to Christopher NUTTER, dec'd, containing 10 acres. Thomas DAVIS & Mary his wife for the sum of £35 sold to Joshua BENNETT the afsd 10 acres. Signed: Thomas DAVIS, Mary DAVIS. Wit: Nehemiah DAVIS, Elias TOWNSEND. Rec: 15 Aug 1789 Nath'l MITCHELL, Proth'y.

O-14:76. Petition. Thomas LAWS, Admin of Wm BAGWELL late of Sussex cnty, DE, dec'd, who d: Intestate prays Court for leave to convey land. Sd William BAGWELL in his lifetime was seized of a parcel of land, part of a larger tract situate in Cedar Creek Hundred, cnty afsd & so being seized by his article of agreement dtd 16 Jan 1777 acknowledged himself to be held bound to John CHANCE of sd cnty in the sum of £37 10s to be paid to sd John CHANCE w/condition sd William BAGWELL or his heirs, Attorney, Admin, Exec convey his title to a tract of land bounded by Joshua SPENCER formerly sold to him by

William BAGWELL, other land of John CHANCE containing 10 acres. William BAGWELL after making sd writing & before he executed a Deed d: Intestate aft having first rec'd sd John CHANCE's £13 9s 2p part of the purchase monies & having since been fully paid & satisfied to the Petitioner. Sd lands together w/other land of sd John CHANCE have been seized, & sold by Peter Fretwell WRIGHT Esq late High Sheriff of Sussex cnty afsd to satisfy a Judgement which James THARP recovered against sd John CHANCE by Deed from sd Peter Fretwell WRIGHT to William BRADLEY of Kent cnty, DE. William BRADLEY afterwards sold all his right & title to sd lands to Mark DAVIS. Petitioner prays the Ct authorize sd Petitioner to execute a Deed to sd Mark DAVIS for the sd land in discharge of the above sd recorded writing to convey sd lands contracted for w/their Decedents. 06 Aug 1789 Signed: Thos LAWS. Nath'l MITCHELL, Proth'y.

O-14:77. Deed. Thomas LAWS, Admin of the estate of William BAGWELL late of Sussex cnty, DE, yeoman, dec'd. William BAGWELL in his lifetime was seized of a parcel of land part of a larger tract situate in Cedar Creek Hundred , sd cnty by his writing Obligatory dtd 16 Jan 1777 bound to John CHANCE of sm cnty in the sum of £37 10s w/condition sd William BAGWELL shall convey title to a tract of land bounded by land of Joshua SPENCER formerly sold to him by William BAGWELL afsd, other lands of John CHANCE containing 10 acres for which land sd John CHANCE bound himself to pay sd William BAGWELL £37 6p per acre & when Bond is complied w/then be void & duly rec: in afsd cnty. Sd William BAGWELL before he executed conveyance to sd John CHANCE for the afsd lands d: Intestate. Whereas the equitable right of sd John CHANCE in the sd lands together w/other lands of John CHANCE hath since been seized & sold by Peter Fretwell WRIGHT, late High Sheriff of Sussex cnty afsd to satisfy a Judgement which James THARP recovered against sd John CHANCE as appears by Deed from sd Peter Fretwell WRIGHT as Sheriff to William BRADLEY of Kent cnty, DE. Whereas sd William BRADLEY for valuable consideration sold the sd lands purchased under the Sheriff's sale afsd to Mark DAVIS (one of the parties to these presents). Whereas Thomas LAWS, Admin of sd William BAGWELL petitioned Ct of Com Pleas which Ct empowered him as Admin for sd William BAGWELL, dec'd, to execute sufficient Deed to sd Mark DAVIS for the lands afsd. Sd Thomas LAWS, Admin of sd William BAGWELL in obedience to sd Order of Court for the sum of £13 19s 2p pad by sd John CHANCE to sd William BAGWELL in his lifetime & in consideration of the sum of £3 5s 10p (being the residue of the purchase money) pd by sd Mark DAVIS the receipt of which I acknowledge thereof convey all the land above cited containing 9 & 1/5 acre of land. Signed: Thomas LAWS, Admin. Wit: William HALL, Thomas HAZZARD. Rec: 15 Aug 1789 Nath'l MITCHELL, Proth'y.

O-14:79. Deed. This Indenture made 30 May 1789 between Hugh STEPHENSON of Sussex cnty, DE & Peggy his wife of the one part & Robert HOOD of cnty afsd of the other part. There is a tract of land situate in Broadkiln Hundred, Sussex cnty, DE on the NW side of Mill Creek Branch containing 161 acres included in the bounds of a patent granted to John RICHARDSON for 500 acres, part of which became the property of Samuel COULTER of Sussex cnty, dec'd. Sd Samuel COULTER d: Intestate, his lands descending to his son, Charles COULTER. Charles COULTER by deed dtd 06 Apr 1779 conveyed sd land to the above Hugh STEPHENSON, the remaining part of the sd 161 acres is included in a survey mad pursuant of a Warrant granted to Peter CROW. Martha CROW, dtr of sd Peter CROW assigned sd Warrant to Wilbour PEERY who assigned part of same to sd Hugh STEPHENSON which sd 161 & 1/4 is bounded by John NEILL's land, land of Robinson SAVAGE, containing & now surveyed for 161 & 1/4 acres. Hugh STEPHENSON & Peggy his wife for the sum of £161 in gold & silver coin sold sd land to Robert HOOD. Signed: Hugh STEPHENSON, Peggy STEPHENSON. Wit: James VENT, Samuel DODD. Peggy STEPHENSON, wife of above Hugh, being of full age, declared she signed & delivered the within Deed of her own free will. Signed: John CLOWES, Justice, Ct of Com Pleas, 07 Aug 1789. Rec: 15 Aug 1789 Nath'l MITCHELL, Proth'y.

O-14:81. Deed. This Indenture made 26 October 1787 between John Wittington ADAMS of Broadkiln Hundred, Sussex cnty, DE, of the one part & John TIMMONS the younger of hund & cnty afsd, yeoman, of the other part. John W ADAMS for the sum of £150 sold to John TIMMONS a parcel of land situate in Broad Creek Hundred, cnty afsd, called Eastwood supposed to contain 200 acres, granted by patent to Alexander ADAMS & by his last will & testament, devised to his son, Samuel ADAMS, fthr of the Grantor in these present. Signed: John W ADAMS. Wit: Joseph MILLER, Davidson DAVID. Rec: 15 Aug 1789 Nath'l MITCHELL, Proth'y.

O-14:81. Deed. This Indenture made 06 May 1789 between Ephraim VAUGHAN of Sussex cnty, DE of the one part & Thomas MOORE of the other part. Ephraim VAUGHAN for the sum of £50 sold to Thomas MOORE all that parcel of land called Poplar Neck (or Ridge) situate in Little Creek Hundred, Sussex cnty, DE containing by estimation 50 acres of land as will more fully appear by Deed from James QUARTARMUS to Ephraim VAUGHAN, fthr of sd Grantor, dtd 19 Nov 1766. Signed: Ephraim MOORE. Wit: Chs MOORE, John MITCHELL. Ephraim VAUGHAN the Grantor above appoints David HALL or Joseph MILLER Esqs at his Attorney. Rec: 15 Aug 1789 Nath'l MITCHELL, Proth'y.

O-14:82. Petition. Ann LACEY, Adminx of John LACEY for leave of Ct of convey land. John LACEY in his lifetime, to wit, on the 30 Mar 1774 by his writing obligate called an alienation Bond obliged himself to convey to Benjamin BENSTON a tract of land in sd Bond mentioned. Benjamin BENSTON by Indorsement on sd Bond assigned sd Bond to his son Benjamin BENSTON Jr which Bond & indorsement thereon were duly proved 12 Feb 1789. Sd John LACY since the execution of sd Bond is dead w/o having made conveyance of the lands in the Bond. Petitioner prays that the Ct empower her to convey sd lands to Benjamin BENSTON Jr the consideration money being paid in discharge of the Obligation. Signed: Ann LACEY. Indorsed on back thereof granted & order made 06 Aug 1789. Nath'l MITCHELL, Proth'y.

O-14:83. Deed. This Indenture made 26 May 1789 between Charles WHEATLY of Dorchester cnty, MD of the one part & Jonathan COPE of Sussex cnty, DE of the other part. For the sum of £244 11s 3p current money of MD paid to sd Charles WHEATLY by Jonathan COPE sd WHEATLY sold to sd COPE part of a tract of land called Lees First Purchase in Sussex cnty, DE containing 150 & 1/2 acres. Signed: Charles WHEATLY. Wit: John TENNENT, Jacob CANNON. Charles WHEATLY appoints Alexander LAWS Esq or Rhoads SHANKLAND Esq as his Attorney. Rec: 15 Aug 1789 Nath'l MITCHELL, Proth'y.

O-14:84. Deed. This Indenture made 26 May 1789 between Charles WHEATLEY of Dorchester cnty, MD of the one part and John ELLIOTT of same cnty & state afsd of the other part. Charles WHEATLY for the sum of £244 11s 3p current money of MD sold to John ELLIOTT part of a parcel of land called Lees First Purchase in Sussex cnty, DE. containing 150 & 1/2 acres. Signed: Charles WHEATLEY. Wit: John TENNENT, Jacob CANNON. Charles WHEATLEY appoints Alexander LAWS Esq or Robert SHANKLAND his Attorney. Rec: 15 Aug 1879 Nath'l MITCHELL, Proth'y.

O-14:85. Deed. This Indenture made 04 Apr 1788 between Nathan WALLER of Sussex cnty, DE of the one part & Matthew CALLAWAY of same place of the other part. Nathan WALLER for the sum of £50 sold to Matthew CALLAWAY part of a tract of land called Swamp surveyed for Nathaniel WALLER Sr 10 Jun 1734 containing by estimation 64 acres more or less as also all the lands surveyed by virtue of a resurvey Warrant granted to sd Nathan WALLER by the Proprietor PENN on afsd tract called Swamp resurveyed 15 May 1776 the whole by estimation containing 294 acres more or less which sd tract called Swamp was devised by Nathaniel WALLER Sr, dec'd, to afsd Nathan WALLER. Nathan WALLER appoints Phillips KOLLOCK, William POLK or Charles MOORE

Esqs of Sussex cnty his Attorney. Signed: Nathan WALLER. Wit: Chas MOORE, William POLK. Rec: 15 Aug 1789 Nath'l MITCHELL, Proth'y.

O-14:86. Deed. Robert JONES & Archabald FLEMING of Sussex cnty, DE, Execs of the last will of John WALKER late of Broadkiln Hundred in afsd cnty, yeoman, dec'd. John WALKER in his lifetime was seized of 436 acres of land, being part of a larger tract situate in Broadkiln Hundred called Millfield. John WALKER made his last will & testament 14 Apr 1788 wherein among other things he did direct his Execs should have full power to sell & dispose of 186 acres of land off the tract that formerly belonged to David RANKIN to be taken off that side of the tract adjoining John HOLLAND proceeds to pay my just debts & appointed sd Robert JONES & Archabald FLEMING his Executors. Robert JONES & Archabald FLEMING, Executors afsd, in pursuance of the trust of sd will & for the sum of £186 sold to Nathaniel MITCHELL the above recited 186 acres of land, being part of the tract of 436 acres conveyed by William PEERY & James MARTIN Esqs, Attorneys, of David RANKIN by Deed dtd 02 Feb 1784 to sd John WALKER. Signed: Robert JONES, Archabeld FLEMING. Wit: Wm MASSEY, George HAZZARD. Rec: 15 Aug 1789 Nath'l MITCHELL, Proth'y.

O-14:87. Deed. This Indenture made 06 Aug 1789 between Nathaniel MITCHELL of Sussex cnty, DE, Esq of the one part and Robert JONES of Broadkiln Hundred, cnty afsd, yeoman of the other part. Nathaniel MITCHELL for the sum of £187 8s sold to Robert JONES a tract of land containing and laid off for 186 acres of land, being part of a larger tract situate in Broadkiln Hundred called Millfield 436 acres whereof was conveyed by William PEERY & James MARTIN Esq, Attorneys of David RANKIN by Deed dtd 02 Feb 1784 to John WALKER, dec'd, who by his last will & testament direct his Execs to sell the above 186 acres of land & in pursuance of that request did by Deed dtd one day before date of this Deed sell sd 186 acres to Nathaniel MITCHELL. Signed: Nath'l MITCHELL. Wit: Wm MASEY, George HAZZARD. Rec: 15 Aug 1789 Nath'l MITCHELL, Proth'y.

O-14:89. Deed. There is a tract of land situate in Cedar Creek Hundred, Sussex cnty, DE called the Brook Tract containing 280 acres being the moiety of a larger tract lying on the N side of Prime Hook bounded by land of Caleb CIRWITHINS, dec'd, land of William BELLAMY. Whereas William CRAMMER by Deed dtd 04 Feb 1721 conveyed the same to John WATSON of Sussex cnty who made his last will & testament dtd 03 Jan 1729 & devised same land to his 3 sons, James, Hezekiah & Luke WATSON all my plantation & land containing 300 acres being in Prime Hook Neck, cnty afsd, sd plantation & land to be equally divided between them & to have their choice according to their age, the eldest first & if any of them die w/o issue then his dividend shall be equally divided between his 2 brothers & the last liver of them to enjoy all the sd land. Whereas sd James WATSON d: Intestate w/o issue by whose death the whole of the sd lands vested in the afsd Hezekiah & Luke WATTSON which sd Luke afterwards dock'd the Entail thereon & his one moiety of sd lands were sold by the Sheriff of Sussex cnty for discharge of his debts & the other moiety descended to Thomas WATTSON by the death of his fthr sd Hezekiah. Sd Thomas afterwards d: Intestate & w/o issue whereby sd moiety descended to the heirs of Elizabeth late the wife of Stephen TOWNSEND, dec'd, one of the dtrs of afsd John WATTSON the Testator, namely 1/2 thereof to Stephen TOWNSEND, Abigail the wife of Aaron OLIVER, Corton TOWNSEND (since dec'd leaving 3 children to wit Littleton TOWNSEND, Elizabeth the wife of Wm WALTON), Betty SPENCER (since dec'd, leaving Samuel, Ebenezer, Sarah & Betty SPENCER & Mary METCALF), Littleton TOWNSEND, Noah TOWNSEND & Jehu TOWNSEND, & the other 1/2 thereof to Isaac TOWNSEND, John TOWNSEND, James Townsend, heirs of Mary late wife of Corton TOWNSEND the elder, dec'd, of the sons of the afsd John WATTSON dec'd. This Indenture made between the afsd Aaron OLIVER & Abigail his wife of the one part & George RICKARDS of Cedar Creek Hundred, Sussex cnty of the other part. Sd Aaron OLIVER & Abigail his wife for the sum of £13 2s 6p sold to George RICKARDS the sd lands containing 9 & 3/8 acres, Aaron OLIVER & Abigail his wife sd lands to George RECARDS against the claim or claims of them sd Aaron OLIVER & Abigail & against Eli, son of Elias TOWNSEND or any other person(s) by from under them, being first interlined, shall & will forever Warrant & defend. Signed: Aaron OLIVER, Abigail A OLIVER (mark). Wit: John CLOWES, Littleton TOWNSEND, Jonathan WILLIAMS. 09 Aug 1787 Abigail OLIVER wife of w/in sd Aaron OLIVER, was examined separated from her husband, declared she became a party to this Deed of her own free will. Signed: John CLOWES. Aaron OLIVER & wife appoint Thomas EVANS of cnty afsd their attorney. Signed: Aaron OLIVER. Wit: Littleton TOWNSEND, Jonathan WILLIAMS, Joseph STOCKLEY. Rec: 15 Aug 1789 Nath'l MITCHELL, Proth'y.

O-14:90. Deed. There is a parcel of land situate in Cedar Creek Hundred, Sussex cnty, DE called Brook Tract containing 280 acres being the moiety of a larger tract lying on the N side of Prime Hook bounding w/land of Caleb CIRWITHIN, land of William BELLAMY. Whereas William CRAMER by Deed dtd 04 Feb 1721 conveyed same to John WATTSON of cnty afsd who afterwards made his will dtd 03 Jan 1729 wherein he devised the sd land to his 3 sons, James, Hezekiah & Luke WATTSON all my plantation & land containing 300 acres lying in Prime Hook Neck, Sussex cnty to be equally divided amongst them to have their choice according to age, the eldest first; if any of them d: w/o issue his dividend to be equally divided between his 2 brothers & the last liver of them to enjoy all sd land. James WATTSON d: Intestate & w/o issue whereby the whole of the sd land vested in the afsd Hezekiah WATTSON & Luke WATTSON. Afterwards Luke docked the entail thereon & his moiety of sd lands was sold by the Sheriff of Sussex cnty for discharge of his debts. The other moiety thereof descended to Thomas WATTSON only son & heir of Hezekiah WATTSON by the death of the sd Hezekiah which sd Thomas WATTSON also d: Intestate whereby 1/2 of his sd moiety descended to the heirs of Elizabeth late the wife of Stephen TOWNSEND the elder, dec'd, one of the dtrs of John WATTSON the Testator & the other 1/2 thereof to Isaac, John & James TOWNSEND sons of Mary late the wife of Corton TOWNSEND, dec'd, another of the dtrs of the sd John WATTSON, Testator. James TOWNSEND lately d: Intestate & Admin of his estate was granted to his brother the afsd Isaac TOWNSEND who on 09 Nov 1786 petitioned setting forth that sd James left no personal estate to pay his just debts, that sd Petitioner has approved Accountings of £26 12s 8p, that sd James d: seized of an undivided right in a tract of land situate in Cedar Creek Hundred known as the Brook containing 150 acres & prayed the Ct grant an order for him to make sale of sd James TOWNSEND's land afsd to discharge his just debts. The Ct so ordered. Sd Isaac TOWNSEND on 24 Jan last put same to public sale the same was purchased by George RICKARDS of Cedar Creek Hundred for the sum £30 he being the highest bidder. This Indenture made between sd Isaac TOWNSEND of the one part & George RICKARDS of the other part. Isaac TOWNSEND for the afsd sum of £30 sold to sd George RICKARDS all the undivided right of the sd James TOWNSEND, dec'd, in the land afsd. Signed: Isaac TOWNSEND. Isaac TOWNSEND appoints Thomas EVANS at his Attorney. Signed: Isaac TOWNSEND. Wit: John METCALF, Sarah CONNER, Joseph STOCKLEY. Rec: 15 Aug 1789 Nath'l MITCHELL, Proth'y.

O-14:92. Deed. Whereas Peter ROBINSON of Sussex cnty, DE at Ct of Com Pleas at Lewes, cnty afsd, at Feb term 1787 before the Justices of sd Ct had recovered against Jacob WILSON, late Sarah STEWART, Exec of the estate of Daniel STEWART, dec'd, a debt of £28 14s 8p which sd Peter in sd Ct were adjudged for his damages he had sustained for his costs & charges by default of her the sd Sarah, of the estate of sd Daniel STEWART in the hand of sd Sarah, he should have that money on Wednesday 07 of May next term at which day sd Sheriff did return that by virtue of the writ directed to him of the lands & tenements of sd Daniel STEWART in the hands of sd Sarah he had seized & taken in execution, two parcels of land situate in Indian River & Broadkiln Hundreds containing in the whole 235 acres w/all improvement to same, which sd land he had appraised by 2 Freeholders of Bailiwick, who found the rents, issues, etc of a clear yearly value insufficient beyond all reprises to satisfy the debt & damages w/in 7 years & that same remained in his hands unsold for want of buyers. Whereas a certain writ 06 Aug 1788 to sd Peter Fretwell WRIGHT directed by which he was ordered sd lands & tenements be him taken he should expose to public sale & have that money before the sd Ct on Wednesday 05 Nov next to render to sd Peter ROBINSON for his debt & damages. Sd Sheriff did return by virtue of that writ, sd land was purchased by afsd Peter ROBINSON for the use of Henry LINGO 01 Nov 1788 for the sum of £30 12s 4p, he being the highest bidder. Whereas sd Peter Fretwell WRIGHT was removed from office of Sheriff before he had executed conveyance to sd Henry LINGO for the lands afsd . Therefore Thomas EVANS Esq for the afsd sum paid doth convey to sd Henry LINGO 2 tracts of land containing in the whole 235 acres. Signed: Thomas EVANS, Sheriff. Wit: John WOOLF, Adam HALL. Peter Fretwell Wright ack rec'pt from Henry LINGO the consideration money mentioned in the above 08 Aug 1789. Rec: 15 Aug 1789 Nath'l MITCHELL, Proth'y.

O-14:93. Deed. Samuel ARNALL late of Lewes, Sussex cnty, DE, pilot, dec'd, in his lifetime was seized of part of an Island of Marsh situate in Lewes Creek commonly called Baily's Island made his last will & testament whereof he apptd Joseph BAILY & William ARNALL both late of the town & cnty afsd, pilots, dec'd, his Execs & afterwards d: seized as afsd in which sd Samuel ARNALL did direct his Execs afsd to sell his land to the best advantage of his estate. Whereas sd Joseph BAILY & William ARNALL both after they had the will duly proved & registered d: Intestate before they had sold sd lands whereof Admin of all & singular which were of sd Samuel ARNALL at the time of his death unadministered by sd Joseph BAILY & William ARNALL were committed by Phillips KOLLOCK Esq Register apptd for Probate granting LOA to William ARNALL of Lewes, Sussex cnty, DE, house carpenter & joyner, party to these present. Whereas the personal estate of the sd Samuel ARNALL proved insufficient to pay & discharge his just debts & support & educate his small children. Whereupon sd William ARNALL, Admin afsd obtained an order from Orphans Ct for the sale of sd land whereof sd Samuel ARNALL d: seized for the purpose afsd. Thereupon sold by public sale on 04 Mar 1789 sd island of marsh when same was purchased by Reece WOOLF party to these presents for the sum of £6 10s he being the highest bidder being 1/8 part thereof as appears by Deed from Stewart BAILY to sd Samuel ARNALL situate on S side of sd Island of Marsh called Baily's Marsh being 1/8 part thereof. 07 Aug 1789 Signed: William ARNALL. Wit: John WOOLFE, Robert SHANKLAND. Rec: 15 Aug 1789 Nath'l MITCHELL, Proth'y.

O-14:95. Bond of Conveyance. Director COSTON of Sussex cnty, DE, yeoman, am firmly bound unto Joshua COSTON of sd cnty, yeoman, in the sum of £50 to sd Joshua COSTON this 25 Jun 1784. Conditions of sd Obligation is such that Director COSTON shall convey at Ct of Com Pleas to be held at Lewes, cnty afsd, at reasonable request of sd Joshua COSTON a parcel of land lying in the forrest of Broadkiln Hundred being part of a parcel of land formerly belonged to Ezekle COSTON which land falls to sd Director COSTON by heirship. Signed: Director COSTON (mark). Wit: Stephen COSTON, Elizabeth SKIDMORE. For the consideration of £27 paid by Stephen COSTON I assign all my right & claim of the within Bond to Stephen COSTON. 28 Mar 1786. Signed: Joshua COSTON. Wit: Somerset DICKINSON, John ROACH (mark). 27 May 1786 Mrs Elizabeth SKIDMORE personally came before me Joseph HAZZARD & made oath she saw the foregoing Bond signed by Stephen COSTON. Signed: Joseph HAZZARD, Esq. Rec'd of Stephen COSTON on his Bond to Somerset DICKINSON who was Exec to the estate of Derector COSTON which Bond was assigned me by Sarah DICKINSON, Exec to sd Samuel DICKINSON's estate for the use of Elisha COSTON a minor son of sd Director COSTON to who I was apptd Guardian whereof I do ack: to have rec'd the full sum due for this w/in land. Signed: Sommerset Dickinson COSTON, Guardian.

O-14:95. Bond of Conveyance. Youfamy COSTON of Sussex cnty, DE, yeoman, am bound to Joshua COSTON of sd cnty, yeoman in the sum of £50 to be paid to sd Joshua COSTON. 25 Jun 1784. Condition of the Obligation is that sd Youfamy COSTON shall convey at the request of sd Joshua COSTON a parcel of land situate in the forest of BroadKill Hundred, it being a parcel formerly belonging to Ezekiel COSTON which lands fall unto one sd Youfamy COSTON by heirship. Signed: Youfamy COSTON (mark). Wit: Stephen COSTON, Elizabeth SKIDMORE (mark). For the sum of £27 pd by Stephen COSTON I assign my right & claim of the w/in Bond unto Stephen COSTON. 23 Mar 1786 Signed: Joshua COSTON. Wit: Somerset DICKINSON, John ROACH. Rec'd 12 Jul 1787 of Stephen COSTON the full sum of £25 being full consideration for which I hold the w/in described lands unto my brother, Joshua COSTON, & the legal interest thereon from 25 Jun 1784 until this day & am fully satisfied & paid according to contract I sold the land afsd. Signed: Youfamy COSTON (mark). Wit: Joseph HAZZARD, N WAPLES.

O-14:96. Bond of Conveyance. Benton COSTON of Sussex cnty, DE, yeoman, am bound unto Joshua COSTON of sd cnty, yeoman, in the sum of £50 to be paid to be paid to sd Joshua COSTON dtd 05 Jun 1784. If sd Benton COSTON conveys at Ct of Com Pleas at the request of Joshua COSTON a certain parcel of land that formerly belonged to Ezekiel COSTON which sd land falls unto me by heirship this obligation to be void. Signed: Benton COSTON (mark). Wit: Stephen COSTON, Elizabeth SKIDMORE. 27 May 1786 Mrs Elizabeth SKIDMORE personally appeared before me & made oath she saw the afsd Bond ack & delivered & saw Stephen COSTON sign same. Signed: Jos HAZZARD Esq.

O-14:96. Bond of Conveyance. Sumerset Dickuson COSTON, millwright, of Sussex cnty, DE am bound unto Stephen COSTON in the penal sum of £200 for which payment to sd Stephen COSTON I hereby bind myself & set my hand this 07 Sep 1789. The condition of such that if sd Somerset Dickerson COSTON upon request of Stephen COSTON assign by sufficient Deed of Sale a certain parcel of land formerly the property of Ezekiel COSTON, dec'd, being undivided right among the several heirs situate in Broadkill Hundred, Sussex cnty, one large tract known as Coston's Content, another named Poplar Ridge & another named Son Ground supposed to contain 50 acres the above obligation to be void. Signed: Sommerset Dickerson COSTON. Wit: John CLOWES, James WILEY. 07 Sep 1789 Rec'd of Stephen COSTON full satisfaction of w/in Bond. Per Somerset D COSTON. Test: Jas WILEY.

O-14:97. Deed. This Indenture made 08 Sep 1789 between Ebenezer PETTYJOHN of Sussex cnty, DE, yeoman, of the one part and William OWENS of same, cordwinder, of the other part. Whereas Thomas TILTON, Elizabeth HILL & Thomas DAVOCK had granted unto them by sundry patents several tracts of land with sd cnty situate being on the N side of Long Bridge Branch & adjoining tracts 500 acres thereof being the most S part of the whole did by sundry conveyances become the separate property of the afsd Thomas DAVOCK. Sd Thomas DAVOCK by his last will & testament dtd 27 Jan 1718 devised to his son, Thomas DAVOCK the above 500 acres. Sd Thomas DAVOCK the younger d: Intestate w/o issue whereupon the afsd 500 acres became the property of his sisters, Mary & Neomy. Sd Mary & Neomy by mutual consent divide sd 500 acres & sd Mary had the lands on the west and sd Neomy the lands on the E side of sd dividing line. Sd Neomy md: Michael GODWIN of Worcester cnty by whom she had issue several children & by her last will & testament executed by her husband sd Michael GODWIN did devise her dividend of the afsd 500 acres of land to her eldest son, William GODWIN. Michael GODWIN by his last will & testament dtd Dec 1765 bequeathed to sd William GODWIN the afsd E division of the afsd 500 acres. Sd William GODWIN did by his Deed of Sale dtd 29 Aug 1772 convey the afsd E division of land containing 250 acres onto Solomon PASIMORE. Solomon PASEMORE by Deed dtd 04 Oct 1788 conveyed to Ebenezer PETTYJOHN 47 acres of land being part of the afsd 250 acres. Ebenezer PETTYJOHN for the sum of £77 10s 8p sold the afsd 47 acres to

William OWENS. Signed: Ebinezer PETTYJOHN, Mary PETTYJOHN. Wit: John REED, William COVERDIL. Mary PETTYJOHN being of full age was examined apart from her husband & declared she became a party thereof of her own free will. 08 Sep 1789 Signed: John CLOWES. Rec: 16 Sep 1789 Nath'l MITCHELL, Proth'y.

O-14:99. Deed. This Indenture made 19 Aug 1789 between Casey THOMPSON of Kent cnty, DE, planter, & William THOMPSON & James THOMPSON & Leah CAREY & Priscilla PHILLIPS & Sarah CASEY & Esther HUTSON, these of Sussex cnty, DE, planters all of these named being of the one part & Benjamin PHILLIPS of Sussex cnty, DE, farmer, of the other part. Whereas there is a parcel of land situate in Sussex cnty being taken by a resurvey of John THOMPSON's old tract of 100 acres taken in way of resurvey by sd John THOMPSON as by pattent of resurvey more at large appears sd parcel or quantity of land beginning at the SE end of the home tract of 100 acres containing 131 acres. The above named parties, each & every one, for the sum of £50 sold the 131 acres to Benjamin PHILLIPS. The afsd, each one of us, appoint John WINGATE or Woolsey BURTON our Attorney. Signed: Cary THOMPSON (mark), William THOMPSON (mark), James THOMPSON (mark), Leah CARY (mark), Priscilla PHILLIPS, (mark), Sarah CARY (mark), Esther HUTSON (mark). Wit: John PHILLIPS, William THOMPSON. Rec: 16 Sep 1789 Nath'l MITCHELL, Proth'y.

O-14:99. Deed. This Indenture made 08 Sep 1789 between Thomas EVANS Esq, High Sheriff of Sussex cnty, DE of the one part & Caleb BALDING of same of the other part. Whereas there is a tract of land situate in Little Creek Hundred, Sussex cnty, DE bounded by lands belonging to James & William WALLER (sons of William WALLER dec'd) who devised sd land to Ephraim WALLER which sd tract contains 50 acres & is called Moors Lott. Whereas Isaac HOSSEY Esq late in Ct of Com Pleas held at Lewes in May term 1780 recovered judgement against the afsd Ephraim WALLER for the sum of £98 14s, debt, & £2 4s 7p which sd Ct adjudged for costs. Afsd Ephraim WALLER was convicted.4 for the sd debt & costs. Writ was issued by sd Ct dtd 05 Nov 1789 to the Sheriff of Sd cnty ordered which Warrant was levied & writ of Venditioni Exponas dtd 06 May year afsd conveyed to sd Caleb BALDING. Signed: Thomas EVANS, Sheriff. Wit: John W BATSON, Josiah GRIFFITH. Rec: 16 Sep 1789 Nath'l MITCHELL, Proth'y.

O-14:100. Deed. This Indenture made 10 Sep 1789 between Abraham HARRIS of Broadkill Hundred, Sussex cnty, DE, carpenter, of the one part & Elizabeth CONNER of same, seamster, of the other part. Abraham HARRIS for the sum of £93 10s sold & conveyed to Elizabeth CONNER a tract of land situate in the

Broadkill forest called Son Ground Tract bounded by Luke THOMAS's fence containing 93 & 1/2 acres whereof sd Abraham HARRIS became lawfully seized. Signed: Abraham HARRIS. Wit: Thomas TAYLOR (mark), Rhoads SHANKLAND. Rec: 16 Sep 1789 Nath'l MITCHELL, Proth'y.

O-14:101. Deed. This Indenture made 10 Sep 1789 between Sarah BURTON, late the wife of John BURTON, dec'd, & dtr of Albertus JACOBS, dec'd, of Lewes & Rehoboth Hundred, Sussex cnty, DE of the one part & John CRAIGE of Lewes of the other part. Whereas there is a parcel of land situate in the town of Lewes on the bank of Lewes Creek joining on the SE side of the house & lot in the possession of William JACOBS being part of 3 lotts originally granted by the Ct of Sussex cnty to John KIPHAVEN who by his last will & testament devised same to his 2 grandsons, John & Albertus JACOBS, who both d: Intestate seized thereof as tenants in common, leaving issue several children. Whereupon James JACOBS, eldest son of sd Albertus JACOBS & Albertus JACOBS, eldest son of sd John JACOBS, after necessary proceedings in Orphan's Ct accepted the sd lotts of land together w/other lands of their fathers at the valuations pursuant to law. Sd James JACOBS & Albertus JACOBS, being so seized to the lotts as tenants in common, sd James JACOBS afterwards d: Intestate leaving Albertus JACOBS, his only child & heir. Sd Albertus JACOBS, son of sd John JACOBS by his last will & testament devised his part of sd lotts as a residuary part of his estate to his dtr, Sarah JACOBS (alias) Sarah BURTON party to these presents. Albertus JACOBS, son of sd James JACOBS & sd Sarah JACOBS alias Sarah BURTON being so seized of sd lotts as tenants in common. Whereupon sd Sarah JACOBS alias Sarah BURTON by her guardian Sarah JACOBS & sd Albertus JACOBS entered an amicable action for division of the sd lotts between them. Whereupon John BOYD had sold from the sd lotts, the house & lott in occupation of Henry NEILL & whereon sd Henry NEILL now dwells, & that James JACOBS in his lifetime had sold & conveyed to Robert SHANKLAND 400 sq ft of land off the NW corner of the sd lotts of sd Sarah JACOBS alias Sarah BURTON & Albertus JACOBS, they did divide the residue of sd lotts bounded by land formerly belonging to Samuel PAYNTER, dec'd, was allotted to sd Albertus JACOBS. Whereas sd Albertus JACOBS & Elizabeth his wife, by their Deed dtd 03 Apr 1782 for the sum therein mentioned sold & conveyed to William JACOBS the part allotted to him the sd Albertus JACOBS was allotted by sd division to Sarah JACOBS alias Sarah BURTON. Sd Sarah BURTON for the sum of £25 sold to John CRAIG the division bounded on the NE by Front St, on the SE by house & lott late the property of Samuel PAYNTER dec'd & whereon the widow of John MARSHALL, dec'd, now dwells, on the SW by Second St & on the NW by afsd house & lott sold by sd Albertus JACOBS & Elizabeth his wife to William JACOBS. Signed: Sally BURTON.

Wit: George PARKER, Sam'l PAYNTER Jr. Rec: 16 Sep 1789 Nath'l MITCHELL, Proth'y.

O-14:103. Deed. This Indenture made 19 Dec 1788 between Nathaniel WEST, Exec of Robert WEST of Sussex cnty, DE of the one part & Jonathan DAZEY of same of the other part. Nathaniel WEST for the sum of £259 to Jonathan DAZEY all that tract of land called West's Addition together w/two parcels more, 50 acres, which was Deeded from William WEST & 50 acres from same William WEST, both parcels named West Recovery bounded by land of William GRAY, land of Elizabeth GRAY, land of Elijah WEST & Black Water Creek containing 130 acres of land. Signed: Nathaniel WEST. Wit: William LOCKWOOD, Thomas WILLIAMS. Rec: 16 Sep 1789 Nath'l MITCHELL, Proth'y.

O-14:104. Deed. This Indenture made 19 Dec 1788 between Jonathan DAZEY of Sussex cnty, DE, planter, of the one part & John HAZZARD of same place, ship carpenter, of the other part. Jonathan DAZEY for the sum of £250 sold to John HAZZARD a parcel of land call West's Addition together w/2 tracts more; one parcel Deeded by William WEST to Robert WEST & the other Deeded by same William WEST to Robert WEST both & each of them 50 acres, both being part of West's Recovery beginning near the mouth of Black Water Creek, being the boundary of West Recovery, S to William GRAY's line til it comes to Elijah WEST's line, W til it comes to Black Water Creek according to several courses of the pattent called West Addition containing & now laid out for 130 acres. Signed: Jonathan DAZEY. Wit: John EVANS, William LOCKWOOD, Thomas WILLIAMS. Rec: 16 Sep 1789 Nath'l MITCHELL, Proth'y.

O-14:104. Deed. This Indenture made 31 Oct 1788 between Gunning BEDFORD of Philadelphia city & Mary his wife of the one part & John YOUNG Jr of same place, merchant, of the other part. Whereas John JONES, John CLOWES Jr & Benjamin MIFFLIN by conveyance purchased sundry tracts of land within Sussex cnty, DE containing in the whole 3630 acres by plots & surveys & sd John JONES, John CLOWES & Benjamin MIFFLIN in order to divide did by Indenture dtd 03 Oct 17--- confirm sd partition in sd Deed the mutually agreeable granted to each other separately the several divisions therein mentioned. The divisions of sd lands laid off for full quota of sd John JONES within one single tract containing 3482 acres bounded by land of Andrew COLLINS, land of Prettyman DAY & sd division laid off for sd John JONES lies E of the above & S of several small tracts belonging to sundry persons containing 1220 acres more or less. Sd John JONES being so seized did by Indenture dtd 10 Nov 1767 convey sd 1220 acres to William BROWN, who being so seized did by

Indenture convey 240 acres lying on E end of sd tract to Richard HARTLEY & 20 Nov in year last afsd sd William BROWN & Rebecca his wife by Indenture conveyed the residue of the sd tract of 1000 acres among other lands to Samuel BILES, John HINCHMAN & Samuel BLACKWOOD in trust they should convey the same of his just debts. Sd BILES, HINCHMAN & LOCKWOOD by Indenture 25 Mar 1769 grant & confirm to John MIFFLIN & Ruser MEREDITH all the residue & remainder of sd tract of 1220 acres as tenants in common. John MIFFLIN by Indenture dtd 12 Apr 1779 for the sum of £1960 lawful money of PA all his one full equal moiety or 1/2 part of the 1220 acres to sd John JONES by sd cited Indenture containing 980 acres to sd Gunning BEDFORD. Whereas Benjamin MIFFLIN being legally vested in the sold property of sundry tracts of land in Sussex cnty, to wit, one tract in the forest of Broadkill Hundred bounded by lands of James REED, Babel DAVIS, Solomon DOD, James PETTYJOHN & by other lands of sd Benjamin containing 100 acres, which he bought of Thomas COLLINGS & John FOWLER & one other tract whereon the sd Benjamin dwelt bounded by the afsd tract and by lands of John FOWLER & James PETTYJOHN, James REED & by other lands of sd Benjamin containing 400 acres which he bought of Solomon & Edward WRIGHT, one other tract called the Green Drains bounded by the last mentioned tract to the E and by lands of Isaac DRAPER, Richard REYNOLDS, James PETTYJOHN, John CLOWES, Andrew COLLINGS, John SPENCER, Fosster DONAVAN & James REED being part of a larger tract purchased in company with sd John CLOWES & John JONES; the sd Benjamin's division bounded afsd being estimated at 750 acres, one other tract within the bounds of the last described tract bought of John PETTYJOHN & whereon he dwelt containing 70 acres; one other tract in the Broadkill Forest afsd called the Water Hole Savannah bounded by lands of Jacob MORRIS, Bevans MORRIS, Thomas DUTTON & James REED & Foster & Woolman DONAVAN containing 125 acres, being part of sd Benjamin's dividend in the Deed of Partition with sd John CLOWES & Jone JONES all which Deeds being recorded in Lewes, Sussex cnty, afsd. Sd Benjamin MIFFLIN by Indenture dtd 06 May 1776 did convey sd 5 tracts to sd John MIFFLIN who by Indenture dtd 12 Oct 1779 for the sum of £5760 did convey all 5 tracts containing in the whole 1440 acres unto sd Gunning BEDFORD as in sd last Deeds more fully appear. This Indenture witnesseth that sd Gunning BEDFORD doth hereby ack: that one moiety or half part of the sum of moneys mentioned above amounting together to the sum of £7720 was the proper monies of sd John YOUNG Jr & the other moiety thereof of sd Gunning BEDFORD & that he hath ever since the above purchases held the lands granted to him by sd John MIFFLIN in trust as to one moiety for the use of John YOUNG & the other moiety to the use of him the sd Gunning BEDFORD. Whereof sd Gunning BEDFORD & Mary his wife for the sum of £3860 the one moiety or half part of the monies above mentioned to them paid by sd John YOUNG grant one full equal & undivided fourth part of sd tract of 980 acres in & by the first Indenture above recited from sd John MIFFLIN to sd Gunning BEDFORD conveyed, situate as above described & also one full equal & undivided moiety or half part of all those afsd 5 tracts in above recited Indenture from John MIFFLIN to sd Gunning BEDFORD containing in the whole 1440 acres. Signed: Gunning BEDFORD, Mary BEDFORD. Wit: John HAZELWOOD, G CONNYHAM. 15 Dec 1788 before Honorable Thomas M KEAN, Esq, Dr of Laws, Chief Justice of the state of PA came above named Gunning BEDFORD & Mary his wife. Mary BEDFORD being of full age and privately examined apart from her sd husband declared she executed above Indenture of her own free will. Signed: Thomas M KEAN. Rec'd of John YOUNG Jr the sum of £3860 the consideration money within mentioned. Signed: Gunning BEDFORD. Wit: John HAZELWOOD, G CONYORSHAM.

O-14:107. Deed of Mortgage. This Indenture made 31 Jan 1789 between John YOUNG Jr of the city of Philadelphia, merchant, & Mary his wife of the one part & Isaac WYKOFF of Monmouth cnty, NJ, Esq of the other part. Where sd John YOUNG by a Bond duly executed dtd date herewith doth stand bound unto sd Isaac WYKOFF in the penal sum of £830 14s 6p gold & silver money of PA conditioned for payment of £415 7s 3p current gold & silver afsd on 27 Nov 1790 together w/lawful interest for same commencing on 02 Feb next. John YOUNG & Mary his wife in consideration of the afsd Debt of £415 7s 3p gold & silver afsd & for better securing the payment w/interest to Isaac WYKOFF in discharge of sd Obligation as of further sum of 5s to sd John YOUNG & Mary his wife paid by sd Isaac WYKOFF at time of execution hereof hath confirmed unto sd Isaac WYKOFF one full & equal undivided fourth all that tract of land situate in Sussex cnty, DE containing 980 acres being part of a large tract of 1220 acres allotted & assigned to John JONES an Indenture tripartite dtd 03 Oct 1765 between sd John JONES, John CLOWES & Benjamin MIFFLIN & also one full undivided moiety or half part of all those 5 tracts of land situate in Sussex cnty, DE to wit one tract in the forest of Broadkill Hundred bounded by land of James REED, Babel DAVIS, Solomon DOD, James PETTYJOHN & Benjamin MIFFLIN containing 100 acres which he bought of Thomas COLLINGS & John FOWLER, one other tract whereon sd Benjamin dwelt bounded by last mentioned tract & lands of John FOWLER, James PETTYJOHN, James REED & sd Benjamin MIFFLIN containing 400 acres which he bought of Solomon & Edward WRIGHT, one other tract called the Green Drains bounded by last mentioned tract to the E & by lands of Isaac DRAPER, Richard REYNOLDS, James PETTYJOHN, John CLOWES, Andrew COLLINGS, John SPENCER, Foster DONAVAN & James REED being part of a large tract purchased in company w/sd John CLOWES & John JONES, the sd Benjamin's dividend bounded as afsd being estimated at 750 acres, one other tract w/in the bounds of last described tract bought of John PETTYJOHN & whereon he dwelt containing 70 acres, one other tract in Broadkill Forest called the Water Hole Savannah bounded by lands of Jacob MORRIS, Bevan MORRIS, Thomas DUTTON, James REED & Foster & Woolman DONAVAN containing 125 acres which one undivided fourth part of sd 980 acres, and one undivided moiety in sd 5 tracts of land being the same which Gunning BEDFORD of sd city of Philadelphia, house carpenter, & Mary his wife by Indenture dtd 31 Oct past conveyed unto sd John YOUNG. Provided if sd John YOUNG doth pay to sd Isaac WYKOFF the afsd Debt on the day hereinbefore mentioned sd recited Obligation shall become void. John YOUNG & Mary his wife appoint Gunning BEDFORD Jr, Attorney General for DE, or Henry FISHER their lawful Attorney. Signed: John YOUNG, Mary YOUNG. Wit: Abm SHOEMAKER, Jos BENNETT Jr. 10 Feb 1789 before Honorable Thomas M KEAN, Esq, Dr of Laws, Chief Justice of Supreme Ct of PA came John YOUNG & Mary his wife. Sd Mary being of full age & privately examined apart from her husband declared she executed above Indenture of her own free will. Signed: Thos M KEAN. Rec: at Philadelphia 24 Jul 1789 James TRIMBLE for Charles BIDDLE, Sec'y.

O-14:109. Deed of Mortgage. This Indenture made 03 Nov 1788 between David MOORE of Sussex cnty, DE of the one part & George MITCHELL of same, merchant, of the other part. David MOORE by his Obligatory Bond dtd as above to sd George MITCHELL in the penal sum of £89 10s 10p in Spanish milled dollars at 7 & 6 or half Joes at £3 each conditioned for the payment of £44 15s 5p in like money. Sd David MOORE for securing sd Bond to sd George MITCHELL & in consideration of the sum of 1s in money afsd paid by sd George MITCHELL grant unto sd George MITCHELL a tract of land called Lanes Adventure situate in Dagsbury Hundred in afsd cnty containing by computation 98 acres bounded at E corner of WATSON's land containing 98 acres but 15 acres have been sold to Joseph HOUSTON & also the right of David MOORE in sd land. Conditioned if sd David MOORE pays unto George MITCHELL the afsd sum of money w/interest afsd then this Indenture shall be void. Signed: David W MOORE (mark). Wit: John WILLIAMS, William FREEMAN, Rhoads SHANKLAND. Deed for this land is recorded in Liber I, folios 165 & 166 at Snow Hill. Feb 14 Oct 1789 Nath'l MITCHELL, Proth'y. On 07 Aug 1793 George MITCHELL, grantor in this Deed of Mortgage ack: recp't of full satisfaction from Grantee principal & interest due & Quit Claimed to the lands in this Deed mentioned. J RUSSELL, Record'r.

O-14:110. Deed. This Indenture made 10 Sep 1789 between Abraham HARRIS of Sussex cnty, DE of the one part & John Wise BABSON of same of the other part. For the sum of £100 Abraham HARRIS sold to sd John W BATSON a tract of land called Low Ground situate in Broadkill Hundred, cnty afsd containing 100 acres being part of the S end of sd tract being part of a tract conveyed by Charles CLARK unto sd Abraham HARRIS. Signed: Abraham HARRIS. Wit: Nath'l MITCHELL, Rhoads SHANKLAND. Rec: 14 Oct 1789 Nath'l MITCHELL, Proth'y.

O-14:110. Incorporation of Trustees for Lewes, Coolspring & Indian River Presby'n Congregation. By Act of the General Assembly of DE passed at Dover 03 Feb 1787 instituted to enable all the religious denominations in this state to appt Trustees who shall be a body corporate for the purpose of taking care of the Temporalities of their respective Congregations it is enacted that each and every religious body of Christians, of whatsoever sect, order or denomination, which now are or hereafter may be in this state entitled to protection in free exercise of their religion by the Constitution & Laws of this state ... We the subscribers pursuant to the privileges vested in religious societies by the above & members of the religious society called Presbyterians met at Coolspring on 01 Sep 1787 did elect Rev Dr Mathew WILSON, Henry NEILL, Simon KOLLOCK, Nathaniel WAPLES & William PEERY Esqs & Dr Joseph HALL & John HOPKINS gent, to be Trustees for the Presbyterian congregations of Lewes, Coolspring & Indian River afsd & sd Trustees have assumed the name of United Presbyterian Congregations of Lewes, Coolspring & Indian River. 24 May 1788. Signed: Matthew WILSON, William PEERY, Henry NEILL, Joseph HALL, Simon KOLLOCK, N WAPLES.

O-14:111. Petition to Convey Lands. James BRATTON, Cyrus MITCHELL & John MITCHELL Execs of John MITCHELL, dec'd. John MITCHELL in his lifetime became bound to John COLLINS of Sussex cnty, DE to convey a tract of land in cnty afsd called Banner Field, sd John MITCHELL since d: & also sd John COLLINS. As money for same has been paid Execs request authority to convey sd land to the heirs of sd John COLLINS. Signed: MITCHELL, BRATTON & MITCHELL. Ct of Com Pleas held 05 Nov 1789 & above Petition was granted. Rec: Nath'l MITCHELL, Proth'y.

O-14:111. Bond of Conveyance. Hinman WHARTON Sr of Worcester cnty, MD am held bound to Joseph DERRICKSON of cnty & province afsd in the sum of £350 current money of MD to be paid to Joseph DERRICKSON of Sussex cnty DE. 01 Jul 1771. Hinsman WHARTON shall on or by 01 Jan next confirm to sd Joseph DERRICKSON the quantity of 175 acres of land situate in cnty afsd in 3 tracts known as Daniel's Luck containing 75 acres, Tarpeun Ridge containing 50 acres & Addition to Taraipen Ridge containing 50 acres, this being done in fee simple & w/o further delay then this Obligation to be void. Signed: Hinsman WHARTON. Wit: William TUNNELL, Elizabeth TUNNELL (mark). Joseph DERRICKSON assigns all right & title to above Bond of Conveyance to George MITCHELL. 15 Jul 1789 Signed: Jos DERRICKSON. Wit: John W BATSON, William FREEMAN. Rec: 27 Nov 1789 Nath'l MITCHELL, Proth'y.

O-14:112. Deed of Conveyance. John LEGGIT of Sussex cnty, DE, yeoman, am bound to Israel HOLLAND of same for the sum of £100. 17 Oct 1788. If sd John LEGGIT conveys sufficient Deed of Sale for a tract of land containing about 50 acres situate in Baltimore Hundred in cnty afsd adjoining the land of George HOWARD, Elizabeth COLLINGS, sd LEGGAT bought above land of Samuel DERRICKSON, to sd Israel HOLLAND then the above Obligation to be void. Signed: John LIGGET. Wit: Thomas EVANS, Edward HITCHENS. Rec 27 Nov 1789 Nath'l MITCHELL, Proth'y.

O-14:112. Deed. This Indenture made 17 Oct 1789 between Jeremiah TOWNSEND & Elizabeth his wife, William FRANKLIN & Sarah his wife, William STEVENSON & Tabitha his wife & William PITTS & Hannah his wife of Worcester cnty, MD of he one part & William SMITH of Sussex cnty, DE of the other part. Jeremiah TOWNSEND & Elizabeth his wife, William FRANKLIN & Sarah his wife, William STEVENSON & Tabitha his wife & William PITTS & Hannah his wife for the sum of £40 current money of MD sold to sd William SMITH all the land formerly belonging to Samuel CAMPBELL, dec'd, near Cedar Creek in Sussex cnty, DE. Jeremiah TOWNSEND & Elizabeth his wife, William FRANKLIN & Sarah his wife, William STEVENSON & Tabitha his wife & William PITTS & Hannah his wife appoint John HOLLAND or Robert STEVENSON their Attorney to complete this conveyance. Signed: Jeremiah TOWNSEND, Elizabeth TOWNSEND (mark), William FRANKLIN, Sarah FRANKLIN (mark), William STEVENSON, Tabitha STEVENSON, William PITTS, Hannah PITTS (mark). Wit: Joseph GREEN, Josiah DALE. Rec: 27 Nov 1789 Nath'l MITCHELL, Proth'y.

O-14:113. Deed. There is a tract of land situate in Baltimore Hundred in cnty afsd containing 100 acres which was conveyed by Henry SMITH to Archibald McFARRAN by Deed dtd 29 Apr 1786 bound by land of John MASSEY Jr purchased of Avery MORGAN called Stockley's Adventure and Marsh Point being part of two tracts, land of Henry SMITH. Whereas Richard DENNIS of the city of Philadelphia in Sussex cnty Ct of Com Pleas at May term 1788 recovered against sd Archibald McFARREN a debt of £600 adjudged to sd Richard, also 40s for his damages by the default of sd Archibald, to be levied.

Whereas by writ issued 06 Feb 1788 Peter Fretwell WRIGHT Esq then High Sheriff of cnty afsd was ordered to secure sd debt from the goods of sd Archibald to be ready on Wednesday 07 May next. Sd Sheriff seized a tract of land situate in Baltimore Hundred containing 100 acres being sd tract described above, he had sd land & premises appraised by 2 Freeholders who did say the rents, issues & profits of sd land were not a clear yearly value sufficient to satisfy the debt & damages w/in 7 years & sd land remained in his hands unsold for want of buyers. Whereas a writ of V E dtd 05 Aug 1789 directed sd Peter Fretwell WRIGHT, Sheriff, to put to public sale & have that money to the Ct on Wednesday 04 Nov next to render to sd Richard & sd WRIGHT exposed the land to sale 02 Nov instant & same was purchased by Littleton TOWNSEND of cnty afsd, yeoman, for the sum of £42 10s he being the highest bidder. Whereas Peter Fretwell WRIGHT was discharged from office of Sheriff before any Deed could be made by him. Thomas EVANS, High Sheriff of Sussex cnty, DE for the sum of £42 10s conveyed to sd Littleton TOWNSEND all that tract of land described above. 04 Nov 1789 Signed: Thomas EVANS, Sheriff. Wit: George HAZZARD, Israel HOLLAND. Rec: 27 Nov 1789 Nath'l MITCHELL, Proth'y.

O-14:114. Deed. This Indenture made 27 Oct 1789 between Nunez DEPUTY of Sussex cnty, DE of the one part & Purnal VEACH of same cnty of the other part. There is a tract of land containing 304 acres situate in Cedar Creek Hundred in cnty afsd adjoining land of Silvester DEPUTY & William DANIEL & Alexander LAYTON , The afsd tract being the portion of land that fell to the sd Nunez DEPUTY at his father's death. Nunez DEPUTY for the sum of £100 paid to him 12 Jan 17 last by Purnal VEACH hath sold to sd VEACH a part of the above mentioned tract containing in all 150 acres & premises. Nunez DEPUTY appoints Curtis SHOCKLEY or John TRUITT his Attorney. Signed: Nunez DEPUTY. Wit: Nehemiah REED, Zachariah REED (mark). Rec: 27 Nov 1789 Nath'l MITCHELL, Proth'y.

O-14:115. Deed. This Indenture made 30 Oct 1789 between Nunez DEPUTY of the one part of Sussex cnty, DE & Joseph TRUITT of the other part of same cnty. Whereas there is a tract of land containing 304 acres situate in Cedar Creek Hundred adjoining lands of Silvester DEPUTY, William DANIEL & Alexander LAYTON, the afsd tract of land being part of a portion of land that fell to sd Nunez DEPUTY by his father, Solomon DEPUTY. Curtis SHOCKLEY paid £41 10s to Nunez DEPUTY sometime in 1787 for the use of Joseph TRUITT & Nunez Deputy hereby ack: recp't & conveys a part of afsd land to Joseph TRUITT which is 150 acres out of above mentioned tract 150 acres of which was sold to Purnall VEACH & sd VEACH to have his laid off first & sd Joseph TRUITT to have his laid off according to the division & to adjoin sd land of

Purnall VEACH. Nunez DEPUTY appoints Joseph MILLER or Joshua FISHER Esq as his Attorney. Signed: Nunez DEPUTY. Wit: John TRUITT, Stephen COSTEN. Rec: 27 Nov 1789 Nath'l MITCHELL, Proth'y.

O-14:116. Deed. This Indenture made 10 Oct 1789 between James JONES of Sussex cnty, DE formerly, now of state of SC, yeoman, of the one part & John KILLINGSWORTH of Sussex cnty, DE, yeoman, of the other part. James JONES for the sum of £50 pad to his grndfthr James JONES & £2 5s paid to James JONES grndsn of sd James JONES dec'd, sold to John KILLINGSWORTH a parcel of land situate in sd cnty, part being part of a tract formerly taken up & surveyed for David SMITH & sold to Samuel OLIVER & part being part of a tract granted by Warrant dtd at Philadelphia 25 Jul 1741 to sd James JONES the elder bounded by John KILLINGSWORTH's land, part of Joshua JONES' (now Silvester WEBB's), Levin DOW's land containing 30 acres; the other parcel bounded by Sevin DORR's land, John LOFLAND's land, containing 65 & 1/2 acres. James JONES appoints Thomas EVANS Esq or John INGRAM, yeoman, his Attorney. Signed: James JONES (mark). Wit: John TRUITT, John KELSO. Rec: 27 Nov 1789 Nath'l MITCHELL, Proth'y.

O-14:117. Bond of Conveyance. 04 Nov 2789. Joshua POLK, Esq, of Nanticoke Hundred, Sussex cnty, DE am bound to James BRATTEN the younger, son of James BRATTEN of Broad Creek Hundred, in the sum of £1000 to be paid to sd James BRATTEN the younger. Joshua POLK Esq is seized of two tracts of land in cnty afsd, one of which contains 100 acres being the same which Joshua POLK purchased by Deed from Josiah HURST of sd cnty called Stayton's Lot, situate in Nanticoke Hundred, the other of which was conveyed to sd Joshua POLK by his fthr, James POLK, dec'd, containing 100 acres adjoining lands now in the tenure of William OWENS. Condition of above Obligation is such that if Joshua POLK shall convey to sd James BRATTEN the younger, or James BRATTEN the elder, the 2 tracts of land w/in reserving to himself & his wife an estate during their natural lives & ack: sd Deed in due form of law the above Obligation to be void. Signed: Joshua POLK. Wit: S KOLLOCK, Jos MILLER. Rec: 27 Nov 1789 Nath'l MITCHELL, Proth'y.

O-14:118. Deed. Henry CANNON late of Sussex cnty, DE, dec'd, was in his lifetime seized of a tract of land situate in Northwest Fork Hundred & afterward made his last will & testament & devised sd tract to his 3 sons, Charles CANNON, Newton CANNON & Willis CANNON & directed Daniel POLK Esq to divide sd parcel into 2 parts; all that part lying on SW side to his sons Charles CANNON &

Newton CANNON equally to be divided between them & the remaining part being one moiety lying on the NE side to his son Willis CANNON. Newton CANNON being seized of 1/4 of afsd land, d: Intestate & Admin of his estate was granted 06 Aug 1786 to his son George CANNON party to these presents. George CANNON at Orphans Ct 08 Nov 1787 set forth the personal estate of sd Newton CANNON was insufficient to discharge his debts, requesting the Ct grant him an order to sell so much of the real estate to enable him to discharge afsd debts. Sd Ct empowered sd George CANNON to sell at public sale the afsd. 07 Apr last did return to sd Ct that on 21 Feb last sd estate was purchased by Jesse GRIFFITH for the sum of £26 15s, he being the highest bidder. It appeared to sd Ct the sd sale was not agreeable to their order & intent sd sale was set aside & a new order granted for selling same by virtue of which George CANNON at public sale did on 27 Apr last sell same to Joshua OBEAR for the sum of £51 all that 1/4 part of afsd land. Signed: George CANNON. Wit: Jeremiah RUST, Jackson NOBLE (mark), Perry OBEAR. Rec: 27 Nov 1789 Nath'l MITCHELL, Proth'y.

O-14:119. Deed. This Indenture made 20 Oct 1786 between Jean WARRING, widow, of Sussex cnty, DE of the one part & Richard HUDSON of same place of the other part. There is a parcel of land situate in cnty afsd in forrest of Cedar Creek Hundred lying on the S side of a tract of land possessed by Alex'r ARGO the elder, being part of a larger tract called Stallon Head bounded by land of William DANIEL, containing 150 acres. Jean WARRING for the sum of £90 sold sd land to Richard HUDSON. Jean WARRING appoints John RODNEY or Phillips KOLLOCK her attorney. Signed: Jean WORREN (mark). Wit: Zachariah CARLISLE, Thomas DANIEL, John VINSON. Rec: 27 Nov 1789 Nath'l MITCHELL, Proth'y.

O-14:120. Petition. Rhoda GODWIN, Admin'x of estate of Thomas GODWIN, late of Sussex cnty, DE, dec'd. Thomas GODWIN by Bond of Conveyance w/a penalty therein mentioned, agreed in his lifetime to make good & sufficient Deed to Pearson ONIONS a tract of land in Baltimore Hundred afsd cnty who has since died/ Sd Bond being assigned to Israel HOLLAND Esq, Petitioner requests Ct of direct her to convey sd land in discharge of sd Bond of Conveyance. Signed: Rhoda GODWIN. Indorsed on back of sd Petition granted & order made 05 Nov 1789. Rec: Nath'l MITCHELL, Proth'y.

O-14:120. Return on Division of Lands. Hinman ROADS & William THOMPSON, both of Sussex cnty, DE by amicable action entered on the records of the Ct of Com Pleas hath agreed to make partition of a tract of land situate in Rehoboth Hundred called Avery's Rest which they hold as tenants in common. By consent of sd parties & rule of sd Ct all matters in variance were referred to William PEERY Esq, Peter MARSH & Thomas MARSH, gent. Sd PEERY, MARSH & MARSH have laid off to William THOMPSON all that part of sd land bounded by William THOMPSON's orchard, Avery's Creek, containing 143 acres of land & marsh. Sd PEERY, MARSH & MARSH laid off to Hinman ROADS all the remaining part of sd land beginning near the mouth of King's Creek, bounded by a branch called Woolf Pit Branch, land of William THOMPSON containing 430 acres of land & marsh. Signed: 07 Oct 1789 Thos MARSH, William PEERY, Peter MARSH. Ack: 05 Nov 1789 Peter F WRIGHT.

O-14:121. Map of above division of land.

O-14:122. Bond of Conveyance. William WILSON, cordwinder, of Sussex cnty, DE am bound unto William HICKMAN, planter, of same place in the full sum of £250. 26 Apr 1784. The condition of sd Obligation is such that if sd William WILSON make good & sufficient Deed at next Ct of Com Pleas to be held at Lewes for a certain parcel of land situate in Slaughter Neck formerly sold out of tract called the Schoolfield by Daniel WILSON, dec'd to sd HICKMAN. Signed: William WILSON. Wit: Neh' DAVIS, William HINDS.

O-14:122. This Indenture made 10 Dec 1789 between Elijah CANNON of Broad Creek Hundred, Sussex cnty, DE, yeoman, of the one part & David HALL of town of Lewes, cnty afsd, Esq of the other part. Elijah CANNON is seized of 2 tracts of land called Folly & the other Handly's Luck situate in sd Hundred & cnty, sd tract called Folly being on SE side of Nanticoke River in a woods in Wimber Succum Neck & bounded by a tract called Mill Lott formerly surveyed for Peter CALLAWAY, containing 75 acres; the other called Handly's Luck beginning on the NE side of a tract called Cannon's Discovery containing 100 acres. Elijah CANNON by Bond stands bound to sd David HALL in the sum of £121 9s 8p conditioned for payment of £60 14s 10p at or before 10 Dec next. Elijah for securing payment of sd sum afsd & interest & further sum of 5s sold to sd David HALL the afsd lands called Folly & Handly's Luck. Condition is if sd Elijah CANNON shall pay sd David HALL the afsd sum on 10 Dec next & interest this Indenture shall be void. Signed: Elijah CANNON. Wit: Simon HALL, Thomas FISHER. Rec: 16 Dec 1789 Nath'l MITCHELL, Proth'y.

O-14:123. 20 Apr 1796. David HALL, Mortgagee in above recorded Deed ack: receiving full satisfaction of mortgage monies & interest from Elijah CANNON, mortgager & quit claims the lands & premises mortgaged in this deed. Rec: Jno RUSSELL, Record'r

O-14:124. This Indenture made 10 Dec 1789 between Elijah CANNON of Broad Creek Hundred, Sussex cnty, DE, yeoman, of the one part & Peter Fretwell WRIGHT of Broadkiln Hundred, cnty afsd, Esq of the other part. Elijah CANNON is seized of two tracts of land called Folly & called Handly's Luck situate in Broad Creek Hundred, cnty afsd. Folly is on N side of SE branch of Nanticoke River in a neck of land called Wimbo Soccum Neck & bounded by a tract called Mill Lot formerly surveyed for Peter CALLAWAY, containing 75 acres. Handly's Luck is on NE side of a tract called Cannon's Discovery containing 100 acres. Elijah CANNON stands bound to Peter Fretwell WRIGHT for the sum of £145 6s 4p conditioned for payment of £65 13s 2p at or before 10 Dec next w/interest grants to Peter Fretwell WRIGHT all tracts of land above described conditioned that if sd Elijah CANNON shall pay the full just sum afsd to sd WRIGHT on or before 10 Dec next this Indenture shall become void. Signed: Elijah CANNON. Wit: Simon HALL, Thomas FISHER. Rec: 16 Dec 1789 Nath'l MITCHELL, Proth'y.

O-14:126. This Indenture made 03 Oct 1788 between Whiteley HATFIELD of Broadkiln Hundred, Sussex cnty, DE, yeoman, of the one part & John LANK of hundred & cnty afsd, blacksmith, of the other part. There is a tract of land situate in the hundred & cnty afsd being part of a larger tract originally granted by Warrant to Timothy DUNNOVAN bounded by land of Charles COULTER & Timothy DUNNAVAN, containing 100 acres. Above land was taken in execution & sold by Peter HALL, then High Sheriff of sd cnty to John DUNNAVAN in satisfaction of debt & damages by Jacob KOLLOCK Esq against afsd Timothy DUNNAVAN, he being the highest bidder. Peter HALL before he executed any Deed to sd John DUNNAVAN for the premises was removed from office & Jacob KOLLOCK Jr Esq who succeeded him by Indenture dtd 06 Sep 1756 did convey same to sd John DUNNAVAN who by his Indenture dtd 08 Sep in year last sd sold & conveyed same to Mary DUNNAVAN who afterwards md: Gabriel POWELL who together w/sd Mary sold same to Jacob KOLLOCK Sr Esq by Indenture dtd 16 Aug 1765 & rec: at Lewes in Liber K-10, Folio 181. Jacob KOLLOCK being so seized by his Bond dtd 01 Mar 1769 bound himself in the penal sum of £120 conditioned that sd Jacob KOLLOCK should at receipt of £60 from sd HATFIELD convey sufficient Deed of Sale & afterwards d: making his last will & testament wherein he appointed Margaret KOLLOCK his sole Exec'x who afterwards by her Deed dtd 09 Sep 1777 conveyed sd lands to sd Whitely HATFIELD in discharge of sd Bond. Whitely HATFIELD & Rhoda his wife for the sum of £150 sold the above described 100 acres to John LANK. Whitely HATFIELD appoints John RUSSELL Esq his Attorney. Signed: Whitely HATFIELD, Rhoda HATFIELD (mark). Wit: John CLOWES, Prisse SIMPLER. Rhoda HATFIELD, wife of Whitely HATFIELD, one of the grantees in the above, being of full age & examined apart from her husband did say that she became a party thereto of her own free will. 03 Oct 1788 John CLOWES. Rec: 16 Dec 1789 Nath'l MITCHELL, Proth'y.

O-14:128. Bond of Conveyance. Thomas MARINER of Sussex cnty, DE, farmer, am bound to Henry LINGO in the penal sum of £160 to be paid to Henry LINGO. 20 Oct 1772. Condition of above Obligation is such that if Thomas MARRINER shall make over right & title to a parcel of land called Dawes' Choice containing about 92 acres at Ct next after this date to Heneary LINGO bounded by land of Robert PRETTYMAN, head of Swan Krick, then above Obligation to be void. Signed: Thomas MARINER. Wit: Allen REID, Samuel LINGO. I sign over all my right & title of this w/in Bond to Jesse DEAN. 14 Jan 1778. Signed: Henry LINGO. Wit: Robert PRETTYMAN, William PRETTYMAN. I assign all my right & title to w/in Bond to Hugh STEPHENSON. 15 Oct 1789. Signed: Jesse DEAN. Wit: James STEPHENSON, James LANK. Rec: 16 Dec 1789 Nath'l MITCHELL, Proth'y. At a Ct of Com Pleas held 04 Feb 1790 Robert PRETTYMAN ....to Wm LINGO ... this Bond ... proved by Wm PEERY Esq & Jesse DEAN.

O-14:129. Deed. This Indenture Tripartite made 01 Dec 1789 between William WILSON of Cedar Creek Hundred, Sussex cnty, DE, William HARRISON of same cnty, & John RUSSELL of same cnty. William WILSON for the sum of 10s doth discharge and hath granted to John RUSSELL all that land which Thomas WILSON of Cedar Creek Hundred by his last will & testament dtd 08 Mar 1727 devised to his son Daniel situate in slaughter Neck, hund & cnty afsd supposed to contain 138 acres the bounds of which may be ascertained in the Deed of Sale from Henry SKIDMORE to Thomas Wilson dtd 05 May 25 & the conveyance from John BOWMAN to Daniel WILSON dtd 05 May 1747 the first containing 55 acres & the last 88 acres. John RUSSELL may be perfect tenant of the freehold & inheritance of the afsd premises against whom common recovery of sd premises may be had as of Nov term this present year before Ct of Com Pleas continued by adjournment in which sd Common Recovery it is agreed sd William HARRISON shall be Demandant, sd John RUSSELL, tenant, & sd William WILSON shall be voucher & he shall Vouch over the Common Voucher after the manner of Common Recovery for the assignance of land. Signed: William WILSON, William HARRISON, Jno RUSSELL. Wit: Thomas EVANS, Jos MILLER. Rec: 16 Dec 1789 Nath'l MITCHELL, Proth'y.

O-14:130. Deed. This Indenture made 11 Dec 1789 between William WILSON of Cedar Creek Hundred, Sussex cnty, DE of the one part & William HINDS of same of the other part. William WILSON for the sum of £50 sold to William HINES two pieces of land which were devised from Thomas WILSON to his son

Daniel WILSON situate in Slaughter Neck hund & cnty afsd, one part of which was conveyed 05 May 1725 from Henry SKIDMORE to Thomas WILSON for 50 acres & the other 50 acres whereof were conveyed on 08 Jul 1759 from Isaac WATSON Jr Exec to Baker JOHNSON, together w/all improvements, etc. Signed: William WILSON. Wit: T WILTBANK, Jos MILLER. Rec: 16 Dec 1789 Nath'l MITCHELL, Proth'y.

O-14:130. Deed. This Indenture made 10 Dec 1789 between Thomas Evans Esq, High Sheriff of Sussex cnty, DE of the one part & William HINES of Cedar Creek Hundred, cnty afsd, of the other part. There is a tract of land situate in Slaughter Neck which by Deed of Sale dtd 05 May 1725 was conveyed by Henry SKIDMORE to Thomas WILSON & on 08 Mar 1727 devised by sd WILSON to his son Daniel WILSON & from thence descended until it became the right of William WILSON son of Daniel & by him sold to Joseph DRAPER now dec'd. Sd tract is situate on S side of Indian Branch containing 50 acres of upland & 5 acres of marsh. There is a parcel of land situate in afsd hund & cnty conveyed by Deed dtd 05 May 1747 from John BOWMAN to Daniel WILSON being part of a larger tract surveyed for Henry BOWMAN containing 88 acres. 50 acres of last cited land was sold 01 Mar 1784 by William WILSON son of sd Daniel, from Isaac WATTSON Jr Exec of sd Daniel WILSON, to Baker JOHNSON late of afsd cnty, dtd 08 Feb 1759. By sale afsd the 50 acres last afsd & also the 50 acres of upland described in Deed from Henry SKIDMORE to Thomas WILSON became the property of sd Joseph DRAPER now dec'd. William HINES, lately in Ct of Com Pleas at May term 1788 recovered Judgement against Elizabeth DRAPER Admin'x of the estate of Joseph DRAPER, for the sum of £113 w/cost of suit. A writ of sd Ct dtd 04 Nov 1788 to Sheriff of Sussex cnty directed sd Sheriff to levy sd recovery, costs against sd estate & he advised sd estate would not w/in 7 years pay the debt & costs. By writ of V E issued 04 Feb 1789 directed sd Sheriff to sell at public sale & have that money to Ct at May term in sd year. Accordingly sd Sheriff sold at public sale to William HINES the afsd lands for the sum of £70 10s 10 Apr last, he being the highest bidder. Signed: Thomas EVANS, Sheriff. Wit: Jos MILLER, J RUSSELL. Rec: 16 Dec 1789 Nath'l MITCHELL, Proth'y.

O-14:132. Deed. This Indenture made 11 Dec 1789 between William WILSON of Slaughter Neck, Sussex cnty, DE, yeoman, of the one part & Rachel HICKMAN, widow, & John HICKMAN, Mary LOFLAND wife of Nutter LOFLAND , Elizabeth RICKARDS, wife of William RICHARDS & Jacob HICKMAN children of William HICKMAN, late of afsd cnty, dec'd, of the other part. William WILSON for the sum of £25 sold to Rachel HICKMAN, widow of John HICKMAN; Mary LOFLAND, Elizabeth RICKARDS & Jacob HICKMAN, children of sd Wm HICKMAN 50 acres of land conveyed by Deed dtd 06 Jul 1753 from Daniel WILSON to William HICKMAN being part of a larger tract called Bowman's Farms situate in Slaughter Neck, Sussex cnty, described in afsd Deed rec: in Liber H:7, folio 380, supposed to contain 38 acres & also the afsd 50 acres in form following: 1/3 part in 3 equal parts to be divided Rachel HICKMAN for her dower during her natural life and remaining 2/3 parts (together w/sd Rachel's 1/3s or dower after her decease) unto sd John HICKMAN, Mary LOFLAND, Elizabeth RICHARDS & Jacob HICKMAN. Signed: William WILSON. Wit: W HARRISON, Jno RUSSELL. Rec: 16 Dec 1789 Nath'l MITCHELL, Proth'y

O-14:133. Deed. This Indenture made 11 Dec 1789 between Margaret KOLLOCK, Exec'x of Jacob KOLLOCK the elder late of Lewes, Sussex cnty, DE, of the one part & Hugh SMITH of sd town, cnty & state, millwright, of the other part. There is a tract of land situate w/in Lewes near the Block House Pond called Mount Pleasant beginning at the S post of Friends Burying Ground on South St, bounded by a ditch & Market St containing 10 acres & 24 sq perches of land & some pond which sd tract Jacob KOLLOCK d: seized of & by his last will & testament directed his Exec to sell except the place where he then lived & the Mill Plantation. Sd Margaret KOLLOCK for the sum of £40 sold to Hugh SMITH the afsd 10 acres & 24 sq perches. Margaret KOLLOCK appoints Phillips KOLLOCK or John RODNEY her Attorney. Signed: Margaret M KOLLOCK (mark). Wit: George HAZZARD, W HARRISON. Rec: 16 Dec 1789 Nath'l MITCHELL, Proth'y.

O-14:133. Deed of Mortgage. This Indenture made 19 Mar 1789 between John WALTON of Sussex cnty, DE, yeoman, of the one part & Thomas FISHER, Samuel Rowland FISHER & Miers FISHER of the city of Philadelphia, gent, Trustees of the estate of Sarah DAWES, dec'd, of the other part. John WALTON by a Bond of Obligation is bounded unto sd Thomas, Samuel & Meirs FISHER in the sum of £600 gold & silver money of PA conditioned as hereinafter stated. John WALTON in consideration of sd debt & to secure payment thereof & the sum of 5s confirms to sd Thomas, Samuel & Meirs FISHER all that parcel of land part of a tract called Farmers Delight situate beginning at a corner post of other part of sd tract now or late belonging to Thomas CAREY Jr (last survey was 1773) & shall include 300 acres, bounded by part of original tract belonging to heirs of Benjamin RILEY, dec'd, & Thomas CAREY Jr's land provided if John WALTON shall pay the just & full sum of £100 with interest from date hereof on £300 on 19 Sep 1790 & further sum of £100 w/interest on £200 on 19 Sep 1791 & further sum of £100 & one year interest on 19 Sep 1792 this Indenture shall become void. John WALTON appoints Nicholas RIDGELY or Joseph MILLER

Esqs his Attorney. Signed: John WALTON. Wit: Joseph WATTSON, Edward STAPLEFORD. Rec: 16 Dec 1789 Nath'l MITCHELL Proth'y.

O-14:135. Article of Agreement Tripartite made 08 Oct 1789 between Isaac DRAPER of Kent cnty, DE, shipwright, of the one part, John CLOWES & Mary his wife of Sussex cnty, DE of the 2nd part & George CONWELL w/Unice his wife of Sussex cnty of the 3rd part. Dr John SPENCER, late of 14th VA Regiment in the service of the USA d: Intestate w/o issue leaving in Sussex cnty real estate which estate by the Laws of DE for lack of issue descended to Isaac DRAPER, Mary CLOWES & Unice CONWELL they being Intestate's brother & sisters of the half blood in equal degree & that divers controversies have arisen between the afsd touching the descent of sd land, all of which are finally now settled by DE Ct of Appeals. Sd Ct decreed all the Intestate's real estate to be equally divided between the afsd brother & sisters of the half blood. Afsd 3 parties therefore choose Joseph HAZZARD Esq, Hap HAZZARD, Jacob HAZZARD, John HOLLAND & Baptist LAY, gent, all of Sussex cnty, DE to take a surveyor unto lands & premises of sd estate & divide same into 3 lots of equal value & if they cannot so equally divide to make sd lots equal in value empower them to make sd lots equal in value by charging most valuable lot debtor to the lots of lesser value (which sums to be recoverable from the person whose name is on such valuable lot by persons whose names are on less valuable lots. After numbering sd lots on the map w/ 1, 2, 3. Numbers to be placed on folded sheets of paper and placed in hat & to be drawn in turn by heirs, they to own lot # drawn, to settle for final division of the estate of sd Dr John SPENCER. Signed: Mary CLOWES, George CORNWALL, Isaac DRAPER, ... bottom of page missing .... Wit: Joseph HAZZARD, Hap HAZZARD, ... bottom of page missing .... Mary CLOWES, wife of John CLOWES Esq & Unice CONWELL, wife of George CONWELL both being of full age and separately examined from their husbands declared they entered into afsd agreement of their own free will. Signed: Peter Fretwell WRIGHT. In pursuance of above sd agreement above lots & tenements were divided as follows: Lot #1 containing 4 acres of land whereon stands the grist mill of late John SPENCER, Lot #2 containing 199 acres & Lot #3 containing 288 acres situate in the forest of Broadkiln hundred, Sussex cnty. We have ascertained that Lot #1 is valued at £20 4s better than Lot #3 & sd Lot #1 is to the value of £4 8s better than Lot #2. We called two indifferent people & Lot #1 was drawn against Isaac DRAPER, Lot #2 against the name of George CONWELL & Eunice his wife, & Lot #3 against the name of John CLOWES & Mary his wife. We order that sd Isaac DRAPER pay to George CONWELL the sum of £4 8s. We laid off Lot #2 containing 198 acres in Broadkiln Hundred to George CONWELL & Eunice his wife. We laid off to John CLOWES & Mary his wife all the lands in Lot #3 containing 288 acres. 18 Jan 1790.

Signed: John HOLLAND, Baptis LAY, Jacob HAZZARD, Hap HAZZARD, Joseph HAZZARD.

O-14:136. Plot map on division of Jno SPENCER's Lands covers further text of above agreement.

O-14:137. Plot map on division of Jno HOPKINS Lands & final paragraphs & signatures of above settlement of Dr John SPENCER's estate.

O-14:138. Whereas John HOPKINS late of Sussex cnty, DE, by his last will & testament dtd 12 Feb 1787 apptd the subscribers to lay off to his widow, Sophia HOPKINS 1/3 part of his lands as her right of Dower & to make partition of the remaining part of his sd lands among his children & devises under his last will. We make partition in the manner following: We have laid off to sd widow that part of sd lands bounded by land of Josiah MARTIN, containing 130 acres, during her natural life. We laid off to Josiah HOPKINS son of sd John HOPKINS that part of sd lands bounded by Roger GUM's Patent, containing 87 acres. We laid off to David HOPKINS son of sd John HOPKINS 52 acres w/bldgs & improvements. We laid off to Samuel HOPKINS son of sd John HOPKINS bounded by David's part a parcel containing 77 acres. We laid off to Cornelius HOPKINS son of John HOPKINS bounded by Samuel's share containing 87 acres. We laid off for Lemuel HOPKINS son of John HOPKINS a part bounded by Josiah's part, containing 87 acres. We laid off for William HOPKINS son of sd John HOPKINS bounded by Lemuel's part, Saunder's Deed, containing 10 acres. We also laid off for Archibald HOPKINS all that part of sd land bounded by William's part, containing 10 acres. We also laid off to John HOPKINS son of late John HOPKINS bounded by Archibald's part, containing 10 acres. We laid off to Robert HOPKINS son of late John HOPKINS all remaining part of lands which late John HOPKINS devised to be equally divided amongst his 4 eldest sons, being 10 acres. 10 Jan 1790 Signed: William PEERY, Maurice VERDEN, Sackes WYATT.

O-14:140. Manumission. Negroes Joseph & Suffiah his wife having served out their time to my satisfaction are at their liberty to bargain for themselves w/any person as other free people. 25 Nov 1784. Signed: Jos CORD

O-14:140. Deed. This Indenture made 26 Jan 1790 between John YOUNG of Sussex cnty, DE, yeoman, of the one part & John MANN & Rachel his wife of cnty afsd of the other part. John MANN & Rachel his wife for the sum of £80 sold to John YOUNG a tract of 173 acres & 50 perches that Samuel DAVIS & Mary BOWMAN sold & conveyed to Nathan YOUNG. Afsd Nathan YOUNG d:

Intestate seized of a tract of land in Slaughter Neck on W side of Delaware Bay & S side of Ceder Creek & left to his wife Mary & 5 children, viz: John YOUNG the eldest, James YOUNG, Sarah YOUNG, Betty YOUNG & Rachel YOUNG. Sd Mary YOUNG having right of Dower to 1/3 sd land & the oldest John YOUNG drawing two shares of all sd land & other 4 heirs equal shares alike. Sd Rachel YOUNG md: John MANN. Sd John MANN & Rachel his wife sell all their right in her Mother's 1/3 lifetime & her brother James YOUNG, dec'd right of the 173 acres & 50 perches of land bounded by land of Joseph STOCKLEY, land of Joshua LOFLAND, Jacob HICKMAN's land containing 173 acres & 50 perches. Signed: John MANN, Rachel MANN. Wit: Jno WILTBANK, James H PRIDE (mark). Rachel MANN being of full age was examined & she declared she entered above agreement of her own free will. Signed: Jno WILTBANK, JP. 05 Feb 1790 Rec'd of John YOUNG the sum of £10 in full for above Deed. Signed: John MANN, Rachel MANN. Rec: 12 Feb 1790 Nath'l MITCHELL, Proth'y.

O-14:142. Deed. This Indenture made 03 Feb 1790 between William BRADLEY of Kent cnty, DE, yeoman, & Mary his wife of the one part & Sylvester WEBB of Sussex cnty, DE, yeoman, of the other part. There is a parcel of land & marsh situate on Cedar Creek Neck on the S side of Mispilion Creek including a place called Gravelly Landing, bounded by Payntor's Gut, containing 190 acres & 16 perches as by a plot of David HILFORD dtd 25d 10m 1771. Sd land & marsh was conveyed to Spencer CHANCE by 2 Deeds of Sale, one made by Jehu SPENCER dtd 04 Aug 1766 rec: Liber K, #10, folio 255, the other made by Ebenezer SPENCER dtd 20 May 1769 rec: Liber L, #11, folio 24 whereby Spencer CHANCE became lawfully seized of sd land & marsh. He afterwards d: Intestate leaving issue a son & 2 dtrs to wit: John CHANCE, Mary CHANCE & Sally CHANCE to whom above land & marsh descended together w/other lands Spencer CHANCE d: possessed of. Application being made to Orphans Ct by William BRADLEY who md: Mary CHANCE for a division of the lands. Sd Ct appt 5 Freeholders to make partition amongst dec'd's several heirs. Sally CHANCE md: David SIMMONS. The above cited lands & marsh divided between Mary BRADLEY & Sally SIMMONS. The above cited 190 acres of land & marsh were sold to George CULLEN late of Kent cnty, DE by William BRADLEY & afsd William BRADLEY had purchased of sd SIMMONS & Sarah his wife executed dtd 20 May 1788. George CULLEN d: before the conveyance was made. Sarah CULLEN, widow, w/son, John CULLEN, were appt'd Exec's of Geo CULLEN's estate. Sarah CULLEN, widow, d: before settlement of George CULLEN's estate. John CULLEN found the personal estate of Geo CULLEN not sufficient to satisfy the just debts. John CULLEN made app to Orphans Ct for an order for the sale of the above cited land & marsh. Ct granted sd app to satisfy creditors of the estate. Sylvester WEBB one of the parties to these presents bought afsd land & marsh for the sum of £325 10s part of which sum was due afsd William BRADLEY from the estate of Geo CULLEN, dec'd, which sum Sylvester WEBB paid to William BRADLEY out of the purchase money. Wm BRADLEY & Mary his wife make good & sufficient Deed to Sylvester WEBB agreeable to the Conveyance Bond assigned him by John CULLEN, Exec of the estate of Geo CULLEN, dec'd. Signed: William BRADLEY, Mary BRADLEY. Wit: Hutter LOFLAND, John HALL. Rec: 12 Feb 1790 Nath'l MITCHELL, Proth'y. 03 Feb 1790 John CLOWES ack: he examined Mary BRADLEY separate from her husband & she declared she executed above Indenture of her own free will. Signed: John CLOWES.

O-14:144. Deed. This Indenture made 20 May 1788 between David SIMMONS of Kent cnty, MD, yeoman, & Sally his wife of the one part & William BRADLEY of Kent cnty, DE, yeoman, of the other part. There is a parcel of land situate in Cedar Creek Neck on S side of Mispilion Creek including a place called Gravelly Landing. bounded by land of Joshua SPENCER & Paynters Gut, containing 190 acres & 16 perches as by a plot of David HILFORD dtd 25d 10 m 1771 which sd land & marsh was conveyed to Spencer CHANCE by two Deeds of sale, one made by Jehu SPENCER dtd 04 Aug 1766, rec: Lib K, #10, folio 255, the other made by Ebenezer SPENCER dtd 20 May 1769 rec: Lib L, #11, folio 27 whereby Spencer CHANCE become possessed of afsd land & marsh. Spencer CHANCE d: Intestate leaving issue: a son & 3 dtrs to wit: John CHANCE, Mary CHANCE & Sally CHANCE to whom afsd land descended together w/other lands of Spencer CHANCE, dec'd. William BRADLEY (who md: Mary CHANCE) made petition to Orphan's Ct for a division of the land of Spencer CHANCE, dec'd, amongst the heirs. Sd Ct apptd 5 Freeholders to make ordered partition who divided afsd 190 acres 16 perches between Mary, wife of William BRADLEY & Sally, party to this Indenture who had md: David SIMMONS. David SIMMONS & Sally his wife for the sum of £235 sold to William BRADLEY their dividend of afsd land. David SIMMONS & Sally his wife appt Messrs Phillips KOLLOCK or Adam HALL of Sussex cnty, DE their Attorney. Signed: David SIMMONS, Sally SIMMONS. Wit: Nehemiah CARY, John CULLEN. 20 May 1788 Wm POLK examined Sally SIMMONS, wife of David, separate from her husband, & she declared she became a party of the same of her own free will. Signed: Wm POLK. Rec: 12 Feb 1790 Nath'l MITCHELL, Proth'y.

O-14:145. Deed. This Indenture made 12 Oct 1789 between James JONES of Lawrence cnty, SC, yeoman, of the one part & John KILLO of Sussex cnty, De, yeoman, of the other part. James JONES, grndfthr of afsd James JONES, by virtue of a Proprietary Warrant granted him at Philadelphia 25 Jul 1745 a tract of land at the head of Slaughter Branch in Cedar Creek Hundred, Sussex cnty, DE,

& sd James JONES by his last will & testament give to his son, Joshua JONES, one moiety of sd tract of land which moiety when surveyed contained 115 & 3/4 acres, which sd land Joshua JONES was seized when he d: Intestate leaving a widow and issue 6 children, viz: James, party to this Indenture & eldest son; Sarah, Izaak, Pheby, Stephen & Joshua to whom by DE Intestate laws sd lands descended. Son Joshua d: in his minority, Intestate, & w/o issue. James JONES, party to this Indenture, hath title to 2/7 parts of the whole by descent from his father & 1/5 of 1/7 part of the whole as heir to his dec'd brother, Joshua's, part, including the widow's right of Dower therein. James JONES having good right & title in fee to 2/7 & 1/5 part of 1/7 of afsd 115 & 3/4 acres of afsd land, adjoining on N land of Nathaniel STOCKLEY, on S lands of William STOCKLEY, on W lands of John PORTER & on E land of John ROBINSON, for the sum of £37 sold to John KILLO sd James JONES rights to 2/7 & 1/5 parts of sd 115 & 3/4 acres (the widow's right of Dower excepted). Signed: James JONES (mark). Wit: John J POSTLES (mark), Peter CLOWES. Rec: 12 Feb 1790 Nath'l MITCHELL, Proth'y.

O-14:147. Deed. This Indenture made 02 Nov 1789 between John POSTLES, Sarah POSTLES,& Selah POSTLES of Sussex cnty, DE of the one part & John KILLO of same, yeoman, of the other part. There is a tract of land in Cedar Creek Hundred, which was granted to James JONES of sd cnty by a Proprietary Warrant dtd at Philadelphia 25 Jul 1741. Sd James JONES by his last will & testament dtd 09 Mar 1768 devised to his 2 sons Jacob & Joshua all the afsd tract to be divided equally between them, Jacob JONES to possess the upper part & Joshua the lower part. Jacob JONES d: Intestate seized of his dividend leaving issue 5 children to whom the sd land descended. Richard STOCKLEY having purchased of sd Jacob JONES, eldest son, all his right to sd Intestate lands, petitioned Orphans Ct for partition & division among the several heirs of sd Jacob. Sd Ct apptd 5 Freeholders to make sd partition & they reported sd land would not partition w/o spoiling the whole whereupon 3 men were apptd to set a true value on sd lands & at return of their report sd Richard STOCKLEY accepted sd lands at their valuation being 115 & 3/4 acres. Richard STOCKLEY by his deed of sale dtd 06 Sep 1786 convey sd 115 & 3/4 acres to afsd John POSTES & sd John POSTTES did by his Deed of Sale convey sd land to afsd Sarah & Selah POSTTES reserving the use thereof to himself during his natural life. Sd John POSTTES. Sarah POSTTES & Selah POSTTES being seized of the afsd 115 & 3/4 acres for the sum of £1-8 10s sold one moiety or 1/2 part of the afsd 115 & 3/4 acres containing 57 acres & 120 sq perches of land to sd John KILLO. John POSTTES, Sarah POSTTES & Selah POSTTES appoint John WILTBANK Esq. Signed: John POSTTES (mark), Sarah POSTTES, Selah POSTTES (mark). Wit: John CLAWS, Casa HALL. Rec: 12 Feb 1790 Nath'l MITCHELL, Proth'y.

O-14:148. Deed. This Indenture made 12 Aug 1789 between Grace LOFLAND of Sussex cnty, DE of the one part & Littleton LOFLAND of same of the other part. There is a tract of land situate in Cedar Creek Hundred containing 400 acres, late the property of William LOFLAND, dec'd, part of which tract, to whit 200 acres, sd William LOFLAND purchased of Dorman LOFLAND & part thereof, to whit, 100 acres sd William LOFLAND purchased of Elias BAKER & part thereof to whit 50 acres thereof sd William LOFLAND purchased of Thomas WHARTON & 14 acres thereof William LOFLAND obtained a Warrant for in his own name from the Proprietary of PA & cntys of Newcastle, Kent & Sussex, DE & remainder of sd tract sd William LOFLAND purchased of Henry HILTIN, sd several purchases making in the whole 400 acres. Sd William LOFLAND by his last will & testament dtd 15 Dec 1785 devised part of afsd 400 acres to his son, Dorman LOFLAND, & residue thereof sd William LOFLAND devised to his wife, Grace LOFLAND, and his son, Dorman LOFLAND, to be equally divided. Dorman LOFLAND, dying w/of issue, by his last will & testament dtd 29 Nov 1788 devised to his mother, afsd Grace LOFLAND, all his land left to him by his father, by which sd Grace LOFLAND became entitled to the whole of the 400 acres of land. Grace LOFLAND for the natural love & affection she hath for her son, Littleton LOFLAND, & for the sum of £150 to be paid by sd Littleton LOFLAND to William, George & Gabriel LOFLAND, sons of Grace LOFLAND, in equal portions of £50 each & for the sum of 20s to her, the sd Grace LOFLAND, hath sold to Littleton LOFLAND the afsd land reserving to herself her own life time in sd land & reserving to her dtr, Margaret, a room in the house in which sd Grace LOFLAND now lives & also a ground for a garden on the N side of sd house so long as sd Margaret shall live unmarried & no longer. Grace LOFLAND appoints John LOFLAND her Attorney. Signed: Grace LOFLAND (mark). Wit: William PEERY, John LOFLAND. Ack: receipt of their portion of purchase sum. Signed: Wm LOFLAND, George LOFLAND, Gabriel LOFLAND. Wit: Wm REDDEN, John LOFLAND. Rec: 12 Feb 1790 Nath'l MITCHELL, Proth'y.

O-14:149. Deed. This Indenture made 13 Oct 1789 between William LOFLAND, George LOFLAND, Gabriel LOFLAND, Margaret LOFLAND, John RYLY & Anna RYLY his wife & Bennet WARRING & Rachel WARRING his wife, of Sussex cnty, DE (brothers & sisters to Dorman LOFLAND, dec'd) of the one part & Littleton LOFLAND of same (one other brother of afsd) of the other part. Dorman LOFLAND by his last will & testament dtd 29 Nov 1788 bequeath to his mother, Grace LOFLAND, all the land that was left to him by his father & to her disposal, all of which land Grace LOFLAND by her Deed of Sale dtd 12 Aug 1789 conveyed to sd Littleton LOFLAND by which Deed & Conveyance it was supposed a tract of land containing 95 & 1/2 acres purchased by the father in his lifetime of Elias BAKER adjoining the afsd lands left by the father to afsd Dorman was included. But by recourse to deed from Elias BAKER to the father, it appears sd Deed was made to sd Dorman LOFLAND in his own right. Sd Dorman not having disposed thereof must have d:Intestate as to the afsd 95 & 1/2 acres whereby the afsd Partys by DE law are equally devised. William LOFLAND, George LOFLAND, Gabriel LOFLAND, Margaret LITTLETON, John RYLEY w/Ann his wife, & Bennett WARRING & Rachel his wife for the sum of £50 have sold unto Littleton LOFLAND their right & title to sd lands. William LOFLAND, George LOFLAND, Gabriel LOFLAND, Margaret LITTLETON, John RYLY w/Ann his wife & Bennet WARRING w/Rachel his wife hereby appoint John WITT & John CLOWES Esqs as their Attorney. Signed: William LOFLAND, George LOFLAND, Gabriel LOFLAND, Margaret LITTLETON (mark). Signed: William REDDEN, John LOFLAND. Rec: 12 Feb 1790 Nath'l MITCHELL, Proth'y.

O-14:151. Bond of Conveyance. John ROBINSON & Jenny his wife, planter & spinster of Sussex cnty, DE, are each of us jointly bound unto Ezekiel WILLIAMS in the penal sum of £200 to which we bind ourselves 05 Jan 1789. Condition of Obligation is such that if John ROBINSON & Jenny his wife convey to Ezekiel WILLIAMS that tract of land on S side of Indian Town Branch being part of a tract resurveyed for sd John ROBINSON to a tract called Summerfield on S side of sd tract & to lay off sd part to sd WILLIAMS. Signed: John ROBINSON, Jenny ROBINSON. Wit: George MITCHELL, Stephen STYER. Rec: 12 Feb 1790 Nath'l MITCHELL, Proth'y.

O-14:151. Bond of Conveyance. Joseph ROBINSON of Worcester cnty, MD, planter, am firmly bound unto William TINGLE of same place, planter, in the full sum of £200 sterling to which payment I do bind myself 16 Mar 1762. Condition of above Bond is such that if above Joseph ROBINSON shall convey to William TINGLE 3 acres of land being part of a tract called Sommerfield lying on E side of the great Branch between Joseph ROBINSON & William ROBINSON beginning near path leading to Daniel ADKINS. Signed: Joseph ROBINSON. Wit: John PERKINS, Parker ROGERS.

O-14:152. Deed. This Indenture made 18 Sep 1789 between William WILLEY of Cedar Creek Hundred, Sussex cnty, DE, yeoman, & Ann his wife of the one part & Joshua WRIGHT of Carlisle cnty, MD, planter, of the other part. John CLIFTON of Sussex cnty being seated on a parcel of vacant land & made some improvement thereon requested Robert SHANKLAND then Deputy Surveyor of Sussex cnty to survey lines to include 200 acres together w/his improvements for confirmation from Proprietary Agents of PA Land Office sd land being situate on W side of Bowmans Branch, one of the branches of Mispilion Creek joining on S side of 200 acres surveyed for Richard HAYS, containing 210 acres but since found to contain more by survey of sd Robt SHANKLAND on 19 Jan 1725 after which John CLIFTON did assign his right & title to Robert WARREN of Sussex cnty on 21 Apr 1744 for valuable consideration, said assignment being witnessed by Wm DANILEY, Wm SHANKLAND & Robert WARREN in the presence of Mary DAVID & Thos POSTTES on 22 Feb 1750/1 unto Richard HAYS Jr. Richard HAYS Jr on 25 Feb 1750/1 for a valuable consideration assign his right & title to sd land to Abraham WYNKOOP in the presence of Nicholas HAMMOND, Mary CANTWELL after which Benjamin WYNKOOP, Exec of last will & testament of sd Abraham WYNKOOP, dec'd di assign title to sd William WILLEY and Evans CLARK for the sum of £60, sd assignment made 27 Feb 1759 witnessed by John RODGERS & Jacob WARRINGTON & sd Evans CLARK on 08 Aug 1761 did sell sd land to Levin WILLEY for the sum of £32 10s in the presence of Benj WYNKOOP & John VANCE after which Levin WILLY & Elizabeth his wife on 24 Sep 1783 assigned their right & title to Henry HUDSON for the sum of £280 entering into an Obligatory writing w/sd William WILLEY that if sd William WILLEY should lay off 100 acres adjoining sd Bowmans Branch of the E part of the tract to the sd Henry HUDSON it being the quantity Levin WILLEY had contracted w/sd Henry HUDSON for, the William WILLEY should have the remainder for sd tract. William WILLEY having laid off sd 100 acres became lawfully possessed of the residue of sd tract as follows: bounded by land of William JOHNSON, land of Henry HUDSON, land of Curtis HAYS, containing 152 acres & 31 sq perches. William WILLEY & Ann his wife for the sum of £210 to Joshua WRIGHT. William WILLEY & Ann his wife appoint Thomas EVANS Esq High Sheriff of Sussex cnty or William HARRISON of Lewes, Sussex cnty their Attorney. Signed: William WILLEY, Ann A WILLEY (mark). Wit: Richard HAYS, Morgan WILLIAMS. 18 Sep 1789 Ann WILLEY, wife of William WILLEY, was examined separate from her husband, declared she became a party of her own free will. Signed: Alex'r LAWS. Rec: 12 Feb 1790 Nath'l MITCHELL, Proth'y.

O-14:154. Deed of Sale. There is a tract of land containing 6 & 1/2 acres being part of a larger tract situate in Broadkiln Hundred originally surveyed for William COULTER & laid out 07 Jan 1790. Sd 6 & 1/2 acres w/appurtenances belonging by sundry conveyances to Thomas WATTKINS , painter, who being seized of sd land eloped from his place of abode being indebted to Levina OAKEY which sd OAKEY at Aug Term 1785 sued a writ of Attachment against sd Thomas WATKINS. The then High Sheriff attached sd parcel of land & improvements.

Nov Term 1786 Ct of Com Pleas rendered judgement & directed sd Sheriff to proceed to sell sd land. By order issued 04 Nov 1789 Sheriff Peter Fretwell WRIGHT on 07 Jan 1790 sold sd land to Israel HOLLAND Esq for the use of Isaac ATKINS of hund & cnty afsd, yeoman, for the sum of £9 14s 1p, he being the highest bidder. Peter Fretwell WRIGHT was removed from office before he executed any Deed for sd 6 & 1/2 acres to Isaac ATKINS. Thomas EVANS, High Sheriff of Sussex cnty, DE & further consideration of 5s made Deed of Conveyance to sd Isaac ATKINS. Signed: Thomas EVANS. Wit: none signed. Rec: 12 Feb 1790 Nath'l MITCHELL, Proth'y.

O-14:156. Deed of Sale. This Indenture made 03 Dec 1789 between John JONES Esq of Sussex cnty, DE of the one part & Dagworthy JONES of same place of the other part. John JONES for the sum of £40 sold to Dagworthy JONES all that tract of land called Chance formerly in Worcester cnty, but now in Sussex cnty, being back in Indian Forest at the head of Martins River laid out for 100 acres, also one half part or moiety of a tract called Unity Grove resurveyed by virtue of a Warrant of Resurvey obtained from John PENN Esq dtd at Philadelphia 10 Oct 1776 & resurveyed 17 Dec following containing an estimated 1080 acres of land. Signed: John JONES. Wit: Benjamin LONG, David MURRAY, Severn JONES. John JONES appoints David HALL or William PEERY Esqs his Attorney. Rec: 12 Feb 1790 Nath'l MITCHELL, Proth'y.

O-14:156. Bond. David HALL, yeoman, of Sussex cnty, DE is firmly bound unto John RECARDS, yeoman, of cnty afsd in the sum of £250 03 Jan 1769. Obligation is such that if David HALL, Exec of the last will & testament of Peter RAZER, Esq, dec'd, shall at reasonable request of John RECARDS convey a certain house & lot in the town of Lewes being the house & lot that belonged to Peter RAZER Esq late of sd cnty, dec'd, & by his last will & testament directed to be sold & John RECORDS has agreed w/sd David HALL, Exec, upon paying to sd heirs the full & just sum of £125 on or before 01 Nov next David HALL shall convey to sd John RECCARDS the sd house & lot & if sd David HALL does convey title to sd house & lot according to above this Obligation to be void. Signed: David HALL. Wit: Jenny HALL, Fenwich STRETCHER. For valuable consideration of the within bond to me in hand paid I sign over all my right of within Bond to Nehemiah DAVIS Jr. Signed: John RECARDS. Wit: William WATTSON, Samuel GLOVER. Rec: 12 FEb 1790 Nath'l MITCHELL, Proth'y.

O-14:157. Petition. 03 Feb 1790. Mary Magdalen HALL, Joseph HALL & David HALL, Admin of the estate of David HALL late of Sussex cnty, DE, Esq, dec'd. Peter RAZOR late of Sussex cnty, DE, dec'd, made his last will &

testament 05 Feb 1766 & apptd above David HALL Esq to be his Exec giving sd Exec full power to dispose of all his estate real & personal. Sd David HALL did sell to John RECCORDS a lot of land in the town of Lewes & by an Obligatory Bond dtd 03 Jan 1769 became bound to John RECARDS in the sum of £250 w/condition if sd David HALL upon reasonable request execute a good Deed conveying sd lot & premises to John RECCORDS on his paying to David HALL the sum of £125 the sd Obligation should be void. Sd John RECCARDS assigned sd Bond unto Nehemiah DAVIS, taylor, of cnty afsd. Consideration money herein had been paid to sd David HALL by Nehemiah DAVIS, David HALL afterwards d: w/o executing Deed conveying sd lot to sd Nehemiah DAVIS. Petitioners pray Ct to grant an order allowing them to execute a Deed to sd Nehemiah DAVIS. Signed: Mary Magdalen HALL, Jos HALL, L HALL. Indorsed on back side: Granted & order made 03 Feb 1790. Rec: Nath'l MITCHELL, Proth'y.

O-14:158. Deed. Mary Magdalen HALL, Joseph HALL & David HALL, Admin of the estate of David HALL, late of Sussex cnty, DE, dec'd. James THOMPSON of Lewes by a Deed dtd 05 Feb 1760 sold to Peter RAZOR of cnty afsd a lot of land in Lewes fronting Second St bounded by land of John SIMONTON, lot late the property of Isaac WILTBANK & a lot in possession of Joseph CORD, which sd lot James THOMPSON purchased of Joshua FISHER of the city of Philadelphia. Peter RAZOR d: having made his last will & testament dtd 05 Feb 1766 whereby he appt'd David HALL, Esq, dec'd, to be his Exec & authorized sd Exec to sell his estate. David HALL sold afsd lot to John RICCORDS of Lewes for the sum of £125 & became bound unto sd John RICCARDS in the penal sum of £250 w/condition sd David HALL should at reasonable request & cost of sd John RICCARDS execute a sufficient Deed conveying afsd lot to John RICCARDS which sd Bond was afterwards assigned to Nehemiah DAVIS of Lewes. David HALL afterwards d: before he executed a conveyance to Nehemiah DAVIS. David HALL d: Intestate, Admin of his estate was granted to sd Mary Magadalen, Joseph & David who petitioned the Ct to empower them to execute a proper Deed for sd land to Nehemiah DAVIS (assignee of John RICCARDS). The Ct so ordered & in consideration of the sum of £125 sd Mary Magdalen, Joseph & David conveyed sufficient Deed for sd land to Nehemiah DAVIS 03 Feb 1790. Signed: Mary Magdalen HALL, Joseph HALL, D HALL. Wit: Jacob HAZZARD, Nathaniel HICKMAN. Rec: 12 Feb 1790 Nath'l MITCHELL, Proth'y

O-14:159. Deed. This Indenture made 27 Nov 1786 between Catherine YOUNG of Sussex cnty, DE, widow, of the one part & John CLOWES of same, Esq, of the other part. Whereas John CLOWES Esq (fthr of afsd Catherine YOUNG & John CLOWES) by his last will & testament bequeathed all his lands to his 7 children to be divided equally by lots fairly drawn which division was made 17 Dec 1772 by which division lot # 6 containing 61 & 3/4 acres of land & marsh in Broadkiln Hundred became the property of Mary the wife of John Sheldon DORMAN, record of same rec: in Liber L # 11, folio 270. Sd John Sheldon DORMAN & Mary his wife by Deed of Sale dtd 29 Jul 1773 convey the afsd Lot #6 to the first mentioned John CLOWES. Sd John CLOWES by his Deed of Sale dtd 14 Feb 1776 convey afsd lot to afsd Catherine YOUNG then the wife of John YOUNG. Catherine YOUNG for the sum of £133 10s sold the 61 & 3/4 acre lot bounded by HAZZARD's land to sd John CLOWES. Signed: Catherine YOUNG. Wit: Samuel GLOVER, Joseph STATON. Rec: 12 Feb 1790 Nath'l MITCHELL, Proth'y.

O-14:160. Deed. This Indenture made 02 Feb 1790 between Shadrach CARTER of Sussex cnty, DE of the one part & James KING of same place, planter, of the other part. Shadrach CARTER is seized of a tract of land called Utter situate in Broad Creek Hundred containing 400 acres. Shadrach CARTER for the sum of £50 & other valuable considerations sold to James KING the afsd tract. Shadrach CARTER appoints David HALL or John Wise BATSON or Samuel HALL of Sussex cnty, DE as his Attorney. Signed: Shadrach CARTER (mark). Wit: Thomas WALLER, Ebenezer CALLAWAY. Rec: 12 Feb 1790 Nath'l MITCHELL, Proth'y.

O-14:161. Deed. This Indenture made 02 Feb 1789 between William COULTER & Sarah his wife of Lewes & Rehoboth Hundred, Sussex cnty, DE of the one part & Robert OAKEY of same, tanner, & Jennet OAKEY of same, spinster, of the other part. William COULTER & Sarah his wife for the sum of £65 sold to Robert OAKEY & Jennet OAKEY a tract of land situate in sd city & hund bounded by lands late the property of Joseph BAILEY, dec'd, containing 4 acres. Signed: Wm COULTER, Sarah COULTER. Wit: Jno WILTBANK, Richard GREEN. Sarah COULTER, wife of William COUTTER, was examined separate from her husband, being of full age, declared she signed above conveyance of her own free will. Signed: Jno WILTBANK. Rec: 12 Feb 1790 Nath'l MITCHELL, Proth'y.

O-14:162. Deed. This Indenture made 01 Aug 1788 between John BROWN of Sussex cnty, DE, planter, & Rebecca his wife of the one part & Daniel POLK of same place, farmer, of the other part. For the sum of £35 paid by Daniel POLK to John BROWN & Rebecca his wife sd John & Rebecca sold to sd Daniel POLK a tract of land called Brown's Regulation situate in Northwest Fork Hundred between where Edward WILLIAMS formerly lived, containing 35 acres. John BROWN & Rebecca his wife appoint John RODNEY or Phillips KOLLOCK of Lewes, Esqs their Attorney. Signed: John BROWN, Rebecca BROWN (mark). Wit: Wm POLK, Caleb HUTTER. Rebekah, wife of John BROWN, was examined separate from her husband declared she became a party to within Deed of her own free will. Signed: Wm POLK. Rec: 12 Feb 1790 Nath'l MITCHELL, Proth'y.

O-14:163. Deed. There is a tract of land situate in Lewes Hundred, Sussex cnty, DE containing about 187 acres called St Giles, being part of a larger tract formerly the property of Jacob WHITE, late of sd cnty, dec'd, who by his last will & testament devised sd land to his son Wrixham WHITE, sd land bounded by land of John PRETTIMAN & Hawks Nest Hammock. Phillip WHITE for the sum of 5s sold sd land & marsh to Wrixham WHITE 02 Jan 1789. Signed: Philip WHITE. Wit: Cornelius WILTBANK Jr, Mary KILLEN. Rec: 12 Feb 1790 Nath'l MITCHELL, Proth'y.

O-14:163. Deed. This Indenture made 30 Jan 1789 between Wrixham WHITE of Sussex cnty, DE of the one part & Jacob WHITE same of the other part. There is a tract of land situate in Lewes & Rehoboth Hundred being part of a larger tract of land granted by Patent to Davis GRAY. A Resurvey made on the Patent by Thomas GRAY & sd Thomas GRAY & Temperance his wife by their Deed of Sale dtd 12 Dec 1727 conveyed 187 acres of sd larger tract unto Phillip RUSSELL which sd 187 acres by sundry more conveyances has now become the property of Wrixham WHITE, sd land bounded by lands of John PRETTYMAN, a beaver dam on Coolspring Creek, Hawk's Nest Hammack & a marsh containing & laid off for 187 acres of land & marsh. Wrixham WHITE for the sum of £157 in gold & silver coin sold sd land & marsh to Jacob WHITE. Wrixham WHITE appoints Robert WHITE as his Attorney. Signed: Wrixham WHITE. Wit: Cornelius WILTBANK Jr, Mary KILLEN. Rec 12 Feb 1790 Nath'l MITCHELL, Proth'y.

O-14:164. Deed. This Indenture made 20 Jan 1789 between Joseph HEBRON & wife of Sussex cnty, DE, hatter, of the one part & James GORDON of same place, carpenter, of the other part. There is a tract of land situate in Lewes & Rehoboth Hundred, Sussex cnty, being part of a tract whereon sd Joseph HEBRON now liveth bounded by the County Road, land of James GORDON, containing 1 acre & 30 sq perches. Joseph HEBRON for the sum of £3 sold sd land to James GORDON. Signed: Joseph HEBRON, Leah HEPBRON. Wit: Jno WILTBANK, Samuel MUSTARD. Leah HEBRON, wife of afsd Joseph, being of full age, was examined apart from her sd husband and declared she became a party to w/in Deed of her own free will. Signed: Jno WILTBANK. Rec: 12 Feb 1790 Nath'l MITCHELL, Proth'y.

O-14:165. This Indenture made 06 Feb 1790 between John RODNEY of Sussex cnty, DE, of the one part & Hugh SMITH of Lewes, cnty afsd, of the other part.

There is a parcel of land w/house in Lewes which Sarah HART & Thomas HART, Execs of John HART, dec'd, conveyed to William Anderson PARKER, late of sd cnty, by Indenture dtd 12 May 1787. Sd parcel is bounded by land of Sarah & Mary, 2 of the heirs of John SIMONTON, dec'd, & contains one acre of land. Sd house & land were sold by the Sheriff at suit of Margaret KOLLOCK, Exec of Jacob KOLLOCK, dec'd, & Daniel RODNEY for the use of John RODNEY became the purchaser. Sd John RODNEY for the sum of £70 sold sd land & house to sd Hugh SMITH. Signed: Jno RODNEY. Wit: William Brittingham ENNIS, Mary LEVICK. Rec: 12 Feb 1790 Nath'l MITCHELL, Proth'y.

O-14:166. Bond. Elijah HALL, planter, of Sussex cnty, DE am firmly bound to James WARD of same in the sum of £500 to which payment I hereby bind myself dtd 26 Jul 1785. Condition of sd Obligation is that Elijah HALL shall give up his rights to a Branch between sd HALL's & Aaron GOLD's, bounded by Ward's Mill , excepted if sd mill is let fall & be void sd HALL to have 1/3 part of the privilege of sd branch for the use of a meadow, then the above Obligation to be void. Signed: Elijah HALL. Wit: George SMITH, Samuel HEARN. Rec: 12 Feb 1790 Nath'l MITCHELL, Proth'y.

O-14:166. Deed. This Indenture made 17 May 1786 between Ephraim KING & Margaret his wife of the one part & John POLK Jr & John BACON of the other part, both of Little Creek Hundred, Sussex cnty, DE. For the sum of £70 Ephraim KING & Margaret his wife sold to John POLK & John BACON all that tract of land called King's Venture situate in Little Creek Hundred bounded w/Job SERMAN's land & w/Hezekiah MORRIS' survey, containing 152 acres of land, 47 acres of patten land & 105 acres vacancy exclusive of 3 acres of the original tract bounded by land of Robert KING which sd 3 acres is the property of Edward CREAGH. The afsd 3 acres were once the dwelling house of Mikial LINTCH but now the property of Edward CREAGHTON; also excluding 3 acres of resurvey from where sd Edward CRAIGH now lives next to Job SERMAN's land known as Craigh's Purchase, which 3 acres John POLK Jr & John BACON claim no right in the whole 3 acres of the resurvey, the above mentioned 47 acres & 152 acres vacancy exclusion of the above 3 acres of land which is the property of the afsd CREAGH. Ephraim KING & Margaret his wife appoint Capt Peter MARSH or Dr Joseph HALL as their Attorney. Signed: Ephraim KING (mark), Margaret KING (mark). Wit: Jobe SERMANS, Edward CREAGH, Marshall SMITH. Rec: 12 Feb 1790 Nath'l MITCHELL, Proth'y.

O-14:167. Deed. This Indenture made 30 March 1789 between Jacob WHITE of Lewes & Rehoboth Hundred, Sussex cnty, DE, yeoman, of the one part & John

WOLFE of same place, cordwinder, of the other part. There is a parcel of marsh situate in the hund & cnty afsd being part of White's Island in Lewes Creek as laid off to sd Jacob WHITE by Rhoads SHANKLAND, Peter Fretwell WRIGHT & William FISHER dtd 06 Feb 1781. Beginning at the 3rd corner of that part allotted to the heirs of Isaac WHITE containing 8 & 1/4 acres. Jacob WHITE for the sum of £9 sold sd parcel to John WOLFE. Signed: Jacob WHITE. Wit: George NOX, James WILLSON. Rec: 12 Feb 1790 Nath'l MITCHELL, Proth'y.

O-14:168. Deed. This Indenture made 25 Jun 1789 between Phebe VINING of the borough of Wilmington, New Castle cnty, DE, widow, & Benjamin WYNKOOP of Philadelphia, gent, surviving Exec of Abraham WYNKOOP heretofore of Sussex cnty, DE, Esq, dec'd, of the one part & Nehemiah CAREY of Sussex cnty, yeoman, of the other part. Abraham WYNKOOP in his lifetime by diverse conveyances became seized of 2 contiguous tracts of land in Cedar Creek Hundred originally granted by 2 patents to Thomas BOSTOCK & Daniel LEACH by the names of Cypress Hall & Pathalia & so being seized made his last will & testament dtd 15 Nov 1753 after giving divers legacies among his children did devise as follows: all lands not above disposed being in Kent & Sussex cntys be sold & monies arising from sd sales be paid in discharge of several legacies or sums of money I have willed & bequeathed to be paid & he did appt Mary WYNKOOP, the sd Phebe & Benjamin & Thomas WYNKOOP Execs, of which Mary & Thomas are since dec'd & sd Phebe & Benjamin remain as Execs. Benjamin WYNKOOP of city of Philadelphia, PA one of the Execs of estate of Abraham WYNKOOP Esq, dec'd, & Attorney for the other Execs by his writing Obligatory dtd 21 Jul 1788 become bound to Benjamin TRUITT of Sussex cnty in the sum of £200 current money of PA w/condition if sd Benjamin WYNKOOP should convey to Benjamin TRUITT a tract of land containing 144 & 1/2 acres situate in Sussex cnty being part of 2 larger tracts called Cyprus Hall & Pathalia together w/improvements then sd Obligation should be void. Sd Benjamin TRUITT afterwards d: Intestate & Admin of his estate was committed to George WALTON the elder of Sussex cnty. Orphans Ct at Lewes 10 Feb 1787 sd George WALTON was empowered to sell sd tract of land to pay the debts & legacies of sd Benjamin TRUITT, dec'd. George WALTON thus sold sd tract to Nehemiah CAREY but no Deed was executed. George WALTON conveyed sd annexed Obligation by Ct order to Nehemiah CAREY & appt'd Benjamin WYNKOOP to convey sd lands & premises to Nehemiah CAREY & delivered sd Obligation to sd Phebe VINING & Benjamin WYNKOOP. Phebe VINING & Benjamin WYNKOOP for the sum of 5s do convey unto sd Nehemiah CAREY all that tract of land situate in Sussex cnty beginning at a corner of land sold to Thomas CAREY, thence by George COWAN's land, by land late of John DRAPER, thence by land of John TRUITT containing 144 & 1/2 acres. Phebe

VINING & Benjamin WYNKOOP appoint Nicholas RIDGLEY or Joshua FISHER Esqs as their Attorney. Signed: Phebe VINING, Benjamin WYNKOOP. Wit: Edmond POTTER, John CHANCE, Miers FISHER. Rec: 12 Feb 1790 Nath'l MITCHELL, Proth'y.

O-14:170. Deed. This Indenture made 01 Aug 1786 between Isaac BENSON & Ester his wife of the one part & Aaron GORDY of the other part. For the sum of £400 Isaac & Ester BENSON sold onto Aaron GORDY a tract of land called Hound's Ditch situate in Little Creek Hundred, Sussex cnty, DE beginning at SW corner of Jane COOPER's land & laid out for 83 acres. Isaac BENSON & Ester his wife, appoint David HALL Esq of Lewes or Wm Marshall SMITH of Broad Creek as their Attorney. Signed: Isaac BENSON, Esther BENSON. Wit: Jas TRUSHAM, Laben TURNER. Rec: 12 Feb 1790 Nath'l MITCHELL, Proth'y.

O-14:170. Deed. This Indenture made 18 February 1788 between Obediah EDGE of Sussex cnty, DE of the one part & Jonathan Green BEACH of same of the other part. Obediah EDGE for the sum of £100 sold to Jonathan Green BEACH all that tract of land called Edge's Right. Obediah EDGE appoints Peter WHITE, Phillips KOLLOCK or Simon HALL as his Attorney. Signed: Obadiah EDGE. Wit: John WILLIAMS, John BACON. Rec: 12 Feb 1790 Nath'l MITCHELL, Proth'y.

O-14:171. Deed. This Indenture made 15 October 1785 between Ephraim HAINS of Little Creek Hundred, Sussex cnty, DE of the one part & William POLK of same place, yeoman & Leah POLK, dtr of sd William POLK of the other part. Ephraim HAINS for the sum of £120 sold to Leah POLK. dtr of William POLK (preserving to sd William POLK & Leah his wife the use of afsd mentioned premises during their natural life) all that tract of land called Hain's Grove, situate in Little Creek Hundred formerly granted to Francis HAINS, dec'd, who by Deed of Gift conveyed same to his son David HAINS, fthr of afsd Ephraim HAINS, bounded by land of Ephraim HAINS between sd HAIN's plantation & Elijah HASTING's plantation, containing 50 acres. Signed: Ephraim HAINS (mark). Wit: Thomas POLLETT Jr, John POLK. Rec: 12 Feb 1790 Nath'l MITCHELL, Proth'y.

O-14:172. Deed. This Indenture made 20 Nov 1789 between Charles BRADLEY of Sussex cnty, DE of the one part & Gideon BRADLEY of the other part. Charles BRADLEY for the sum of £21 sold to Gideon BRADLEY all that part of a tract called Taylor's Chance Deeded to Charles' grndfther, John BADLEY by William TAYLOR dtd 05 Nov 1742 as rec: in Summerset cnty, MD, which part of sd land was devised by sd John BRADLEY unto his son Dean BRADLEY. Likewise Dean BRADLEY devised sd land to afsd Charles BRADLEY for 1/2 or moiety of sd land now lying in Little Creek Hundred in

Sussex cnty, DE. Signed: Charles BRADLEY (mark). Wit: Chas MOORE, William B COOPER. Rec: 12 Feb 1790 Nath'l MITCHELL, Proth'y

O-14:173. Deed. This Indenture made 05 May 1789 between Thomas FIGGS of Sussex cnty, DE of the one part & William POLK of same of the other part. William FIGGS was seized of 50 acres of land, part of a tract called Glasses situate on the S side of Broad Creek in Little Creek Hundred, sd William FIGGS being dec'd. Thomas FIGGS his eldest brother & Admin of his estate. Thomas FIGGS for the sum of £5 sold sd 50 acres to William POLK. Thomas FIGGS appoints David HALL or Peter WHITE of Sussex cnty his Attorney. Signed: Thomas FIGGS. Wit: John WILLIAMS, Samuel WILLIAMS Jr. Rec: 12 Jan 1790 Nath'l MITCHELL, Proth'y

O-14:174. Deed. Cornelius KOLLOCK late of Sussex cnty, DE, Esq was seized in his lifetime of a certain lot of ground commonly called Savannah Lot situate in the town of Lewes bounded on the NE by 3rd Street, on the SE by South Street, on the SW by Front St, & on NW by the lot devised by Samuel PAYNTER late of the cnty afsd to his dtr Hannah now the wife of George PARKER. Cornelius KOLLOCK made his last will & testament & after devising part of his estate to certain persons gave & devised residue to his 4 children: Royal KOLLOCK, Lemuel KOLLOCK, William KOLLOCK, Mary NEILL & his grnddtr Hester GRIFFITH, now Hester LITTLE wife of Nicholas LITTLE of cnty afsd to be equally divided among them of which above land is a part. Whereas Royal KOLLOCK, Lemuel KOLLOCK, William KOLLOCK and Leah his wife, and Nicholas LITTLE & Hester his wife by their Indenture dtd 04 Jan 1785 did sell to Henry NEILL all their undivided equal 4/5 parts in 5 parts to be divided. Whereby Henry NEILL named 4 parts in 5 in his own right & the other 5th part to sd Henry & Mary his wife. Whereas sd Henry NEILL & Mary his wife by their Indenture dtd 07 Jun 1785 conveyed afsd lot to Isaac TURNER of Lewes. Isaac TURNER by his Indenture dtd 05 Nov 1785 conveyed to Evan McHAM of Lewes one moiety or half part of afsd lot. Whereas Riece WOOLF of the cnty afsd lately in a Ct of Com Pleas recovered judgement against sd Evan McHAM for a debt of £27 as 44s 7p adjudged for damages sd Evan McHAM was convicted. Ct issued a writ 08 Nov 1786 directing Peter Fretwell WRIGHT Esq High Sheriff of sd cnty to levy the debt & damages by which writ sd Sheriff seized sd 1/2 lot bounded as afsd w/a blacksmith shop thereon & same remained in his hands unsold due to no buyers. Ct issued write of V E & sd 1/2 was exposed to sale & same was purchased by John WOOLF 27 Apr 1787 for £18 12s 6p. Sd Sheriff did execute Deed of Conveyance to John WOOLF the afsd 1/2 lot. John WOOLF & Mary his wife for the sum of £37 10s sold sd 1/2 lot to

George PARKER. 09 Aug 1789 Signed: John WOLFE, Mary WOLFE. Wit: Phillips KOLLOCK, W HARRISON. 16 Sep 1789 Mary WOOLF wife of John WOOLF, was examined separate from her husband declared she became a party to this Indenture of her own free will. Signed: Jno WILTBANK. Rec: 12 Feb 1790 Nath'l MITCHELL, Proth'y

O-14:176. Deed. This Indenture made 24 Oct 1788 between William COLEMAN of Lewes, Sussex cnty, DE, silversmith, of the one part & Whittington CLIFTON of same, cordwinder, of the other part. William COLEMAN for the sum of £10 sold to Whitington CLIFTON a lot of land in Lewes on the NW side of South St adjoining the burying ground of the people called Quakers containing 1200 sq ft of land being part of a parcel of land Joseph CORD & Jane his wife conveyed by Deed dtd 30 Jul 1784 to Anderson PARKER who by Deed of Gift conveyed 03 Nov 1784 conveyed the same to William COLEMAN (Quit Rents excepted). Signed: William COLEMAN, Eleanor COLEMAN (mark). Wit: Abr'm HARGIS, Caleb RODNEY. Eleanor COLEMAN, wife of William, being of full age, was examined separate from her husband and declared she became a party thereto of her own free will. Signed: Jno WILTBANK. Rec: 12 Feb 1790 Nath'l MITCHELL, Proth'y.

O-14:177. Deed. Lydia WEST of Sussex cnty, DE at Ct of Com Pleas Feb Term 1787 recovered against John MORRIS & Eleanor his wife late Eleanor WEST, Admin of the estate of Joseph WEST, dec'd a debt of £182 10s 8p & £3 7s 11p damages. By writ dtd 07 Nov 1787 Peter Fretwell WRIGHT Esq seized 2 tracts of land in Indian River & Angola Hundred containing 300 acres & it was found rents, etc from sd land was not sufficient to pay sd debt w/in 7 years. By writ of V E dtd 04 Feb 1789 Peter Fretwell WRIGHT Esq exposed sd tracts of land to public sale & same was purchased by David HAZZARD 19 Mar 1789 for the sum of £129, he being the highest bidder. Peter Fretwell WRIGHT was removed from office of Sheriff before he executed Deed for sd lands to David HAZZARD. Thomas EVANS Esq for the sum of £129 paid to Peter Fretwell WRIGHT by David HAZZARD conveyed Deed for sd lands to David HAZZARD for 2 tracts of land; the first situate on the SW side of Herring Creek containing 200 acres; the other being part of a tract situate in Indian River Hundred on the NE side of Goldsmith or Herring Creek bounded by land formerly of one SHEPPARD containing 200 acres (formerly thereout sold 21 acres). 02 Mar 1790 Signed: Thomas EVANS, Sheriff. Wit: D HALL, James ? WILSON. Rec: 06 Mar 1790 Nath'l MITCHELL, Proth'y.

O-14:178. Deed. There is a tract of land situate in Baltimore Hundred, Sussex cnty, DE originally by the Proprietary of MD by Patent dtd 09 Apr 1689 to William WITTINGTON & afterwards by several conveyances became the property of Joshua HILL late of Sussex cnty. Sd tract of land is called Springfield bounded by a beaver dam, house where Rhoads CLANK formerly lived & Spring Gut containing 486 acres. 12 Mar 1777 by Indenture Joshua HILL for the sum of £800 sold sd land to Ann CLAY of Newcastle, DE. Ann CLAY at a Ct of Com Pleas 04 Feb 1784 obtained a judgement against Levin HILL tenant of the land. Levin HILL by Writ of Certiorari removed the proceedings of Ct of Com Pleas to the Supreme Ct which 24 Apr 1787 confirmed the Ct of Com Pleas judgement & issued a Writ 24 Oct 1787 directing Peter Fretwell WRIGHT, High Sheriff, to levy the sum of £800 w/interest from 12 Mar 1787 abating £300 & £16 to Ann CLAY. Sd Sheriff seized the tract of land of Joshua HILL Sd Supreme Ct issued a Writ of V E 30 Apr 1788 & Sheriff put sd land to public sale & it was purchased by Ann CLAY 28 Oct 1788 for the sum of £600, she being the highest bidder. Signed: Thomas EVANS, Sheriff. Wit: Jno WILTBANK, Geo MITCHELL. Rec: 06 Mar 1790 Nath'l MITCHELL, Proth'y.

O-14:180. Deed. This Indenture made 25 Sep 1789 between Cornelius COFFIN and Abner COFFIN both of Sussex cnty, DE of the one part & Benjamin HAMBLIN of Worcester cnty, MD, planter, of the other part. Cornelius & Abner COFFIN for the sum of £127 10s sold to Benjamin HAMBLIN a tract of land formerly surveyed for Ambros WHITE called Schotish Plot by patent dtd 30 Apr 1689 which by sundry conveyances became the property of John COFFIN, dec'd. John COFFIN by his last will & testament gave to his son Cornelius COFFIN 125 acres of afsd land in the head of Herrin Creek & if afsd Cornelius d: w/o a lawful heir to fall to his son Abner COFFIN, sd land bounded by 25 acres of land sd Cornelius COFFIN and Abner COFFIN sold to Thomas TAYLOR, containing 100 acres (Quit Rents only excepted). Signed: Cornelius COFFIN, Abner COFFIN. Wit: Ananias HUDSON, Ezekiel WILLIAMS. Rec: 06 Mar Nath'l MITCHELL, Proth'y.

O-14:181. Deed. This Indenture made 02 Mar 1790 between John WHEETON & Sarah his wife of Kent cnty, DE of the one part & Joseph STOCKLEY, blacksmith, of Sussex cnty, DE of the other part. John WHEETON & Sarah his wife for the sum of £275 sold to Joseph STOCKLEY a tract of land called Cod's Quarter that Avery DRAPER bought of Thomas TILL by a Deed of Sale rec: at Lewes Liber H, No.8, folio 203 &204. Avery DRAPER by Deed of Gift gave sd land to his son Henry DRAPER dtd 08 May 1776 rec: Liber M, No.12, folio 96 for 200 acres lying in Slaughter Neck, Sussex cnty, DE. Henry DRAPER d: seized of sd land leaving two dtrs, Elizabeth & Sarah, which lands were devised by Order of Orphans Ct by David Thornton STRINGER, Tilney Robert YOUNG, John MIDCALF & Elias MORRIS, gents. Sarah DRAPER md: John WHEETON & they sold sd land to Joseph STOCKLEY. Sd land bound by land of Stephen TOWNSEND, land of Charles DRAPER, land of John YOUNG & land of Joshua LOFLAND containing 110 acres & being part of a patten called Edmon Furlong & of the Big Island & joining the lands of Thomas DAVIS & land of John MIDCALF who owns part of the afsd patten which Avery DRAPER, dec'd, d: seized of. Signed: John WHEETTON, Sarah WHEETTON. Wit: William HINDS, Wm DAVIS. 03 Mar 1790 Sarah WHEETTON, wife of John, was examined separate from her husband & she declared she became a party to the above Deed of her own free will. Signed: Jno WILTBANK. Rec: 06 Mar 1790 Nath'l MITCHELL, Proth'y

O-14:182. Deed. This Indenture made 02 Mar 1790 between Sylvester WEBB of Sussex cnty, DE, yeoman, of the one part & John LOFLAND, yeoman, of same of the other part. There is a tract of land situate on S side of N branch of Primehook Creek sometimes called Beaver Dam Branch in Cedar Creek Hundred which land by virtue of a Proprietor's Warrant was surveyed for James JONES of sd cnty. Sd James JONES by his last will & testament bequeathed sd tract to his son Joshua JONES. Joshua JONES by Deed of Sale conveyed 90 & 1/2 acres, part of sd tract, to Mark DAVIS. Mark DAVIS conveyed sd 90 & 1/2 acres to sd Silvester WEBB. Sylvester WEBB & Meram his wife for the sum of £90 10s sold sd 90 & 1/2 acres to John LOFLAND, sd land being W most part of the whole tract. Signed: Sylvester WEBB, Merom WEBB (mark). Wit: Joshua LOFLAND (mark), Smart LOFLAND, Thomas EVANS, George HAZZARD. Merom WEBB, wife of Sylvester, was examined separate from her husband & declared she became a party to above Deed of her own free will. Rec: 06 Mar 1790 Nath'l MITCHELL, Proth'y.

O-14:183. Deed. There is a tract of land situate in Rehoboth Neck, Sussex cnty, DE originally granted by Warrant dtd 10 Dec 1754 to John NEWBOLD late of sd cnty, dec'd, who d: Intestate seized of sd land leaving issue several children to whom sd land descended. James NEWBOLD one of the sons & heirs of sd John NEWBOLD petitioned Orphas Ct 28 Aug 1773 asked sd Ct to appt 5 Freeholders to partition thereof among the heirs. Sd Ct appt'd Messrs Stephen GREEN, John HARMONSON, Samuel DARBY, Reice WOOLF & Peter F WRIGHT to make division thereof among the heirs. Sd Freeholders laid of to William NEWBOLD one of the sons & heirs a parcel of land part of the afsd tract for his share containing 50 acres. James THOMPSON at Feb term 1788 of Ct of Com Pleas recovered against sd William NEWBOLD a debt of £40 65s 8p whereof sd William NEWBOLD was convicted. By order of sd Ct Peter Fretwell WRIGHT, High Sheriff, levied same & seized sd 50 acres being in Lewes & Rehoboth

Hundred to be sold at public sale. Same was purchased by James THOMPSON for the use of Robert WEST for the sum of £78, he being the highest bidder. Peter Fretwell WRIGHT was discharged from office of Sheriff before conveyance to sd Robert WEST. Therefore Thomas EVANS doth convey unto sd Robert WEST the afsd 50 acres. 04 Mar 1790 Signed: Thomas EVANS, Sheriff. Wit: D HALL, George HAZZARD. Rec: 06 Mar 1790 Nath'l MITCHELL, Proth'y

O-14:185. Deed. This Indenture Tripartite made 01 Mar 1790 between Jacob WHITE of Lewes & Rehoboth Hundred, Sussex cnty, DE, William HARRISON of same cnty & Simon HALL of same cnty. Jacob WHITE for the sum of 10s & for other good causes thereunto moving sold to Simon HALL all that land which Jacob WHITE of Lewes, Sussex cnty, DE by his last will & testament dtd 11 Dec 1769 devised unto sd Jacob WHITE situate in Lewes & Rehoboth Hundred supposed to contain 166 acres of land including the whole of a tract purchased by sd Jacob WHITE, dec'd, from Jacob WALKER & William BURTON for the use of sd Simon HALL to the purpose that sd Simon HALL may be a perfect tenant of the Freehold & Inheritance of against whom a common recovery of the lands continued by adjournment Feb Term before the Ct of Com Pleas in which Common Recovery it is agreed that sd William HARRISON shall be Demandant & sd Simon HALL tenant & sd Jacob WHITE voucher. Signed: Jacob WHITE, W HARRISON, Simon HALL. Wit: D HALL, Rhoad SHANKLAND. Rec: 06 Mar 1790 Nath'l MITCHELL, Proth'y

O-14:185. Deed. There is a tract of land situate in Baltimore Hundred, Sussex cnty, DE commonly called Whorton's Folley, originally granted by patent dtd 10 Jun 1734 to Francis WHORTON for 100 acres on E side of E branch of Vines' Creek & S side of Indian River containing 100 acres & whereas there is a parcel of land situate in sd cnty & hund afsd containing 78 acres of land it being part of a Resurvey made by Francis WHORTON on Hog Quarter containing 70 acres pattent & 416 Vacancy added called Hog Quarter which sd parcel of land was held by Joseph WHARTON to the W of the house Harvey WHORTON lived in & where Benjamin CLARK now lives by an alienation by Francis WHARTON to sd Joseph WHORTON dtd 20 Nov 1785 & rec: 1790 bounded by line of Resurvey of Samuel DIRRECKSON owns, being 78 acres. Whereas Joseph WHARTON became seized of one other tract of land by virtue of a Survey granted to him by Warrant dtd 17 Apr 1776 called Stringle beginning near Mill Pond thence near a tract of land called Partnership to the line of Truman's Addition, with John DAGWORTHY'S line containing 48 acres. Whereas Francis WHORTON at a Ct of Com Pleas Feb term 1788 recovered judgement against Joseph WHORTON for the sum of £96 debt & 44s 7p damages whereof sd Joseph was convicted. By writs of FF dtd 07 May 1788 & write of V E dtd 07

Aug 1788 Sheriff Peter Fretwell WRIGHT seized & sold by public sale the sd 3 tracts of land 10 Nov 1788 for the sum of £93 10s to George MITCHELL of sd cnty & in consideration of 1s to Thomas EVANS paid by sd George MITCHELL sd Thomas EVANS conveyed sd tracts to sd George MITCHELL. Signed: Thomas EVANS, Sheriff. Wit: John W BATSON, Peter WHITE. Rec: 06 Mar 1790 Nath'l MITCHELL, Proth'y.

O-14:187. Bond of Conveyance. Joseph WARRINGTON of Sussex cnty, DE, farmer, am firmly bound unto Robert HOLMES 06 Feb 1777. Condition of sd Obligation is Joseph WARRINGTON shall at next Ct of Com Pleas ack: a good deed of Release duly executed by sd WARRINGTON to Robert HOLMES 153 acres of land situate in Indian River hundred, part of a tract surveyed to sd WARRINGTON by virtue of a Warrant granted to James McALVAIN & John WARRINGTON & by them assigned to Joseph WARRINGTON being the SW part of sd land. Signed: Joseph WARRINGTON. Wit: Francis JOHNSON, Rhoads SHANKLAND. Robert HOLMES for the sum of £75 assign my right to the w/in Bond of Conveyance for certain land therein mentioned to George BLACK for the use of Betty HOLMS now a minor 04 Jul 1777. Signed: Robert HOLMES. Wit: Wm HAZZARD, Magdalene OWENS. Robert HOLMES mentioned in w/in Bond for the sum of £100 assign my right to within Bond to Robert WHITE. 27 Jan 1781. Signed: Robert HOLMES. Wit: Wrixam WHILY, Rhoad SHANKLAND. For the sum of £175 in gold & silver coin to be paid by Thomas WALKER I hereby assign to Thomas WALKER all my right to w/in Bond. 15 Nov 1788 Signed: George WALKER. Wit: Catharine GORDON, Peter HARMANSON. Rec: 06 Mar 1790 Nath'l MITCHELL, Proth'y.

O-14:188. Bond. Joseph WARRINGTON of Sussex cnty, DE am bound to Robert HOLMES of sd cnty in the sum of £48. 04 Jul 1777. Condition of sd Obligation is such that if sd Joseph WARRINGTON do convey a sufficient Deed w/a Common Warrantee confirming unto Robert HOLMES all that tract of land situate in Sussex cnty, part of Welches Folley adjoining the S side of the 150 acres sd HOLMES bought of sd WARRINGTON & the N side of Warrington containing 61 acres this Obligation to be void. Signed: Joseph WARRINGTON. Wit: Thomas DAZEY, Rhoad SHANKLAND. Robert HOLMES mentioned in w/in Bond assigns all right & interest in sd w/in Bond to Robert WHITE for the sum of £60 in country produce except 54 acres part of the w/in Bond which I already sold to Stephen ATKINS to be laid out at SW end of sd land. 24 Jan 1781 Signed: Robert HOLMES. Wit: Newcom WHITE, Rhoad SHANKLAND. For the sum of £175 in gold or silver coin to be paid by George WALKER I hereby assign to him the sd George WALKER all my right & interest to w/in Bond. 09

Apr 1782. Signed: Robert WHITE. Wit: William PEERY, Mary PEERY. For the sum of £175 in gold or silver coin secured to be paid by Thomas WALKER I hereby assign to sd Thomas WALKER all my title to w/in Bond. 15 Nov 1788. Signed: George WALKER. Wit: Catharine GORDON, Peter HARMONSON. Rec: 06 Mar 1790 Nath'l MITCHELL, Proth'y.

O-14:189. Petition. Rhoad SHANKLAND, Exec of Joseph WARRINGTON, states Joseph WARRINGTON in his lifetime became obligated in 2 Bonds of Conveyance to Robert HOLMES; one for 61 acres & the other for 153 acres situate in Indian River Hundred for which sd Robert HOLMES was satisfied. Sd Bond of Conveyance by sundry assignments has since become the right of Thomas WALKER. Petitioner humbly prays Ct to grant him the right to execute a Deed of Conveyance agreeable to sd Contract in discharge of the sd Bonds. 02 Mar 1790. Signed: Rhoads SHANKLAND. Read & granted 02 May 1790. Signed: Nath'l MITCHELL, Proth'y.

O-14:189. Deed. This Indenture made 02 Mar 1790 between Rhoads SHANKLAND, Exec of the estate of Joseph WARRINGTON, lately dec'd, of the one part & Thomas WALKER of Lewes & Rehoboth Hundred, Sussex cnty, DE, of the other part. Joseph WARRINGTON in his lifetime by 2 Conveyance Bonds, 1 dtd 06 Feb 1777 & the other dtd 04 Jul 1777, became bound in certain penalties specified set forth in sd Bonds to Robert HOLMES of cnty afsd to make over to sd HOLMS by sufficient Deed 153 acres of land situate in Indian River Hundred being part of a tract of land secured by virtue of a Warrant originally granted to James McALVAIN & John WARRINGTON & by their assignment to sd Joseph WARRINGTON, & also 1 other part of a tract of land called Welches Folley adjoining the S side of sd 153 acres of land. Whereas by Bonds of Conveyance for the sd tracts of land by sundry assignments duly executed have become the property of sd Thomas WALKER of hund & cnty afsd. Sd Bonds of Conveyance have been legally rec. Whereas Rhoads SHANKLAND, Exec afsd, was granted petition to convey sufficient Deed to sd Thomas WALKER to the 2 tracts of land afsd in discharge of sd Bonds. Sd petition was granted. Rhoads SHANKLAND, Exec for the estate of Joseph WARRINGTON, dec'd, for the sum of £91 paid to sd Joseph WARRINGTON in his lifetime & for the further sum of 10s paid to Rhoads SHANKLAND, Exec afsd, by sd Thomas WALKER conveys unto sd WALKER all that above mentioned land laid off by survey for 160 acres. Signed: Rhoads SHANKLAND, Exec'r. Wit: Jos MILLER. Rec: 06 Mar 1790 Nath'l MITCHELL, Proth'y

O-14:190. Deed. Thomas EVANS Esq, High Sheriff of Sussex cnty, DE. Baptis

LAY of cnty afsd in our Ct of Com Pleas at Lewes Nov term 1785 recovered against Robert MILLER of cnty afsd a debt of £86 11p which sd LAY was adjudged for damages & 68s 5p for his charges for suit & sd MILLER was convicted. Sd Ct issued a writ dtd 09 Nov to Peter Fretwell WRIGHT Esq, then High Sheriff, to levy sd debt & damages against the goods & chattels of sd MILLER's lands & tenements. Sd Sheriff seized in execution a parcel of land situate in Cedar Creek & Slaughter Neck Hundred containing 30 acres which 2 Freeholders found to be not sufficient to repay sd debt & damages w/in 7 years. B writ of V E issued 08 Feb 1786 sd Sheriff WRIGHT put to public sale & same was purchased by Luke WATSON of Cedar Creek & Slaughter Neck Hundred 15 Apr year afsd, he being the highest bidder, for the sum of £25. Whereas sd Peter Fretwell WRIGHT was from office of Sheriff before he had executed any Deed to sd Luke WATSON for sd lands. Thomas EVANS for the sum of £25 paid to sd WRIGHT sells to Luke WATSON the land afsd being part of a larger tract formerly belonging to Isaac KELLY situate in Slaughter Neck in Cedar Creek Hundred bounded on SE by lands of Baker JOHNSON, on SW by lands of Branson LOFLAND, on NW by lands of Levi TURNER & NE by lands of Jacob HICKMAN containing 30 acres. 05 Mar 1790 Signed: Thomas EVANS, Sheriff. Wit: D HALL, W HARRISON. Rec: 06 Mar 1790 Nath'l MITCHELL, Proth'y

O-14:192. Deed. This Indenture made 04 Mar 1790 between Jacob WHITE of Lewes, Rehoboth Hundred, Sussex cnty, DE, farmer, & Sarah his wife, of the one part & William JEFFERSON of Broadkiln Hundred, cnty afsd, yeoman, of the other part. Jacob WHITE, dec'd, in his lifetime was seized of a plantation made his last will & testament dtd 11 Dec 1769& among other things devised to his grandson, Jacob WHITE, son of Wrixham WHITE the land & plantation which he bought of Warrington WOOLF on the S of Warrington's Plantation to the plantation of John CRAIG, dec'd, but my will is that sd Wrixham WHITE shall have the use & profits of sd plantation devised to my grandson until he attains the age of 21 years & in case he should d: w/o issue then it was his will that the same lands should descend to his son, Phillip: and in case he should die before sd grandson comes of age, sd land should descend unto his 2 sons Isaac & Robert to be equally divided between them. Sd Jacob WHITE & Sarah his wife for the sum of £125 sold to William JEFFERSON that plantation situate in Lewes, Reboboth Hundred, Sussex cnty, DE adjoining on the N side of sd land which Jacob WHITE, dec'd, purchased of William BURTON being formerly the land of Francis WOOLF, dec'd, & on E side of land sd Warrington WOOLF sold to William DAVIS & on S side of Peter PARKER's mill pond & on W side of sd Jacob WHITE's, dec'd, land containing 112 acres. Signed: Jacob WHITE. Wit: Dan'l RODNEY, D HALL. Sarah WHITE, wife of sd Jacob WHITE, was privately examined separate from her husband, being of full age, and declared she entered above agreement of her own free will. Rec: 06 Mar 1790 Nath'l MITCHELL, Proth'y

O-14:193. Deed. Whereas Purnell JOHNSON, late of Sussex cnty, dec'd by Deed of Sale dtd 05 May 1761 sold to Samuel MUNTFORD late of sd cnty, dec'd, 100 acres of land & marsh situate in Broadkill Hundred being part of a larger tract of 400 acres called Luck by Chance originally granted by Warrant from Deal Court dd 28 Feb 1600 to Harmanias WILTBANK. Whereas Isaac WILTBANK by Deed of Sale dtd 02 May 1764 sold to sd Samuel MUNTFORD 130 of land part of a larger tract granted to afsd Harmenias WILTBANK. Whereas afsd Samuel MUNTFORD afterwards by his last will & testament dtd 10 Aug 1784 gave unto his wife Frances MUNTFORD all his estate, lands, etc to dispose of as she thought fit . Whereas William FENWICK & Agness his wife by their Deed of Sale dtd 05 Feb 1789 did sell to sd Frances MUNTFORD a parcel of land situate in Broadkill Hundred containing 29 & 1/4 acres adjoining the first above sd 100 acres. Sd Frances MUNTFORD for the natural love & affection for John KING & Margaret his wife of Washington cnty, PA & for the sum of £10 grants unto sd John KING & Margaret his wife in right of sd Margaret an equal 1/3 part of the above sd 3 parcels of land. Sd Frances MUNTFORD reserves a right of occupancy during her natural life. Signed: Frances MOUNTFORD (mark). Wit: John CLOWES, Geo MITCHELL. Frances MOUNTFORD appoints John WILTBANK, Phillips KOLLOCK or Joseph MILLER Esqs her Attorney. 23 Jun 1789 Signed: Frances MOUNTFORD (mark). Wit: John CLOWES, Geo MITCHELL. Rec: 06 Mar 1790 Nath'l MITCHELL, Proth'y.

O-14:194. Deed. This Indenture made 03 May 1790 between Lucilla POLK, Admin'x of James POLK late of Sussex cnty, DE, dec'd, of the one part & James POLK, John POLK, Robert POLK & William POLK, minor sons of John POLK, son of Jas, late of cnty afsd, of the other part. Lucilla POLK (agreeable to a Conveyance Bond give by her dec'd husband, James POLK, to Francis JOHNSON, John NORMAN & John POLK of John dtd 12 Nov 1787 for the sum of £1000) sold all that parcel of land that was late in the possession of John POLK of Jas situate in Sussex cnty near the NE fork of Nanticoke River in a neck of land called John's Neck, the afsd lands containing 250 acres. Sd Lucilla POLK appoints Wm PEERY Esq or Col David HALL her Attorney. Signed: Lucilla POLK. Wit: Joshua POLK, Nancy POLK, William OWENS. Nath'l MITCHELL, Proth'y.

O-14:195. Deed. This Indenture made 05 May 1790 between Thomas INGRAM of Sussex cnty, DE, farmer, of the one part & William JONES of sd cnty of the other part. There is a parcel of land situate in Nanticoke Hundred being part of a larger tract of land surveyed for Thomas INGRAM called Ingrams Chance containing & laid off for 11 acres. Thomas INGRAM for the sum of £5 sold to William JONES sd 11 acres. Signed: Thomas INGRAM (mark). Wit: Phillips KOLLOCK, William BURCHER Sr.

O-14:196. Deed. This Indenture made 05 May 1790 between Lydia DODD, late Lydia HARMANSON of Sussex cnty, DE of the one part & Jacob STOCKLEY of sd cnty of the other part. Mary ELDRIDGE, late of afsd cnty, widow, was in her lifetime seized of a parcel of land & plantation in Lewes, Rehoboth Hundred by Deed of Sale from Joshua FISHER & Peter HARMANSON of sd cnty to William COLEMAN of same place containing 83 acres. Mary ELDRIDGE being so seized afterwards d: first making her last will & testament & therein devised sd land to her 2 grndsns, Thomas HARMONSON & afsd Joshua FISHER. Thomas HARMONSON thereafter d: leaving afsd Peter HARMONSON & sd Lydia HARMONSON his brother & sister by the father his nearest of kin & heirs & to whom the right of sd Thomas HARMONSON to the moiety or half of sd land descended in equal portions to Lydia DODD, late Lydia HARMONSON, became seized of 1/2 of sd moiety or 1/4 part of the whole & sd Peter in like manner. Lydia DODD, late Lydia HARMONSON, for the sum of £53 sold to Jacob STOCKLEY above sd land. Signed: Lydia DOOD. Wit: Joseph COULTER, Rhoads SHANKLAND.

O-14:1997. Deed. This Indenture made 18 Dec 1786 between Luke SPENCER of Sussex cnty, DE of the one part & Charles DRAPER of cnty afsd, innholder, of the other part. There is a tract of marsh situate in Cedar Creek Neck containing 22 acres & 152 perches of marsh being part of a larger tract of marsh & land now the property of sd Luke SPENCER, left to sd Luke SPENCER by his fthr's last will & testament which land & marsh is called Harts Delight now in the possession of sd Charles DRAPER. Luke SPENCER for the sum of £51 12s 9p sold afsd marsh to Charles DRAPER. Luke SPENCER appoints John RODNEY Esq or John CLARK his Attorney. Signed: Luke SPENCER. Wit: Catharine SPENCER, Rhoda MASON. Rec: 05 May 1790 Nath'l MITCHELL, Proth'y

O-14:198. Bond of Conveyance. We, Cornelius COFFIN & Abner COFFIN, of Sussex cnty, DE, yeomen, are firmly bound unto Thomas TAYLOR of same, planter, in the penal sum of £500 08 Dec 1787. Condition of this Obligation is such that if they, Cornelius & Abner, or either of them shall at reasonable request of Thomas TAYLOR make over a parcel of land part of a tract called Scottish Plot containing 25 acres situate on the N side of the road leading to Rumly Marsh the above Obligation to be void. Signed: Cornelius COFFIN, Abner COFFIN. Wit: Arthur WILLIAMS, Jonathan DAZEY, Ezekiel WILLIAMS. Rec: 05 May 1790.

O-14:198. Bond of Conveyance. William ROSS (of James) of Sussex cnty, DE, planter, am held firmly bound unto Trustin Laws POLK of same, planter, in the sum of £114 2s 6p in Spanish milled dollars at 7s 6p each to be paid to sd Trustin Laws POLK dtd 09 Feb 1784. Condition of this Obligation to be such that if William ROSS shall convey unto sd Trustin Laws POLK part of a tract of land called Hogg Range situate in Northwest Ford Hundred containing 41 & 1/2 acres of land: sd ROSS to make a Deed of General Warrantee, at any reasonable request of of sd Trustin POLK this Obligation shall be void. Signed: William ROSS. Wit: Clement POLK, Daniel POLK. Rec: 05 May 1790.

O-14:199. Deed. This Indenture made 03 May 1790 between Samuel DIRRICKSON of Sussex cnty, DE of the one part & John LEGATE of same of the other part. Samuel DIRRICKSON for the sum of £83 sold to John LEGATE a parcel of land situate in Baltimore Hundred, afsd cnty, being part of a tract containing 190 acres of land called Chance which sd land was Resurveyed & patented by Thomas COLLINS, dec'd in 1755. Levi COLLINS, son of sd Thomas COLLINS 04 Aug 1784 sell to Jonathan NOTINGHAM by Deed of Sale 50 acres of land part of the above tract called Chance. 03 Jan 1785 Jonathan NOTTINGHAM by Deed of Sale made over to Samuel DIRRICKSON above sd parcel of land. Samuel DIRRICKSON appoints Benjamin HOLLAND or Phillips KOLLOCK as his Attorney. Signed: Samuel DIRRICKSON. Wit: Thomas HAZZARD, Jos DIRRICKSON. Rec: 05 May 1790.

O-14:200. Deed. This Indenture made 29 Apr 1785 between John ROBINSON of Sussex cnty, DE of the one part, & Solomon EVANS, Arthur WILLIAMS, Andrew WILLIAMS, William POWELL & Ezekiel WILLIAMS of same & James LAW, John AYDELOTT, John DIER & John COE of Worcester cnty, MD of the other part. For the sum of 20s current money of DE by the sd Solomon EVANS, Arthur WILLIAMS, Andrew WILLIAMS, William POWELL, Ezekiel WILLIAMS, James LAW, John AYDELOTT, John DIER & John COE to sd John ROBINSON & for diverse other considerations as ROBINSON thereunto moving, sold & conveyed unto sd Solomon EVANS, Arthur WILLIAMS, Andrew WILLIAMS, William POWELL, Ezekiel WILLIAMS, James LAW, John AYDELOTT, John DIER & John COE all that part of a tract of land called Summerfield containing 1 acre of land & premises to the express purpose of a preaching house or chapel for the use of the Methodist or those of the clergy of the Church of England that are friendly thereto shall be erected & built thereon & they the sd Trustees shall forever permit the people called Methodists in America to preach and expound God's Holy Word therein & no others & sd persons preach no other doctrine then contained in Rev Mr John WISTLY's notes on the New

Testament & 4 Vols of sermons. Signed: John ROBINSON. Wit: Rackisse CONNOR, Robert WILDGOOSE (mark) Thomas McGAU (mark). Rec: 05 May 1790.

O-14:201. Deed. Luke SPENCER, surviving Admin of the estate of Alexander McCAY, late of Sussex cnty, DE, dec'd. There is a parcel of land situate in Cedar Creek Hundred on S side of Mispillion Creek called Pennington surveyed & laid out for 400 acres of land & marsh 08 Mar 1688 by Joshua BARKSTEAD then Dept'y Surveyor of cnty afsd, at the request of Henry PENNINGTON who sold same unto Thomas MAY who by Deed of Sale conveyed same to his son, Thomas MAY who by his last will & testament devised same to his son Jonathan MAY who afterwards d: seized thereof Intestate leaving issue two sons, Thomas & Draper MAY to whom sd tract descended. Sd Thomas MAY & Mary his wife & Draper MAY & Ann his wife by their Deed of Sale dtd 02 Nov 1772 sold 100 acres part of the afsd 400 acres being the uppermost end thereof to Alexander McCAY & afterwards by his Deed of Sale sold 50 acres, the one moiety of sd 100 acres unto William McCAY & afterwards made his last will & testament 06 Aug 1783 wherein he directed that all his land may be sold to the best advantage & his just debts paid & apptd his dtr, Catharine McCAY & his brother in law Luke SPENCER Exec's. Luke SPENCER hath survived sd Catharine & sd Luke SPENCER for the sum of £145 sold to John CLANDANIEL of Sussex cnty, yeoman, the one moiety of the above mentioned 100 acres of land sd Alexander McCAY directed be sold in his last will & testament, sd land bounded by land of John KIRK in the line of Harts Pattent & corner of George WALTON & John PLOWMAN's land & Flax Pond Branch containing 50 acres of land surveyed & divided 02 Nov 1772 by David HILFORD. Signed: Luke SPENCER. Wit: Jno RUSSELL, Sylvester WEBB. Rec: 05 May 1790.

O-14:203. Deed. This Indenture made 03 Apr 1790 between Cornelius COFFIN & Abner COFFIN of Sussex cnty, DE, planters, of the one part & Thomas TAYLOR of same, planter, of the other part. Cornelius COFFIN & Abner COFFIN for the sum of £65 sold to Thomas TAYLOR all that parcel of land situate in Baltimore Hundred called Scottish Plot being part of tract granted by the Proprietor of MD to Thomas FENWICK by Patten dtd 30 Apr 1689. Thomas FENWICK & Mary his wife by Deed of Conveyance sold same to George LAYFIELD dtd 04 Apr 1699. George LAYFIELD & Priscilla his wife conveyed same to Hugh TINGLE & of sd land by sundry conveyances John COFFIN became seized. Sd John COFFIN in his last will & testament bequeathed to his son Cornelius COFFIN 125 acres of sd land & if Cornelius d: w/o lawful heir then to his son Abner COFFIN. Sd Cornelius COFFIN & Abner COFFIN agree to make over 25 acres of sd land beginning near the road leading from

Joseph WILDGOOSE's to Rumly Marsh, bounded by land of Thomas GRAY to Thomas TAYLOR. Cornelius COFFIN appoints William BRUINTON, or Peter WHITE or John Wise BATSON his Attorney. Signed: Cornelius COFFIN. Wit: Ezekial WILLIAMS, Thomas COFFIN. Rec: 05 May 1790.

O-14:204. Deed. This Indenture made 06 May 1790 between Isaac COOPER of Sussex cnty, DE of the one part & Samuel TULLY of Broad Creek Hundred, cnty afsd, yeoman, of the other part. There is a tract of land situate in Broad Creek Hundred, cnty afsd, containing 232 acres being part of 3 tracts of land called Cypress Swamp Outlet & Addition which sd tracts were sold by Peter F WRIGHT, High Sheriff, & deeded unto Isaac COOPER 11 Aug 1786. Isaac COOPER for the sum of £77 6p sold sd 232 acres to Samuel TULLY. Signed: Isaac COOPER. Wit: John W BATSON, Barkley TOWNSEND. Rec: 06 May 1790.

O-14:205. Deed. This Indenture made 01 Mar 1782 between George WALTON & Mary WALTON his wife of Sussex cnty, DE of the one part & George BLACK, yeoman, of same of the other part. There is a tract of land containing 362 acres & 62 perches situate in Cedar Creek Hundred, cnty afsd, on the W side of the main branch of Mill Creek called Herring Branch, part of a larger tract called Sawmill Range purchased by John WALTON, dec'd (fthr of afsd George WALTON) from John BOWMAN, dec'd, dtd 06 of 6th mo 1748 & rec: in Lib H, No.7, folio 179. John WALTON by his last will & testament dtd 18 Jul 1751 bequeathed sd 362 acres 62 perches to be equally divided between his 2 sons, George & Samuel WALTON. George WALTON & Mary his wife for the sum of £550 sold to George BLACK 167 acres of land part of sd George WALTON's sd dividend of afsd sd tract beginning by the old shipyard, corner of Benjamin WYNKOOP's land, S side of Landing Road, edge of Old County Road & Mill Creek (only reserving to sd George WALTON 1/4 of an acre of sd land for the use of a burying ground where his fthr & mthr are buried). George & Mary WALTON appoint John WILTBANK or John RODNEY Esqs their Attorney. Signed: George WALTON, Mary WALTON (mark). Wit: Wm HAZZARD, Jno WILTBANK. Mary WALTON was examined apart from her husband & declared she signed above Deed of her own free will. Signed: Jno WILTBANK. Rec: 06 May 1790.

O-14:207. Deed. This Indenture made 06 May 1790 between Charles MASON Admin of the estate of Jonathan MANLOVE, late of Cedar Creek Hundred, Sussex cnty, DE, dec'd, of the one part & Wm BURROUGHS of same of the other part. Jonathan MANLOVE at the time of his death was seized of a tract of land situate in hund & cnty above being part of a larger tract called Morris' Folly originally surveyed for Henry MOLISTON. Henry MOLISTON sold sd land to John Morris. John MORRIS sold sd land to Edward BURROUGHS. Edward BURROUGHS by Deed dtd 03 Aug 1743 sold part of sd land to his son John BURROUGHS. John BURROUGHS sold sd part to Jonathan MANLOVE. Jonathan MANLOVE d: seized of sd part of sd tract of land beginning near a fork of Mispillion Creek, up to Tanjoft Branch, along line of William BURROUGHS' containing 170 acres & 67 sq perches of land. Jonathan MANLOVE being so seized d: Intestate & Admin committed to Charles MASON. Charles MASON petitioned Orphans Ct for permission to sell sd land to pay the estate's outstanding debts. Order was so made 08 Mar 1785. 07 Apr last sd land was sold at Public Vendue to William BURROUGHS, he being the highest bidder, for the sum of £250. Signed: Charles MASON. Wit: George HAZZARD, Kendle BATSON. Rec: 06 May 1790.

O-14:209. Deed. There is a tract of land situate in Broadkiln Hundred, Sussex cnty, DE originally granted to Cornelius WILTBANK late of sd cnty, dec'd, by Warrant dtd 01 Mar 1685 containing 425 acres. Cornelius WILTBANK in his lifetime sold a part of sd tract to Abraham PARSLEY & Frances his wife & by his last will & testament appointed William BEKET & Jacob KOLLOCK his Execs & authorized his sd Execs to convey to sd Abraham PARSLEY & Frances his wife the lands sold to them afsd by virtue of which sd William BUKET & Jacob KOLLOCK by Deed of Sale dtd 07 May 1724 did convey to sd Abraham & Frances his wife the afsd land. Abraham PARSLEY & Frances his wife by their Deed dtd 04 May 1725 did convey sd land containing 275 acres to James FENWICK who afterwards by his last will & testament dtd 21 Dec 1732 devise the same to his 5 children: Thomas, William, James, Mary & Sidney FENWICK, Sd Thomas, James & Sidney d: w/o issue & their parts became the right of sd Mary & William. Sd Mary & William by Indenture dtd 04 Nov 1765 conveyed to Samuel TOM of Sussex cnty a part of the lands afsd before any division was had between the sd Mary & William & sd part was afterwards allotted to sd Mary as her part of the whole by 2 Freeholders nominated by sd William FENWICK & afsd Samuel TOM. Sd William FENWICK & Agness his wife for the sum of £100 sold to James DOUGHERTY all that part of the lands allotted to sd William by the afsd 2 Freeholders (exclusive of 6 acres reserved by them sd William & Agness) bounded by Broadkiln Creek, Fenwick's Landing, containing 100 acres. 06 May 1790 Signed: William FINWICK, Agness FINWICK (mark). Wit: Phillips KOLLOCK, Wm HARRISON. Agness FINWICK was examined separate from her husband, William, & being of full age, declared she became a party to above Deed of her own free will. Signed: Peter F WRIGHT. Rec: 06 May 1790.

O-14:210. Deed. George SMITH of Little Creek Hundred, Sussex cnty, DE in his lifetime was seized of one moiety or half part of a messuage, plantation & tract of land being part of a larger tract called Turkey Trap situate in Little Creek Hundred on Bald Cypress Branch w/the moiety of the saw mill & grist mill thereon (sd moiety lying on the W side of sd Branch) together w/5 acres at the E end of Mill Dam & on E side of sd Branch, all which premises were granted by Pattent by the Proprietary of MD to Thomas ADAMS who by his last will & testament devised same to Caleb BALDERY & sd Caleb BALDERY by his Deed dtd 17 Mar 1769 sold to William VENABLES, who by his Bond of Conveyance dtd 01 Dec 1774 sold sd premises to George SMITH (son of Andrew) & Marshall SMITH who by assignment of sd Bond dtd 11 Mar 1785 did transfer to George SMITH, dec'd, first mentioned, all their right to the tract of land above described. George SMITH being seized of sd land made his last will & testament dtd 14 Sep 1786 appointing Isaac COOPER Exec of his estate. Isaac COOPER 06 May 1789 petitioned Orphans Ct stating sd personal estate was insufficient to discharge all debts whereupon sd Ct ordered sd COOPER to dispose of lands at public sale. Isaac COOPER returned to the Ct that he had sold sd lands viz: 50 acres of part of Turkey Trap to Athanatious MARTIN & the remainder of sd moiety & part of Turkey Trap & dividend of the Grist & Saw mill & privilege of 5 acres at E end of Mill Dam to Barkley TOWNSEND for the sum of £91, they being the highest bidders. Isaac COOPER for the sum of £91 sold above described lands to Barkley TOWNSEND excepting 50 acres sold to Athanatias MARTIN as afsd. 07 May 1790 Signed: Isaac COOPER, Exec. Wit: John W BATSON, Geo MITCHELL.

O-14:212. Barkley TOWNSEND's Survey of Laurel Town. Beginning on a hill on the S side of Broad Creek near the creek swamp & N side of County Road leading from Shingle Landing to Broad Creek Bridge. 32 Lotts.

O-14:215. Bill of Sale. Henry SAFFORD, planter, of Sussex cnty, DE for the sum of £63 sold to Jonathan WOOTTEN 2 cows & yearlings, 1 heifer, 1 horse, 4 beds & furniture, 4 chests, 2 cupboards, 3 linen wheels, 1 woolen wheel, 3 iron pots, 1 tea kettle, 1 iron spider, 3 pewter basins, 6 pewter plates 31 May 1790. Signed: Henry SAFFORD. Wit: Robert ROBINSON, William SAFFORD.

O-14:215. Lease. This Indenture made 31 Jan 1789 between Barkley TOWNSEND of Sussex cnty, DE of the one part & Henry EDGES, blacksmith, of same, of the other part. Barkley TOWNSEND for the yearly rents hereinafter mentioned doth devise unto Henry EDGES a lot of ground, No 15, in Laurel Town & in like manner afsd the quantity of 60 ft sq of ground in lot No 7 in sd town for the convenience of building a blacksmith shop & coal house for the term of 7 years paying sd Barkley TOWNSEND yearly rent of £2 5s 301 Jan each year during the above term of time. If it should happen sd rent or any part thereof be unpaid six months after any of sd days afsd from thenceforth it shall be lawful for sd Barkley TOWNSEND to re-enter sd premises & enjoy as in his own. Further if sd Henry EDGE should build store houses or enter into mercantile line & import any quantity of goods exceeding the sum of £40 in one year & suffer them to be sold on either of the lots from thenceforth it shall be lawful for sd Barkley TOWNSEND to re enter sd premises & enjoy as his own. Neither is afsd Henry EDGES to purchase with cash more than £40 in one year unless he should first take a new lease of £5 per year then he is not to be limited importing or exporting any quantity of goods. It is further agreed if sd EDGES should be desirous to enter into the mercantile business afsd Barkley TOWNSEND doth oblige himself to execute a new lease at £5 the year. If sd Henry EDGES should be desirous to rent/lease sd lots after sd term of 7 years sd Barkley TOWNSEND doth oblige himself to renew & give a new lease to sd Henry EDGES for 7 years on same terms as above. Signed: Barkley TOWNSEND, Henry EDGES. Wit: Henry EDGES Jr, Samuel HEARN.

O-14:217. Negro Finder Manumission. To all whom this may Concern I do hereby certify to all persons that I have set a liberty the Bearer as my Negro Woman Finder & I Desire all persons not to Intercept her or render her in any of the Lawful Business or proceeds given under my hand this 14 Jun 1790. She hath enjoyed her freedom 2 years & 5 months. Signed: Abraham HARRIS.

O-14:217. Deed. Jonathan FOWLER at the time of his death was seized of 2 parcels of land situate in Nanticoke Hundred, Sussex cnty, DE. The first parcel is Pattent land bounded by Arthur FOWLER's lands, land of John LAWS Esq, dec'd, surveyed for 89 acres & 118 sq perches; the other parcel called Fern Pond Tract surveyed for Jonathan FOWLER 14 Apr 1757 by William SHANKLAND, Surveyor, beginning at a path leading from sd FOWLER's to his father, Arthur Fowler, bounded James OWENS' lands, containing 37 acres & 107 sq perches of land. Jonathan FOWLER being so seized made his last will & testament whereof he apptd Rachel FOWLER his wife his Exec & afterwards d: at the time of his death being indebted to sundry persons in considerable sums of money. Solomon TAYLOR, Atty for sd Rachel FOWLER petitioned Orphans Ct 07 Dec 1789, obtained an order for the sale of afsd land & at public sale under the hand of Phillips KOLLOCK Clk of Orphans Ct sold sd 2 parcels of land 02 Jan 1790 to Joseph RICKARDS for 15s 7p per acres the pattent land containing 89 acres & 118 sq perches amounting to £69 8s 8 1/2p & the 60 acres tract for the sum of £13 10s 6p, Joseph RICKARDS being the highest bidder. Rachel FOWLER for the sum of £82 19s 2p & 1/2p paid by Joseph RICKARDS to Solomon TAYLOR my

Atty hath sold sd lands to Jonathan FOWLER this 06 May 1790. Signed: Rachel FOWLER.

O-14:219. Deed. This Indenture made 07 Jun 1790 between John TINGLE, Priscilla TINGLE wife of sd John TINGLE, formerly Priscilla WAPLES, & William BUTCHER all of Sussex cnty, DE of the one part & Henman WHARTON of same of the other part. Whereas Benjamin AYDELOT formerly of Worcester cnty, MD, now dec'd, was seized in his lifetime by the Proprietary of MD Pattent dtd 10 Nov 1709 of a tract of land called Duck Head being then in Worcester cnty, MD but at this time being in Sussex cnty, DE on S side of Indian River. By his last will & testament Benjamin AYDELOT gave sd land Duck Head to his dtr Neomy AYDELOT who afterwards md: John MUMFORD. John MUMFORD & Neomy his wife did Deed sd tract of land to William WHARTON who by his Deed of Sale w/his wife, Elizabeth WHARTON, Quit Claimed dtd 31 Jul 1753 & sold to Elihu HEWES then of Worcester cnty, MD part of sd tract called Duck Head. Elihu HEWES afterwards sold same to John WAPLES who by his last will & testament bequeathed same to his dtr Priscilla WAPLES now Priscilla TINGLE above mentioned. Priscilla TINGLE w/her mthr Mary WAPLES by her Bond or Obligations dtd 16 Apr 1779 did bind herself i the penal sum of £200 gold or silver to convey to Robert BUTCHER the above mentioned part of the sd tract called Duck Head that was Deeded the sd Elihu HEWES who sd Robert BUTCHER from date of above Obligation seized until he d: when sd land to have been conveyed to sd Robert BUTCHER was sold by virtue of an order of Orphans Ct by William BUTCHER, Admin of the estate of Robert BUTCHER, sd Robert BUTCHER having d: Intestate and in debt. Sd John TINGLE, Priscilla TINGLE & William BUTCHER for the sum of £26 sold to sd Hinman WHARTON the sd part of Duck Head being the same that was sold off sd tract to Elihu HEWES afterwards purchased by sd John WAPLES that was afterwards sold to sd Robert BUTCHER containing 23 acres. John TINGLE, Priscilla TINGLE & William BUTCHER appoint M Woolsey BURTON or Thomas EVANS of Sussex cnty, DE their Attorney. Signed: John TINGLE, Priscilla TINGLE (mark), William BURCHER Sr. Wit: Robert HORESTON, Wm BURTON Joyner. 08 Jun 1790 Priscilla TINGLE, wife of John, was examined separate from her husband & did declare she signed sd Deed of her own free will. Signed: Peter F WRIGHT.

O-14:221. Bond of Conveyance. John BELL of Sussex cnty, DE, yeoman, is firmly bound in the sum of £300 to Jonathan CALHOUN, yeoman, of sd cnty 11 May 1787. Condition of sd Bond is such that if above sd John BELL shall by sufficient Deed convey unto sd Jonathan CALHOON 26 acres of land being part of the tract of land John BELL now lives on beginning at a corner of sd BELL's, sd CALHOON's land & land of Edmun DICKERSON at reasonable request of sd Jonathan CALHOON then this Obligation shall be void. Signed: John BELL. Wit: John CLOWES, John RILEY. Rec: 08 Jun 1790.

O-14:222. Deed. This Indenture made 02 Apr 1790 between Morgan WILLIAMS Jr of Sussex cnty, DE, gent, of the one part & Trustin S POLK, farmer of same place of the other part. For the sum of £115 Morgan WILLIAMS sold to Trustin S POLK a tract of land called Nobel Quarter & also part of a tract called William's Vexaction situate in Northwest Fork Hundred, sd cnty, bounded by land of William MELONEY, containing 164 acres. Sd Morgan WILLIAMS Jr appoints Phillip KOLLOCK or Thomas EVANS of Lewes, Esqs, as his Attorney. Signed: Morgan WILLIAMS Jr. Wit: Israel BROWN, Daniel ROGERS. Rec: 08 Jun 1790

O-14:223. Deed. This Indenture made 08 Jun 1790 between Hinman WHARTON of Sussex cnty, DE, yeoman, of the one part & Robert HOUSTON of same, yeoman, of the other part. Whereas James ROUNDS of Worcester cnty, MD was seized of a parcel of land called Self Defence being formerly in Worcester cnty, MD but now in Sussex cnty, DE on the S side of Indian River in a neck called Piney Neck which was surveyed to sd ROUNDS dtd 15 Mar 1753. Part of sd land was Deeded to John SMITH & at this time owned part thereof by Paul WAPLES & part by Job INGRAM of sd cnty & the remaining of sd tract called Self Defense sd James ROUNDS sold to Joshua ROBINSON now dec'd who dying in debt sd land sold to him by sd ROUNDS of the tract called Self Defense was in 1788 sold by Sheriff of Sussex cnty for sd debts when above mentioned Hinman WHARTON became the purchaser thereof. Hinman WHARTON for the sum of £40 sold to Robert HOUSTON all that part of land being part of Self Defense & a part of that part that was sold Joshua ROBINSON by James ROUNDS supposed to contain upwards of 30 acres. Signed: Hinman WHARTON. Wit: Peter F WRIGHT, Wm BURTON joyner. Rec: 08 Jun 1790.

O-14:225. Bond of Conveyance. Isaac WATTSON, carpenter of Sussex cnty, DE is bound to William HILL, farmer of sd cnty in the sum of £200 27 Apr 1775. .... Modey Branch Plantation, --ngeman WINCOP & John CARLILE .... at reasonable request of William HILL. Isaac WATTSON is to Warrant & defend above sd land from Arter VANCEARK & Andrew COCHRON & Richard LONCOME & John MAY & Joseph LANE & Levi LEWES & Simon LEWES & Purnal WATTSON & above sd William HILL is to pay the sum of £1 7s 6p per acre for as many acres as is laid off to him then the above Obligation is to be void. Signed: Isaac WATTSON. Wit: John YOUNG, James YOUNG. Rec'd 14 Dec 1776 from William HILL the sum of £55 11s 6p part of the w/in Bond. Signed:

Isaac WATTSON. 21 Nov .... William HILL the sum of £10 it being part of the w/in Bond. Signed: Isaac WATTSON. Rec: 09 Jun 1790.

O-14:225. Bond of Conveyance. Purnal WATTSON of Sussex cnty, DE is bound to Isaac WATTSON of same, house carpenter, in the sum of £185 to be paid to sd Isaac WATTSON dtd 25 Aug 1766. Condition of sd Obligation is such that if Purnal WATTSON convey to Isaac WATTSON a parcel of land lying on the Modey Branch being the same land Purnal WATTSON now lives on containing 94 acres at the reasonable request of Isaac WATTSON this Obligation to be void. Signed: Purnal WATTSON. Wit: Jonathan MAY, Thos MAY. Rec: 09 Jun 1790.

O-14:226. Deed. This Indenture made 03 Jun 1790 between John YOUNG of Sussex cnty, DE, yeoman, of the one part & Nehemiah DAVIS Sr & Sarah his wife & John HAYS & Betty his wife of cnty afsd of the other part. Nehemiah DAVIS Sr & Sarah his wife & John HAYS & Betty his wife for the sum of £100 sold to John YOUNG a tract of 173 acres & 50 perches of land that Samuel DAVIS & Mary BOWMAN sold to Nathan YOUNG & sd Nathan YOUNG d: Intestate & seized of in Slaughter Neck Hundred on W side of Delaware Bay & S side of Cedar Creek bounded by land belonging to Joseph STOCKLEY called Cods Quarter, land of Joshua LOFLAND. land of Jacob HICKMAN. Signed: Nehemiah DAVIS, Sarah DAVIS, John HAYS, Betty HAYS. Wit: Bethuel WATTSON Jr, Avery DRAPER. Sarah DAVIS & Betty HAYS being of full age were examined separate from their husbands & declared they signed above Deed of the own free will. Signed: Peter F WRIGHT. Rec: 09 Jun 1790.

O-14:227. Deed. There is a tract of land situate in Cedar Creek Hundred, Sussex cnty, DE beginning at a beaver dam in Cedar Creek Neck, bounded by land formerly of Abraham WYNKOOP, lands formerly of Widow HALL, containing 94 acres being part of a larger tract originally granted to Arthur VANKIRK & by sundry conveyances to Simeon LEWIS who by Deed of Sale dtd 04 Sep 1755 conveyed afsd land to Purnal WATTSON. Purnal WATTSON by a Bond dtd 25 Aug 1766 became bound to Isaac WATTSON in the sum of £185 w/condition if sd Purnal WATTSON should by sufficient Deed of Conveyance to Isaac WATTSON afsd Bond to be void. Purnal WATTSON d: Intestate before he executed a Deed of Conveyance. Admin of the estate of Purnal WATTSON was granted to afsd Mary now the wife of Isaac BEAUCHAMP & party to these presents. Sd Isaac BEAUCHAMP & Mary his wife petitioned Orphans Ct to execute Deed of Conveyance for land afsd to Robert WATTSON, Exec of estate of Isaac WATTSON, & sd petition was granted. Isaac BEAUCHAMP & Mary his wife confirm & convey sd 94 acres unto Robert WATTSON, Exec of sd Isaac

WATTSON. Signed: Isaac BEAUCHAMP, Mary BEAUCHAMP. Wit: Avery DRAPER, W HARRISON. Rec: 09 Jun 1790.

O-14:229. Release. Reese WOOLF appeared before John WILTBANK Esq, Chief Justice of the Ct of Com Pleas of Sussex cnty, DE & deposed he was personally present & witnessed, as did Hap HAZZARD, Peter ROBINSON. son of Burton ROBINSON Esq of Sussex cnty, DE, sign & seal this Release, and further that he has been acquainted w/sd Peter & Burton ROBINSON & knows them to be surviving brothers of Thomas ROBINSON, dec'd, who was b: in this county & about 1776 joined the Armies of the King of Britain, resided some time in NY, & afterwards in Nova Scotia, returning to Sussex cnty, DE & died here & that his son Thomas ROBINSON named an Exec in his fthr's will d: by drowning in Nov last & was buried in this cnty. Signed: Reece WOOLF. 06 Jul 1790 Jno WILTBANK. Rec: 06 Jul 1790 Nath'l MITCHELL, Proth'y.

Peter ROBINSON & Burton ROBINSON of Sussex cnty, DE, Esqs who survived Thomas ROBINSON which sd Peter, Burton & Thomas were Execs in the will of Thomas ROBINSON the elder, Esq, some time of Sussex cnty but late of Nova Scotia dec'd. Thomas ROBINSON the elder in his lifetime constituted Benjamin & William WADDINGTON of London, merchants, his Receiver of monies due & belonging to him in England who in virtue of such appt received diverse sums of money for & on acct of sd Thomas ROBINSON & 31 Dec 1786 transmitted to America an acct of their recpts & pymnts leaving a balance of £1081 sterling money of Grt Britain due to sd Thomas ROBINSON which acct (sd Thomas having in meantime d:) came to the hands of his Execs. Whereas sd Peter & Burton ROBINSON (sd Thomas the younger being then in Nova Scotia) as Execs of Thomas ROBINSON the elder drew certain Bills of Exchange dtd Sussex cnty, DE 30 Dec 1787 directed to sd Benjamin & William MADDINGTON to pay unto Thomas, Samuel & Miers FISHER the sum of £1081 sterling w/interest thereon & to charge the same to sd Thomas ROBINSON's estate. Whereas sd Benjamin & William WADDINGTON did pay same to sd Ralph ---- & Warren ---- for acct of sd Thomas, Samuel & Mier FISHER the sum of £1134 sterling. Sd Thomas, Samuel & Meirs FISHER have fully paid & satisfied Peter ROBINSON acting Exec of sd Thomas ROBINSON the sum of £1984 10s lawful money of PA. Therefore Peter ROBINSON & Burton ROBINSON do release Benjamin & William MADDINGTON & to sd Ralph ---- & Warren ---- & sd Thomas, Samuel & Meirs FISHER. 14 May 1790 Signed: Peter ROBINSON, Burton ROBINSON. Wit: Reece WOOLF, Hap HAZZARD. Rec: 06 Jul 1790.

O-14:232. James P WILSON & Elizabeth WILSON vs Peter MARSH & Mary his wife, William PEERY & Margaretta his wife & Theodore WILSON.

Amicable action in partition of the lands Rev Matthew WILSON d: seized. 30 Jun 1790 all matters in variance in this cause by consent of parties & rule of Ct are referred to Peter WHITE, John RUSSELL & Adam HALL who are to 1st lay off the house & one small lot below the garden as the Dower of Elizabeth WILSON, in sd lands & make partition of remaining 2/3 of sd lands among the others equably to true intent of last will & testament of sd Matthew WILSON, dec'd. Rec: 06 Jul 1790. Peter WHITE, John RUSSELL & Adam HALL were sworn for the purpose afsd 28 Jul 1790 before William PEERY. Whereas Matthew WILSON late of Sussex cnty, DE by his last will & testament dtd 29 Mar 1790 duly proved before Phillips KOLLOCK, Esq, Reg for Probate of Wills & granting Letters of Administration, did devise all his real estate & direct it be disposed of among his legal reps Elizabeth WILSON, his widow, James P WILSON, Theodore WILSON, Mary MARCH & Margaretta PEERY. Whereas sd Elizabeth WILSON, James P WILSON, Theodore WILSON, Mary MARCH & Margaretta PEERY by an amicable action in Ct of Com Pleas did appt Peter WHITE, John RUSSELL & Adam HALL to make partition of the lands, 1st laying off the mansion house together w/the outhouses (except the stable) and on small lot of ground bounded on the NW by sd garden, on NE & SE lands late of David HALL, dec'd, & on SW by land herein after to be laid off to Elizabeth WILSON, sd widow, as her Dower. Sd WHITE, RUSSELL & HALL made partition of sd lands among the widow, 2 sons & 2 dtrs as follows: sd lot & house to widow as Dower as above, to James P WILSON, eldest son, as one of his 2 shares one moiety of a lot of land adjoining the widows third; to Theodore WILSON, second & youngest son, the other moiety of the lot last afsd bounded by land of Peter WHITE, land now in the possession of the HALLs; to Peter MARSH & Mary his wife 1/3 part of the meadow; to William PEERY Esq & Margaretta his wife the remaining 1/3 part of the meadow. 28 Jul 1790 Signed: Peter WHITE, Jno RUSSELL, Adam HALL.

O-14:234. Plat map of above division of lands amongst Elizabeth WILSON, James P WILSON, Mary MARSH & Margaretta PEERY.

O-14:234. Commission. The Delaware State to Peter Fretwell WRIGHT of Sussex cnty, DE, Esq. Greetings: Whereas our President & General Assembly on 23 Jan last past did by joint Ballot elect and appoint you, the sd Peter Fretwell WRIGHT, Third Justice of the Ct of Com Pleas & Orphans Ct of & for sd cnty of Sussex. Know Ye therefore in pursuance of sd Appt we do by these present commission you, sd Peter Fretwell WRIGHT, to be Third Justice of sd Ct of Com Pleas & Orphans Ct of & for sd cnty of Sussex Requiring you to do therein that which of Right according to the laws of sd state out to be done and performed. In Testimony whereof we have caused our Great Seal to be hereunto affixed. Wit:

His Excellency Joshua CLAYTON, Esq, our Presidential Commander In Chief at Newcastle 05 Feb 1790 and in the 14th year of our Independency. Signed: James CLAYTON. Attest: Jas BOOTH, Sec'y.

O-14:235. Deed. This Indenture made 15 Oct 1789 between William WALLER (of Thos) of the Dorchester cnty, MD of the one part & Charles MOORE of Sussex cnty, DE of the other part. William WALTER (of Thomas) for the sum of £25 hath sold to Charles MOORE all that tract of land called McGlastin's Choice (or Chance) situate in Little Creek Hundred in Sussex cnty being the land that McGLASLEN Deed to sd William WALLER as appears in Somerset cnty, MD containing 50 acres of land unto Charles MOORE. William WALLER appts Peter WHITE or Joseph MILLER Esqs his Attorney. Signed: William WALLER. Wit: Joshua WRIGHT, John TWYFORD.

O-14:236. Deed of Gift. Michael McDADE of Sussex cnty, DE, farmer, for the love which I have towards my children viz: Elizabeth McDADE, Hanna McDADE & Michael McDADE of same parish & cnty have granted all my goods & chattels in my dwelling house in sd cnty, the following articles: To dtr Elizabeth McDADE 2 beds & furniture belonging to them, to dtr Hannah McDADE 1 bed & furniture belonging to same, likewise I give my dtr Elizabeth 1 cow & calf & to my dtr Hanna 1 cow & calf; likewise to dtrs Elizabeth & Hannah 1 mare, 1 cupboard, 1 sq table, 1 round table, 1 chest, 1/2 dozen of chairs, 2 spinning wheels, 1 doz of earthenware. 12 doz pewter plates & tin cups, 2 earthen pans & dish, 2 flat irons, 1 hackle, 2 iron pots, 2 earthen pots, 9 spoons & 2 mugs, 1 loom & tackling, 3 pound thread, 4 pound of Flax, 10 bushels of corn, 5 pounds of Flax not drext, 2 ploughs, 2 sets of harrow teeth, 1 stone jug, 4 bottles, 1 tea pot, 2 soughs & their pigs. I likewise give to my dtrs Elizabeth & Hanna McDADE 5 shoats, 130 weight of pork. I likewise give to my son Michael McDADE 2 guns as his own property. 16 Feb 1789 Signed: Michael McDADE (mark). Wit: James DENNISON, James ONEAL.

O-14:236. Thomas ROBINSON, Parker ROBINSON & Peter ROBINSON, minors vs their Guardian John ROBINSON. Amicable action in partition for the lands whereof Thomas ROBINSON, their father, d: seized. All variances in this cause by consent of all parties & rule of this Ct referred to William PEERY, Woodman STOCKLEY, Newcomb WHITE, George WALTON & William MATTHEWS on 4 days notice. Rec: 13 Apr 1790. Nath'l MITCHELL, Proth'y. Within named STOCKLEY, WHITE, WALTON & PEERY were sworn in due form of law 04 Aug 1790 before Rhoads SHANKLAND. 06 Aug 1790 Wm MATTHEWS was legally qualified for the purpose above before Jno WILTBANK.

Whereas Thomas ROBINSON late of Sussex cnty, DE by his last will & testament dtd 25 Mar 1790 duly approved before Phillips KOLLOCK Esq, Reg for Probate & grants of LOA for cnty afsd, devise all his lands to his 6 sons to wit: Benjamin, William, Thomas, Parker, John & Peter ROBINSON to be equally divided among them. Whereas sd Benjamin, William, Thomas, Parker, John & Peter ROBINSON by amicable action in Ct of Com Pleas, sd Benjamin & William in person & sd Parker, Thomas, John & Peter by their Guardian, being w/in the age of 21 years did appoint William PEERY, Woodman STOCKLEY, Newcomb WHITE, George WALTON & William MATTHEWS to make partition of sd lands of their dec'd father. Partition as follows: To Benjamin ROBINSON, eldest son of sd Thomas ROBINSON 140 acres & 1/6 part of land sd Thomas purchased of Yates CONWELL adjoining lands of Painter STOCKLEY, dec'd. To William ROBINSON 140 acres & 1/6 part of above described. To Thomas ROBINSON 140 acres & 1/6 part of afsd. To Parker ROBINSON 115 acres & 1/6 part afsd. To John ROBINSON 115 acres & 1/6 part afsd. To Peter ROBINSON all the remaining of sd land containing 130 acres & remaining 1/6 afsd. Signed: William PEERY, Woodman STOCKLEY, Newcomb WHITE, George WALTON, William MATTHEWS.

O-14:239. Petition. Purnal WATTSON, dec'd, by his Bond of Obligation dtd 25 Aug 1766 became bound unto Isaac WATTSON late of Sussex cnty, DE, dec'd, in the sum of £185 w/the Condition Purnal WATTSON should convey a sufficient Deed of Sale to Isaac WATTSON for a parcel of land situate in Cedar Creek Hundred containing 94 acres. Sd Purnal WATTSON d: Intestate before he executed sd Deed. Petitioner Isaac BEAUCHAMP & wife Mary late Mary WATTSON, his wife, asks Ct to grant an order to execute sd Deed to Robert WATTSON, Exec of sd Isaac WATTSON, dec'd. Signed: Isaac BEAUCHAMP, Mary BEAUCHAMP. Granted & Rec: 09 Jun 1790.

O-14:239. Deed. This Indenture made 21 Jun 1790 between Phillips KOLLOCK of Sussex cnty, DE, Esq & Penelope, his wife, of the one part & John BURTON of same, yeoman, of the other part. There is a tract of land situate in Broadkiln Hundred containing 825 acres called Finch Hall which tract of land was granted by Warrant of Resurvey to Jacob PHILLIPS, Andrew FULLERTON & Charles COULTER late of Sussex cnty, dec'd. Division of sd tract Jacob PHILLIPS, Andrew FULLERTON & Charles COULTER in which division all that part of sd tract on SE side of the head of Round Pool Branch containing 275 acres was laid off to Jacob PHILLIPS as his 1/3 of sd tract as may appear by William SHANKLAND's plot. Jacob PHILLIPS d: seized of sd 275 acres & by his last will & testament dtd 07 Mar 1760 appt Jacob KOLLOCK Esq to be his sole Exec. Jacob KOLLOCK by Deed of Conveyance dtd 28 Aug 1771 sold sd 275 acres to

Phillips KOLLOCK party to these presents. Phillips KOLLOCK by Deed of Conveyance same date reconveyed same to afsd Jacob KOLLOCK. Jacob KOLLOCK did not dispose of afsd tract by his last will & testament leaving Margaret his widow & 7 children: Jacob KOLLOCK, Magdalen SWIFT, Hannah NUNEZ, Catharine WILTBANK, Hester KOLLOCK, Mary FIELD & Phillips KOLLOCK & also 2 grandchildren: Susannah LEWIS & Hester LEWIS, dtrs of Wrixom LEWIS by Jane his wife, late Jane KOLLOCK, dec'd dtr of sd Jacob KOLLOCK, to whom sd land descended. Margaret KOLLOCK & Phillips KOLLOCK 10 Oct 1772 obtained an Order of sd Ct appt'g Gilbelsher PARKER & Parker ROBINSON Esqs, Thomas SKIDMAN, John WALLER & Stringer TILNEY, gent, to make division of sd tract among the heirs of sd Jacob KOLLOCK, dec'd. Sd Freeholders laid off to Margaret KOLLOCK 92 acres of sd land in full for her Dower & remaining 2/3 would not admit of partition among the remaining heirs w/o spoiling the whole. 31 Oct 1772 Phillips KOLLOCK obtained an Order of the Ct appt'g afsd Gilbelsher PARKER Esq, John WALLER & Stringer TILNEY, gent, to appraise the value of the remaining 2/3 of afsd tract of land which sd Freeholders appraised remaining 2/3 of sd land containing 183 acres was worth 15s per acres amounting to the sum of £137 5s. Jacob KOLLOCK, eldest son of Jacob KOLLOCK, dec'd, by written instrument dtd 08 Dec 1772 refused to accept afsd 2/3 of afsd land evaluation whereupon the Ct adjudged the sd 2/3 to Phillips KOLLOCK to the other heirs their shares of the evaluation. Phillips KOLLOCK conveyed sd 2/3 tract to Robert BURTON Sr by Deed of Conveyance. Margaret KOLLOCK thereafter d: whereby afsd 92 acres of land become subject to division among afsd heirs whereupon Phillips KOLLOCK petitioned Ct to appt 5 Freeholders to make partition of the afsd 92 acres amongst the heirs. Ct apptd Hap HAZZARD, Nathaniel HICKMAN, Jacob HAZZARD, John Abbott WARRINGTON & John HOLLAND to make partition which sd Freeholders reported sd 92 acres would not admit of equal partition w/o damaging the whole. Phillips KOLLOCK obtained an Order of the Ct appt'g Hap HAZZARD, Nathaniel HICKMAN & John Abbott WARRINGTON to make estimate of the intrinsic value thereof & they reported sd land to be valuated at 18s 9p per acre. Whereupon sd Ct adjudged sd 92 acres to Phillips KOLLOCK he paying the other heirs their share of the value. Phillips KOLLOCK & Penelope his wife for the sum of £126 10s sold to John BURTON all that parcel of land laid off to afsd Margaret KOLLOCK as her 1/3 or Dower of the 275 acres of land beginning at a pillar of brick in the line of Thomas SKIDMAN's land, containing 92 acres. Signed: Phillips KOLLOCK, Penelope KOLLOCK. Wit: William BRERETON, Burton JOHNSON. Penelope KOLLOCK, wife of Phillips, was examined separate from her husband, did declare she became a part to above Deed of her own free will. 22 Jun 1790 Signed: Jno WILTBANK. Rec: 29 Jul 1790.

O-14:242. Deed. This Indenture made 16 Feb 1786 between Gamage Evans HODGSON & Ann his wife of Sussex cnty, DE of the one part & Zachariah HARRIS of same of the other part. There is a parcel of land in sd cnty containing 125 acres situate on N side of the head of Indian River being part of a larger tract formerly the property of Thomas CAREY, dec'd, called the Vineyard being the E most end of sd tract which sd Thomas CAREY by his last will & testament dtd 04 May 1766 bequeathed to his son Ebenezer CAREY. Ebenezer CARY by Deed of Sale conveyed sd 125 acres to George WALKER. George WALKER by Deed of Sale dtd 07 May 1780 conveyed sd 125 acres to Gamage Evans HODGSON. Gamage Evans HODGSON & Ann his wife for the sum of £120 sold sd 125 acres to Zachariah HARRIS; sd land bounded by land of Benjamin BENSTON, land now in possession of Latherbury BARKER, called the Vineyard. Gamage Evans HODGSON appts Robert Wattson McCALLEY or Elisha DICKENSON as his Attorney. Signed: Gamage Evans HODGSON (mark), Ann E HODGSON (mark). Wit: Simon KOLLOCK, John HARRIS.

O-14:244. Deed. There is a tract of land & marsh situate on Rehoboth Bay, Sussex cnty, DE called Horse Island containing 107 acres which was the property of William HOUSTON formerly of formerly of cnty afsd. Thomas & Peter ROBINSON by virtue of Power of Attorney from sd William HOUSTON by Deed of Sale dtd 25 Jan 1764 conveyed sd tract to Hamilton CRAIG late of cnty afsd, dec'd, Sd Hamilton by his last will & testament dtd 20 Mar 1777 bequeathed to his son John CRAIG 5 acres of marsh part of the afsd Horse Island & did also by his last will & testament bequeathed to his son Edward CRAIG 5 acres of marsh part of sd Horse Island adjoining sd John CRAIG's 5 acres. Sd Edward CRAIG being seized of sd 5 acres of marsh d: having made his last will & testament appt'g Rhoads SHANKLAND to be his Exec. At Sussex cnty Orphans Ct RhoadS SHANKLAND petitioned sd Ct that the personal estate of sd dec'd was not sufficient to discharge his debts & sd Ct ordered sd Rhoads SHANKLAND expose to Public Sale all real estate of sd dec'd in Sussex cnty to discharge sd debts. Sd SHANKLAND did sell all sd Edward CRAIG'S marsh land to Woodman STOKLEY Sr for the sum of £8 15s, he being the highest bidder. 02 Aug 1790 Signed: Rhoads SHANKLAND. Wit: Nicholas SMITH, W HARRISON.

O-14:245. Deed. This Indenture made 17 May 1787 between Richard CLIFTON & Susannah his wife of Sussex cnty, De, yeoman & seamster, of the one part & Maitelda BOUNDS of Somerset cnty MD of the other part. Richard CLIFTON & Susannah his wife hath sold unto Mattilda BOUNDS by Bond of Conveyance dtd 17 May 1787 a tract of land called Daniel's Adventure, his part to sd tract being 57 & 1/2 acres, also all their title to a Resurvey on the sd Daniels' Adventure by

Warrant of Nanticoke Hundred dtd 15 Jul 1776 to resurvey sd tract originally 12 Apr 1747 for Daniel CLIFTON & since granted to sd CLIFTON by the Proprietary of MD for 100 acres & from a Certificate from Thos WHITE surveyor of part of Sussex cnty has added vacant land to afsd original tract of 58 acres w/allowance of 6 & reduced the whole entire tract now called Richard's Venture, bounded by land called Clifton's Range, containing 115 & 1/2 acres. Richard CLIFTON & Susannah his wife appoint Joshua POLK or John LAWS Jr, Esqs their Attorney. Signed: Richard CLIFTON, Susannah CLIFTON (mark). Wit: Joshua POLK, William OWENS, Jonathan BOUNDS. 17 May 1787 Susannah CLIFTON was examined separate from her husband & declared she signed above Deed of her own free will. Signed: Joshua POLK.

O-14:246. Deed. This Indenture made 02 AUG 1790 between William HALL of Sussex cnty, DE of the one part & Samuel HALL of cnty afsd, taylor, of the other part. There is a tract of land situate in Broadkiln Hundred being part of a tract whereof George WEST late of sd cnty, dec'd, who in his lifetime was seized of, dying Intestate & leaving children who were legal heirs. George WEST, son of George WEST, dec'd, petitioned Orphans Ct to appt 5 Freeholders to make partition of sd land among the heirs which Ct granted & 5 Freeholders returned that sd land would not be divided w/o marring the whole whereupon 3 Freeholders were appt'd to set a value on sd land. Sd land bounded by land of the heirs of David McILVAIN, land of the heirs of James WALKER, dec'd, containing 10 acres. William HALL & Barsheba HALL his wife for the sum of £80 sold to Samuel HALL the sd 10 acres. Signed: William HALL, Bathsheba HALL. Wit: Aaron PEERY, James STEPHENSON. 04 Aug 1790 Bathsheba HALL was examined separate from her husband & did declare she signed sd Deed of her own free will. Signed: Peter F WRIGHT.

O-14:248. Petition. John BELL in his lifetime was seized of a parcel of land containing 26 acres being part of a larger tract situate in Broadkiln Hundred, Sussex cnty, DE by his Bond dtd 11 May 1781 bound himself unto Jonathan CALHOON of sd cnty, yeoman, in the sum of £300 w/Condition John BELL should by sufficient Deed convey to Jonathan CALHOON the afsd 26 acres being part of a larger tract John BELL then lived on beginning at a corner of sd BELL's, sd CALHOON's & Edmond DICKERSON's lands, then sd Obligation should be void. Sd John BELL after making sd Bond & before executing a Deed for same d: Intestate. Admin of his estate was committed to William BELL Jr. Sd William BELL Jr petitioned Orphans Ct for order to execute sufficient Deed to Jonathan CALHOON for the sd 26 acres in discharge of afsd Bond. 04 Aug 1790 Signed: William BELL Jr, Admin. Petition granted 04 Aug 1790,

O-14:248. Deed. John BELL in his lifetime was seized of a parcel of land containing 26 acres being part of a larger tract situate in Broadkiln Hundred, Sussex cnty, DE by his Bond dtd 11 May 1781 bound himself unto Jonathan CALHOON of sd cnty, yeoman, in the sum of £300 w/Condition John BELL should by sufficient Deed convey to Jonathan CALHOON the afsd 26 acres being part of a larger tract John BELL then lived on beginning at a corner of sd BELL's, sd CALHOON's & Edmond DICKERSON's lands, then sd Obligation should be void. Sd John BELL after making sd Bond & before executing a Deed for same d: Intestate. Admin of his estate was committed to William BELL Jr. Sd William BELL Jr petitioned Orphans Ct for order to execute sufficient Deed to Jonathan CALHOON for the sd 26 acres in discharge of afsd Bond 04 Aug 1790. Ct granted above petition & William BELL Jr, Admin of the estate of John BELL late of Broadkiln Hundred, Sussex cnty, DE. yeoman, dec'd, conveyed Deed of Sale to Jonathan CALHOON for above sd lands 04 Aug 1790. Signed: William BELL Jr, Admin. Rec: 04 Aug 1790 Nath'l MITCHELL, Proth'y.

O-14:251. Deed. This Indenture made 26 Jul 1790 between William JOHNSON of Sussex cnty, DE of the one part & Thomas BLIZZARD of same of the other part. There is a tract of land situate in Indian River Hundred on SW side of Hairfield's Branch containing 93 acres, part of a larger tract granted by Warrant dtd 23 Sep 1740 to Philip WASTCOAT who endorsed sd Warrant assigned same to Thomas BRYAN & Thomas BRYAN by Deed of Sale dtd 06 Jan 1755 conveyed the lands surveyed of the above Warrant to John Bounds JUMP & Samuel JUMP in Joint Tenancy. Sd John Bounds JUMP d: before division of sd lands was made between him & Samuel JUMP & sd lands became the property of Samuel JUMP who by his Deed of Sale dtd 15 May 1773 conveyed sd land to above mentioned William JOHNSON. Now William JOHNSON for the sum of £40 hath sold to Thomas BLIZZARD 93 acres of land, part of the tract of land above described. Signed: William JOHNSON. Wit: John DUTTON, Abraham HARRIS. Rec: 04 Aug 1790.

O-14:252. Deed. This Indenture made 29 Nov 1788 between Manlove CLIFTON & Tabitha his wife of Kent cnty, DE of the one part & William CARLISLE of Sussex cnty, DE of the other part. Manlove CLIFTON & Tabitha his wife for the sum of £100 sold to William CARLISLE part of a tract of land over & above what is sold to John JOHNSON, the land lying in Hinds' Neck surveyed 10 Jan 1745 & known as Clifton's Folly containing 138 acres of land. Manlove CLIFTON & Tabithy his wife appoint John WILTBANK or Alexander LAWS Esqs their Attorney. Signed: Manlove CLIFTON, Tabithy CLIFTON (

mark). Wit: William OWENS, Thomas LEVESTY, Joseph MURPHY. 29 Nov 1788 Tabitha CLIFTON, wife of Manlove, was examined separate from her husband, declared she became a party thereto of her own free will. Signed: Alex'r LAWS. Rec: 04 Aug 1790.

O-14:253. Deed. This Indenture made 04 Jun 14th year of Independence & 1790 between Henry EDGES, farmer, & Peggy his wife of Dorchester cnty, MD of the one part & George VINSON, merchant, of Sussex cnty, DE of the other part. Perry EDGES, wife of Henry EDGES, stands seized of 200 acres of land called Warland's Adventure situate in Worcester cnty (at time of granting, but now in Sussex cnty) beginning at the head of Broad Creek on the E side of the main branch abt 3/4 mile S of Benston's Mill, containing 204 acres of land. Henry EDGES & Perry his wife, for the sum of £10 sold to George VINSON all of the afsd 204 acres of land. Signed: Henry EDGES (mark), Peggy EDGES (mark). Wit: Robt HOUSTON Sr, George FARMAN, Elsey MOORE. Henry EDGES & Peggy EDGES his wife appoint Phillips KOLLOCK or Thomas EVANS, Esqs as their Attorney. Signed: Henry EDGES (mark), Peggy EDGES (mark). Rec: 04 Aug 1790.

O-14:254. Deed. This Indenture made 04 Jun 1790 between John RILEY & Ann RILEY his wife & Bennett WARREN & Rachel WARREN his wife of Sussex cnty, DE of the one part & Littleton LOFLAND of same of the other part. There is a parcel of land situate in Cedar Creek Hundred being part of a larger tract called Riley's Fortune which sd larger tract was formerly the property of Benjamin RILEY, dec'd. Benjamin RILEY in his lifetime bound himself to convey 100 acres of sd larger tract to Thomas WHARTON. Sd Thomas WHARTON assigned sd Obligatory Bond to Hugh BAKER, & Thomas RILEY, George RILEY, Execs of late will & testament of sd Benjamin RILEY by their Deed of Sale dtd 02 May 1764 conveyed sd 100 acres of land to sd Hugh BAKER having first obtained an Order of the Ct of Com Pleas. Sd Hugh BAKER by his Deed of Sale dtd 10 Jan 1787 conveyed sd 100 acres to Dorman LOFLAND of cnty afsd, dec'd. Dorman LOFLAND d: Intestate as to sd 100 acres of land & w/o issue. Sd land descended to his brothers & sisters, the above Ann RILEY & Rachel WARREN being 2 sisters. John RILEY & Ann his wife, Bennett WARREN & Rachel his wife, for the sum of £16 3s hath sold to sd Littleton LOFLAND all of the afsd 100 acres of land. Signed: John RILEY, Ann RILEY (mark), Bennett WARREN, Rachel WARREN (mark). Wit: Peter F WRIGHT, George LOFLAND. John RILEY, Ann RILEY, Bennett WARREN & Rachel WARREN appoint William PEERY or Thomas EVANS Esqs as their Attorney. 14 Jun 1790 Ann RILEY & Rachel WARREN were examined separate from their husbands & each declared she became a party to above Deed of her own free will. Signed: Peter F WRIGHT. Rec: 04 Aug 1790.

O-14:256. Deed. This Indenture made 16 Mar 1790 between Robert JUETT, Jessey GRIFFITH & Mary GRIFFITH his wife, of Sussex cnty, DE of the one part & John HOOPER of same, yeoman, of the other part. Robert JUETT, Jessey GRIFFITH & Mary GRIFFITH his wife, for the sum of £160 11s 3p hath sold to John HOOPER part of a tract of land situate in NW Fork Hundred being part of a tract called Marin's Hundred which formerly belonged to William JUETT late of Sussex cnty, dec'd, containing 91 & 3/4 acres. Robert JUETT, Jesse GRIFFITH & Mary his wife appt William PEERY or Rhoads SHANKLAND at their Attorney. Signed: Robert JUETT, Jesse GRIFFITH, Mary GRIFFITH. Wit: Newton CANNON, Joshua OBIER, John TENNENT. Mary GRIFFITH was examined separate from her husband & ack: she did sign above Deed of her own free will. Signed: Peter F WRIGHT. Rec: 04 Aug 1790.

O-14:257. Deed of Gift. Charles JOHNSON & Phebe JOHNSON his wife of Sussex cnty, DE for the sum of £5 for natural love & other consideration we moving have Quit claimed unto William JOHNSON a tract of land situate in Indian River Hundred granted to my father, Samuel JOHNSON, dec'd, by Proprietaries Warrant dtd at Philadelphia 03 Jul 1754 for 200 acres of land. 18 May 1790 Signed: Charles JOHNSON, Phebe JOHNSON (mark). Wit: Isaac ATKINS, Sarah BLIZARD (mark). 04 Aug 1790 Phebe JOHNSON was examined separate from her husband & ack: she became a party to the above Deed of Gift of her own free will. Signed: Peter F WRIGHT.

O-14:258. Deed. This Indenture made 04 Aug 1790 between Thomas NEWCOMB & Elizabeth his wife, of Sussex cnty, DE, yeoman, of the one part & George BAINUM of same, yeoman, of the other part. Thomas NEWCOMB & Elizabeth his wife for the sum of £3 sold to George BAINUM all that part of a tract of land situate in Broadkiln Hundred late the property of William LIGHT, dec'd being on N side of the County Road from Lewes town to Evans Saw Mill near the corner of John CAREY's land, bounded by Robert HOOD's land. Signed: Thomas NEWCOMB, Elizabeth NEWCOMB (mark). Wit: Phillips KOLLOCK, Robert HOOD. 04 Aug 1790 Elizabeth NEWCOMB was examined separate from her husband & did declare she signed the above of her own free will. Signed: Jno WILTBANK.

O-14:259. Deed. This Indenture made 04 Aug 1790 between Robert HOOD of Sussex cnty, DE, yeoman, of the one part & George BENNUM of same, yeoman, of the other part. Robert HOOD for the sum of £15 sold to George BENNUM a parcel of land situate in Broadkiln Hundred, land sd Robert HOOD purchased of Paul SIMPLER, sd land bounded by Thomas NEWCOMB's land, containing 60 acres. Signed: Robert HOOD. Wit: Thomas EVANS, Milby SIMPLER. Rec: 04 Aug 1790.

O-14:260. Deed. This Indenture made 04 Aug 1790 between Peter Fretwill WRIGHT of Sussex cnty, DE, Esq of the one part & James WILEY of same, Innholder, of the other part. There is a tract of land situate in Broadkiln Hundred containing 216 acres called Hashold's Fortune which sd tract by sundry conveyances became the property of Purnall JOHNSON late of Sussex cnty, dec'd who by Deed dtd 30 Aug 1777 conveyed sd tract to Peter Fretwell WRIGHT. Peter Fretwell WRIGHT for the sum of £9 sold to James WILEY a parcel of land, part of afsd tract, containing 16 acres. Signed: Peter F WRIGHT. Wit: Jno WILTBANK, W HARRISON. Rec: 04 Aug 1790

O-14:261. Deed. This Indenture made 10 Aug 1789 between Mary WILLEY & Sarah HURLLEY, Execs of Richard CROCKETT & John CROCKETT, dec'd, of Sussex cnty, DE of the one part & Robert LAMBDEN of same of the other part. Mary WILLY & Sarah HURLLY, Execs afsd for the sum of £75 sold to Robert LAMBDEN all that parcel of land being part of a tract called Outtin's Mistake situate in Nanticoke Hundred bounded by Joseph BAYER's plantation, containing 100 acres. Sarah HURLEY & Mary WILLEY appt Isaac TURNER as their Attorney. Signed: Sarah HURLEY, Mary WILLEY (mark). Wit: Pharoah HARLEY, Hales SPICER.

O-14:262. Deed. This Indenture made 20 Mar 1790 between John FUTCHER of Rehoboth Neck, Sussex cnty, DE, yeoman, & Sarah his wife of the one part & William SHANKLAND Jr, merchant, of Philadelphia in PA of the other part. John FUTCHER & Sarah his wife for the sum of £71 5s sold to William SHANKLAND Jr a parcel of land in Angola Neck part of a larger tract granted by pattent to John JOHNSON 29 Sep 1677 beginning at a line agreed upon between John FUTCHER to Mills & Moses SHANKLAND dtd 13 May 1769 containing 20 acres of land & marsh (surveyed 26 Oct 1783). Signed: John FUTCHER. Wit: N WAPLES, Robert HOUSTON.

O-14:262. Bond of Conveyance. John BELL of Sussex cnty, DE, yeoman, is bound to William PASSEMORE in the sum of £3600 dtd 20 Mar 1783. William PASSEMORE purchased from John BELL 570 acres of land + John BELL's 1/2 of a Grist mill on the premises, sd land not yet surveyed & it is therefore agreed if sd land measures more William PASSEMORE is to pay in proportion for what is over & if measured less will pay less in proportion. Condition of sd Obligation is if John BELL shall at reasonable request of William PASSEMORE convey sufficient Deed of Sale w/common Warrantee therein confirmed to sd William PASSEMORE all that tract of land where John BELL now dwells & sd BELL's 1/2 of sd Grist mill & sd land situate on S side of Long Bridge Branch adjoining lands in possession of John ROUSE, James HALL, William FITCHETT, Jonathan CALHOON, George CONWELL & Richard ABBOT in Broadkiln Hundred, this Obligation to be void. Signed: John BELL. Wit: John CLOWES, Thomas BELL. Know all those present that I w/in named William PASSEMORE for the love & affection I bare my well beloved son William PASSEMORE Jr & in consideration of the sum of £5 I assign all my claim, title & interest to the w/in Bond & also the lands & premises therein mentioned unto sd William PASSEMORE Jr. 04 Aug 1790 Signed: Wm PASSEMORE. Wit: Rhoads SHANKLAND, J RUSSELL. Rec: 05 Aug 1790.

O-14:263. Petition. William BELL Jr, Admin of estate of John BELL, late of Sussex cnty, DE, yeoman, dec'd, 05 Aug 1790. John BELL in his lifetime was seized of a tract of land containing by estimation 575 acres situate in Broadkiln Hundred & so being seized bound himself dtd 20 Mar 1783 setting forth William PASSEMORE of Accomack cnty, VA had purchased the 575 acres & sd 1/2 of a Grist mill on the premises which land was not then surveyed for the sum of £3600 current money of DE w/Condition sd John BELL should convey sufficient Deed for sd land & premises bounded by lands of John ROUSE, James HALL, William FITCHETT, Jonathan CALHOON, George CONWELL & Richard ABBOT in Broadkiln Hundred then sd Bond to be void. John BELL after making sd Bond & before conveyance of sd land d: Intestate whereof Admin of his estate were committed to sd Petitioner Wm BELL Jr. The money for which above sd lands were sold was in part paid unto sd John BELL in his lifetime & residue hath since been paid to Petitioner. Sd William PASSEMORE by his assignment endorsed on sd Bond hath transferred all his right & claim to lands & premises afsd to William PASSEMORE Jr. Petitioner requests an Order authorizing him to execute sufficient Deed to sd land & premises to William PASSEMORE Jr. Signed: William BELL Jr, Admin. 05 Aug 1790 Petition read & granted. Signed: Nath'l MITCHELL, Proth'y.

O-14:264. Deed. John BELL in his lifetime was seized of a tract of land containing by estimation 575 acres situate in Broadkiln Hundred & so being seized bound himself dtd 20 Mar 1783 setting forth William PASSEMORE of Accomack cnty, VA had purchased the 575 acres & sd 1/2 of a Grist mill on the premises which land was not then surveyed it was therefore agreed if sd land measures more William PASSEMORE is to pay in proportion for what is over & if measured less will pay less in proportion & sd John BELL ack: himself to be bound for the sum of £3600 w/Condition sd John BELL should convey sufficient Deed for sd land & premises bounded by lands of John ROUSE, James HALL, William FITCHETT, Jonathan CALHOON, George CONWELL & Richard ABBOT in Broadkiln Hundred then sd Bond to be void. John BELL after making sd Bond & before conveyance of sd land d: Intestate whereof Admin of his estate were committed to afsd William BELL Jr, Admin of John BELL's estate. Whereas the money for which above sd lands were sold was in part paid unto sd John BELL in his lifetime & residue hath since been paid to William BELL Jr Admin & party to these present. Whereas sd William PASSEMORE by his assignment endorsed on sd Bond hath transferred all his right & claim to lands & premises afsd to William PASSEMORE Jr. William BELL Jr petitioned Ct for Order to convey afsd lands to William PASSEMORE Jr & Ct granted same. Now sd William BELL Jr , Admin of John BELL, dec'd, in pursuance of sd Order of the Court & for the sum of £1687 10s in part paid to sd John BALL in his lifetime. the residue thereof since paid to William BELL Jr, Admin, & in further consideration of 5s paid by sd William PASSEMORE Jr doth grant, sell & convey to sd William PASSEMORE Jr sufficient Deed to afsd lands & premises bounded by land formerly belonging to Thomas DAVOCK, John HALL's line, Joseph CORD's land, Stephen REVAT's line, land for John SPENCER Esq, dec'd, in all containing 588 1/2 acres of land resurveyed by Caleb CIRWITHIN at the instance of Henry SMITH 23 Oct 1772. (always excepting & reserving 26 acres which were sold by John BELL in his lifetime to Jonathan CALHOON by a Deed dtd 04 Aug 1790 from afsd William BELL, Admin). 05 Aug 1790 Signed: William BELL Jr, Admin. Wit: Jno RUSSELL, Wm COULTER.

O-14:267. Deed. 05 Aug 1790 Levi HALL of Sussex cnty, DE of the one part for the sum of £25 hath sold to Thomas KILLAM of same of the other part all that parcel of land situate on the S side of Indian River called Hall's Choice, being a tract taken up by Joseph HALL of Worcester cnty which sd land was granted to afsd Joseph HALL by a Proprietaries Warrant dtd 24 Oct 1749 who afterwards d: leaving the afsd child Levy HALL sd land containing 45 acres. Signed: Levi HALL. Wit: Daniel RODNEY, Caleb RODNEY.

O-14:268. Deed. 26 Feb 1790 Joshua TAYLOR of Sussex cnty, DE, planter, of the one part for the sum of £50 current money of MD hath sold to James FASSETT of Worcester cnty, MD of the other part all that tract of land called Hog Quarter situate formerly in Worcester cnty but now in Sussex cnty, DE granted 09 Mar 1761 to Charles NICKOLS containing 40 acres. Sd Charles NICKOLS 29 Mar 1765 by Deed conveyed sd land to Peter JOHNSON. Sd Peter JOHNSON 22 Oct 1767 by Deed conveyed sd tract of land unto John TAYLOR, fthr of above Joshua TAYLOR. John TAYLOR by his last will & testament dtd 22 Oct 1786 devised sd land to sd son Joshua TAYLOR & Joshua TAYLOR now conveys sd land to James FASSITT. Joshua TAYLOR appoints John W BADSON or Peter WHITE of Sussex cnty, DE his Attorney. Signed: Joshua TAYLOR. Wit: John POSTLY, Elijah FOSSITT. Rec: 05 Aug 1790.

O-14:269. Deed. 21 Sep 1787 Custis RODGERS of Sussex cnty, DE of the one part for the sum of £47 & for diverse other good causes him thereunto moving hath sold to John GODDARD, son of Francis Lane GODDARD of same, gent, of the other part the one moiety or part of a tract of land situate on S side of rode leading from Broad Creek to Salisbury lying upon the head of a tract of land called Days Beginning near Jobe Simmon's Plantation & tract of land called Callaways's Intention which formerly belonged to John CALLOWAY, the fthr of Peter CALLOWAY, containing 30 & 1/2 acres. Custis RODGERS appoints Col Nathaniel WAPLES or Dr Joseph HALL as his Attorney. Signed: Custis RODGERS. Wit: William POLK, William VAUGHAN. Rec: 05 Aug 1790.

O-14:270. Deed. This Indenture made 30 Jan 1790 between William HARGIS of state of VA, yeoman, of the one part & Joseph HOUSTON of Sussex cnty, DE, yeoman, of the other part. Hinman WHARTON was by Proprietary of MD pattent dtd 23 Jul 1739 seized of a tract of land called Lanes' Adventure situate in Sussex cnty containing 300 acres of land & is the tract of land David MOORE owns part of at this time, all which tract called Lane's Adventure having since been sold by sd Hinman WHARTON; 100 acres of sd land became the property of William HARGIS by heirship laying at the W end of sd tract. Sd William HARGIS having by his Bond dtd 24 Mar 1772 bound himself in the penal sum of £92 current money of cnty of Worcester, MD to convey unto John HOLLOWAY of Worcester cnty, MD 100 acres of land lying in Piney Neck & part of tract of land called Lane's Adventure containing 300 acres, which Bond sd John HOLLOWAY 22 Mar 1773 did assign to John DARBY. John DARBY 13 Nov 1773 assigned sd Bond to Joseph HOUSTON, party afsd. For the sum of £41 William HARGIN sells to Joseph HOUSTON sd 100 acres. Mary HARGIS, wife of sd William HARGIS, doth freely surrender her right of Dowry & right of thirds in sd land to Joseph HOUSTON. William & Mary HARGIS appoint Simon KOLLOCK Esq, Robert HOUSTON, Isaac ATKINS or George FRAMES, yeomen, as their Attorney. Signed: William HARGIS. Wit: William BENSTON, James BURSTON (Benston?), Wm DOWNING. Rec: 05 Aug 1790.

O-14:272. Deed. This Indenture made 04 May 1782 between John CRAPPER, yeoman, of Sussex cnty, DE & Mary CRAPPER, his wife, of the one part &

George BLACK, yeoman, of same of the other part. There is a tract of land situate in Sussex cnty containing 800 acres called Farmers Delight granted by pattent 05 Jan 1687 to Henry SKIDMORE & by sundry conveyances became the property of Abraham WYNKOOP Esq, dec'd, who sold 200 acres part thereof to afsd John CRAPPER by Deed of Sale dtd 04 Aug 1752. John CRAPPER & Mary his wife for the sum of £23 sold to George BLACK 7 acres & 106 & 1/2 sq perches of land, part of the afsd 200 acres joining on the Herring Branch bounded by land of Daniel DINGUS. John CRAPPER & Mary his wife appoint John WILTBANK or John RODNEY as their Attorney. Signed: John CRAPPER, Mary CRAPPER (mark). Wit: Wm HAZZARD, George CORVEN. Mary CRAPPER was examined separate from her husband & declared she executed above Deed of her own free will. Signed: Wm POLK. Rec: 05 Aug 1790.

O-14:273. Deed. James BAILY, late of Sussex cnty, DE, dec'd, was in his lifetime seized of certain lands situate on Lewes Creek & by his last will & testament dtd 29 Apr 1745 devised unto his 4 children: James BAILY, Hannah BAILY, Ann BAILY & Stewart BAILY, all his estate to be equally divided between them. After the estate was equally divided, Ann BAILY by Indenture dtd 08 Apr 1767 for the sum of £27 sold to Jacob KOLLOCK of Sussex cnty a lot of land containing 138 ft front & 200 ft back lying between a graveyard & a piece of 8 ft front & 200 ft back laid out for Samuel ARNALL, who purchased the undivided right of Stewart BAILY of the lands of afsd James BAILY; also one moiety of the land divided between sd Ann BAILY & sd Samuel ARNALL, sd Ann's part lying next to the marsh, likewise all sd Ann's part of the marsh lying between Jacob's part & Lewes Creek which sd divident appear by Deed of Release from sd Samuel ARNALL to sd Jacob KOLLOCK. Sd Indenture provided if sd Ann BAILY should pay to Jacob KOLLOCK the sum of £27 w/lawful interest then sd Indenture should be void. Margaret KOLLOCK, Exec of the last will & testament of sd Jacob KOLLOCK 08 Nov 1786 obtained judgement against sd Ann BAILY for the principal & interest monies in sd Indenture plus legal costs & charges. A Ct of Com PLeas order dtd 09 May 1787 directed Peter Fretwell WRIGHT, High Sheriff, to make sale of the mortgaged premises & render to sd Margaret KOLLOCK the principal, interest, charges & costs monies. 08 Aug 1787 sd WRIGHT did report he had sold sd land at public sale 18 Jun last afsd to sd Margareat KOLLOCK for the use of William HARRIS for the sum of £24, she being the highest bidder. Sd Peter Fretwell WRIGHT was removed from office of Sheriff before he executed Deed of Conveyance for sd lands. Thomas EVANS, High Sheriff of Sussex cnty for the sum of £24 pd to Peter WRIGHT by William HARRIS has conveyed by this Deed afsd lot, land, marsh & premises to sd William HARRIS. Signed: Thomas EVANS, Sheriff. Wit: John TENNENT, W HARRISON.

O-14:274. Deed. 30 Oct 1789 William GREAR & Elizabeth his wife, of Sussex cnty, DE of the one part for the sum of £100 sold to George MOORE of same of the other part all that parcel of land called Rough Savannah situate in Little Creek Hundred, cnty afsd, whereon William GREAR lives laid off for 50 acres of land as appears by Deed of Sale from Thomas WALLER to afsd William GREAR dtd 08 Feb 1759, rec: Sommerset cnty, MD. William GREAR & Elizabeth his wife appoint Peter WHITE, Phillips KOLLOCK or Joseph MILLER their Attorney. Signed: William GREAR (mark), Elizabeth GREAR (mark). Wit: Chas MOORE, Jonathan BUCK, John BRADLEY.

O-14:275. Deed. This Indenture made 06 Aug 1790 between Benjamin BURROUGHS of Kent cnty, Admin of the estate of Bridget MANLOVE late of Sussex cnty, DE, dec'd, of the one part & William BURROUGHS of cnty afsd of the other part. There is a parcel of land, part of a larger tract of 400 acres situate in Broadkiln Hundred, cnty afsd, which by sundry conveyances became the property of William Lord CARHART, who w/Rosanna his wife by Deed of Sale dtd 29 Aug 1766 conveyed same to Boaz MANLOVE, late of Sussex cnty. By Act of Assembly of DE sd parcel of land & all of the estate of Boaz MANLOVE was confiscated for use of sd DE & sold by Levin DERRICKSON Esq, Commissioner , & same was purchased by John CLOWES Esq for the sum of £143 15s. John CLOWES by his Bond dtd 06 Oct 1778 became bound to Bridget MANLOVE in the sum of £2000 w/condition if sd John CLOWES or sd Levin DERRICKSON or his Successor should by good & sufficient Deed convey to sd Bridget MANLOVE the afsd parcel of land purchased by John CLOWES as part of the confiscated Estate of afsd Boaz MANLOVE then the Obligation should be void. Bridget MANLOVE thereafter d: Intestate possessed of the parcel of land afsd & Admin of her estate was granted to afsd Benjamin BURROUGHS who at Orphans Ct obtained a Order for sale of sd lands to discharge debts of sd dec'd & made return to sd Ct he did expose sd lands to public sale & same was purchased 27 Mar 1787 by sd William BURROUGHS for the sum of £75 he being the highest bidder. Benjamin BURROUGHS for the afsd sum by this Deed conveys 120 acres to William BURROUGHS. Signed: Benj'm BURROUGHS. Wit: John PARKER, W HARRISON.

O-14:277. Deed. This Indenture made 06 Aug 1790 between William BURROUGHS of Kent cnty, DE of the one part & Jacob HAZZARD of Sussex cnty, DE of the other part. Whereas Bridget MANLOVE, late of Sussex cnty, dec'd, was in her lifetime possessed of a parcel of land situate in Broadkiln Hundred, d: Intestate & Admin of her estate was granted to Benjamin BURROUGHS who at Orphans Ct obtained a Order for sale of sd lands to discharge debts of sd dec'd & made return to sd Ct he did expose sd lands to public sale & same was purchased 27 Mar 1787 by sd William BURROUGHS for the sum of £75 he being the highest bidder. Sd parcel of land being part of a tract of 400 acres called Swan Point containing 120 acres. William BURROUGHS for the sum of £100 sold to Jacob HAZZARD the afsd 120 acres. Signed: William BURROUGHS. Wit: Charles DRAPER, W HARRISON.

O-14:278. Deed. 06 Aug 1790 Thomas PASSEMORE of Sussex cnty, DE of the one part for the sum of £60 sold to Josiah TRUITT of same of the other part all that parcel of land situate in Broadkiln Hundred, cnty afsd, called Security being on SE side of Nanticoke River & NE side of Broad Creek in Wimbosoccum Neck & S of a tract of land surveyed for Matthew PASSEMORE containing 50 acres & also 10 acres of land adjoining Security being part of a tract granted to Matthew PASSEMORE 14 Nov 1738 (called Little Worth) which was transferred to Jehu PARAMORE by Ezekiel PASSEMORE & 10 Jun 1765 was transferred by Jehu PASSEMORE to Charles COTTINGHAM of Sommerset cnty, MD. Sd Charles COTTINGHAM by his last will devised sd land to his son, William COTTINGHAM, who 11 Jan 1771 transferred sd land to afsd Matthew PASEMORE who dying sd land became the property of his son, Thomas PASSEMORE who 27 Apr 1789 transferred sd land to Nathan CARMENE & sd Nathan CARMENE 10 Dec 1789 transfered sd land to John WILLIAMS & sd John WILLIAMS 21 Dec 1789 transferred sd land to afsd Thomas PASSEMORE in the right of Patrick PASSEMORE, dec'd, & Thomas PASSEMORE Jun 1790 obtain an Orphans Ct Order to sell sd lands to discharge debts of sd Patrick PASSEMORE, dec'd. Signed: Thomas PASSEMORE (mark). Wit: Thomas FISHER, W HARRISON.

O-14:279. Deed of Gift. Elizabeth ROBERTS of Sussex cnty, DE for the natural love & affection I bare unto my children, namely Mary ROBERTS & Tabitha ROBERTS & for other consideration, me thereunto moving, hath given & confirmed unto sd Mary & Tabitha ROBERTS all my goods, chattels to be equally divided between them. Signed: 30 Jul 1790 Elizabeth ROBERTS (mark). Wit: Sanders ROBERTS, Nehemiah HOWARD.

O-14:280. Deed. 29 Aug 1790 Morgan WILLIAMS of Sussex cnty, DE, yeoman, of the one part for the natural love & affection he bears his son Robert WILLIAMS of same, yeoman, of the other part & for the sum of £5 hath confirmed unto his son, Robert WILLIAMS, a parcel of land called Coopers Blind situate in Northwest Fork Hundred on NW side of dwelling plantation Thomas WILLIAMS formerly lived but now belonging to Tustin S POLK laid out for 50 acres of land. Morgan WILLIAMS also grants unto sd Robert WILLIAMS all that part of a tract of land called Morgan's Venture situate on the E side of

County Road leading from Bridge Branch to Clear Brook Branch. Sd Morgan WILLIAMS appoints Francis JONSON or Joseph RICARDS his Attorney. Signed: Morgan WILLIAMS. Wit: Joseph RICARDS, Fran's JOHNSON. Rec : 09 Sep 1790.

O-14:281. Bond of Conveyance. Smith FRAME of Sussex cnty, DE is firmly bound unto William PEERY of cnty afsd in the sum of £80 dtd 25 May 1785. Condition is such that if bound Smith FRAME by Deed of Sale confirm unto sd William PEERY all his right to a parcel of land situate in Broadkiln Hundred containing 52 acres being part of a larger tract called Timber Hill late the property of Archibald SMITH of sd cnty, dec'd, which sd 52 acres was lately surveyed by Rhoads SHANKLAND of cnty afsd this Obligation to be void. Signed: Smith FRAME. Wit: Job INGRAM, William FRAME. Rec: 09 Sep 1790.

O-14:282. Deed. Job INGRAM at a Ct of Com Pleas recovered against Nunez DEPUTY late of Sussex cnty a debt of £300 & £3 4s 3p costs & damages. Sd Ct ordered 05 Aug 1789 Thomas EVANS, High Sheriff, to seize a parcel of land situate in Broadkiln Hundred containing 100 acres adjoining lands of John COLLINS & land whereon Nunez DEPUTY now lives sd to be the property of John CLOWES Esq which sd tract of land he had appraised by 2 Freeholders who evaluated sd land as to not be sufficient to satisfy sd debt & damages w/in 7 years. 04 Nov 1789 Ct ordered sd Sheriff to expose sd lands to public sale & same was purchased by Job INGRAM 19 Dec 1789 for the sum of £30 he being the highest bidder. Thomas EVANS for the sum of sd £30 hath sold & conveyed unto sd Job INGRAM the afsd 100 acres. Thomas EVANS, Sheriff. Wit: James P WILSON, Nath'l MITCHELL. Rec: 09 Sep 1790.

O-14:283. Deed. John Sheldon DORMAN by virtue of Deed of Sale from John CLOWES Esq, dec'd, dtd 01 Mar 1776 was seized of 4 allotments of land in pursuance of the last will of John CLOWES the elder, Esq, dec'd, to wit: lotts # 1 & 2 containing 2 & 1/2 acres of land & lotts # 3 & 4 containing 100 & 1/2 acres. Sd John Sheldon DORMAN being so seized of sd lands 13 Aug 1785, John CLIFFORD, assignee of William MILLARD by consideration of Ct of Com Pleas recovered judgement against sd John Sheldon DORMAN for the sum of £186 10s together w/costs of suit. By Ct Order Peter Fretwell WRIGHT, then High Sheriff, to levy sd debts & cost to chattels, good & lands of sd DORMAN. Whereas Richard BASSETT of Kent cnty, DE also by consideration of Ct of Com Pleas recovered judgement against sd John Sheldon DORMAN & Lawrence RILEY for the sum of £600 together w/costs of suit. May term 1787 sd Ct ordered sd Sheriff to levy sd sum of damages & costs to the goods & chattels of sd John Sheldon

DORMAN & Lawrence RILEY. Sd Sheriff, Peter Fretwell WRIGHT, returned he had taken in execution sundry goods, chattels & several parcels of land & 2 Freeholders who reported the rents, issues, etc of sd lands were not sufficient to satisfy sd debts & damages w/in 7 years. Whereupon sd Ct issued writs ordering sd Sheriff to expose the lands to public sale. 24 Jul 1790 sd Sheriff sold the Drawbridge Plantation to John CLARK, gent, for the sum of £75, he being the highest bidder. Sd Peter Fretwell WRIGHT was removed from the office of Sheriff before making Deed to John CLARK for the afsd land. Thomas EVANS Esq, High Sheriff of Sussex cnty, DE for the further sum of 5s conveys unto sd John CLARK all that above describe 103 acres of land & premises of the lotts called Drawbridge Plantation of John Sheldon DORMAN 07 Sep 1790. Signed: Thomas EVANS, Sheriff. Wit: Jos MILLER, William PEERY.

O-14:285. Deed. There is a tract of land situate in Broadkiln Hundred, Sussex cnty, DE containing 227 acres John Sheldon DORMAN was seized of 2/3 parts of in his own right & 1/3 thereof in rights of his wife, Mary DORMAN. Sd John Sheldon DORMAN being indebted to sundry persons endeavors sums of money, who obtained judgements in the Ct of Com Pleas against sd John Sheldon DORMAN & executions being issued on sd judgements the then Sheriff of cnty afsd, Peter Fretwell WRIGHT, seized sd tract of land & exposed same to public sale & sd tract of land was struck off to William HALL of same cnty, blacksmith, he being the highest bidder. Sd Peter Fretwell WRIGHT was removed from office of Sheriff before executing conveyance of the land to sd William HALL. Thomas EVANS Esq who succeeded sd Peter Fretwell WRIGHT as Sheriff duly executed & conveyed sd land to sd William HALL. Sd land is situate on the SE side of Mill Creek near Fishers Landing, bounded by lands late of John WALKER, dec'd, & William WYATT, line of Samuel RUSSELL, line late of Levi ROBINS, dec'd, containing 227 acres. But as sd John Sheldon DORMAN was seized of 1/3 part of sd tract of land in right of his wife, sd Mary DORMAN, the Deed from Sheriff of Sussex cnty could only convey an Estate for life in the sd 1/3 part of he sd tract to sd William HALL. John Sheldon DORMAN & Mary DORMAN his wife for the sum of £20 have quit claimed unto sd William HALL all their right & claim to sd land. 04 Sep 1790 Signed: John S DORMAN, Mary DORMAN. Wit: Jno WILTBANK, William PEERY. Mary DORMAN was examined separate from her husband and declared she signed the w/in Deed of her own free will. Signed: Jno WILTBANK. John Sheldon DORMAN & Mary DORMAN his wife appoint Peter Fretwell WRIGHT Esq their Attorney. Signed: John S DORMAN, Mary DORMAN. Wit: Jno WILTBANK, William PEERY. Rec :10 Sep 1790. Nath'l MITCHELL, Proth'y.

O-14:287. Deed. This Indenture made 10 Sep 1790 between James KING of Broadkiln Hundred, Sussex cnty, DE, yeoman & Ann his wife, of the one part & William HALL of Lewes, Rehoboth Hundred, Sussex cnty, DE, blacksmith, of the other part. There is a tract of land situate in Broadkiln Hundred containing 200 acres being part of a larger tract originally granted to Garthright EVERSON called Orphans Choice which sd 200 acres of land being the SW end of sd larger tract; by sundry conveyances became the property of Hugh KING, dec'd who by his last will & testament devised the 200 acres to be equally divided between his 2 sons, James & Hugh KING which sd James KING d: Intestate before any division was made leaving sd 200 acres of land to William KING & James KING, party to these presents. Hugh KING the younger & afsd William & James KING, sons of James KING, dec'd, made division of the 200 acres among themselves, Hugh KING to have all that part of sd land lying on the NW of the middle dividing line & William KING & James KING to have all the part of the 200 acres lying on the SE side of middle dividing line & by their several deeds of release had surveyed 108 acres divided between themselves, William KING to have all that part of sd 108 acres on the NE side of the dividing line containing 72 acres & James KING to have all that part lying on the SW side of the dividing line containing 36 acres of land. Now sd James KING & Ann his wife for the sum of £60 had sold to William HALL the sd 36 acres surveyed by Rhoads SHANKLAND Esq 28 Aug 1790. Signed: James KING, Nancy KING. Wit: Peter F WRIGHT, Joshua HALL. Ann, wife of James KING, was examined separate from her husband & being of full age did declare she became a party to the above Deed of her own free will. Signed: Peter F WRIGHT.

O-14:289. Deed. This Indenture made 04 Sep 1790 between William HALL of Sussex cnty, DE, blacksmith, & Betty his wife of the one part & Mary DORMAN present wife of James Sheldon DORMAN & Nehemiah DORMAN, son of sd John Sheldon DORMAN of same cnty of the other part. There is a parcel of land situate in Broadkiln Hundred late the property of afsd John Sheldon DORMAN & Mary DORMAN his wife containing 227 acres of land. Sd John Sheldon DORMAN being indebted to sundry persons who obtained Judgements against him in the Ct of Com Pleas & execution being issued directing Sheriff to seize & put to public sale at which time afsd parcel of land was struck off to be afsd William HALL he being the highest bidder. Peter Fretwell WRIGHT, then High Sheriff was removed from office before executing Deed for sd land to William HALL, Thomas EVANS, Esq, who succeeded sd WRIGHT as Sheriff by Deed of Sale executed under his hand & seal conveyed sd land to sd William HALL. As John Sheldon DORMAN was seized of only 2/3 of sd land in his own right & of the other 1/2 in right of his wife, the afsd Mary, Mary DORMAN together w/her husband, John Sheldon

DORMAN, released their claim & right to sd land & afsd William HALL became seized of sd land. William HALL & Betty his wife for the sum of £13 paid by Mary & Nehemiah DORMAN had sold unto afsd Mary DORMAN during the term of her natural life & after her decease to sd Nehemiah DORMAN all sd William & Betty HALL's claim to 50 acres of sd tract of land. Signed: William HALL, Betty HALL. Wit: Jno WILTBANK, William PEERY. Betty HALL was examined separate from her husband & did declare she signed the w/in Deed of her own free will. Signed: Jno WILTBANK.

O-14:290. Deed. This Indenture Tripartite made 09 Sep 1790 between Samuel DODD of Broadkiln Hundred, Sussex cnty, DE, farmer, Phillips KOLLOCK of same, Esq & William HARRISON of same, scrivener. Samuel DODD for the sum of 10s paid to him by William HARRISON doth discharge sd William HARRISON, sd Samuel DODD thereunto moving, hath granted & sold to sd HARRISON all that part of land & plantation called The Forrest Plantation which Moses DODD by his last will & testament dtd 19 Nov 1779 devised unto Samuel DODD situate in Broadkiln Hundred & called in the survey Ragged Woods bounded by land surveyed for Nicholas McGLANDER containing 367 acres of land. William HARRISON may be tenant of the Freehold against whom a common recovery of the land & premises before the Ct of Com Pleas in which sd common recovery Phillips KOLLOCK shall be demandant, William HARRISON tenant & Samuel DODD voucher. Signed: Samuel DODD, Phillips KOLLOCK, W HARRISON. Wit: D HALL, Nath'l MITCHELL.

O-14:292. Deed. This Indenture made 04 Aug 1790 between Thomas EVANS Esq High Sheriff of Sussex cnty, DE of the one part & William HALL of same, blacksmith, of the other part. There is a tract of land situated in Broadkiln Hundred containing 227 acres formerly the property of John FISHER, dec'd. Sd John FISHER d: Intestate & sd land was divided among his several heirs by order of Orphans Ct by their several Deeds of Sale conveyed sd tract of land to Edward LAY. Sd Edward LAY d: Intestate & not having personal estate sufficient to discharge debts, Ann LAY, Admin of sd estate petitioned sd Ct empowering her to sell sd tract of land to enable her to discharge sd debts which sd Ct granted. Ann LAY at public sale sold sd land to Thomas STATON, he being the highest bidder. Sd Thomas STATON by his last will & testament dtd 11 Apr 1751 devised sd land to his son, Hill STATON. Hell STATON by his Deed of Sale dtd 04 Feb 1767 conveyed sd land to David CLOWES. David CLOWES by his last will & testament dtd 13 Apr 1770 devised sd land to his dtr Hannah, but if sd Hannah should d: w/o heirs of her body then sd David CLOWES devised sd land to his brother John CLOWES & his 2 sisters Catharine & Mary to be divided equally. Sd Hannah d:

w/o issue & sd land became the property of sd John, Catharine & Mary. Sd John CLOWES & Catharine, by the name of Catharine YOUNG, by their Deed of Sale dtd 08 Feb 1786 conveyed their share of sd land to John Sheldon DORMAN. John Sheldon DORMAN before that time had md: Mary CLOWES whereby he became seized of 2/3 of sd tract of land in his own right & of the other 1/3 part in right of Mary, his wife, sd 227 acres of land bounded by land late of John WALKER, dec'd, & lands now belonging to William WYATT, lands of Samuel RUSSELL, lands late of Hugh KING, dec'd. Sd John Sheldon DORMAN being indebted to Richard BASSETT Esq of Kent cnty, sd BASSETT obtained Judgement against sd John Sheldon DORMAN & legal costs & Ct of Com Pleas ordered Peter Fretwell WRIGHT, sheriff of Sussex cnty, to expose sd lands to public sale & sd land was struck off to William HALL for the sum of £130 , he being the highest bidder. Thomas EVANS, current Sheriff, conveys Deed of Sale to William HALL. Signed: Thomas EVANS, Sheriff. Wit: George HAZZARD, Isaac TURNER. Rec'd 05 Aug 1790 from William HALL, blacksmith, £130. Peter F WRIGHT, Sheriff.

O-14:294. Bill of Sale. Robert GRIFFITH of Sussex cnty, DE for the sum of £50 sold to Jonathan BRADY of Queen Ann's cnty, MD 1 bay mare, one black ditto, 1 black coat, 1 sorrel ditto, 7 head of cattle, 15 head hogs, 27 head geese, 4 feather beds & furniture, 1 dish, 1 walnut table, 1 cupboard, 8 setting chairs, 1 horsecart, 1 plow, 1 harrow, 1 axe, 1 grubbing hoe, 3 iron pots, 1 frying pan, 1 iron pott rack, 1 loom, 3 spinning wheels, some pewter & earthen ware, 1 case & bottles this 14 Oct 1790. Signed: Robert GRIFFITH. Wit: Philip HUGHES, Thomas LAWS.

O-14:294. Return on Division of Henry HOOPER's Lands. John HOOPER, Henry HOOPER & Thomas HOOPER of Sussex cnty, DE, yeoman, pursuant to the last will & testament of our fthr, Henry HOOPER, late of sd cnty, dec'd, have w/assistance of a surveyor divided land devised to us in the following manner: to John HOOPER a part S of the home line of Martins Hundred which is 325 & 7/10 acres which is 72 & 3/10 acres more than his proper share devised him which sd overage sd Thomas has exchanged w/sd John for the same # of acres of a tract which sd John bought of Robert JUETT; to Henry HOOPER all that part lying between sd John & sd Thomas's divisions of sd land containing 253 & 4/10 acres which is N of division line of Martins Hundred; to Thomas the remainder containing 180 & 6/10 acres which is 71 & 8/10 acres his share exchanged for other land as above mentioned. 26 Oct 1790 Signed: John HOOPER, Henry HOOPER, Thomas HOOPER. Wit: John TENNENT, William POLK, Write Brown SMITT.

O-14:295. Return & Description of 1 Acre of Land Devised Jno TENNENT by

H HOOPER. John HOOPER & Henry HOOPER Execs apptd by last will & testament of Henry HOOPER late of sd cnty, dec'd, convey unto John TENNENT 1 acre of ground out of land called Hoopers Lott as directed by sd will & w/assistance of a surveyor hath laid off same to John TENNENT. 16 Sep 1790 Signed: John HOOPER, Henry HOOPER. Wit: Ezekiel BROWN, Edward BROWN.

O-14:295. Deed. 03 Nov 1790. For the sum of £176 Peter RUST of Sussex cnty, DE, planter, & Sally his wife, of the one part sold to John NEAL of same, planter, of the other part all that tract of land called Hard Fortune situate in Northwest Fork Hundred beginning at an old road across the Neck to the Old Chapel being the beginning of a resurvey by Peter RUST to a line of land called Grape Vine Thicket to land of George SMITH containing 148 & 1/2 acres of land & also their right & title to 9 & 1/2 acres of land bought of John TENNENT. Peter & Sally RUST appoint John WHEELBANK or Phillips KOLLOCK their Attorney. Signed: Peter RUST, Sally RUST. Wit: Thomas EVANS, Chas MOORE. 03 Nov 1790 Sally, wife of Peter RUST was examined separate from her husband declared she became a part to afsd Deed of her own free will. Signed: Peter F WRIGHT.

O-14:297. Deed of Mortgage. This Indenture made 11 Jan 1790 between Benjamin WYNKOOP of the city of Philadelphia, PA, merchant, of the one part & Phebe VINING of Wilmington, DE, widow, of the other part. Benjamin WAYNKOOP by his Obligation dtd 10 Jun 1789 stands bound unto sd Phebe VINING in penalty conditioned for payment of £2500 & to secure payment & interest it is the intent of sd Benjamin WYNKOOP to convey to sd Phebe VINING his right & estate in premises hereinafter mentioned & also his right to certain sums of money due him. Benjamin WYNKOOP is seized of a tract of land situate in Cedar Creek Hundred, Sussex cnty, DE called Cedar Town containing 878 acres & 119 perches adjoining S side of Mispillion Creek which sd Benjamin WYNKOOP by articles of agreement dtd 25 May 1781 did covenant to make over to Samuel FOUNTAIN upon complete payment by sd FOUNTAIN of £2634 in gold & silver coin w/interest from 19 Aug 1783. Samuel FOUNTAIN hath since departed this life & Benjamin WYNKOOP hath begun suit for recovery of sd sums against the Representatives of sd Samuel FOUNTAIN. Benjamin WYNKOOP is seized of a plantation & 2 tracts of land in Kent cnty, DE which James JOHNSON & Mary his wife, Admin of Zadok CRAPPER, dec'd, by Indenture dtd 15 Aug 1782 recorded in Kent cnty Liber M, folio 177 conveyed to Benjamin WYNKOOP in due form of law which sd plantation & 2 tracts of land last mentioned sd WYNKOOP by Articles of Agreement consented to convey to Dr Nathaniel SISSON on payment of a sum of money & suit hath been commenced against sd SISSON in order to recover the sums of money stipulated in Agreement. Sd Benjamin WYNKOOP to better secure to sd Phebe VINING the payment of the sum of money & interest thereof for the sum of 5s lawful money of PA hath granted & sold to sd Phebe VINING the several plantations, parcels & tracts of land before described & agreements, suits & judgements afsd & all sums of money due or to become due Provided that is sd Benjamin WYNKOOP shall pay unto sd Phebe VINING the sum of money & interest due on 01 May 1791 this Obligation shall become void. Benjamin WYNKOOP appoints Dyer KEARNEY, Joshua FISHER or Nicholas RIDGELY Esqs of Dover, DE his Attorney. Signed: Benja WYNKOOP. Wit: Joseph BARNES, Joseph WYNKOOP. Joshua BARNES appeared before Samuel PARVEL Esq, Mayor of Philadelphia & swore he witnessed he saw Benjamin WYNKOOP, merchant in sd city, sign & seal this Indenture. Signed: Samuel PORVEL, Mayor. Rec: 03 Nov 1790, Sussex cnty, DE. Nath'l MITCHELL, Proth'y.

O-14:299. Deed. This Indenture made 29 Oct 1790 between Casey THOMPSON, James THOMPSON, Priscilla PHILIPS, Sarah CAREY, Esther HUDSON & Leah CAREY of Sussex cnty, DE of the one part & William THOMPSON of same, yeoman, of the other part. John THOMPSON of Worcester cnty, MD was seized of a tract of land called Second Chance containing 100 acres of land, on which 1759 he resurveyed & enlarged sd tract to 577 acres of land as appears in Certificate of Resurvey in Land Office of MD dtd 18 Dec 1759 & confirmed to him, sd John THOMPSON & his heirs, by the State of MD Patent dtd 06 Dec 1787. John THOMPSON by Bond dtd 17 Mar 1762 bound himself to sd William THOMPSON his Attorney & Exec in the penal sum of £200 current money of MD to convey to sd William THOMPSON 100 acres, part of afsd tract whereon sd William THOMPSON then lived & by his one other Bond dtd 15 Apr 1767 bound himself unto John THOMPSON Jr his Attorney & Exec in the penal sum of £200 current money of MD to convey 84 acres, part of afsd tract whereon sd John THOMPSON Jr then lived which last sd Bond John THOMPSON Jr 25 Apr 1767 assigned to John WINGATE of sd cnty who again on 18 Apr 1768 did assign & convey to William THOMPSON, the conditions of which 2 conveyances having not yet been fulfilled & sd John THOMPSON the obligee being dec'd it devolves unto sd Casey THOMPSON, James THOMPSON, Priscilla PHILIPS, Sarah CAREY, Esther HUDSON & Leah CAREY to make the legal Deed to him the sd William THOMPSON being 184 acres the contents of the two Bonds together. Sd Casey THOMPSON, James THOMPSON, Priscilla PHILIPS, Sarah CAREY, Esther HUDSON & Leah CAREY make good & sufficient Deed to William THOMPSON for 100 acres of land as agreed to above mentioned conveyance Bonds devolved unto us from the death of sd John THOMPSON. Sd Casey

THOMPSON, James THOMPSON, Priscilla PHILIPS, Sarah CAREY, Esther HUDSON & Leah CAREY make good & sufficient Deed to William THOMPSON for all that parcel of land being part of afsd Resurvey tract called Second Chance of 577 acres which call for 184 acres of land out of sd resurvey. Sd Casey THOMPSON, James THOMPSON, Priscilla PHILIPS, Sarah CAREY, Esther HUDSON & Leah CAREY appoint Wolsey BURTON, Job INGRAM, Elisha DICKERSON or John MORRIS of Sussex cnty, DE their Attorney. Signed: Cary THOMPSON, James THOMPSON (mark), Priscilla PHILLIPS (mark), Sarah CARY (mark), Esther HUTSON (mark), Leah CARY (mark). Wit: Truitt THOMPSON, William THOMPSON.

O-14:301. Deed. This Indenture made 28 Oct 1790 between John OLDHAM Atty for Isaiah JONES, both of Pendleton cnty, SC of the one part & John KILLINGSWORTH of the other part. John OLDHAM in consideration of the report of John INGRAM & John LOFLAND elected to set a valuation of a piece of land belonging to the heirs of Joshua JONES, dec'd, father of sd Isaiah JONES but now the property of John KILLINGSWORTH by report of the above named arbitrators of which sd John OLDHAM Atty of sd JONES doth ack: himself satisfied & granted doth absolutely grant unto sd John KILLINGSWORTH all his right of inheritance to afsd tract of land situate on the head of Primehook Creek in Sussex cnty part thereof being part of a tract formerly surveyed for David SMITH & sold to Samuel OLIVER & part being part of land granted by Warrant dtd at Philadelphia 25 Jul 1741 to James JONES, grndfthr to Isaiah JONES the elder bounded by land of John KILLINGSWORTH, part of Joshua JONES' land (now John LOFLAND's), land of Levin DOWS containing 31 acres of land. John OLDHAM appoints Thomas EVANS or John INGRAM, yeomen, as his Attorney. Signed: John OLDHAM. Wit: William KILLINGSWORTH, John KELLO.

O-14:301. Deed. This Indenture made 20 Aug 1790 between Anderton BROWN Sr of Sussex cnty, DE, yeoman, of the one part & Anderton BROWN Jr, son of afsd Anderton BROWN, of same, yeoman, of the other part. Anderton BROWN Sr in consideration of the natural love & affection he bears unto his son, Anderton BROWN Jr as well as for the sum of 5s has sold to his son, Anderton BROWN Jr, all that tract of land called Turkey Ridge situate in Northwest Fork Hundred on N side of Clearbrook Branch out of the NE fork for Nanticoke River above where Charles ROLLINS formerly lived containing 327 & 1/2 acres (excepting 29 & 1/2 acres which Anderton BROWN Sr sold to Charles BROWN of Joseph); also 1 other tract of land called Safety granted by patent to Charles HINES by the Proprietary of MD & sold by him to Jonathan WILLIAMS & then became the property of John WILLIAMS son to sd Jonathan WILLIAMS & sold by him to

Joseph ENNALS & sold to sd Anderton BROWN Sr situate in cnty & hund afsd containing 50 acres, intent of sd Anderton BROWN Sr is to retain possession & use of Safety during his natural life & after his decease to be & remain the property of sd Anderton BROWN Jr.; also 40 acres of land, part of a tract of land called Browns Outlet which shall be laid off where it lies most convenient to lands already given. Anderton BROWN Sr appoints Thomas LAWS or Robert LAWS his Attorney. Signed: Anderton BROWN. Wit: Thomas LAWS, Robert LAWS, Robert WILLIAMS.

O-14:303. Deed. 03 Nov 1790 Woolsey HATHAWAY of city of Edenton, NC, mariner, of the one part for the sum of £72 17s 4p current money of DE hath sold unto William FOSSETT of Sussex cnty, DE, mason, of the other part a parcel of land in Indian River Hundred on N side of Abraham Branch being part of a larger tract granted to John HERMMAN by a Proprietary Warrant dtd 09 Oct 1746, surveyed by William SHANKLAND 15 Jan 1747/8 called Murraies Folly. John HERMMONS 06 Sep 1748 sold sd land to William MARRINER who devised same unto Thomas MARRINER who conveyed the afsd part to Arbuckle ROGERS containing 130 acres. Arbuckle ROGERS d: Intestate & his widow, Elizabeth ROGERS, Admin of his estate by virtue of Ct Order conveyed afsd parcel of land unto Woolsey HATHAWAY. Signed: Woolsey HATHAWAY. Wit: Benjamin BURTON, Thos HERMMONS, Jos PRETTYMAN.

O-14:304. Deed. This Indenture made 04 Nov 1790 between Stephen COSTON of Sussex cnty, DE, yeoman, of the one part & Robert PRETTYMAN of same, yeoman, of the other part. There is a parcel of land in Broadkill Hundred, part of a larger tract of land called Content formerly taken up by Benton COSTON & has become the property of sd Stephen COSTON. Sd tract begins on the NE side of Water Hole Savannah & is bounded by PRETTYMAN's other land & sd COSTON's, containing 200 acres. Stephen COSTON for the sum of £175 hath sold land afsd to Robert PRETTYMAN. Signed: Stephen COSTON. Wit: Rhoads SHANKLAND, Thomas INGRAM (mark).

O-14:305. Deed. This Indenture is made 03 Nov 1790 between Joseph MORRIS of Sussex cnty, DE, yeoman, of the one part & Joseph MORRIS Jr of same, yeoman, of the other part. There is a tract of land situate on the S side of Pemberton's Branch in Broadkill Hundred which by Proprietary Warrant dtd Philadelphia 07 Jun 1737 to John HALL & John READ, which land being divided between sd HALL & READ sd John READ did by Deed of Sale convey his moiety to John CROTHERS, containing 150 acres. John CROTHERS by Letter of Attorney to Lawrence RILEY & sd RILEY did grant a Deed of Sale for the 150 acres dtd 07 Aug 1770 to afsd Joseph MORRIS. Joseph MORRIS for the sum of £131 5s paid to Zadock LINDAL, hath sold sd land to Joseph MORRIS Jr. Sd land beginning at the NW fork of Pembertons Branch bounded by Robert COLE's land, land formerly laid out for Peter LEWES now in possession of William MILTEN, containing 150 acres. Signed: Joseph Morris LITTLE. Wit: John CLOWES, Robert WHITE.

O-14:307. Deed. 08 Oct 1790 Charles MOORE of Sussex cnty, DE of the one part for the sum of £50 hath sold unto William SKELEY of same of the other part all that tract of land called McGlaclin's Choice or Chance situate in Little Creek Hundred being land young Baily McGLACLIN deeded to William WATER containing 50 acres of land. Charles MOORE appoints Phillips KOLLOCK or Joseph MILLER Esqs as his Attorney. Signed: Chas MOORE. Wit: Isaac COOPER, Shiles MOORE.

O-14:307. Deed. This Indenture made 15 Jun 1790 between William SLAYTON of Baltimore, MD of the one part & Cyrus MITCHELL of Dorchester cnty, MD of the other part. William SLAYTON in virtue of a land Warrant granted to Thomas KIMMERLY dtd Philadelphia 25 Jun 1776 (which by sd KIMMERLY assigned to John POLK who sold sd Warrant to sd SLAYTON) had surveyed to him the sd SLAYTON a tract of land called William's Burrough situate adjoining the lands of William LAWS & William OWENS near St Johns Town in Sussex cnty, DE per survey in Rhoads SHANKLAND Esq's office. William SLAYTER for the sum of £10 current money of DE had sold to Cyrus MITCHELL all that part of sd survey on SW side of William LAWS' land called Rich Land, S of Great Landing Road leading thru St John's Town to Milford containing by estimation 4 acres of land. William SLAYTON appoints David HALL or William PEERY Esqs as his Attorney. Signed: Wm SLAYTON. Wit: William OWENS, Anna POLKE.

O-14:308. Deed. This Indenture made 02 Nov 1790 between William CALDWELL of Sussex cnty, DE, gent, of the one part & Barkley TOWNSEND of same, gent, of the other part. Ezekiel JACKSON of cnty & state afsd being seized of a tract of land called Batchelors Contrivance originally granted by Lord Proprietary of MD to James WYTHE and Marmaduke MISTER, sd tract of land lying in cnty & state afsd on the E side of Nanticoke River on S side of Broad Creek W of Whore Kill Road, containing 150 acres. Same was sold by Ezekiel JACKSON to Thomas CALDWELL who afterwards d: leaving William CALDWELL his only surviving son & heir. William CALDWELL for the sum of £5 sells unto Barkley TOWNSEND all that tract of land afsd called Batchelor's Contrivance. Signed: William CALDWELL (mark). Wit: Isaac COOPER, John

PATRICK. William CALDWELL appoints David HALL or Joseph HALL Esqs as his Attorney.

O-14:309. Deed. 04 Nov 1790 Barkley TOWNSEND of Sussex cnty, DE of the one part for the sum of £33 6s 8p hath sold to Isaac COOPER of same of the other part all that parcel of land situate in Laurel Town # 4 on the S side of Broad Creek & N side of Front Street in the swamp, bounded by Wheat Street. Signed: Barkley TOWNSEND. Wit: Phillips KOLLOCK, William VAUGHAN.

O-14:310. Deed. Nov 1790 Mitchel JACKSON of Worcester cnty, MD of the one part for the sum of £60 current money of Kent, Newcastle, Sussex cntys, DE hath sold to John JONES of Sussex cnty, DE of the other part for the use of Abigail BENSTON wife of Benjamin of Sussex cnty part of a tract of land situate on the N side of Indian River in Indian River Hundred it being part of a tract taken by Proprietors Warrant granted to William CARY who assigned his right to Thomas & Peter ROBINSON & sd ROBINSONs conveyed by Deed of Sale to sd Michael JACKSON, sd land bounded by BUCHER's land, LACEY's land, containing 100 acres, to sd John JONES for the use & benefit of sd Abigail BENSTON. Signed: Mitchell JACKSON. Wit: William WYATT, Robert PRETTYMAN.

O-14:311. Deed. This Indenture made 03 Nov 1790 between Woolsey HATHAWAY of Edenton, NC & Robert PRETTYMAN of Sussex cnty, DE, cordwinder (son of William PRETTYMAN late of cnty afsd, dec'd) of the one part & Thomas WAPLES, smith, (son of Thomas WAPLES, dec'd) of the town of Warwick of the other part. Woolsey HATHAWAY by his Attorney Leatherbery BARKER 27 Feb 1787 by Alienation Bond of Conveyance sold to Robert PRETTYMAN 2 lots of land & a small island of marsh in Indian River containing 3 acres, for the sum of £75 & 01 Sep 1789 Robert PRETTYMAN contracted w/Thomas WAPLES for his purchase of the afsd 2 lots of land & the island & put sd Thomas WAPLES in full possession of same who holds the full possession thereof 1 of which lots of land by several conveyances became vested in Elizabeth TULL & by her Deed of Conveyance dtd 08 Aug 1783 conveyed sd lot w/premises to Woolsey HATHAWAY which Deed is recorded in Sussex cnty Liber M, # 12, folio 569 & the other lot of land was leased by Woolsey BURTON Esq unto Thomas CLIFTON for a term of years under the yearly rent of 6s 8p & afsd island of marsh by a Warrant was surveyed unto sd Thomas & Thomas CLIFTON sold his right of sd island & his term of sd lease thereunto belonging to William DUNLAP & sd William DUNLAP it appears sold same to Samuel GALE & by several assignments the sd lot of land & marsh became vested in Martha FINNEY who by her Alienation Bond dtd 07 Feb 1774 sold her right of same to the above mentioned Woolsey HATHAWAY, sd several documents recorded in Land Office at Lewes, Sussex cnty, together w/this Deed. Sd Leatherbury BARKER, Attorney to sd Woolsey HATHAWAY d: before any Deed for the afsd 2 lotts of land & island was executed & sd Woolsey HATHAWAY now being in Sussex cnty, DE undertakes to make this Deed. Sd Woolsey HATHAWAY for the sum of £75 paid by Robert PRETTYMAN to his Attorney Leatherbury BARKER & sd Robert PRETTYMAN for the sum of £50 pad to him by the afsd Thomas WAPLES sold to Thomas WAPLES all that messuage of 2 lots of land situate in Indian River Hundred in the town of Warwick on Water Street each lot 60 ft in breadth & 200 ft in length adjoining each other, one of which formerly belonged to William BURTON & sd William BURTON by his last will & testament devised same to his dtr, Elizabeth, who had md: Woolsey BURTON Esq who leased sd lot to Thomas CLIFTON & after the death of Woolsey BURTON the afsd Elizabeth md: William PRETTYMAN by whom she had a son, to whit, the above named Robert PRETTYMAN & sd William PRETTYMAN dying before the afsd Elizabeth the sd Elizabeth by her last will & testament dtd 04 Feb 1777 devised all land she held in her own right to her son Robert PRETTYMAN part to these presents & sd lease to Thomas CLIFTON being subjected to pay the yearly which at the death of sd Elizabeth the right became vest in sd Robert PRETTYMAN her son which now leaves this lot being part of the land devised by Elizabeth to her son Robert PRETTYMAN & also the small island of marsh. Woolsey HATHAWAY & Robert PRETTYMAN convey unto sd Thomas WAPLES all of the above 2 lots of land & small island of marsh containing 3 acres afsd. Signed: Woolsey HATHAWAY, Robert PRETTYMAN. Wit: Thomas WALKER, William BURCHER Sr.

O-14:313. Deed. This Indenture made 13 Oct 1788 between Robert PRETTYMAN, cordwinder, of Sussex cnty, DE (son of William PRETTYMAN & Elizabeth PRETTYMAN, his wife, both late of Sussex cnty, DE, dec'd) of the one part & Thomas WAPLES, blacksmith (son of Thomas WAPLES, dec'd) of the other part. There is a tract of land situate in Indian River Hundred called Warwick which sd tract of land was granted to William KENNING for 300 acres of land 26 Mar 1684 by William PENN Esq, Proprietary of PA & 3 lower cntys on DE which sd 300 acres by sundry conveyances became vested in Will BURTON by Deed of Sale from Abraham INGRAM dtd 07 Nov 1733 to William BURTON rec'd in Sussex cnty Liber G, #6, folio 43. William BURTON by his last will & testament dtd 07 Apr 1744 then of MD having laid out 6 lotts of ground sd to contain 10 acres each for a town 100 poles in length from Indian River back & for breadth from William WAPLES line. Wm BURTON by his last will & testament afsd did bequeath his dtr Elizabeth BURTON then wife of Woolsey BURTON Esq of Sussex cnty 1 of the afsd 6 lotts of land. Afsd Elizabeth after the death of her husband afsd md:

William PRETTYMAN, fthr of above Robert PRETTYMAN, who also predeceased her. Elizabeth PRETTYMAN by her last will & testament dtd 04 Feb 1777 among other things bequeathed to her son the afsd Robert PRETTYMAN all the land she held in her own right near or about Warwick afsd (which sd 6 lotts of land being part of the afsd 300 acres laid out by William BURTON's will for a town) and the lott of land hereby to be granted being one of the afsd 6 lotts bequeathed to Elizabeth by her fthr & by her to her son Robert PRETTYMAN & is the 3rd lot laid off from William WAPLES' line (which sd William WAPLES being now dec'd sd land is held by his son, Burton WAPLES Esq who also purchased the lot adjoining him & his son Burton WAPLES Jr now dec'd having in his lifetime purchased the 2nd lott & now held by the heirs of sd Burton WAPLES Jr, dec'd) being one of the afsd 6 lots & also is bounded on the N with the 3rd lott as laid out from the afsd & containing 10 acres. Robert PRETTYMAN for the sum of £25 hath sold to Thomas WAPLES the above described parcel of land. Signed: Robert PRETTYMAN. Wit: Elizabeth WAPLES (mark), Isaac ATKINS, N WAPLES.

O-14:314. Map of six lots in Warwick as above.

O-14:314. Deed. This Indenture made 05 Feb 1790 between David CONWELL of Sussex cnty, DE, yeoman, of the one part & George Hardy FISHER of same, farmer, of the other part. There is a tract of land on E side of Nanticoke River in Nanticoke Hundred surveyed for William TOADWINE per pattent dtd 19 Aug 1748 & by sundry conveyances & devises became the property of afsd David CONWELL which sd land begins on W side of Newbolds Road abt 1/2 mile from Unity Forge containing 100 acres of land called Drawn Forward. 15 Feb 1788 David CONWELL obligated himself to convey to George Hardy FISHER 50 acres of afsd land for the sum of £35. David CONWELL appoints Elias CONWELL or Hercules KOLLOCK as his Attorney. Signed: David CONWELL. Wit: John FISHER, Thos GRAY. Rec: 04 Nov 1790.

O-14:315. Deed. Oct 1790 James NICOLLS of Sussex cnty, DE, planter, & Diana NICOLLS his wife, of the one part for the sum of £100 sold 100 & 1/2 acres of land in sd cnty to Ralph ROBINSON of same, blacksmith, of the other part; 75 acres of which is called Hog Neck & was originally granted to Edward LUDENHAM by Charles, Proprietor of MD by patent dtd 20 Dec 1741 & 25 & 1/2 acres more adjoining sd Hog Neck, being in the whole 100 & 1/2 acres. Sd James & Diana NICOLLS appoint Phillips KOLLOCK or Peter Fretwell WRIGHT Esqs their Attorney. Signed: James NICOLLS. Wit: Daniel POLK, Henry SMITH.

O-14:316. Deed. This Indenture made 19 Oct 1789 between Sarah NICOLLS, Nehemiah NICOLLS & Comfort NICOLLS his wife, Elizabeth NICOLLS, William WRIGHT & Lovey WRIGHT his wife, James SPENCER & Jewel SPENCER his wife, Stacey NICOLLS, William NICOLLS & Levin NICOLLS of Sussex cnty, DE of the one part & James NICOLLS of same of the other part. There is a parcel of land in sd cnty now in the possession of James NICOLLS which sd land was by the last will & testament of Nehemiah NICOLLS, dec'd devised onto his son, John NICOLLS, which sd John NICOLLS dying w/o issue sd land by heirship fell to the afsd Sarah, Nehemiah & Elizabeth NICOLLS, Lovey RIGHT, Jewel SPENCER, Stacey, William, Levin & James NICOLLS. Afsd Sarah NICOLLS, Nehemiah NICOLLS & Comfort his wife, Elizabeth NICOLLS, William WRIGHT & Lovey his wife, James SPENCER & Jewel his wife, Stacy NICOLLS, William NICOLLS & Levin NICOLLS for the sum of £40 sold to James NICOLLS the afsd land sd to contain 75 acres. Parties of the first part appoint Phillips KOLLOCK or Peter Fretwell WRIGHT as their Attorney. Signed: Sarah NICOLLS (mark), Nehemiah NICOLLS, Comfort NICOLLS (mark), William WRIGHT (mark), Lovey WRIGHT (mark), Elizabeth NICOLLS (mark), Wm NICOLLS, James SPENCER Jr (mark), Jewel SPENCER (mark), Stacey NICOLLS, Levin NICOLLS. Wit: Oliver JUMP, Levy STAFFORD (mark), Henry SMITH, William WHITE Sr. Rec: 04 Nov 1790.

O-14:317. Deed. This Indenture made 17 Sep 1790 between Benjamin BENSTON of Sussex cnty, DE, & Abigail his wife (later Abigail JONES) of the one part & Jacob HAZZARD of same of the other part. Griffith JONES 06 May 1782 petitioned Orphans Ct setting forth that Isaac JONES late of afsd cnty, dec'd, in his lifetime was seized of lands & tenements situate in Broadkiln Hundred & d: Intestate leaving Abigail his wife & 8 children, namely: Martha, Sarah, Mary, Isaac, Griffith, Elias, Abigail & John to whom sd lands descended & sd Griffith asked Ct to order 5 Freeholders to lay off the Widows Dower & make partition of the remaining 2/3 among the heirs. Sd Petition was granted. Joseph HAZZARD Esq, Messrs Rhoads SHANKLAND, David THORNTON, Thomas GROVE & John HAZZARD w/assistance of a surveyor laid off the Widows Dower & of the remaining 2/3 laid off to Abigail JONES, present wife of Benjamin BENSTON, all that part of the Neck tract along the line of the widow's dividend containing 78 acres. Benjamin BENTSON & Abigail his wife for the sum of £136 10s sold all the afsd allotment of land containing afsd to Jacob HAZZARD. Signed: Benjamin BENSON Jr, Abigail BENSTON. Wit: Seth GRIFFITH, Mary McILVAIN. 19 Oct 1790 Abigail BENSTON, wife of Benjamin, was examined separate from her husband, being of full age, did declare she became a party to above deed of her own free will. Signed: Peter F WRIGHT.

O-14:319. Deed. This Indenture made 15 Jun 1790 between George VINSON of Sussex cnty, DE of the one part for the sum of £10 sold to Joseph CANNON Sr of same of the other part part of a tract of land called Wailands Adventure granted unto Benjamin WAILAND under the Great Seal of MD in 1748, sd land now in Sussex cnty, DE, laid off for 95 & 1/4 acres. George VINSON appoints Joseph MILLER or John W BATSON or Phillips KOLLOCK Esq his Attorney. Signed: George VINSON. Wit: Joseph CANNON Jr, Levi CANNON, Sam'l HEARN. Rec: 05 Nov 1790.

O-14:320. Deed. 14 Sep 1789 Micajah WATES of North West Fork Hundred, Sussex cnty, DE, farmer, & Liner his wife of the one part for the sum of £117 14s 1p sold to Elijah ADAMS of same, house carpenter & joyner, of the other part all that tract of land called Mount Pleasure situate in cnty afsd bounded by Rick Swamp near the W end of a tract formerly surveyed for Capt Charles NUTTER, land of Thomas LAYTON, W side of NE fork of Nanticoke River, containing 89 acres. Elijah WATES appoints Alexander LAWS or Joseph MILLER as his Attorney. Signed: Micajah WAITS (mark), Linah WAITS (mark). Wit: Isaac BRADLEY, Thomas NUTTER. Rec: 05 Nov 1790.

O-14:321. Deed. This Indenture made 01 Nov 1790 between William MORRIS of Sussex cnty, DE, yeoman, of the one part & Armwell LOCKWOOD of same of the other part. Bevins MORRIS, late of cnty afsd, dec'd, died seized of sundry tracts of land situate in Dagsberry Hundred about a mile SE of Dogsberry Town & S side of Peppers Creek Branch, amongst which is a tract of land called Turtle Swamp that was first owned by Daniel WHARTON by virtue of Proprietary of MD Patent dtd 10 Dec 1714 for 78 acres, another tract called Batcherlors Lot that was first granted to Bevins MORRIS, fthr of afsd Bevins MORRIS by Proprietary of MD Patent dtd 29 Aug 1756 for 75 acres and a 3rd tract of Resurvey called Gaility, all which tract of land sd Bevins MORRIS having d: Intestate were divided by order of Orphans Ct amongst his several children, 80 acres to his son, the afsd William MORRIS. William MORRIS for the sum of £31 10s hath sold unto Armwell LOCKWOOD all that 80 acres of land. William MORRIS appoints William BURSTON, Phillips KOLLOCK or Edward DINGLE his Attorney. Signed: William MORRIS. Wit: Thomas HAZZARD, William LOCKWOOD.

O-14:322. Deed. This Indenture made 11 Sep 1790 between Benjamin WYNKOOP of Philadelphia, gent, & Sarah his wife of the one part & Phebe VINING of the borough of Wilmington, DE, widow, of the other part. Benjamin WYNKOOP by sundry conveyances became seized of four contiguous tracts of land situate on S side of Mispillion Creek in Sussex cnty, DE containing on the whole 881 acres; on tract containing 129 acres, part of a larger tract called Pennington which was seized & execution of to satisfy a debt due from William LETTRIDGE & Lucilla his wife to Trustees of the General Loan Office by William SHANKLAND Esq, High Sheriff, to Abraham WYNKOOP Esq, fthr of sd Benjamin; another tract containing 430 acres part of a tract called Cedar Town which William MANLOVE, Daniel CLIFFTON & Tabitha his wife & Joseph BOOTH by Indenture dtd 21 May 1730 conveyed to sd Abraham WYNKOOP, 1 other of sd tracts containing ? acres, part of a larger tract surveyed for Arthur Johnson VANKIRK which Thomas COVENDALE & Mary his wife by Indenture dtd 29 Jul 1734 conveyed to sd Abraham WYNKOOP; & the other of sd tracts containing 222 acres is other part of Cedar Town tract which Catherine SAMPLES by virtue of Orphans Ct Order by Indenture dtd 06 May 1737 conveyed to sd Abraham WYNKOOP, all of which sd conveyances from original purchases downward are duly rec: in Sussex cnty in the title of sd Benjamin WYNKOOP, devised under the will of his sd fthr & of his brother, Thomas WYNKOOP. Benjamin WYNKOOP being so seized 25 May 1781 agreed to sell same to Samuel FOUNTAIN for the price of £2634 gold & silver. Sd Samuel FOUNTAIN d: Intestate w/o paying off the sd monies whereupon Benjamin WYNKOOP instituted suit against his Admins & obtained judgement & execution for sd monies & interest by means whereof Benjamin WYNKOOP is now seized of the legal estate in same. Benjamin WYNKOOP being indebted to sd Phebe VINING by obligation in the sum of £2400 did by Indenture dtd 11 Jan last past sell sd 4 tracts of land to sd Phebe VINING in mortgage to secure payment of sd debt. Sd parties to these present being agreeable sd lands should be sold for such reasonable price as can be obtained have entered into treaty w/diverse persons for the sale of diverse parts thereof monies from sd sale to be paid to sd Phebe VINING, Signed: Benjamin WYNKOOP, Sarah M WYNKOOP. Wit: Joseph MOORE, Miers FISHER. Sarah WYNKOOP, wife of sd Benjamin, was examined separate from her husband, being of full age, & did declares she became a party to the above of her own free will. 11 Sep 1790 Signed: Sam'l MILES.

O-14:324. Bill of Sale. Levi POLLOT of Sussex cnty, DE, for the sum of £15 sold to John BURBAGE 1 bay horse w/a star in his forehead abt 9 yrs old, 1 cow & calf, 2 small hogs, 1 bed & furniture, 1 loom & tackling, 1 chest. 4 chairs, 1 table, 2 pewter dishes, 6 pewter plates, 1 pewter basin, 1 iron pott & 1 copper tea kettle. 13 Dec 1790 Signed: Levi POLLOT (mark). Wit: Jno RUSSEL, Joseph RUSSEL.

O-14:324. Deed. Mary Magdalen HALL, Joseph HALL & David HALL, Admin of David HALL, dec'd, recovered against Jacob KOLLOCK at May term 1785 of Ct of Com Pleas a debt of £484 8s 4p & 61s sp for damages & costs & sd Ct issued an order to Peter Fretwell WRIGHT, High Sheriff, 03 May 1786 & he seized 2 tracts of land & tenements of sd Jacob KOLLOCK in Lewes, Rehoboth Hundred, one whereon sd KOLLOCK now dwells containing 100 acres, the other whereon Brinkley EVIN then dwelt containing 100 acres. 2 Freeholders determined the rents & issues of sd lands was not sufficient to satisfy sd judgement w/in 7 years. 04 Aug 1790 sd Ct directed sd lands to be sold at public sale & land Brinkley EAVEN lived was purchased by the afsd David HALL 25 Sep 1790 for the sum of £37 10s, he being the highest bidder; sd Peter Fretwell WRIGHT was then removed from office of Sheriff, Thomas EVANS, High Sheriff, therefore grants the afsd lands & premises to sd David HALL, his heirs & Admin. One tract on S of Pothooks Creek near the Flat Lands bounded by land formerly patented by Alexander MORRIS, line of the heirs of Joseph ELDRIGE & line of the heirs of Jonathan BAILEY, line of William HENRY, by a dividing line between John MAXWELL & sd William HENRY containing 8 acres & 106 sq perches of land as by survey dtd 31 Mar 1756; the other tract adjoining the above on the SW side containing 20 acres. 05 Nov 1790 Signed: Thomas EVANS, Sheriff. Wit: Jeremiah CANNON, Kendle BATSON.

O-14:326. Deed. Planner WILLIAMS May term 1788 Ct of Com Pleas recovered against John COLLINS of Sussex cnty, carpenter, a debt of £104 13s & £4 6s 6p damages & costs levied by writ dtd 06 May 1789 to Sheriff, Thomas EVANS. Solomon BRADEY & Robert TRUITT evaluated sd 60 acres & premises to not be of sufficient value to satisfy sd levy w/in 7 years. 04 Nov 1789 sd Ct ordered sd lands & premises sold at public sale & sd was purchased by John LEARMONTH of Lewes, pilot, on 03 Feb 1790 for the sum of £5 1s, afsd land being conveyed to sd John COLLINS by Planner WILLIAMS by Deed dtd 15 Jun 1774 containing 60 acres. 05 Jul 1790 Signed: Thomas EVANS, Sheriff. Wit: D HALL, George HAZZARD.

o-14:328. Deed. William COLEMAN late of Sussex cnty, DE, dec'd, & Hannah his wife by their Indenture dtd 24 Mar 1748/9 sold to Fenwick STRETCHER a parcel of land standing on Lewes Creek containing 34 acres of land & 1 other parcel adjoining sd land bounded by land of William CLARK, dec'd, Lewes Creek, land formerly of Phillips RUSSELL containing 37 acres. Fenwick STRETCHER being seized of sd 2 parcels of land by his last will & testament dtd 04 Apr 1750 apptd Shephard KOLLOCK & David HALL his Exec. David HALL, surviving Exec of Fenwick STRETCHER by Indenture dtd 02 Aug 1773 sold afsd lands to Jacob KOLLOCK except a small part thereof 9-10 acres formerly sold by Peter HALL to Joshua FISHER. Hance BRASTON late of Sussex cnty, dec'd, was in his lifetime seized of a tract of land bounded on NE by

Lewes Creek, on NW land of Stephen GREEN & SE by lands afsd. Hance BRUSTON mortgaged same to Trustees of GLO of Sussex cnty for the sum of £20 in bills of credit & not being paid sd lands by writ were sold by William SHANKLAND, High Sheriff, to Abigail, Elizabeth, Ann & Hannah AUBRY. Sd Abigail afterwards md: Joseph SIMS, sd Elizabeth md: William HENRY & sd Joseph SIMS & Abigail his wife by their Deed dtd 05 Sep 1758 & William HENRY & Elizabeth his wife by their Deed dtd 09 Aug 1758 & afsd Ann AUBRY by her Deed dtd 31 Jan 1763 sold land last mentioned to Jacob KOLLOCK. At Ct of Com Pleas 09 Nov 1785 Mary Magdalen HALL, Joseph & David HALL, Admin, of the estate of David HALL Esq, dec'd, obtained a judgement against sd Jacob KOLLOCK for a debt of £480 8s 4p & 61s 3p damages & costs & by Ct order Peter Fretwell WRIGHT, High Sheriff, seized a parcel of marsh on Lewes Creek opposite afsd lands granted by Warrant to sd Jacob KOLLOCK & Wrixham LEWIS, dec'd, containing 100 acres. 2 Freeholders reported sd lands were not of sufficient yearly value to satisfy afsd judgement w/in 7 years. Sd Sheriff WRIGHT seized afsd lands & exposed them to public sale & same was purchased on 25 Sep last by Peter ROBINSON Esq for the use of Richard BASSETT Esq for the sum of £200 he being the highest bidder. Thomas EVANS, current High Sheriff, conveys to sd Richard BASSETT all the afsd lands, marsh & premises 06 Nov 1790. Signed: Thomas EVANS, Sheriff. Wit: Dan'l RODNEY, W HARRISON.

O-14:330. Deed. This Indenture made 21 Sep 1790 between William BURR of Burlington, NJ in his own right & as Attorney of Thomas EVANS of same, yeoman, of the one part & John RUSSELL of Lewes, Sussex cnty,DE, scrivener, of the other part. Joseph ELDRIDGE late of Sussex cnty, carpenter, dec'd was seized of 5 & 1/2 lotts of land by virtue of a Deed dtd 09 Aug 1722 from James FENWICK & by his Deed dtd 04 Feb 1728 sold one lott of land containing 12,000 sq ft to John CLOWES, merchant. Joseph ELDRIDGE by his last will & testament dtd 10 Mar 1762 devised the remaining lots unto his 2 grndchldrn Thomas EVANS & Phibe LIPPINCUT. Phebe LIPPINCUT md Hudson BURR by whom she had issue & survived sd Hudson BURR her husband. Sd PHebe BURR made her last will & testament dtd 15 Mar 1789 wherein she devised all right in sd lots unto above William BURR. Sd Thomas EVANS by his POA dtd 16 Mar 1790 apptd sd William BURR his attorney to make sale of his interest in sd lotts. William BURR on behalf of himself & as Atty for Thomas EVANS for the sum of £15 sold to John RUSSELL all that part of afsd lots of land situate on S side of South St, near the town of Lewes bounded by land on County Rd formerly belonging to John BYWATER but lately to heirs of William PILES, dec'd, now in the tenure of John DAVIS, & part of afsd lands purchased by Andrew WILLEY, NW line of John RUSSELL's lot purchased of John CLOWES containing 19,007 sq ft of land. Signed: William BURR, Thomas EVANS (by his Atty, Wm BURR). Wit: Peter F WRIGHT, W HARRISON. William BURR & Thomas EVANS have apptd William PEERY or James Patriot WILSON their Attorney.

O-14:333. Deed. This Indenture made 22 Nov 1790 between Shiles MOORE of Little Creek Hundred, Sussex cnty, DE, gent, of the one part & Philip SCROGIN of Broad Creek Hundred, cnty afsd, planter, of the other part. John COLLINS late of Broad Creek Hundred was seized of sundry tracts of land situate in Little Creek Hundred & in his last will & testament dtd 22 Apr 1787 devised unto Isaac HORSEY and Shiles MOORE all the following tracts of land, to whit: one tract called Lott containing 9 acres, one tract called Chance containing 12 acres, all that part of Aarons Folly bound by the Mill Pond & 400 acres of MD Warrant land adjoining same, in all 421 acres to sell & convey, the money arising from sd sale to be applies as followeth, viz: after he is satisfied for his trouble the remainder to be divided between sd COLLINS' 3 dtrs viz: Polly COLLINS, Jeany COLLINS & Peggy COLLINS, each an equal part. By public sale sd lands were sold to above Philip SCROGIN as being the highest bidder, for the sum of £18 10s by Shiles MOORE. Signed: Shiles MOORE. Wit: Barkley TOWNSEND, Amelia MOOR. Shiles MOORE appts David HALL or Thomas EVANS or John W BATSON his Attorney.

O-14:334. Deed of Mortgage. This Indenture made 09 Dec 1790 between William FRAME of Broadkiln Hundred, Sussex cnty, DE, yeoman, of the one part & Joseph HALL of town of Lewes, cnty afsd, Esq, of the other part. William FRAME by his Bond & Warrant of Attorney dtd above is bound to sd Joseph HALL as guardian of his dtr Lydia HALL in the sum of £80 conditioned for payments of £40 on 01 Dec next. William FRAME for the sum of 5s sold to Joseph HALL a parcel of land situate in Broadkiln Hundred on Beaver Dam Branch containing 200 acres which tract is part of two larger tracts, one of which was granted to John COULTER & other two tract by sundry conveyances became the property of sd William FRAME. If above William FRAME shall pay to Joseph HALL the afsd £40 on day afsd w/interest this Indenture shall be void. Signed: William FRAME. Wit: Elijah HALL, Mary HALL.

O-14:335. Deed. 07 Dec 1790 Wolsey HATHAWAY of NC, mariner, of the one part Woolsey HATHAWAY for the sum of £93 hath sold to Joseph WAPLES all that tract of land situate in Indian River Hundred lying between lands of Burton WAPLES & lands of Thomas PRETTYMAN & William HAMSEY at edge of a road leading from Charles VAUGHAN's to St George's Chappel, Cross Roads, containing 93 acres being part of 200 acres granted by Proprietary Warrant dtd 21

Mar 1734/5 to John MARINER who d: leaving 2 sons Joshua & Jacob MARINER to whom he devised sd land to be divided equally. & Joseph WAPLES of Sussex cnty, DE, planter, of the other part. Jacob MARINER sold his division of sd land to Thomas PRETTYMAN between whom & sd Joshua MARINER sd lands of John MARINER laid out. Signed: Woolsey HATHAWAY. Wit: William NEWBOLD, Stephen STYER.

O-14:336. Deed. This Indenture made 04 Aug 1790 between Thomas EVANS Esq, High Sheriff of Sussex cnty, DE of the one part & John HOLLAND of same of the other part. There is a tract of land situate in Broadkiln Hundred, cnty afsd, containing 120 acres formerly the property of William ROBINSON formerly of same cnty, dec'd. William ROBINSON by his last will & testament devised sd 120 acres to his grnddtr Mary STEWART. Sd Mary STEWARD w/Edward STAPLEFORD & Edward STAPLEFORD & Mary his wife sold sd tract to Lawrence RILEY who obliged himself to convey sd land unto John Sheldon DORMAN of cnty afsd. Sd land is bounded by Mill Creek, lands formerly of David SCUDDER, lands now in the possession of Charles CONNALLY formerly James WATKINS, lands now in the possession of Archabald FLEMING formerly William STEWART's. Richard BASSETT Esq of Kent cnty obtained judgement against sd DORMAN for monies due him in the Ct of Com Pleas plus damages & costs. Sd Ct ordered the Sheriff to seize the land & possession of sd DORMAN & expose it to evaluation by 2 Freeholders of the cnty which sd Freeholder reported the issues & rents from the land were not sufficient to repay sd judgement, costs & damages w/in 7 years. Sd Ct directed the Sheriff to expose sd land to public sale which he did & 24 Jul 1790 sd land was sold to John HOLLAND, he being the highest bidder, for the sum of £62. Peter Fretwell WRIGHT, then Sheriff of sd cnty, was afterwards removed from office before any Deed was made to sd HOLLAND. Thomas EVANS, current Sheriff of Sussex cnty, DE duly conveys title to sd lands unto sd John HOLLAND for the debt & costs afsd. Signed: Thomas EVANS, Sheriff. Wit: William PEERY, Newcomb WHITE.

O-14:338. Deed to Lead the Uses of A Common Recovery. This Indenture tripartite made 01 Dec 1790 between Joseph WATTSON of Sussex cnty, yeoman, George HAZZARD & John RUSSELL of same. Joseph WATTSON for the sum of 5s & diverse other good causes, the sd Joseph moving, hath sold to John RUSSELL all that parcel of land which was devised to sd Joseph by the last will & testament of Isaac WATSON, his fthr, one part whereof containing 227 acres granted unto sd Isaac WATSON in his lifetime & other part containing 150 acres granted unto Luke TOWNSEND, dec'd, together w/one other parcel of 202 acres devised by sd Isaac WATSON, dec'd, to his son Isaac. Sd George HAZZARD to be Demandant, John RUSSELL to be the Tenant & Joseph WATSON to be Vouchee in this Common Recovery. Signed: Joseph WATTSON, George HAZZARD, Jno RUSSELL. Wit: Jos MILLER, Thomas EVANS.

O-14:339. Manumission. Negro RHODES from Abraham CONWELL. 08 Jan 1791. This is to certify that the Bearer hereof RHODES by name is this day set at liberty to act and contract for himself as a free man of the state of DE. Signed: Abraham CONWELL.

O-14:339. Deed. 21 May 1790 Jacob CONWELL, pilot, of Lewes, Sussex cnty, DE, of the one part for the sum of £34 had sold unto John RODNEY of same, merchant, of the other part, a lot of land situate on the S side of Pilot Town Road between lots of Luke SHIELD & William WARE in the part of LEWES called Pilot Town containing 1 acre of land. Provided sd Jacob CONWELL to pay to John RODNEY the sum of £34 on or before 01 May 1791 w/lawful interest for same & this Indenture shall cease. Signed: Jacob CONWELL. Wit: Caleb RODNEY, Simon MARINER. Rec: 05 May 1791 Nath'l MITCHELL Proth'y.

O-14:340. Bond of Conveyance. John CLOWES of Sussex cnty, DE, mariner, is bound to Isaak JOHNSTON of same, yeoman, for the sum of £100. Izaak JOHNSTON this day purchased from John CLOWES 140 acres of land in Broadkill Forrest in sd cnty adjoining lands now in the possession of Obediah & Nehemiah MASSEY, being the lands sd CLOWES purchased of Joseph LUFTON, Jane KIMMEY. LUFTON's 100 acres is a PA survey & KIMMEY's 40 acres of MD patent, which sd 140 acres afsd Izaak JOHNSTON shall possess as his freehold under conditions & restrictions stated, viz: he paying yearly £3 rent for same during the full term of 10 years or until full payment of £50. Signed: John CLOWES. Wit: Essabella ARNETT, Zadock LINDELL. Izaak JOHNSTON for the sum of £77 2s 6p hath sold to Neunez DEPUTY all my right & title unto this Bond & all lands thereby held. Signed: Izaak JOHNSTON (mark). Wit: John CLOWES, Jewel MESSEX (mark).

O-14:341. Commission. 25 Oct 1790. Whereas Our President & General Assembly by joint ballot elect & appoint Charles POLK Fourth Justice of the Court of Common PLeas and Orphans Court for the cnty of Sussex, DE. Wit: His Excellency Joshua CLAYTON, Esq, President & Commander in Chief at New Castle cnty, DE 08 Nov 1790. Attest: Jas BOOTH, Sec'y.

O-14:342. Bond of Conveyance. 11 Nov 1790. Isaac MOORE, Joshua MOORE & William MOORE of Sussex cnty, DE for the sum of £300 bind themselves to

Jonathan CATHALL. Condition of sd Bond shall be that if afsd Isaac, Joshua & William MOORE convey unto afsd CATHIEL all their title to a tract of land called Moore's Lott containing 86 & 3/4 acres of land which is part of a tract Joshua MOORE, dec'd, deeded to David GREEN, now dec'd this contract shall be void. Signed: Joshua MOORE, Isaac MOORE, William MOORE. Wit: Mitchell KERSHAW, William VAUGHAN.

O-14:342. Deed. This Indenture made 09 Feb 1791 between Thomas EVANS Esq, High Sheriff of Sussex cnty, DE of the one part & William ROSS of Northwest Fork Hundred, afsd cnty & state, of the other part. Ct of Common Pleas by writ issued to Thomas EVANS dtd 03 Nov 1791 to recover against Levi STAFORD, late of Sussex cnty, a debt of £72 11s plus 34s damages sd Ct adjudged to William BERRY whereof sd Levi STAFORD was convicted. The 5 parcels of land containing 185 acres lying in Northwest Fork Hundred on which Levi STAFORD now liveth was evaluated to be not sufficient to satisfy the debt & sd Sheriff was ordered to expose sd lands to public sale. Wit: John WILTBANK Esq at Lewes 03 Nov 1790. Thomas EVANS, Esq sold to William ROSS the afsd lands bounded by lands of William NICKOLS, Thomas LEDNUM & Sarah NUTTER & Marshope Branch, for the sum of £111, he being the highest bidder. Signed: Thomas EVANS. Wit: John W BATSON, Clement JACKSON. Thomas FISHER. Nath'l MITCHELL, Proth'y.

O-14:344. Bond of Conveyance. 08 Oct 1779. Thom's CAREY of Sussex cnty, PA, planter, is bound unto William REYNOLDS of sd cnty, planter, in the sum of £1000 lawful money of PA. Condition of sd Obligation is that if sd Thomas CAREY delivers good title to a tract of land called The Vineyard situate in Sussex cnty on the N side of Indian River to afsd William REYNOLDS sd Obligation to be void. Signed: Thom's CAREY (mark). Wit: William KOLLOCK, Elisha DICKERSON.
William REYNOLDS Sr of Sussex cnty, DE for the sum of £350 assign my title to w/in Bond to Elisha DICKERSON. Signed: William REYNOLDS. Wit: Wm KOLLOCK, Magdaline PEERY.
09 Feb 1791. Elisha DICKERSON of Sussex cnty, DE for the sum of 25s assign my claim & title in sd Bond to Benjamin WOORRONTON. Signed: Elisha DICKERSON. Wit: Neh COFFAN, William HARRIS.

O-14:345. Deed. 26 Sep 1787 Woolsey HATHAWAY & Agnes his wife of Chauwan cnty NC & Luke & Patience BURTON of Sussex cnty, DE, yeoman, of the one part for the sum of £70 sold to James HATHAWAY of afsd Sussex cnty, mariner, of the other part a parcel of land situate between Indian River &

Rehoboth Bay in Long Neck bordered by the Great Slash, the BURTONs & the BAGWELLs containing 5 & 3/4 acres, part of a tract of land bequeathed to John BURTON Sr by his father, Woolsey BURTON, dec'd. Signed: Woolsey & Agness HATHAWAY, Luke BURTON, Patience BURTON. Wit: James BURTON, Cornelia BURTON.
I hereby assign all my right to the w/in Deed to James F BAYLES. 05 Dec 1788. Signed: Jas HATHAWAY. Wit: Isaiah BURTON, Edward JOHNSON (mark), Lydia BURTON.

O-14:346. Deed. This Indenture made 09 Feb 1791 between Jane CORD of Sussex cnty, DE, widow, of the one part & her son, William CORD of the other part. There is a parcel of land situate on the SE side of Broad Kill Creek, part of a larger tract of land containing 300 acres conveyed by Deed from John SPENCER to Jos CORD & Jane his wife dtd 06 Sep 1758 which sd land is bounded by where a Tan Yard stood near the marsh side, containing 4 acres & 17 perches. Jane CORD for the sum of £200 sold to sd William CORD the afsd 4 acres & 17 perches of land. Signed: Jane CORD. Wit: Benjamin BURTON, Rhoad SHANKLAND.

O-14:347. Deed. 10 Dec 1790 John DENNIS of Worcester cnty, MD of the one part for the sum of £30 sold to Jesse GRAY of same of the other part 20 acres of land being part of a larger tract called Buckridge situate formerly in Worcester cnty, MD but now in Sussex cnty, DE which tract of land 05 Feb 1749 under MD Right granted to Samuel SMALLWWOOD bounded on the NW of the Cnty Rd from Snow Hill up to Frame's Saw Mill, containing 52 acres of land. The sd part being sold is bounded by a road leading from John HUDSON's to the Cnty Rd towards VERDIMAN's, containing 20 acres. John DENNIS appoints William PEERY or John Wise BATSON his Attorney. Signed: John DENNIS. Wit: Joseph ROGERS, John POSTLY.

O-14:348. Deed. This Indenture made 1791 between William THOMPSON of Sussex cnty, DE, yeoman, Casey THOMSON of Kent cnty, DE, farmer, James THOMPSON of Sussex cnty, DE, yeoman, Priscilla PHILLIPS of Sussex cnty, DE, spinster, Sarah CAREY of Sussex cnty, DE, spinster, Esther HUDSON of Sussex cnty, DE, spinster, & Leah CAREY of Sussex cnty, DE, spinster, of the one part & Crafford SHORT of Sussex cnty, DE of the other part. John CAREY, dec'd, was seized of a tract of land called Second Chance containing 577 acres that now lays in Sussex cnty, DE as will appear by MD Patent dtd 06 Dec 1787, same was surveyed to sd CAREY 08 Dec 1759 as appears by afsd Patent. John CAREY by his Bond dtd 22 Jun 1761 obligated himself in the sum of £80 that he would convey to Jean SANDERS, an inhabitant of Sussex cnty, 89 acres, part of the afsd tract called Second Chance which sd Bond Jean SANDERS 21 Oct 1771 did assign to Jacob SHORT late of Sussex cnty, dec'd, father of the above named Crafford SHORT to whom this Deed is made for the sd 89 acres, he being the lawful heir. This Indenture witnesseth the sd William THOMPSON, Carey THOMPSON, James THOMPSON, Priscilla PHILLIPS, Sarah CAREY, Esther HUDSON & Leah CAREY for the sum of £40 sold and conveys to sd Crafford SHORT all that parcel of 89 acres, part of the above Second Chance of 577 acres lying in Sussex cnty, DE. The sd William THOMPSON, Carey THOMPSON, James THOMPSON, Priscilla PHILLIPS, Sarah CAREY, Esther HUDSON & Leah CAREY appoint Elisha DICKERSON, John MORRIS, William NEWBOLD and/or Job INGRAM their Attorney. Signed: Priscilla PHILLIPS (mark), Carey THOMPSON, Esther HUDSON (mark), William THOMPSON (mark), Sarah CAREY (mark), James THOMPSON (mark), Leah CAREY (mark). Wit: Samuel SHORT, Job SHORT.

O-14:350. Deed. This Indenture made 03 Dec 1790 between Philip SCROGIN of Broad Creek Hundred, Sussex cnty, DE, planter, of the one part & Barkley TOWNSEND of Little Creek Hundred, Sussex cnty, DE, gent, of the other part. John COLLINS, late of Broad Creek Hundred, dec'd, was seized of sundry tracts of land situate in Little Creek Hundred & by his last will & testament dtd 22 Apr 1787 devised unto Isaac HORSEY & Shiles MOORE the following parcels of land: one tract called Lott containing 9 acres, a tract called Chance of 12 acres, & all that part of Aaron's Folly that is covered by the waters of Little Creek or rather a mill pond called Big Mills. Philip SCROGGIN for the sum of £21 sold to Barkley TOWNSEND all the above mentioned parcels of land. Signed: Philip SCROGGIN. Wit: Benjamin READY, Charles VAUGHAN. Philip SCROGGIN appoints Thomas EVANS, David HALL or John W BATSON his Attorney. Signed: Philip SCROGGIN. Wit: Benjamin READY, Charles VAUGHAN.

O-14:351. Deed. This Indenture made 04 Jun 1782 between Rulany BURK of Sussex cnty, DE & John COLLINS of same of the other part. John BURK of Somerset cnty, MD, dec'd was seized of a tract of land called Chance containing 12 acres & another called Lott containing 9 acres by virtue of then Lord Baltimore granted under the Great Seal of MD situate now in Little Creek Hundred, Sussex cnty, DE at & near the mouth of Little Creek. Sd John BURK d: Intestate leaving issue: 4 dtrs to wit: Betty, Peggy, Terreacey & the sd Rulaney to whom sd land descended. By the deaths of sd Betty & Peggy same descended to sd Terreacey & Rulaney & sd Terreacey or Terry hath heretofore by Deed conveyed her moiety of sd land together w/the moiety that descended to sd Rulaney, then a minor, by virtue of an Act of Assembly for division of Intestate land to Moses LYNN, he paying the valuation thereof to sd Rulany or her Guardian. Moses LYNN being so seized of sd 2 tracts of land conveyed same by

Deed to John COLLINS. Sd Rulany BURK who became of lawful age Feb last for the sum of £4 10s sold to sd John COLLINS the sd moiety of sd 2 tracts of land . Sd Rulany BURK appoints Jacob MOORE, Simon KOLLOCK or John CLOWES of Sussex cnty, DE her Attorney. Signed: Rulany BURK (mark). Wit: James COOPER, Job SIRMAN.

O-14:352. Deed. Oct 1790 Robert LAWS & Mary his wife of Sussex cnty, De, planter, of the one part for the sum of £300 sold to Tristin Laws POLK of same place, planter, of the other part, all that parcel of land called Taylor's Hill containing 200 acres and also another parcel of land called Law's Addition containing 46 acres situate in Northwest Fork Hundred. Robert LAWS & Mary his wife appoint John WILTBANK or Phillips KOLLOCK their Attorney. Signed: Robert LAWS, Mary LAWS (mark). Wit: Robert SHANKLAND Jr, Seth GRIFFITH, Thomas LAWS. 20 Oct 1790 Mary LAWS, wife of Robert, was examined separate from her husband and declared she became a party to the w/in Deed of her own free will. Signed: Peter F WRIGHT.

O-14:354. Deed. This Indenture made 11 Nov 1790 between George GREER of Sussex cnty, DE of the one part, planter, & Jonathan CATHELL of same of the other part. Joshua MOORE, dec'd, had granted unto him under the Great Seal of MD 333 & 3/4 acres of land called Moor's Lott 15 Jun 1759. George GREER for the sum of £50 sold to Jonathan CATHELL all that part of sd parcel of land containing 86 & 3/4 acres. George GREER appoints Simon HALL, Thomas EVANS or Phillips KOLLOCK his Attorney. Signed: George GREER. Wit: Mitchell KRISHAW, William VAUGHAN.

O-14:355. Deed. 02 Oct 1790 John FUTCHER of Sussex cnty, DE, yeoman, & Sarah his wife of the one part for the sum of £2 5s sold to Aaron BURTON of sd cnty, joyner, of the other part, all that parcel of land containing 2 & 1/2 acres situate in Indian River Hundred bordered by land of Micajah HOUSTON, Moses MARRINER. Signed: John FUTCHER. Wit: Sukey FUTCHER, Robert MARRINER. John FUTCHER appoints Phillips KOLLOCK or Daniel RODNEY as his Attorney.

O-14:356. Deed. There is a parcel of land within the Liberties of Lewes, Sussex cnty, DE containing 33 acres which James CLAYPOOLE died seized of which was by Order of Orphans Court laid out to James CLAYPOOLE the son of sd James CLAYPOOLE, dec'd, bounded by lands of Jonathan BAILY, dec'd, and Dr Henry FISHER, dec'd. Thomas LAWRENCE of Philadelphia & Co & Ryves HOLT of Sussex cnty recovered two judgements against sd James CLAYPOOLE the younger for 2 sums of money by virtue whereof 2 writs of Execution were directed to Peter CLOWES Esq High Sheriff. Sd Sheriff seized among other things the afsd land and by public sale sold same to Richard METCALF. Richard METCALF by Indenture dtd 03 Dec 1748 conveyed unto William ROWLAND the younger one moiety of the afsd tract. Sd William ROWLAND made his last will & testament dtd 13 Mar 1758 & devised afsd 1 moiety unto his son, David ROWLAND part to these presents. David ROWLAND for the sum of £20 sells to James ROWLAND all that moiety of land afsd containing half an acre. Signed: David ROWLAND. Wit: Phillips KOLLOCK. Peter WHITE.

O-14:357. Deed. This Indenture made 03 Feb 1780 between John CLOWES of Sussex cnty, DE, mariner, of the one part & Jacob CARPENTER of sd cnty, yeoman, of the other part. There is a tract of land in Broad Kill Forrest granted to afsd CLOWES by virtue of a Proprietary Warrant for 150 acres which when laid out agreeable to the location was found to contain nearly 200 acres. John CLOWES for the sum of £75 sells unto Jacob CARPENTER 150 acres of the above cited tract bound by land of Jane KIMMERY near Carpenter's Field, a MD tract of 40 acres, Obediah MESSIX's, land now made for Andrew COLLINGS' new survey. Signed: Jacob CARPENTER (mark). Wit: Eli PARKER, James WOOD. Jacob CARPENTER assigns all right & title to w/in above Deed except 20 acres where Eli CARPENTER now lives to Stephen REDDEN for the sum of £100. 11 Sep 1789. Jacob CARPENTER (mark). Wit: George MESSICK, Jesse BOUNDS.

O-14:358. Bond of Conveyance. Jacob IRONS & Thomas GODWIN of Sussex cnty, DE, planter are bound unto John MORRIS of same in the sum of £1000 dtd 10 Jul 1779. The Condition of sd obligation is that if Jacob IRONS shall make over to John MORRIS all his right & title to a certain parcel of land containing 50 acres which was bequeathed to afsd Jacob IRONS by his grndfthr Michael GODWIN's last will & testament, sd land ling in Broadkiln Hundred near the Old Chapple then sd Obligation to be void. Signed: Jacob IRONS, Thomas GODWIN. Wit: Noah COLLINS, Rhoda GODWIN.

O-14:359. Bond of Conveyance. William POLK of Little Creek Hundred, Sussex cnty, DE, yeoman, is firmly bound unto Custus ROGERS of Accomack cnty, VA, yeoman, in the sum of £200 dtd 22 Apr 1785. Condition of sd Bond is such that whereas William POLK hath included in his Warrant of resurvey on a tract of land called Good Luck some vacant land that was contiguous unto sd Custis ROGERS & whereas sd Custis ROGERS hath agreed to pay proportionate part of all costs & charges that may accrue for securing sd land in sd resurvey according to the quantity hereinafter mentioned & that if sd William POLK shall convey by sufficient Deed called a Specialty all his right & title to that part of sd resurvey south of land laid off for the heirs of James BOWMAN & north of Job SIMMON's land & also a moiety of that part of sd resurvey that lay between where Custis ROGERS formerly dwelled and Francis GODDARD's, then the above Obligation to be void. Signed: William POLK. Wit: Edward CREAGH, Aaron CALLAWAY (mark). Custis ROGERS assigns all his right & title to above sd land to Thomas WALTER. 07 Nov 1785. Signed: Custis ROGERS. Wit: Edward CREAGH, Aaron CALLAWAY (mark).

O-14:360. Deed. This Indenture made 13 Oct 1790 between Pariz GRIFFITH of Sussex cnty, DE, farmer, and Sarah his wife, of the one part & James LOWRY of same, merchant, of the other part. There is a parcel of land situate in Northwest Fork Hundred on W side of Nanticoke River surveyed for Salathiel GRIFFITH & by his Deed of Sale conveyed to afsd Pariz GRIFFITH dtd 04 Jan 1774. sd land bounded by land of George WALLACE formerly surveyed for Henry WILLIAMS dtd 24 Oct 1759 & William WALLACE's field, containing 197 acres. Sd Pariz GRIFFITH & Sarah his wife for the sum of £150 sold to James LOWRY afsd land. Pariz GRIFFITH & Sarah his wife appoint Seth GRIFFITH or Thomas GRAY their Attorney. Signed: Paris GRIFFITH, Sarah GRIFFITH. Wit: Henry SMITH, Betsey GRIFFITH (mark). Sarah, wife of Paris GRIFFITH, was examined separate from her husband and did declare she signed, sealed & delivered the w/in Deed of her own free will. Signed: Peter F WRIGHT. Rec'd of James LOWRY the sum of £150 in full for the w/in mentioned land. Signed: Paris GRIFFITH. Wit: Robert SHANKLAND Jr.

O-14:362. Deed. This Indenture made 04 Oct 1790 between Edward WILLIAMS of Rockenham cnty, NC of the one part & William OWENS, planter, of Sussex cnty, DE of the other part. John POLK Sr, late of Sussex cnty, was in possession of a tract of land called Conclusion situate in a neck of land called John's Neck & near the New Bridge. Afsd John POLK, dec'd, did by his last will & testament bequeath part of sd land called Conclusion to his 4 dtrs Mary WILLIAMS, Nancy MAXWELL, Jane POLK who md: William POLK, and Nelly POLK bounded by the division line of James POLK (son of James) & sd John POLK (dec'd), land of John LAWS Sr formerly surveyed for William POLK of Sommerset cnty, surveyed & laid out for 267 acres & 63 perches. Sd Mary WILLIAMS having right to 1/4 part of afsd land & 1/4 part of her sister Nelley POLK'S share the sd Nelley POLK being dec'd leaving no issue. Mary WILLIAMS in Open Ct made over all her title to above mentioned land by her Power of Attorney unto her husband Edward WILLIAMS. Sd Edward WILLIAMS for the sum of £80 sold unto William OWENS all his title in the tract of land called Conclusion. Edward WILLIAMS appoints William PEERY or Joseph MILLER his Attorney. Signed: Edward WILLIAMS. Wit: James KOLLOCK, John MARSH, John POLK.

O-14:363. Deed. This Indenture made 01 Oct 1788 between Clement BAILY of the one part & Jesse BOUNDS of the other part, both of Sussex cnty, DE. The Lord Proprietary of MD granted to Robert GIVEN his deed to all that tract of land called White Oak Swamp containing 200 acres of land situate in Worcester cnty otherwise called Somerset cnty then but since taken into Sussex cnty, DE on the S side of Nanticoke River as a Patent thereof. Afsd Robert GIVEN conveyed by his Deed indented 90 acres of sd land to John PHILLIPS as recorded in the records of Somerset cnty afsd. John PHILLIPS by his Deed recorded in Worcester cnty conveyed afsd 90 acres to Jaret WYLE, sd land now known as Phillips' Lott. Afsd Jaret WYLE by Deed recorded in Worcester cnty conveyed to John SCARBOROUGH the afsd 90 acres. John SCARBOROUGH by Deed recorded in Worcester cnty conveyed unto Thomas WINGATE the afsd 90 acres. Thomas WINGATE by Deed recorded in Worcester cnty conveyed sd 90 acres unto Clement BAYLEY. Clement BAYLEY for the sum of £174 lawful money of DE sold to Jesse BOUNDS all that parcel of land called Phillipses' Lott being part of afsd tract of land granted to Robert GIVEN containing 200 acres called White Oak Swamp containing 90 acres. Signed: Clement BAYLEY, Margery BAYLEY. Wit: Jeremiah CANNON, William ADAMS, Isaac WINGATE. Clement BAYLEY appoints Rhoads SHANKLAND Esq or William HALL, blacksmith, his Attorney. Signed: Clement BAYLEY, Margery BAYLEY. Wit: Jeremiah CANNON, Wm ADAMS, Isaac WINGATE.

O-14:364. Deed. 10 Feb 1791 Stephen COSTON of Broadkiln Hundred, Sussex cnty, DE, farmer, of the one part for the sum of £163 sold to Charles MACKALON (MACKULEN) of Cedar Creek Hundred, farmer, of the other part all that tract of land situate in Broadkiln Hundred bounded by land of Stephen PASSMORE, land of heirs of William CLARK, dec'd, Clark's Bridge which crosses to Joseph COULTER's, containing 81 & 1/2 acres of land. Signed: Stephen COSTON. Wit: Phillips KOLLOCK, Nathl MITCHELL.

O-14:365. Deed. 15 Jan 1791 Wallace HARMONSON of Lewes & Rehoboth Hundred, Sussex cnty, DE, house carpenter & joyner, of the one part for £5 sold to Adam HALLL of same, taylor, of the other part, that parcel of land situate on the SE side of South Street, part of a larger parcel of land, containing 7 acres whereof John HALL, late of sd cnty, blacksmith, d: intestate and seized, leaving 6 children: James, Lydia, Mary, John, Elizabeth & Adam to whom sd lands descended. Sd Lydia thereafter md: John HARMONSON by whom she had issue, the afsd Wallice, Mary & Elizabeth & afterwards d: under coverture the wife of the sd John HARMONSON, who is also since dec'd. Orphans Ct ordered division of the lands of sd John HALL, dec'd, among his heirs in which division there was laid off & allotted to afsd Wallice, Mary & Elizabeth HARMONSON all that piece of land binding on the SE side of South Street afsd between parts allotted to John HALL, John PILES & Mary his wife, late Mary HALL. Signed: Wallace HARMONSON. Wit: Jno RUSSELL, Elizabeth RUSSELL.

O-14:367. Deed. This Indenture made 19 Jan 1788 between Eli BARKER, one of the heirs of Perry BARKER of Sussex cnty, De, of the one part & Benjamin ROBINSON & Nancy MILBY of same of the other part. There is a parcel of land situate in Indian River Hundred bounding lands of Joseph WEST, dec'd & land formerly belonging to Jesse ENNES, late the property of Perry BARKER, dec'd, who d: intestate leaving a widow & several children whereof afsd Eli BARKER was the eldest. Sd land became subject to division among the widow & children afsd by Orphans Ct at the request of Ann BARKER, widow of Perry BARKER, dec'd. 5 Freeholders of the cnty by order of the Ct made division & laid off the widow's 1/3 & returned that the residue could not be divided amongst the several children whereupon the Ct appointed 3 Freeholders to evaluate sd lands. Eli BARKER for the sum of £104 12s 6p sold to Benjamin ROBINSON & Nancy MILBY all that parcel of land situate as afsd, bounded by WEST's Old Plantation, widow BARKER's 1/3, containing 139 & 1/2 acres. Signed: Eli BARKER. Wit: Robert BURTON Jr, Newcom WHITE, J F BAYLES.

O-14:368. Power of Attorney. Nehemiah GREEN of Philadelphia, taylor, appoints Joseph MILLER Esq of Sussex cnty, DE my lawful Attorney relative to the estate of William GREEN, late of Sussex cnty, mariner, dec'd. Signed: Nehemiah GREEN. Wit: Richard LITTLE. 10 Feb 1791.

O-14:369. Deed. There is a parcel of land & marsh situate in Lewes & Rehoboth Hundred, Sussex cnty, DE on the SW side of Lewes Creek & SE side of Lewes being part of a larger tract called Middleborough being the E corner of afsd tract bounded by CORD's 20 acres of land, Jacob WHITE's 7 acres, the Patent line of Middleborough & Pothook's Gut containing 52 acres. Sd piece of land & marsh by Indenture dtd 24 Feb 1776 was conveyed by John LEWIS, yeoman, to the heirs of Stephen GREEN, late of sd cnty, dec'd, recorded in Liber M, No 12, folio 85. Since the execution & delivery of sd Indenture several of the heirs have d: intestate, William GREEN, John GREEN, Nelly GREEN & Polly GREEN & another of sd heirs had d: after having first made his last will & testament, Stephen GREEN, one of the sons of sd Stephen GREEN, the elder, dec'd, by which will he devised his share of sd land to Ambrose GREEN one of the other heirs of the sd Stephen GREEN, dec'd, & brother to sd Testator. Nehemiah GREEN, to whom Administration of the estate of William GREEN, late dec'd, in due form petitioned Orphans Ct the personal estate of sd William was insufficient to satisfy sd William's debts & requested an order to convey sd real estate for the purpose afsd. Ct so ordered. Nehemiah GREEN, Admin of the estate, & Richard GREEN & Ambrose GREEN, surviving heirs of sd Stephen GREEN, dec'd, for the sum of £90 sold to Samuel PAYNTER the elder, of Lewes, Sussex cnty, all their right & title to the above described 52 acres. Signed: Nehemiah GREEN by Jos MILLER his Attorney, Richard GREEN, Ambrose GREEN, Violettia TINDLE. Wit: Noble LEWIS, Saml PAYNTER Jr, Jesse DUTTON. 10 Feb 1791 Nath'l MITCHELL, Proth'y.

O-14:371. Deed. This Indenture made 15 Jan 1791 between Uriah HAZZARD of Lewes, Sussex cnty, DE, cartwheelwright, & Sarah his wife, of the one part & Richard LITTLE of same, gent, of the other part. Thomas FENWICK, late of Sussex cnty, was seized of 12 acres of land in Lewes between Market & South streets on one of the branches of Pagen Creek & by his last will & testament dtd 02 Mar 1707/8 devised afsd land to his son, James FENWICK who by his Deed dtd 30 Jul 1722 conveyed sd lands to Simon KOLLOCK, Esq, who by Deed of Sale dtd 04 Mar 1729 conveyed sd land to John PRICE. John PRICE by his writing Obligatory dtd 27 Sep 1737 sold sd lands to John SIMONTON & afterwards d: Intestate before he had executed any Deed of Conveyance for same. Whereupon William TULL, Admin of the estate afsd John PRICE in pursuance of an Order of Ct of Com Pleas by Deed of Sale conveyed afsd lands to John SIMONTON who afterwards d: having first made his last will & testament dtd 29 May 1751 wherein he devised the house wherein he dwelled & a small piece of land thereto adjoining called a Garden unto his son, John SIMONTON & devised the remainder of the afsd 12 acres to his 2 youngest dtrs, Comfort & Elizabeth SIMONTON to be equally divided between them. John SIMONTON, the younger, & sd Comfort SIMONTON afterwards d: Intestate & w/o issue leaving 4 sisters: Jennet the wife of Nathaniel BAILY, Sarah the wife of John SHANKLAND, Mary the wife of James DAVISON & the afsd Elizabeth the wife of Noble LEWIS to who sd land so devised to them descended. Nathaniel BAILY & Jennet his wife, John SHANKLAND & Sarah his wife, James DAVISON & Mary his wife, by their several Deeds of Release, did convey all their right & title to the afsd lands divided by the afsd John SIMONTON the elder, to the afsd John SIMONTON, the younger, & the afsd Comfort SIMONTON to the afsd Noble LEWIS & Elizabeth his wife who being so seized of the afsd 12 acres of land by their Deed of Sale dtd 29 May 1773 conveyed sd lands unto Phillip KOLLOCK

Esq who by Deed of Sale under the hand of sd Phillips KOLLOCK & Penelope his wife dtd 24 Mar 1779 conveyed afsd lands unto Uriah HAZZARD. Sd Uriah HAZZARD & Sarah his wife, for the sum of £125 sold to Richard LITTLE the above described lands bounded N side of Pagan Creek, Market Street, lands now the property of Hugh SMITH, South Street containing 12 acres of land. Signed: Uriah HAZARD, Sarah HAZARD. Wit: Hercules KOLLOCK, W HARRISON. Sarah, wife of Uriah HAZZARD, being of full age, was examined separate from her husband & declared she became a part to the above of her own free will 22 Jan 1791. Signed: Jno WILTBANK.

O-14:374. Deed. This Indenture made 20 Jan 1791 between Richardson CADE, Charles COVERDALE & Ann COVERDALE his wife & Zipporah WHALEY of Sussex cnty, DE of the one part & Isaac MITTEN, of same place, farmer, of the other part. There is a parcel of land situate in the fork of Pembertons Branch being part of a larger tract granted by Proprietaries Warrant to John REED & John HALL who conveyed same to Robert CADE, fthr to afsd Richardson CADE & grndfther to afsd Ann COVERDALE & Zipporah WHALEY who was in his lifetime seized of sd land & sd CADE being so seized gave his Bond of Conveyance to his son, Richardson, afsd for all his part of sd tract of land excepting for his own use 40 acres on the E most part & on S most fork of sd Branch after which sd Robert CADE d: Intestate leaving issue: Richardson CADE, Elizabeth WHALEY & Magdaline WEBB & sd Magaline d: leaving issue: afsd Ann now the wife of Charles COVERDALE, party to these presents, & the afsd Elizabeth WHALEY d: Intestate leaving issue, the afsd Zipporah WHALEY party to these presents; sd land containing & now laid out for 40 & 1/4 acres. Richardson CADE, Charles COVERDALE & Ann COVERDALE his wife & Zipporah WHALEY for the sum of £50 sold unto afsd Isaac MITTEN the afsd 40 & 1/4 acres of land. Richardson CADE, Charles COVERDALE, Ann COVERDALE & Zipporah WHALEY appoint Thomas EVANS High Sheriff of Sussex cnty or Thomas FISHER, Sub Sheriff, their Attorney. Signed: Richardson CADE, Charles COVERDALE (mark), Ann COVERADLE (mark), Zepeah WHALEY (mark). Wit: Zadock LINDALL, William MITTEN.

O-14:375. Deed. This Indenture made 10 Feb 1791 between Samuel SPENCER of Sussex cnty, DE, yeoman, William PEERY of sam, Esq, & John FISHER of same, Esq. Sd Samuel SPENCER for the sum of 5s & diverse other considerations & sd Samuel SPENCER thereunto moving, had sold to sd John FISHER all that parcel of land formerly the property of William ROBINSON formerly of same cnty which sd William ROBINSON by his last will & testament devised to his grnddtr Mary STEWART mthr of afsd Samuel, situate in Broadkiln

Hundred bounded by land formerly of David SCUDDER, land now in the possession of Charles CONNOLLY formerly James WALKER's, lands now in the possession of Archibald FLEMING formerly William STEWART's, containing 120 acres. William PEERY shall be Demandant, sd John FISHER tenant & sd Samuel SPENCER shall be Vouchee. Signed: Samuel SPENCER, William PEERY, John FISHER. Wit: James P WILSON, George HAZZARD.

O-14:376. Deed. This Indenture made 11 Jan 1791 between Levi RUSSELL of Broadkiln Hundred, Sussex cnty, DE, yeoman, & Sarah his wife (late Sarah JONES, one of the dtrs of Isaac JONES, dec'd) of the one part & James REED of same, yeoman, of the other part. Griffith JONES (son of the afsd Isaac JONES) at a Ct of Orphans held at Lewes 06 May 1782 petitioned sd Ct that Isaac JONES in his lifetime was seized of lands & tenements situate in sd Hundred and d: Intestate leaving Abigail, his widow, & 8 children: Martha, Sarah (one of the parties to these presents), Mary, Isaac, Griffith, Elias, Abigail & John, to whom sd lands descended, to appt 5 Freeholders to lay off the widow's Dower and make division of the residue 2/3 amongst the heirs. Sd Ct ordered Joseph HAZZARD Esq, Rhoads SHANKLAND, David THORNTON, Thomas GROVE & John HAZZARD, gent, to survey & lay off the sd Widow's Dower & make partition of the residue 2/3 of land amongst the heirs if it would admit thereof w/o spoiling the whole. 05 Feb 1783 term of Orphans Ct held at Lewes sd Freeholders reported they had laid off the widow's 1/3 and allotted to Sarah RUSSEL wife of Levi RUSSEL (parties to these presents) part of the Intestate lands being a corner of the PA Survey by Aaron CLIFTON's land, bounded by Griffith JONE's dividend, John COVERDALE's land, containing 175 acres of land. Sd Levi RUSSEL & Sarah his wife, for the sum of £150 sold to James REID all the above described 175 acres. Signed: Levi RUSSEL, Sarah RUSSEL. Wit: Peter F WRIGHT, Rachel RUSSEL. Sarah, wife of Levi RUSSEL, was examined separate from her husband and declared she became a party to the above of her own free will. Signed: Peter F WRIGHT.

O-14:378. Deed. This Indenture made 10 Feb 1791 between Nehemiah REED of Sussex cnty, DE, yeoman, & Isabella his wife, of the one part & Jesse DUTTON of same of the other part. There is a parcel of land being part of a larger tract of land in the forest of Broadkiln Hundred containing 300 acres commonly called Collins Folly originally surveyed to Joshua COLLINS 02 Dec 1752 by William SHANKLAND then Deputy Surveyor of cnty afsd by virtue of a Proprietaries Warrant for that purpose dtd at Philadelphia 09 Jun 1743. Sd Joshua COLLINS by Indenture dtd 05 Jan 1753 sold same unto Isaac BRITTINGHAM of Worcester cnty, MD which sd BRITTINGHAM by Indenture dtd 01 Apr 1760 sold same to Edward STEPHENSON which sd STEPHENSON by Indenture dtd

07 May 1778 sold same unto the above Nehemiah REED which sd parcel of land is on the N side of the main road leading from John COLLIN's to John CLOWES between where Nehemiah REED formerly dwelt & Zachariah REED's, containing 80 & 1/2 acres. Afsd Nehemiah REED & Isabella his wife, for the sum of £80 sold to Jesse DUTTON the above described 80 & 1/2 acres. Signed: Nehemiah REED, Isabella REED (mark). Wit: Robert P CAMPBELL, Jos MILLER. Isabella REED, wife of Nehemiah, was examined separate from her husband & she did declare she was a party thereto of her own free will. 10 Feb 1791. Signed: Peter ROBINSON.

O-14:380. Deed. This Indenture made 01 Feb 1791 between John BURTON, Mary BURTON his wife, & William VAUGHAN of Sussex cnty, DE of the one part & Thomas SHIRMAN of same of the other part. There is a parcel of land situate in Indian River Hundred which is part of a larger tract of land which was formerly surveyed unto Francis POPE on 19 Apr 1722 & afterwards was resurveyed unto John HOLMES by virtue of a Warrant of Resurvey from Thomas PENN Esq dtd 22 Feb 1739 & surveyed by William SHANKLAND then Deputy Surveyor of Sussex cnty for 372 acres of land dtd 12 Jan 1742 for the afsd John HOLMES . Sd John HOLMES & Ann HOLMES his wife, by Deed of Sale dtd 08 May 1755 conveyed 98 & 1/2 acres (being a part of the afsd 372 acres of land) unto William VAUGHAN of Sussex cnty which sd Deed is recorded in Liber I, # 8, folio 95. William VAUGHAN by his last will & testament dtd 20 Feb 1775 devised sd parcel of land unto his son, Nathaniel VAUGHAN, & Nathaniel VAUGHAN dying before he came of age 21 the afsd parcel of land fell to his brother, William VAUGHAN & sister Mary & John BURTON parties to these presents, sd John having md: the dtr of above name William VAUGHAN, the elder. The bounds of sd divident of land bounded by a tract of land called Warwick, a tract of land formerly surveyed to Edward SUTHERN & now held by Nathaniel WAPLES Esq, land of Samuel WAPLES & a part sd John HOME sold to Joseph HICKMAN & now held by Samuel WAPLES containing 98 & 1/2 acres. John BURTON, Mary BURTON & William VAUGHAN for the sum of £105 gold & silver coin lawful money of DE sold unto Thomas SHERMAN the above described 98 & 1/2 acres. Signed: John BURTON, Mary BURTON, William VAUGHAN. Wit: Peter ROBINSON, William HARRIS, Marshall SMITH. Mary BURTON, wife of John, was examined separate from her husband & declared she signed the w/in Deed of her own free will. 11 Feb 1791. Signed: Peter ROBINSON.

O-14:382. Deed. This Indenture made 15 Mar 1790 between William MULLENIX of Cedar Creek Hundred, Sussex cnty, DE, yeoman, & Unice his wife, of the one part & Richard HUDSON Jr of same, yeoman, of the other part. There is a tract of land situate in the Forest of Cedar Creek Hundred between the head of Bowman's Branch & the side of Wolf Den Swamp, commonly known as Jone's Adventure, containing 395 acres & another parcel formerly taken up by John MORRIS & sold by him to Alexander ARGO containing 99 & 3/4 acres which sd 2 tracts was purchased by William MULNEX the elder, father of sd William MULNEX party to these presents who by his last will & testament devised unto 2 of his sons, Richard & William MULNEX the above sd 2 tracts of land which was since conveyed unto Jane MULNEX, widow & Executrix of William MULNEXT the elder, dec'd, in right of his children by afsd Alexander ARGO & Bethuel WATTSON his Attorney by Deed dtd 08 Nov 1770. Sd William MULNEX the younger sold his part of the afsd land to John RICKARDS for the sum of £100 & gave a Conveyance Bond for same John RICKARDS who for a valuable sum assigned sd Conveyance Bond (which is dtd 11 Feb 1776) to Thomas FISHER 04 Nov 1777 who gave a Conveyance Bond for sd land to Zachariah CARLISLE who for a valuable consideration assigned same to above named Richard HUDSON which sd parcel of land was devised as afsd to sd William MULNEX after being laid off is bounded the line of John RICKARD's 50 acres, containing 100 acres. Sd William MULNEX & Unice his wife, for the sum of £100 paid by John RICKARD's & also 5s paid by sd Richard HUDSON sold to Richard HUDSON all the described 100 acres. William MULNEX & Unice his wife appoint Messrs Phillips KOLLOCK or William HARRISON of Lewes their Attorney. Signed: William MULNIX. Unice MULNIX (mark). Wit: Robert HART (mark), Zachariah CARLISLE, Nehemiah TATMAN.

O-14:384. Petition. Ct of Common Pleas, Sussex cnty, DE 10 Feb 1791. Mary CLOWES & Isaac CLOWES, Execs of the last will & testament of John CLOWES late of Sussex cnty, Esq, dec'd. John CLOWES was seized in his lifetime of 140 acres of land situate in the forest of Broadkiln Hundred & by his Bond dtd 07 Sep 1772 bound himself to Isaiah JOHNSON of sd cnty, yeoman, in the sum of £100 w/condition that whereas the above Isaiah JOHNSON on the day & year last purchased of sd John CLOWES 140 acres of land situate in Broadkiln forest adjoining land then in the possession of Obediah & Nehemiah MESSICK, it being the lands the sd CLOWES purchased of Joseph LUFTON & Jane KIMMERY. LUFTON's 100 Acres is a PA Survey & KIMMERY's 40 acres a MD patent, which sd 140 acres of land & premises sd Isaiah JOHNSTON shall have under the conditions hereafter mentioned, viz: he shall pay yearly & every year £3 as rent for same during the full term of 10 years or until the payment of £50 be made by sd Isaiah JOHNSTON to sd John CLOWES & if sd £50 not be paid at the end of sd term then sd Isaiah JOHNSTON shall give up all title to sd land w/1 log house 18' x 20'& 1 other 12' x 14', fit for a tenant to dwell & also 50 acres of cleared land fit for the plough under good fence, but at the end of the term sd Isaiah JOHNSTON shall have a Did for the afsd land made by sd

John CLOWES to sd Isaiah forever as he shall pay yearly forever to sd John CLOWES the sum of £3 ground rent for same. Condition of the w/in is such that if the above Bounded John CLOWES upon receipt of the above sum of £50 w/interest w/in 10 years by Deed of Sale convey to sd Isaiah JOHNSTON the above described 140 acres of land & premises & above Obligation to be null & void. Isaiah by his written assign on sd Bond dtd 22 day of Mar 1776 for the sum of £77 2s 6p sold all his title in sd Bond & lands thereby held to Nunez DEPUTY. A dispute thereafter arose between sd John CLOWES & sd Nunez DEPUTY & to settle the dispute by their several Bonds dtd 13 Mar 1789 became bound each to the other in the sum of £200 to abide by the final determination of Joseph HAZZARD, Nathaniel WAPLES, Esqs & John INGRAM, gent, any 2 of them so as the sd aware be made in writing to be delivered to sd parties on or before 01 May next ensuring the date of the sd Obligations. After duly considering the proofs & allegations of both sd parties two of sd Arbitrators, Joseph HAZZARD & Nathaniel WAPLES published their award dtd 11 Apr 1789 wherein they awarded sd Nunez DEPUTY should pay unto John CLOWES the sum of £50 on or before 01 Jan 1791 w/interest & upon payment sd John CLOWES should duly confirm unto sd Nunez DEPUTY all his title to the 140 acres of land above. Nunez DEPUTY by his Indorse on the Award delivered by sd Arbitrators dtd 30 Dec 1790 for the sum of £55 3s 4p by Richard HUDSON paid to your Petitioners sd Nunez DEPUTY did assign all his title & claim to sd award unto sd Richard HUDSON. Sd John CLOWES d: before he executed any Deed of Conveyance for sd lands having first made his last will & testament wherein among other things he apptd Petitioners his Execs. Petitioners request an Order authorizing them to execute a Deed of Conveyance for sd lands & premises to sd Richard HUDSON who is assignee of sd Nunez DEPUTY who is assignee of sd Isaiah JOHNSTON the original Obligatoree. Signed: Mary CLOWES, Isaac CLOWES.

O-14:386. Deed. Mary CLOWES & Isaac CLOWES, Execs, of the last will & testament of John CLOWES late of Sussex cnty, dec'd. John CLOWES was seized of 140 acres of land situate in the forest of Broadkiln Hundred & by his Bond Obligatory dtd 07 Sep 1772 bound himself to Isaiah JOHNSON of sd cnty, yeoman, in the sum of £100 w/Condition that Isaiah JOHNSON purchased of sd John CLOWES 140 acres of land situate in Broadkiln Forest in Sussex cnty adjoining lands of Obediah & Nehemiah MESSICK being lands John CLOWES purchased of Joseph LUFTON & Jane KIMMERY whereon sd Isaiah JOHNSON shall occupy as his Freehold under conditions hereafter mentioned, to wit: he paying each & every year £3 as above sd rent for the full term of 10 years or until the payment of £50 by Isaiah JOHNSON to John CLOWES then upon such payment the above rent to cease. But if above sum of £50 not be paid by end of sd term then afsd Isaiah JOHNSON shall give up all right to sd land w/one logged house 18' x 20' & another 12' x 14', fit for tenant to dwell, also 50 acres of afsd land cleared for the plough, under good fence. It was further agreed that at the end of the term sd Isaiah JOHNSON should have a Deed for the afsd land made by sd John CLOWES to Isaiah JOHNSON., he paying yearly rent £3 for same. Condition of sd Obligation is such if John CLOWES at any time w/in the term of 10 years on rcpt of £50 w/interest shall release a sufficient Deed of Sale to sd Isaiah JOHNSON for the afsd 140 acres of land & premises then above Obligation shall be void. 27 Mar 1776 Isaiah JOHNSON assigned on back of sd Bond for the sum of £77 his claim to afsd lands to Nunez DEPUTY. Controversy arose between John CLOWES & Nunez DEPUTY re sd lands & by their sundry Bonds dtd 13 Mar 1789 became bound to each other in the penal sum of £200 to abide the award & final determination of Joseph HAZZARD, Nathaniel WAPLES Esqs & John INGRAM, gent, sd award to be made in writing on or before 01 May next. Sd Arbitrators after fully examining & duly considering the proofs & allegations of both parties did write their decision dtd 11 Apr 1789 wherein among other things they did award sd Nunez DEPUTY should pay to John CLOWES the sum of £50 on or before 01 Jan 1791 w/interest from date of award & sd John CLOWES at cost of sd Nunez DEPUTY should by Deed of Sale duly executed make over conveyance unto sd Nunez DEPUTY all his title & claim to the sd 140 acres. Nunez DEPUTY by his assignment indorsed on sd aware delivered to him 13 Dec 1790 for the sum of £50 3s 4p by Richard HUDSON paid to Mary & Isaac CLOWES, parties to these presents, sd Nunez DEPUTY did assign all his right to sd aware unto sd Richard HUDSON. Whereas sd John CLOWES d: before executing any Deed of Conveyance having first made his last will & testament wherein he apptd his wife, Mary CLOWES, and heir, Isaac CLOWES, his Execs sd Execs petition Ct of Com Pleas to cause an order to be made empowering them to execute Deed of Conveyance for sd lands & premises to sd Richard HUDSON. Ct so ordered. Mary CLOWES & Isaac CLOWES make Deed of Sale to Richard HUDSON 12 Feb 1791. Signed: Mary CLOWES, Isaac CLOWES. Wit: Daniel ROGERS, Jno WILTBANK.

O-14:389. Sheriff's Deed. John RUST in the Aug 1785 term of the Ct of Com Pleas held at Lewes recovered against Thomas LAWS & Isaac BRADLEY, both of Sussex cnty, for the use of James DOUGLAS, a debt of £513 plus £4 14s 7p for damages. 05 May 1790 sd Ct of Com Pleas directed Thomas EVANS, Sheriff, to collect sd monies to deliver to sd RUST Wed 04 Aug next. By virtue of sd Order Thomas EVANS seized two tracts of land; one tract situate in Cedar Creek Hundred, Sussex cnty, containing 250 acres & the other tract situate in Northwest Fork Hundred, Sussex cnty, containing 250 acres. Sd land was valued by 2

Freeholders who found the rents, issues & profits of afsd lands were not sufficient to satisfy sd debt w/in 7 years. Ct of Com Pleas 03 Nov year last sd ordered afsd lands to be sold at Public Sale and sd Sheriff to make return on Wed 09 Feb the next. Same was purchased by James DOUGLASS 19 Jan 1791 for the sum of £250, he being the highest bidder, sd lands being one tract situate in Cedar Creek Hundred on SE side of a branch of Mispillion Creek called Pond Branch being the same tract sd Thomas LAWS purchased of Saul DAVIS beginning near William PAYNTER's land, bounded by Peterkins' Overgoing, Meeting House Branch, containing 243 acres & 29 perches of land, one other tract situate in Northwest Fork Hundred called Gladstower on the E side of Chesapeake Bay at the head of Nanticoke River laid out for 100 acres and another tract situate in Hundred & cnty afsd called Clearance on the E side of a swamp at the head of Bridge Branch out of the NE fork of Nanticoke River bounded by a tract of land called Gladstower, sd tract containing 94 acres. Signed: Thomas EVANS, Sheriff. Wit: D HALL, Nath'l MITCHELL.

O-14:392. Deed. This Indenture made 12 Feb 1791 between Nathaniel HICKMAN of Broadkiln Hundred, Sussex cnty, DE, yeoman, & Phebe his wife, of the one part & Peter Fretwell WRIGHT of same, Esq, of the other part. Samuel ROWLAND, late of sd cnty, pilot, dec'd, by his last will & testament dtd 15 Dec 1765 devised his lands & tenements to be equally divided among his children after the death of his wife. Sd widow has since died. Division of sd lands amongst the sd children: James, Samuel & Comfort who md: Stephen WARRINGTON, was submitted to Parker ROBINSON, Hap HAZZARD & William PEERY. Sd ROBINSON, HAZZARD & PEERY by their award dtd 09 Mar 1783 published they had divided unto afsd James ROWLAND a parcel of land containing 45 acres situate in Broadkiln Hundred on the W side of Coolspring Creek. Sd James ROWLAND & Deborah his wife by Deed dtd 06 May 1784 sold sd 45 acres of marsh to the above named Nathaniel HICKMAN. Sd Nathaniel HICKMAN & Phebe his wife for the sum of £31 5s sold to sd Peter Fretwell WRIGHT 25 acres of marsh. Signed: Nathaniel HICKMAN, Phebe HICKMAN. Wit: Hap HAZZARD, Nath'l MITCHELL. Phebe, wife of above named Nathaniel HICKMAN, being of full age, was examined separate from her husband and declared she became a party to above Deed of her own free will. Signed: Nath'l MITCHELL, Proth'y.

O-14:393. Sheriff's Deed. Samuel PLEASANTS, assignee of Robert SMYLEY in the Ct of Com Pleas of Sussex cnty, DE recovered against Edmund BLADES & Train GIBBONS late of sd cnty, yeomen, a debt of £175 11s 4p plus 44s 7p for damages, to be levied. Sd Ct 09 Aug 1786 directed Peter Fretwell WRIGHT Esq, then High Sheriff of sd cnty, who in execution thereof seized a tract of land situate in Broad Creek Hundred, Sussex cnty, DE containing 170 acres which sd land & premises he had appraised by 2 Freeholders who upon their solemn oaths sd the income from same was not sufficient to satisfy the sd debt w/in 7 years. Sd Ct then issued writ for the Public Sale of sd land 06 Feb 1788.20 Mar 1788 Sd land was purchased by Robert SMYLEY for the sum of £115, he being the highest bidder. Sd Peter Fretwell WRIGHT was discharged from Office of Sheriff before he executed deed for conveying sd land to sd SMYLEY. Thomas EVANS doth convey unto sd Robert SMYLEY all that before mentioned parcel of land containing 170 acres. Signed: Thomas EVANS, Sheriff. Wit: Phillips KOLLOCK, W HARRISON.

O-14:395. Sheriff's Deed. This Indenture made 10 Mar 1791 between Thomas EVANS, Sheriff of Sussex cnty, DE, of the one part & James BRATTEN of same, merchant; John MITCHELL of same, merchant & Cyrus MITCHELL of Dorset cnty, MD, gent, of the other part. There is a tract or parcel of land situate in Little Creek Hundred in Sussex cnty containing 200 acres called part thereof Howns Ditch, another part thereof Addition to Howns Ditch and the rest Trushams Choice which sd tract of land became the right of Benjamin WOOTEN & by sundry conveyances became the land of James TRUSHAM. James BRATTEN, for the use of the Executors of John MITCHELL, late of Sussex cnty, dec'd, in the Aug 1788 term of the Ct of Com Pleas recovered judgement against James TRUSHAM & Elijah WOOTEN each for the sum of £300 & 44s 7p damages. 2 writs dtd 06 Aug 1788 ordered the Sheriff of Sussex cnty to levy sd judgements against the goods, chattels & lands of sd Elizah WOOTEN & James TRUSHAM. Sd Sheriff returned he had seized sd lands, caused 2 Freeholders to evaluate sd lands who reported the income & profits from sd lands were insufficient to satisfy the debts w/in 7 years whereupon sd Ct ordered sd lands sold at Public Sale to satisfy sd judgements dtd 04 Nov 1789. Whereupon sd Sheriff, Thomas EVANS Esq for the sum of £50 to Cyrus MITCHELL, he being the highest bidder. Signed: Thomas EVANS, Sheriff. Wit: James P WILSON, Nath'l MITCHELL.

O-14:396. Deed. This Indenture made 02 Mar 1791 between John Alburtus STEWART of Sussex cnty, DE, yeoman, & Rachel his wife, of the one part for the sum of £143 sold to George DURHAM of same, yeoman, of the other part, 2/3 of a parcel of land late the property of Jonathan SCUDDER who d: Intestate leaving issue, Rachel, party to these presents unto whom sd lands descended, bounded by lands of Archibald FLEMMING, John WALKER's heirs, William PEERY Esq & Archibald HOPKINS' land, containing 94 & 2/3 acres of land, reserving the other 1/3 part to the widow of sd Jonathan SCUDDER during her natural life. Signed: John Allburtiz STEWART, Rachel STEWART (mark). Wit: John CLARKE, David STEWART. 11 Mar 1791 Rachel STUART whose mark is hereto affixed, was examined separate from her husband & did declare she signed the w/in Deed of her own free will. Signed: Charles POLK.

O-14:397. Deed. James FINNWICK & Sidney his wife, by Indenture dtd 09 Aug 1722 sold to Joseph ELDRIDGE late of Sussex cnty, DE, 5 lotts of ground situate in the Town of Lewes bounded as follows: by land of John BYWATER, the County Rd, lotts of Phillips RUSSELL. Joseph ELDRIDGE by Deed dtd 04 Feb 1728 sold to John CLOWES Esq, dec'd, part of the afsd 5 lotts. Joseph ELDRIDGE thereafter made his last will & testament dtd 10 Mar 176? and therein gave to his grndsn Thomas EVANS & his grnddtr Phebe LIPPINGCUT each a lot of ground in Lewes town (being the remainder of sd lotts conveyed to Joseph ELDRIDGE by sd James FINEWICK & Sidney his wife afsd). Phebe LIPPINGCUT md: Hudson BURR by whom she had issue several children and afterwards d: having first made her last will & testament dtd 15 Mar 1789 thereby devising to her son William BURR the lott of ground devised to her by her sd grndfther, the afsd Joseph ELDRIDGE, by which sd devise the 2 lots of ground being the remainder of the 5 lotts) became the property of the afsd Thomas EVANS and William BURR. Thomas EVANS 26 May 179? authorize sd William BURR to take possession of a lott of ground in the town of Lewes devised to him by his grndfthr, sd Joseph ELDRIDGE, & to convey by a sufficient deed to such person as would purchase same giving William BURR full power to transact all matters. William BURR for the sum of £15 sold unto Andrew WILEY all that part of the afsd lotts of ground devised by Joseph ELDRIDGE to sd Thomas EVANS & Phebe LIPPINGCUT beginning at the corner of 4th & South Sts, to the corner of John RUSSELL's lott commonly called the Church Lott to land late of William PILE's formerly called Bywater Lot, now owned by John DAVIS, to 4th St, containing 30,130 feet. William BURR doth appt David HALL or Phillips KOLLOCK his Attorney. Signed: Thomas EVANS (by William BURR, his Atty), William BURR. Wit: Peter F WRIGHT, W. HARRISON.

O-14:399. Power of Attorney. Know by all men presents that I, Thomas EVANS, of Evesham in the cnty of Burlington, NJ, yeoman, one of the grndsns of Joseph & Mary ELDRIDGE formerly of Sussex cnty, DE. dec'd, by their dtr Rachel, also dec'd, have made, ordained & constituted and by these presents do make, ordain and constitute and in my place and stead, put and depute, William BURR, of the same place, carpenter, a grt grndsn of the said Joseph & Mary, my true & lawful attorney. Signed: Thomas EVANS. Wit: Jabez Maud FISHER, Miers FISHER. 06 Oct 1790.

O-14:400. Deed of Gift. George Howard AYDELOTT, Phillips WHITE & Matthias AYDELOTT for the natural love & affection we bare unto Sarah HAZZARD, wife to Uriah HAZZARD, and for other good causes us thereunto moving have given unto the sd Sarah HAZZARD a woman called Gin and her increase. We forever discharge the Executor to the estate of John AYDELOTT Sr, dec'd, for them to be possessed & enjoyed by sd Sarah HAZZARD during her natural life to descend to her children: Oliver & Felix HAZZARD, to be equally divided. 17 Mar 1791. Signed: George H AYDELOTT, Philip WHITE, Matthias AYDELOTT. Wit: John HAZZARD, Thomas HAZZARD.

O-14:401. Mortgage. This Indenture made 08 Mar 1791 between William SALMON of Sussex cnty, DE of the one part & George MITCHELL of same of the other part. William SALMON by his Bond dtd above for securing the payment thereof stands bound unto sd George MITCHELL in the sum of £109 10s 4p in gold & silver coin conditioned for the payment of the sum of £54 15s 2p w/Interest in gold & silver. William SALMON for securing payment of sd Bond to George MITCHELL & for the sum of 1s doth grant unto sd George MITCHELL all those several tracts of land: one tract of land called Fancy granted unto Benjamin AYDELOTT by Patent dtd 08 Nov 1709 containing 100 acres that lies on the SW side of the main County Rd from Indian River to Dagsbury; all that part of a tract of land called Salmon's Addition granted to Benjamin SALMON by Patent dtd 24 Jan 1748 containing 100 acres lying on the SW side of the road afsd; and all that part of a tract called Conclusion granted unto Joshua BURTON containing 1000 acres according to a bond of conveyance by Jacob BURTON to sd William SALMON dtd 08 Feb 1775 containing 22 acres of land; all that part of a tract called Willeys Invention, exclusive of what was sold out of same to Woolsey BURTON) granted unto Soloman WILLEY by Patent dtd 18 Jul 1776 containing 37 acres 93 perches & 95/100 of land that Solomon WILLEY gave his Bond dtd 11 Feb 1779 to convey unto sd William SALMON all his right to same & also the right unto the afsd tracts of land claimed by sd William SALMON, he Warranting & defending same provided always on the condition that if sd William SALMON shall pay to sd George MITCHELL the afsd principal sum of money with interest for same from date of sd Bond this Indenture shall cease and above sd lands the property & right of sd William SALMON. William SALMON appts Phillips KOLLOCK Esq as his Atty. Signed: William SALMON. Wit: Thomas WILDGOOS, Isaac HUTCHINS.

O-14:402. Woolsey HATHAWAY of the state of NC, mariner have constituted & appointed Woolsey BURTON of Sussex cnty, DE, yeoman, my lawful Attorney to recover all such sums of monies, rents, demands, whatever, which are due me & also in my name & stead to bargain and sell to such persons as he shall think fit. 02 Apr 1791. Signed: Woolsey HATHAWAY. Wit: Daniel BURTON, Benjamin BURTON.

O-14:403. Deed. 11 Apr 1791 Samuel DIRECKSON of Sussex cnty, DE of the one part by his Bond dtd same w/this Indenture stands bound to Woolsey BURTON of same of the other part in the sum of £150 conditioned for payment of the sum of £75. Samuel DIRICKSON for the securing of sd payment & for the sum of 7s 6p pd by sd Woolsey BURTON doth discharge & confirm unto sd Woolsey BURTON all that parcel of land called Babells Addition situate in Sussex cnty & in Baltimore Hundred of sd cnty, DE, which sd land was granted to Joseph DIRECKSON by Patent dtd 29 Sep 1761 provided on the condition that if sd Samuel DIRECKSON shall pay sd Woolsey BURTON the afsd sum w/interest from date of sd Bond then this Indenture shall cease. Signed: Samuel DIRECKSON. Wit: Benjamin BURTON, Thomas HAZZARD.

O-14:404. This Agreement made 22 Mar 1791 between Matthew WHARTON of the one part & Jonathan DAZEY of the other part, both of Sussex cnty, DE. Sd Matthew WHARTON & Jonathan DAZEY hereby agree under Penalty of £100 to set, keep up & support a sufficient fence between them that divides the Plantations of both parties beginning on the N side of the county road that rums from the sea side to Dagsbury & sd fence shall be kept up that each party shall have equal quantity of panels to keep up & support sd fence. Signed: Matthew WHARTON, Jonathan DAZEY. Wit: Stephen STYER, Polly WALTER.

O-14:404. There are several accounts depending & divers controversies lately arisen between John CLOWES Esq of Sussex cnty, DE & Nunez DEPUTY of same, all of which chiefly concern 140 of land w/in sd cnty which sd John CLOWES contracted for the sale thereof 07 Sep 1772 w/Isaiah JOHNSON. Sd Isaiah JOHNSON 22 Mar 1776 assigned all his title & claim of sd Bond of Conveyance & the lands thereby held onto the above named Nunez DEPUTY. To put an end to sd differences John CLOWES & Nunez DEPUTY by their several Bonds dtd 13 Mar 1789 became bound to each other in the penal sum of £200 to abide the award & determination of Joseph HAZZARD & Nathaniel WAPLES, Esq & John INGRAMS, gent, all of Sussex cnty, DE or any 2 of them. Sd Arbitrators having fully examined the proofs & allegations of both sd CLOWES & DEPUTY publish this Award in manner following: further controversy of sd lands shall cease, each of sd parties shall bear his own costs & charges, sd DEPUTY shall pay sd CLOWES the sum of £50, Spanish milled dollars at 7s 6p each on or before 01 Jan 1791; upon payment of sd sum w/lawful interest to sd

John CLOWES, then sd John CLOWES agreeable to his Bond dtd 07 Sep 1772 unto Isaiah JOHNSON & by sd JOHNSON to sd Nunez DEPUTY 22 Mar 1776 at cost & charge of sd Nunez DEPUTY sd John CLOWES by Deed of sale duly executed shall make over conveyance unto sd DEPUTY all his right, title & claim to 140 acres of land & as well all Patents, Warrants, etc concerning same; & further if Default of non payment be made by sd Nunez DEPUTY to sd John CLOWES, sd DEPUTY shall peacefully & quietly leave & yield up to sd CLOWES sd 140 acres together w/all Bonds, conveyances, Patents, Deeds, etc. & then only payments to sd John CLOWES the sum of £10 for use & rent of sd lands & tenements; lastly we do award & order sd John CLOWES & Nunez DEPUTY to abide peacefully by the above. 13 Mar 1789. Signed: Joseph HAZZARD, N WAPLES, J INGRAM.

O-14:406. Nunez DEPUTY for the sum of £55 1s 8p paid by Richard HUTSON to sd DEPUTY, sd DEPUTY assigned all right, title & claim to w/in award to sd Richard HUTSON 30 Dec 179?. Signed: Nunez DEPUTY. Wit: James WILEY, Hugh PATTERSON.

O-14:407. Sheriff's Deed. This Indenture made 04 May 1791 between Thomas EVANS Esq, High Sheriff of Sussex cnty, DE of the one part & Daniel POLK of same, farmer, of the other part. William HITCH of same was seized of certain lands & premises situate in Northwest Fork Hundred, cnty afsd, & being considerably indebted unto sundry persons. 06 May 1789 Sussex cnty, DE Ct of Comm Pleas issued a writ directing Thomas EVANS, Sheriff, to levy against the goods, chattels, lands of William HITCH a debt of £50 19s 8p which Milkey ECCLESTON in the Ct of Comm Pleas recovered against William HITCH as well 44s 7p her damages & costs. Sd Sheriff returned that for want of good & chattels sufficient belonging to sd HITCH he had seized in execution all that part of a tract of land belonging to sd HITCH situate in the Northwest Fork Hundred near Bridge Branch called Haile's Choice containing 27 acres which sd lands were appraised by 2 Freeholders who found the rents & issues of sd lands were not sufficient to satisfy sd debt w/in 7 years. 04 Aug 1790 by order of sd Ct exposed sd lands to public sale & same were purchased by Daniel POLK 14 Oct for the sum of $40, he being the highest bidder. Thomas EVANS, Sheriff, for the sum of $40 hath granted & sold unto Daniel POLK the parcel of land called Haile's Choice containing 27 acres. Signed: Thomas EVANS, Sheriff. Wit: John FISHER, Nath'l MITCHELL.

O-14:408. In pursuance of an Act by the General Assembly of DE at Dover Jan 1791 to remove the Seat of Justice from Lewes to a more Central part of Sussex cnty wherein George MITCHELL, Robert HOUSTON, William MOORE, John

COLLINS, Rhoads SHANKLAND, William PEERY, Woodman STOCKLEY, Thomas BATSON, Nathaniel YOUNG & Daniel POLK were apptd Commissions for buying land to build the Ct House & Prison agreeable to sd Act. The subscribers (except Thomas BATSON, lately dec'd), being a majority, met at Abraham HARRIS's 09 May proceed to purchase lands & tenements situate w/in 2 miles of the house where Ebenezer PETTYJOHN now resides w/in Broadkiln Hundred near the center of Sussex cnty. Rhoads SHANKLAND, Surveyor of sd Cnty, laid out the lands so purchased, being bounded by Abraham HARRIS' land, land of ---- BUTLER, land of Rowland BEVINS, land of Joshua PEPPER, containing & laid out for 76 acres of land. 09 May 1791, in the 15th year of the Independence of DE state. Signed: John COLLINS, Rob't HOUSTON, Rhoads SHANKLAND, Will MOORE, Daniel POLK, Geo MITCHELL.

O-14:409. Deed. This Indenture made 23 Apr 1791 between Purnal LOFLAND of Kent cnty, DE of the one part & Ahab CLENDANIEL of Sussex cnty, DE of the other part. There is a tract of land containing 110 acres situate in Cedar Creek Hundred, Sussex cnty, DE adjoining lands of Jacob TOWNSEND & Richard COVERDILL Jr & Dennis MORRIS & Avra CLENDANIEL Sr, part of the survey called John DAVISES. Purnal LOFLAND for a sum of money paid by Avarey CLENDANIEL hath sold unto sd Ahab CLINDANIEL the above mentioned tract of land, except the Widow LOFLAND's thirds which has been laid off. She is now the wife of Joseph LINDON. Purnal LOFLAND appoints Curtis SHOCKLEY or Thomas EVANS his Attorney. Signed: Purnal LOFLAND. Wit: Jonathan BROWN, Purnal VEACH, Avarey CLINDANIEL.

O-14:410. Sheriff's Deed. Abraham JACOBS recovered judgement against Levi COLLINS, yeoman, of Sussex cnty, DE for a debt of £15 6s 8p w/cost of suit in Sussex cnty, DE Ct of Com Pleas May 178?. Cord HAZZARD Esq, the Sheriff of Sussex cnty was ordered by sd Ct to levy debt upon the goods & chattels & lands of sd Levi COLLINS. Sd Sheriff returned by virtue of sd writ he had seized in execution a tract of land situate in Baltimore Hundred, cnty afsd, containing 33 & 1/3 acres, that 2 Freeholders had valued rents & issues from sd lands insufficient to satisfy afsd debt & damages w/in 7 years. Whereas sd Sheriff was ordered to sell sd land at Public Sale. 15 Sep year afsd Sd Sheriff Cord HAZZARD for the sum of £37 10 sold sd land unto Nehemiah HOWARD, he being the highest bidder. Sd Cord HAZZARD was removed from office of Sheriff before he made any Deed to sd Nehemiah HOWARD for the lands & premises. Thomas EVANS, Sheriff, for the sum of £37 10s paid to Cord HAZZARD, late Sheriff, hath granted and sold unto sd Nehemiah HOWARD all the afsd 33 & 1/3 acres of land (part of a larger tract called TimberLand Enlarged, surveyed 06 May 1760 for John DAGWORTHY

Esq, dec'd) who by Deed conveyed afsd land to sd Levi COLLINS, bounded by Robert McCRAY's home line, Levi COLLINS' other land. 04 May 1791. Signed: Thomas EVANS, Sheriff. Cord HAZZARD, late Sheriff. Wit: Mark DAVIS, Nath'l MITCHELL.

O-14:412. Deed. This Indenture made 07 Feb 1791 between Jacob CARPENTER of Sussex cnty, DE, farmer, of the one part & Stephen REDDEN, yeoman, of the other part. There is a tract of land in Broadkill Forest, Sussex cnty, DE granted to John CLOWES Esq by virtue of a Proprietor's Warrant conveyed from sd CLOWES to afsd Jacob CARPENTER for 135 acres which was found to have 150 acres. Jacob CARPENTER for the sum of £100 has sold unto Stephen REDDEN 130 acres of the afsd land beginning at a corner of a tract of land formerly called Jane KIMMERY's land but now the property of sd Stephen REDDEN near sd Jacob CARPENTER's field to the corner of a MD tract of 40 acres, six perches, then to Obediah MESSICK's land to a corner of Andrew COLLIN'S new survey to a county road. Signed: Jacob CARPENTER. Wit: Sommerset Dickerson COSTON, Isaac MESSICK.

O-14:413. Deed. This Indenture made 04 May 1791 between Wallace HARMONSON of Lewes, Rehoboth Hundred, Sussex cnty, DE. house carpenter & joyner, of the one part & Mary HARMONSON of same, widow of Peter HARMONSON, of the other part. Wallace HARMONSON for the sum of £123 15s sold to sd Mary HARMONSON all that parcel of land situate in hundred & cnty afsd which was devised unto him by the last will & testament of his father, John HARMONSON, dec'd, which was laid off to sd Wallace HARMONSON by David HAZZARD, Peter MARSH & Thomas MARSH apptd by sd John HARMONSON for that purpose & dtd 06 Feb 1788, rec: Liber N-13, folio 472, beginning at a small ditch out of Lewes Creek that proceeds out of Rehoboth Bay which divides lands of the late John HARMONSON, dec'd, from the lands of Joseph DARBY, containing 110 acres of land & marsh. Signed: Wallace HARMONSON. Wit: Hap HAZZARD, George WALTON.

O-14:414. Power of Attorney. Samuel SPENCER of Cumberland cnty, NJ for diverse good causes & considerations he hereunto moving appoint William PEERY of Sussex cnty DE his lawful Attorney to make & convey a Deed of Sale to William HOLLAND, minor son of John HOLLAND to all my right & title to a tract of land situate in Broadkiln Hundred, cnty afsd, containing 120 acres being the same land in Deed of Sale from Thomas EVANS, Sheriff of Sussex cnty, to sd John HOLLAND. 11 Feb 1791. Signed: Samuel SPENCER. Wit: George HAZZARD, Andrew WILLY.

O-14:414. Deed. This Indenture made 04 May 1791 between William PEERY of Broadkiln Hundred, Sussex cnty, DE, Esq & Samuel SPENCER of Cumberland cnty, NJ yeoman, by the afsd William PEERY as Power of Attorney dtd 11 Feb year afsd, of the one part & William HOLLAND, minor, son of John HOLLAND of Broadkiln Hund, cnty & state afsd, dec'd, of the other part. There is a parcel of land, part of a larger tract situate in Broadkiln Hundred in a place called Kimbells Neck whereof William ROBINSON died seized & by his last will & testament devised to his grnddtr, Mary STEWART, mother of afsd Samuel SPENCER. Upon the death of the sd Mary, the estate vested in the afsd Samuel SPENCER of the lands & premises so devised by sd William ROBINSON subject to the life estate of Edward STAPLEFORD w/whom sd Mary married & had issue & whose wife she was at the time of her death. Samuel SPENCER at a Ct of Com Pleas, Nov term 1790, caused a Common Recovery to be had of the land & premises devised by sd William ROBINSON to his grnddtr Mary STEWART afsd. Sd William PEERY & Samuel SPENCER for the sum of £150 hath sold unto William HOLLAND (subject to the life estate of afsd Edward STAPLEFORD which by sundry conveyances is vested in John HOLLAND, father of afsd William HOLLAND) all that parcel of land above recited bounded by land formerly of David SCUDDER, lands now in the possession of Charles CONNOLLY, formerly James WALKER's, land in the possession of Archibald FLEMING, formerly William STEWART's, containing 120 acres of land. Signed: William PEERY, Samuel SPENCER by William PEERY his Attorney. Wit: J RUSSELL, Nath'l MITCHELL.

O-14:416. Deed. This Indenture made 23 Apr 1791 between Purnal LOFLAND of Kent cnty, DE, yeoman, of the one part & Avery CLINDANIEL of Sussex cnty, DE, farmer, of the other part. There is a tract of land situate in Cedar Creek Hundred, Sussex cnty on the W side of a fresh marsh, part thereof taken up & surveyed for John LOFLAND 25 Feb 1715 being part of two surveys John LOFLAND Jr, dec'd, died seized of & intestate & was accepted by afsd Purnal LOFLAND at a valuation, adjoining on the S side of land Patrick LINGO formerly dwelt & on the N side of land whereon John LOFLAND Sr formerly dwelt beginning in a swamp bounded by Ahab CLENDANIEL's land, Avery CLENDANIEL's fence, widow LOFLAND's plantation, containing 126 acres. Purnal LOFLAND 25 Mar 1782 obligated himself to convey afsd land & premises to William POLK of Sussex cnty, afsd & sd William POLK by his assignment on sd Obligation 08 Jan 1783 assigned all his claim unto afsd Avery CLENDANIEL and sold to him the afsd 174 & 3/4 acres. Purnal LOFLAND hereby appoints Thomas EVANS, Sheriff, or Joseph MORRIS his Attorney. Signed: Purnal LOFLAND. Wit: Asa MANLOVE, Purnal VEACH.

O-14:417. Deed. This Indenture made 26 Oct 1790 between Isaac MORRIS of Sussex cnty, DE, yeoman, of the one part & Benjamin LOCKWOOD of same, yeoman, of the other part. Bevins MORRIS, late of cnty afsd, dec'd, died seized of sundry tracts of land situate in afsd cnty in Dagsbury Hundred a mile or so to the SE of Dagsbury Town & SW side of Pepper Creek Branch, amongst which is a tract called Turtle Swamp that was first owned by Daniel WHORTON by virtue of the Proprietary MD Patent dtd 04 Dec 1714 for 78 acres land then called Bachelor's Lot, first granted to Bevins MORRIS, fthr of afsd Bevins MORRIS by the Proprietary of MD by Patent dtd 29 Aug 1756 for 75 acres of land & a third tract of survey called Civility, all which sundry tracts the sd Bevins MORRIES having d: intestate was divided by persons apptd by Orphans Ct amongst the several children of whom the afsd Isaac MORRIS was one and to whom was granted of the three mentioned tracts 80 acres of land as his full part of his father, sd Bevin MORRIS' landed estate. Sd 80 acres on the W side of the road that formerly lead from Dagsbury Church by Samuel LOCKWOOD's to Snow Hill excepting 1/2 or 1/4 acre that lays on the E side of sd road. Isaac MORRIS for the sum of £60 sold to sd Benjamin LOCKWOOD the 80 acres laid off to him as his share of his father Bevins MORRIS landed estate. Isaac MORRIS appoints William LOCKWOOD, Woolsey BURTON, Hinman WHARTON or John MORRIS as his Attorney. Signed: Isaac MORRIS. Wit: Thomas HAZZARD, Edw'd DINGLE.

O-14:419. Deed. This Indenture made 04 May 1791 between Zechariah READ of Sussex cnty, DE of the one part & Edmund DICKERSON of same of the other part. Richard PETTYJOHN late of Sussex cnty made his last will & testament dtd 14 Mar 1751 & thereby devised unto his son, John PETTYJOHN his dwelling plantation called PH together w/all lands thereunto. John PETTYJOHN thereafter d: intestate and Admin of sd dec'd was granted unto Hannah PETTYJOHN widow of sd dec'd, who afterwards also d: intestate w/o fully administering the estate & credits of sd dec'd. LOA 23 Jan 1780 were granted unto above Zechariah READ. At Orphans Ct 04 Nov 1789 sd Zechariah REED petitioned afsd Hannah PETTYJOHN had overpaid the personal estate of sd dec'd 17s 6p and several debts remained still unpaid asking sd Ct to grant an Order to sell as much of the Real Estate of sd dec'd as thought sufficient to discharge the debts due & such was granted. Ct ordered sd Zechariah READ to sell at Public Sale all the Real Estate of sd dec'd for the purpose afsd. Zechariah READ sold sd land to Edmund DICKERSON for the sum of £30, he being the highest bidder. Sd land called PH situate in Broadkiln Hundred bounded by James PETTYJOHN's LAND, Josiah ROTTON's land, BUTLER's line, BEVINS' corner, John CLOWES' and Gunning BEDFORD's land containing 154 acres of land. Signed: Zechariah PETTYJOHN (mark). Wit: J WILTBANK, W HARRISON.

O-12:420. Deed. 04 Aug 1788 John HUBBART of Sussex cnty, DE, farmer, & Elizabeth his wife of the one part for the sum of £35 sold to Peter RUST of same, farmer, of the other part all that part of a tract of land called Smiths Range & Addition to Smiths Range being land whereon John ---- now lives & heretofore was sold by patented claim of James SMITH to Peter RUST situate as the last will & testament of James SMITH to his son Joseph SMITH & all the estate title whatsoever of sd John HUBBART & Elizabeth his wife. John HUBBART & Elizabeth his wife appoint John RODNEY or Phillips KOLLOCK as their Attorney. Signed: John HUBBART, Elizabeth HUBBART (mark). Wit: William CAUSEY, James SAFFORD, Nathan GLADSON, John EVANS, Owen EVANS, Nehemiah TATEMAN.

O-14: 421. Deed. This Indenture made 27 Oct 1788 between Mary DARBY & William NEWBOLD, Admin of the estate of John DARBY late of Sussex cnty, DE, dec'd of the one part & Zachariah JONES of same of the other part. There is a tract of land situate in Dagsbury Hundred in cnty afsd containing 300 acres, 100 acres of which was granted by Patent dtd 03 Jul 1741 to William PHILLIPS & sd William PHILLIPS by Deed dtd 16 Aug 1760 conveyed same to Henry WALLER who by Deed dtd 18 Mar 1763 conveyed sd 100 acres of land to Zachariah JONES. Sd Zachariah obtained a Warrant resurvey of sd 100 acres to include any vacant lands adjoining same which sd Zachariah caused sd resurvey on 15 May 1776 & added 200 acres of vacant land thereto making the whole 300 acres of land and known by the name of Dispute Disputed which sd 300 acres of land is bounded by a tract called Double Purchase, Isaac SHORT's land, Broad Creek Road. Zachariah JONES by his last will & testament dtd 25 May 1780 devised sd tract to his son, Zachariah JONES which sd Zachariah JONES the younger & Margaret his wife by Deed of Sale dtd 04 Feb 1786 conveyed sd 300 acres of land to John DARBY & John DARBY being indebted at the time of his death more than his personal estate was sufficient to discharge the above named Mary DARBY & William NEWBOLD, Admins afsd, petitioned Orphans Ct to grant permission to sell sufficient of the land as to discharge sd debts which sd Ct granted. Mary DARBY & William NEWBOLD, Admins afsd, sold by Public Sale to Zachariah JONES the afsd 300 acres for the sum of £155, he being the highest bidder. Signed: Mary DARBY (mark), William NEWBOLD. Wit: William LOCKWOOD, David LONG, Robert HOPKINS.

O-14:423. Deed. This Indenture made 1791 by Ezekiel SMITH of Sussex cnty, DE, planter, of the one part & Curtis JACOBS of same, planter, of the other part. For the sum of £50 Ezekiel SMITH sold to Curtis JACOBS all that parcel of land called Wolf Swamp in Northwest Fork Hundred being surveyed for sd Ezekiel

SMITH 10 Mar 1784 bounded by a Resurvey called White Levil belonging to Hezekiah SMITH, containing 68 acres & the allowance of 6 perches. Ezekiel SMITH appoints John WILTBANK or Phillips KOLLOCK his Attorney. Signed: Ezekiel SMITH. Wit: Ennalls ADAMS, Daniel POLK.

O-14:424. Deed. This Indenture made 28 Apr 1791 between Isaiah JOHNSON of Sussex cnty, DE, planter, of the one part & Jacob CARPENTER of same, planter, of the other part. There is a tract of land in Sussex cnty, DE containing 180 acres called Good Hope being in Dagsbury Hundred in a neck of land between Shealous Branch & Shappen Branch that issueth out of Indian River was granted by the Proprietary of PA to David ROTTON by Warrant dtd Philadelphia 11 Mar 1776 & surveyed to him by Rhoads SHANKLAND then Surveyor of Sussex cnty 30 Apr 1776. David ROTTON by Deed of Sale dtd 27 Mar 1786 conveyed his right & title to afsd Isaiah JOHNSON. Isaiah JOHNSON for the sum of £100 has sold to Jacob CARPENTER all the afsd tract called Good Hope bounded by Simon KOLLOCK's land, the country road from Broad Creek over Ingram's Mill to the landing at the head of Indian River, Samuel TINDAL's land, MOTT's land, containing 180 acres of land. Isaiah JOHNSON appoints William NEWBOLD, Woolsey BURTON or Job INGRAM as his Attorney. Signed: Isaiah JOHNSON (mark). Wit: Simon KOLLOCK, David MARVEL.

O-14:425. Deed. This Indenture made 13 Apr 1789 between Mary DARBY & William NEWBOLD, Admins of the goods & chattels of John DARBY late of Sussex cnty, DE, dec'd, of the one part & Robert HOOD of same of the other part. There is a parcel of land situate in Dagsborough Hundred, Sussex cnty, which was granted to Simon KOLLOCK containing 76 acres being part of a larger tract called Good Hope. Sd Simon KOLLOCK conveyed sd tract of land unto Lazarus ---- who conveyed same to Ebenezer JONES. Sd Ebenezer JONES d: Intestate the tract descended to his eldest son Thomas JONES as Heir at Law. Thomas JONES conveyed 76 acres of sd tract to his son Ebenezer JONES which sd Ebenezer JONES & Ann his wife conveyed sd 76 acres to afsd John DARBY, bounded by land laid off to Zachariah JONES. There is one other tract situate in afsd Hundred & cnty containing 70 acres being part of a larger tract granted to Robert INGRAM lying on the head of Sheep Pen Branch that runs to Indian River. Sd Robert INGRAM conveyed the afsd 70 acres part of the sd tract to the last mentioned Ebenezer JONES. Sd Ebenezer JONES & Ann his wife conveyed same to John DARBY, bounded by Zachariah JONES' land, the Cripple of Sheep Pen Branch. There is one other tract of land in Hundred & cnty afsd containing 100 acres called Jone's First Choice which was granted by Warrant dtd 12 Mar 1776 bounded by the dividing line of lands of Ebenezer & Zacharias JONES containing & surveyed for 100 acres. Sd 100 acres of land

Ebenezer JONES & Ann his wife by Deed of Sale dtd 04 Feb 1786 conveyed to afsd John DARBY. Sd John DARBY being indebted at the time of his death more than his personal estate was sufficient to discharge, the above named Mary DARBY & William NEWBOLD petitioned Orphans Ct for an Order of Sale of so much of the lands of John DARBY sufficient to discharge the remaining debts which Petition was granted. Mary DARBY & William NEWBOLD put sd lands to Public Sale & 29 Sep 1787 sold the three parcels of land to Robert HOOD for the sum of £155, he being the highest bidder. Signed: Mary DARBY (mark), William NEWBOLD. Wit: Seth GRIFFITH, William LOCKWOOD.

O-14:427. Petition of Nelly CAREY, Exec'x of last will & testament of Thomas CARY (son of Thomas) to convey lands to Benjamin WARRINGTON. Thomas CARY 08 Oct 1779 did exchange a parcel of land lying on Indiana River in Indian River Hundred w/William RUNNELS for a parcel of land lying in Broadkiln Hundred, cnty afsd. Thomas CARY by Bond of Conveyance to sd William RUNNELS obligated himself o convey sd land unto William RUNNELS & William RUNNELS by endorsement on back of sd Bond assigned sd Bond to Elisha DICKERSON who also assigned his right thereto unto Benjamin WARRINGTON the Execution of which duly proved in Ct of Com Pleas. Thomas CARY dec'd before he executed a Deed of Sale. Petitioner asks sd Ct to issue Order to execute Deed of Conveyance for sd land. 28 Feb 1791. Indorsed on back side 02 May 1791. Signed: Nelley CARY (mark).

0_14:428. Deed. This Indenture made 04 May 1791 between Nelley CARY of Sussex cnty, DE, Exec'x of the last will & testament of Thomas CARY late of same, dec'd, of the one part & Benjamin WARRINGTON of Indian River Hundred, Sussex cnty, ship carpenter, of the other part. There is a parcel of land situate in Indian River Hundred on the N side of Indian River called the Vinyard surveyed by Thomas PEMBERTON by Warrant given by Ct of Sussex cnty & laid out by Order of William CLARK Chief Surveyor of same & for the sum of £25 sold same to William CLARK. Thomas BEDWELL & Honour his wife, Exec's of the last will & testament of sd William CLARK for the sum of £12 being part of a Judgement of Ct obtained in Sussex cnty against the estate of sd William CLARK by James WALKER conveyed same to James WALKER. Richard POULTNEY, Admin of the estate of sd James WALKER conveyed same unto Joseph CARTER of Sussex cnty, merchant, for the sum of £40 10s by Deed of Sale dtd 17 Apr 1730 & ack sd Deed in Open Ct 23 Apr. Sd lands by several conveyances became vested in sd Joseph CARTER who 06 Jun 1735 obtained Warrant of Resurvey on afsd land called Vinyard & by virtue of afsd Warrant same was surveyed to sd Joseph CARTER 10 Jul 1735 for 291 acres of land in the original tract & 38 & 1/2 acres of marsh & land added as appears by William SHANKLAND's certificate of Survey. Joseph CARTER by Deed of Sale dtd 08 Jan 1736 conveyed sd 329 acres of land & marsh to James COULTAS of Philadelphia for the sum of £75 & ack same in Ct of Com Pleas held 08 Jan afsd. Sd James COULTAS by Letter of Attorney dtd 10 Oct 1739 nominated Christopher TOPHAM of Sussex cnty to be his Attorney. Christopher TOPHAM for the sum of £90 by Deed of Sale dtd 10 Jan 1742 sold sd lands to Thomas CARY. Thomas CARY by his last will & testament dtd 22 Jul 1777 devised part of afsd tract unto his sn Thomas CARY. Thomas CARY 08 Oct 1779 did give the afsd tract devised to him by his father afsd in exchange w/William RUNNELS for a tract of land situate in Broadkiln Hundred & each did receive of the other peaceable possession of sd lands. Thomas CARY on day & year afsd executed a Bond of Conveyance to sd William RUNNELS & sd William RUNNELS by Indorsement on back of sd Bond assigned his right therein unto Elisha DICKERSON of sd cnty who also assigned his right thereto unto afsd Benjamin WARRINGTON. Thomas CARY dying before he had executed Deed of Sale for same, the afsd Nelly CARY, Exec'x of last will & testament of Thomas CARY petitioned Ct of Com Pleas for Order to execute a Deed in discharge of sd Bond which sd Ct granted. Sd land bounded by Benjamin BENSTON's plantation, formerly John LACEY's, containing 184 acres of land & marsh. Nelley CARY in consideration of sd William RUNNEL's exchanging of sd tracts of land w/her husband Thomas CARY & delivering up to sd Thomas CARY the land in Broadkiln Hundred afsd, doth ack & discharge sd Benjamin WARRINGTON & convey & confirm unto sd Benjamin WARRINGTON all the above described 184 acres of land & marsh. Signed: Nelley CARY (mark). Wit: Isaac ATKINS, Nicholas LITTLE, Stephen REDDEN.

O-14:430. Deed. May 1791 Barkley TOWNSEND of Sussex cnty, DE, gent, of the one part for the sum of £50 sold unto William MOORE of same, Esq, of the other part one lott of land No. 5, situate in Little Creek Hundred in cnty afsd in a town called Laurel Town, sd lott part of an original tract called the Indian Land on S side of Baron Creek, N side of Front St, to Corn St to main water of Baron Creek. Signed: Barkley TOWNSEND. Wit: Geo MITCHELL, Jon BOYCE

O-14:431. Deed. 04 May 1791 George CLAYPOOLE of Sussex cnty, DE, yeoman, of the one part for the sum of £25 sold unto John FLEETWOOD of same, yeoman, of the other part a parcel of land situate in Broadkiln Hundred bounded by the cnty road in the line of Jeremiah CLAYPOOLE's deed, Beaver Dam Branch, Andrew SIMPLER's line containing 28 acres. Signed: George CLAYPOOLE. Wit: J RUSSELL, --- PAYNTER Jr.

O-14:432. Deed. This Indenture made 05 May 1791 between Joseph WILDGOOSE of Sussex cnty, DE, yeoman, & Jane WILDGOOSE his wife, late Jane ROBINSON, Exec of the estate of John ROBINSON late of sd cnty, of the one part & Gracy ARON of same, yeoman, of the other part. John ROBINSON at the time of his death was seized of a tract of land situate in Baltimore Hundred, Sussex cnty, called Sumerfields, originally granted by Propr. of MD Patent dtd 09 Jun 1695 unto William WITTINGTON near the mouth of Shrimp Gut on the E side & on S side of Asswamon Creek also bounded by a tract called Johnson's Lott, a tract called Scott's Plott, & laid out for 150 acres. Sd John ROBINSON not having sufficient personal estate at the time of his death to discharge his just debts the afsd Joseph WILDGOOS & Jane his wife, Exec's, after having fully executed the personal estate of sd dec'd ROBINSON petitioned Orphans Ct to make an order for the sale of the above sd lands for the purpose of discharging the just debts of sd dec'd ROBINSON & for raising & educating the children. Sd petition was granted & they did sell by public sale to afsd Gracy ARON all the above described lands for the sum of £162 1s, she being the highest bidder. Signed: Joseph WILDGOOS, Jane WILDGOOS. Wit: G HAZZARD, Nath'l MITCHELL.

O-14:433. Bond of Conveyance. Phillips FORGUSSON of Baltimore, MD is firmly bound unto Caleb BALDIN of Sussex cnty, DE in the penal sum of £1600. Dtd 14 Jun 1781. Condition of sd Bond is such that if Phillips FORGUSSON shall be proper Deed of Sail make over unto sd Caleb BALDING all his claim to a tract of land in Sussex cnty, Little Creek Hundred deeded to afsd FURGUSSON by John COLLINS upon payment of two Bonds for £400 the above Obligation shall be void. Signed: Phillips FARGUSSON. Wit: James WALSH, Abraham COMRON. Cyrus MITCHELL 05 May 1791 attested to the signature of James WALSH.

O-14:434. Deed. This Indenture made 05 May 1791 between Gracy ARON of Sussex cnty, DE, yeoman, of the one part & Joseph WILDGOOS of same, yeoman, of the other part. Gracy ARON for the sum of £162 1s sold unto Joseph WILEGOOS all that tract of land situate in Baltimore Hundred, Sussex cnty, called Sumerfields originally granted by Prop of Md Patent dtd 09 Jun 1695 unto William MILLINGTON, situate near the mouth of Shrimp Gut on the S side of Asswomin Creek, bounded by land called Johnson's Lott, land called Scottish Plott, laid out for 150 acres of land. Gracy ARON by sundry conveyances became lawfully seized of sd land. Signed: Gracey ARON. Wit: Nath'l MITCHELL, Geo MITCHELL.

O-14:435. Deed. This Indenture made May 1791 between Barkley TOWNSEND of Sussex cnty, DE, gent, of the one part & Thomas ROBINSON of same, physician, of the other part. Barkley TOWNSEND for the sum of £30 sold to Thomas ROBINSON part of a tract of land (being part of an original tract called Indian Lands, situate in Little Creek Hundred, on S side of Broad Creek) which sd part of a tract is a Lott in the tow of Laurel Town bounded as followeth: beginning on S side of Market Street, W side of Wheat Street, running S w/Wheat St. Signed: Barkley TOWNSEND. Wit: Geo MITCHELL, Jona BOYCE.

O-14:436. Deed. This Indenture made 11 Feb 1790 between Morgan WILLIAMS Jr of Sussex cnty, DE, yeoman, of the one part & Thomas GRAY of same, schoolmaster, of the other part. There is a tract of land situate in Northwest Fork Hundred, Sussex cnty, DE near Unity Forge being part of a larger tract formerly the property of Thomas WILLIAMS & by sundry conveyances became the property of the afsd Morgan WILLIAMS Jr, party to these presents, bounded by land of William MELONEY & a small parcel of land purchased by afsd GRAY of afsd MELONEY, land called Golden Grove belonging to Anderton BROWN, containing 10 acres of land. Morgan WILLIAMS by his writing Obligatory dtd 28 Jul 1787 obligated himself to convey the above land by a General Warrant for the sum of £20 to Thomas GRAY. Signed: Morgan WILLIAMS Jr. Wit: Edw'd POLK, Betsey PEAKE (mark).

O-14:437. Deed. This Indenture made 14 Apr 1789 between Robert HOOD of Sussex cnty, DE, of the one part & William NEWBOLD of same of the other part. There is a parcel of land situate in Dagsborough Hundred containing 76 acres being part of a larger tract which was granted to Simon KOLLOCK called Good Hope. Sd Simon KOLLOCK conveyed sd tract to Lazarus KIMONY who conveyed same to Ebenezer JONES. Sd Ebenezer JONES dying intestate, sd tract of land descended to Thomas JONES eldest son of sd Ebenezer. Sd Thomas JONES conveyed 76 acres, part of sd tract, to his son Ebenezer JONES which last mentioned Ebenezer JONES & Ann his wife conveyed sd 76 acres to John DARBY. Sd 76 acres is bound by land laid off to Zachariah JONES. There is one other tract of land situate in hundred & cnty afsd containing 70 acres being part of a larger tract granted to Robert INGRAM lying at the head of Sheep Pen Branch that runneth into Indian River. Sd Robert INGRAM conveyed sd 70 acres unto the above named Ebenezer JONES who with Ann his wife conveyed same 70 acres to above name John DARBY. There is also one other tract of land situate in hundred & cnty afsd containing 100 acres called Jones' First Choice which was granted by Warrant dtd 12 Mar 1776 to above & last named Ebenezer JONES which sd Ebenezer JONES & Ann his wife conveyed to the above named John DARBY. John DARBY, now dec'd & being indebted at the time of his death more than his personal estate was sufficient to discharge, ---- DARBY & William NEWBOLD, Admin's of sd John DARBY by order of Orphans Ct sold the above

3 described parcels of land unto above Robert HOOD. Robert HOOD for the sum of £155 hath sold to William NEWBOLD all his title to the herein described parcels of land. Signed: Robert HOOD. Wit: William LOCKWOOD, Seth GRIFFITH.

O-14:439. Deed. This Indenture made 13 Feb 1790 between Bakor JOHNSON & his wife Sarah JOHNSON of Sussex cnty DE of the one part & John WILLSON of same, yeoman, of the other part. There is in Slaughter Neck, Sussex cnty, DE a small plot of land containing 83 acres part of two tracts conveyed to Daniel WILLSON by Deed dtd 02 May 1747 duly executed by James WHITE & Margaret WHITE his wife which sd Margaret was Admin'x to John LONGEN which sd LONGEN had contract w/sd Daniel WILLSON to convey part of sd two tracts recourse to sd Bond rec'd in Lib H, No 7, folio 123. Sd Daniel WILLSON afterward d: having first made his last will & testament in which he apptd Isaac WATTSON of cnty afsd his Exec. Sd Isaac WATTSON petitioned Orphans Ct that sd Daniel WILLSON was indebted to sundry persons & his personal estate was insufficient to discharge sd debts, requesting an Order to sell sd lands as would enable him to discharge sd debts. Order was granted & Isaac WATTSON put sd lands to Public Sale & sold same to Baker JOHNSON the 83 acres dtd 03 Aug 1758, sd 83 acres being bounded by land of Nehemiah DAVIS, William HICKMAN, Luke DAVIS & William WILLSON. Baker JOHNSON & Sarah his wife for the sum of £278 sold unto John WILLSON the afsd 83 acres. Signed: Baker JOHNSON, Sarah JOHNSON. Wit: Brantson LOFFLAND, Mary LOFLAND. Sarah JOHNSON was examined separate from her husband & did declare she signed the above of her own free will. Jno WILTBANK.

O-14:440. Deed. This Indenture made 11 Sep 1790 between Joseph WATSON of Sussex cnty, DE, yeoman, & Mary his wife of the one part & Phebe VINING of the Borough of Wilmington, DE, widow, of the other part. Joseph WATSON by his Bond dtd herewith stands bound unto sd Phebe VINING in the sum of £1320 conditioned for payment of £660 in manner hereinafter mentioned. Joseph WATSON & Mary his wife in consideration of sd debt & to secure the payment thereof & of the sum of 5s do grant & confirm to sd Phebe VINING all those 350 acres of land situate on the S side of Mispelion Creek in Sussex cnty, part of an original tract called Cedar Town (which by Indenture dtd herewith Phebe VINING executed immediately granted & conveyed unto sd Joseph WATSON) provided sd Joseph WATSON shall well & truly pay to sd Phebe VINING the sum of £210 on or before the 1st day of Jan next w/interest & further sum of £450 w/in fore years from date hereof w/interest this sd Obligation shall be void. Signed: Joseph WATTSON, Mary WATTSON. Wit: George PARKER. We the Subscribers Adorns in Fact to Phebe VINING the Mortgagee in the foregoing

Mortgage named do acknowledge to have received full satisfaction of the Principal & Interest therein mentioned for which we signed the above written acknowledgement as we believe in 1793 but the same being eaten by Mice we again sign this page in acknowledgement 11th month 12, 1795. Samuel Mier FISHER. Wit: Esther DRAPER. Jno RUSSELL, Rec'r.

O-14:441. Deed. 05 May 1791 Walter HUDSON of Sussex cnty, DE, blacksmith, & Mary his wife, of the one part for the sum of £115 sold unto Benjamin McILVAIN of same, taylor, of the other part. all that parcel of land containing 29 & 1/2 acres (being part of a larger tract containing 62 acres, situate in Angola Neck in Indian River Hundred which Henry NEILL & Mary his wife by Deed dtd 06 Feb 1789 sold to the afsd Walter HUDSON & sd Walter HUDSON & Mary his wife by Deed dtd 07 May year afsd sold to the afsd Benjamin McILVAIN, 32 & 1/2 acres of the afsd larger parcel of land) which sd 29 & 1/2 acres beginning at Bundock's Bridge on W side of road leading from Lewes Town to St Georges Chappel bounded by land of Jonathan STEPHENSON, to Bundocks Branch to a dam crossing same (excepting & reserving unto afsd Henry NEILL a clearance on the water course sufficing to prevent obstruction to a mill in case there should be one built & on road that crosses Bundocks Branch sufficient quantity of land for building a dam & mill house is reserved to prevent condemnation of sd stream of obstruction of a mill & all such land that be under water by raising a damn shall be subject to sd Henry NEILL w/o any restitution on behalf of sd Walter HUDSON whatsoever). Signed: Walter HUDSON, Mary HUDSON. Wit: Jno WILTBANK, ? PAYNTER Jr. Mary HUDSON, wife of Walter, was examined separate from her husband & did declare she became a party to these presents of her own free will. ? WILTBANK.

O-14:443. Deed. This Indenture made 07 Apr 1791 between George READ of New Castle, DE, gent, & Gertrude his wife, of the one part & William KENDRICK of Primehook Neck, Sussex cnty, DE, husbandman, of the other part. By Articles of Agreement dtd 30 Aug 1774 between Nathaniel YOUNG of Sussex cnty as the Attorney of the sd George READ of the one part & Samuel TRUITT of Sussex cnty of the other part it was agreed on behalf of sd George READ & Gertrude his wife that upon payment of £100 by Samuel TRUITT sd George READ w/in 4 weeks from date of same & the further sum of £35 w/lawful interest w/in 2 years after sd George & Gertrude would convey unto sd Samuel TRUITT 1/2 of that tract of land situate in Primehook Neck containing 200 acres & one undivided 1/5 part of a parcel of marsh containing 50 acres being in the marsh called Watsons Marsh w/a Covenant of Warranty hereinafter set forth by the same Articles of Agreement. Sd Samuel TRUITT having made his 1st payment of £100 w/in the time limits & thereof afterwards on 20 Jan 1779 by

Indorsement on sd Articles made in the presence of two attesting witnesses for the sum of £950 assigned all his right & title to sd Article unto Colling TRUITT. Sd Collins TRUITT afterwards 30 Dec 1780 by like Indorsement on same Articles for the sum of 1400 bushels of Indian Corn assigned all his right to sd Article unto Thomas WILSON who afterwards 03 Aug 1790 by written Agreement duly executed did contract w/sd William KENDRICK for the sale of all his right in the premises afsd & for obtaining a Deed from sd George READ & Gertrude his wife unto him sd William KENDRICK. George READ & Gertrude his wife in consideration of the sum of £35 & accruing interest together w/the afsd £100 heretofore paid grant & confirm unto sd William KENDRICK the one moiety of all that tract of land in Primehook Neck on Slaughter Creek being the upper corner of Mark DAVIS' land, land sold to John RICKETS, containing 200 acres & undivided 1/5 part of a tract of marsh containing 50 acres in the marsh called Watsons Marsh on the N side of a ditch in sd marsh & adjoining Caleb CIRWITHINS, late of Sussex cnty, dec'd, 21 Jun 1671 granted by Patent from Col Francis LOVELACE then Governor of NY to Richard PARROTT by Deed 04 Jan 1672 conveyed same unto Richard PERROTT his son upon whose death same descended to Richard PERROTT who by Deed dtd 29 Oct 1718 conveyed same to Bukley CODD Esq who having first granted divers tracts lying on S side of sd Neck by his last will dtd 29 Sep 1723 devised same residue to his wife Mary CODD who by her last will dtd 26 Sep 1733 devised same residue to her grt grndsn Thomas TILL who Oct 1760 d: Intestate w/in since DE state) leaving sd Gertrude his widow & only child William who after attained the age of 5 years 3 months 11 Dec 176? d: w/o siblings leaving Gertrude his mother to which the same residue of the neck of land afsd descended. Sd Gertrude afterwards md: sd George READ both now parties to these presents. Sd George & Gertrude READ guarantee against any claims to sd lands from John BELLAMY formerly f Sussex cnty, dec'd; or from Gabriel THOMAS also formerly of same cnty, dec'd; or from Capt Nathaniel PUKLE formerly of the city of Philadelphia, dec'd; or from the heirs of William TILL, dec'd; or from the heirs of Hezekiah WATSON, dec'd; or any of them, & shall warrant & forever defend by these presents conditioned upon sd William KENDRICK shall give notice in writing after commencement of such suit to sd George & Gertrude READ. George & Gertrude READ appoint Henry NIELL or Phillips KOLLOCK their Attorney. Signed: George READ, Gertrude READ. Wit: T McDONOUGH, John READ, Nicholas RIDGELY. 07 Apr 1791 Gertrude READ, wife of George, was examined separate from her husband and did declare she executed the above of her own free will. Signed: Tho McDONOUGH.

O-14:445. Deed. This Indenture made 26 Apr 1791 between Jacob WHITE & his wife Sarah of Sussex cnty, DE of the one part & Cornelius WILTBANK of cnty afsd, yeoman, of the other part. There is a parcel of marsh situate in Lewes, Rehoboth Hundred, cnty afsd, being part of a larger tract of land & marsh conveyed by Deed to the afsd Jacob WHITE dtd 30 Jan 1789 by his father Wixam WHITE which sd marsh is on W side of Elizabeth Drain, edge of Pagan Creek, road leading to Hawks Nest Hammock containing 40 acres of marsh. Jacob WHITE & Sarah his wife for the sum of £30 sold sd 40 acres to Cornelius WILTBANK. Jacob & Sarah WHITE appoint Rhoads SHANKLAND their Attorney. Signed: Jacob WHITE, Sally WHITE. Wit: Jno WILTBANK, Sarah WELSH (mark). Sarah WHITE, wife of Jacob, was examined separate from her husband and did declare she became a party thereto of her own free will. Signed: Jno WILTBANK.

O-14:446. Deed. This Indenture made 08 Jun 1790 between Nehemiah CAREY of Cedar Creek Hundred, Sussex cnty, DE, yeoman, & Elizabeth his wife of the one part & George RICKARDS of same, yeoman, of the other part. Abraham WYNKOOP in his lifetime by divers conveyances was seized in 2 contiguous tract of land in afsd hundred & cnty originally granted by 2 Patents to Thomas BOSTOCK & Daniel LEAK called Cyprus Hall & Pathalia & so being seized made his last will & testament dtd 15 Nov 1753 giving divers legacies to his children & devised as follows: all of my lands no above disposed being in Kent & Sussex cntys be sold & money therefrom be paid in discharge of the legacies I have bequeathed & appt'd Mary WYNKOOP, his wife; Phebe, Thomas & Benjamin WYNKOOP, his children, his Exec's which Mary & Thomas are since dec'd & sd Phebe & Benjamin survived. Benjamin WYNKOOP of city of Philadelphia, PA, one of the Exec's & Attorney for the other Exec's 21 Jul 1768 became bound Benjamin TRUITT of Sussex cnty in the sum of £200 conditioned if sd Benjamin WYNKOOP or Exec' of sd Abraham WYNKOOP should convey to sd Benjamin TRUITT a tract of land containing 144 & 1/2 acres situate in Sussex cnty being part of 2 larger tracts called Cyprus Hall & Pathalia & give Warrant to defend same from heirs of Abraham WYNKOOP & the heirs of Thomas BOSTOCK & Daniel LEAK, then sd Obligation to be void. Benjamin TRUITT thereafter d: Intestate & Admin was made to George WALTON the Elder of Sussex cnty. 10 Feb 1787 sd George WALTON was authorized to make sale of sd tract of land by Orphans Ct to pay debts & legacies of sd Benjamin TRUITT & sd George WALTON did sell afsd land unto sd Nehemiah CAREY but no Deed having been executed by sd Exec's of Abraham WYNKOOP to sd Benjamin TRUITT no lawful conveyance could be made to sd Nehemiah CAREY. Wherefore sd George WALTON as Admin by his Indorsement on sd Obligation did transfer to sd Nehemiah CAREY the above cited Obligation & by virtue of Order of Orphans Ct all claim & title sd Benjamin TRUITT had in the lands for value rec'd did thereby direct sd Benjamin WYNKOOP to convey sd lands & premises unto sd Nehemiah CAREY. (At execution of Deed of Indenture from sd Phebe VINING & Benjamin WYNKOOP, surviving Execs of sd Abraham WYNKOOP, dec'd, dtd 25 Jun 1789 unto sd Nehemiah CAREY). Nehemiah CAREY & Elizabeth his wife, for the sum of £247 sold to George RICKARDS all that part of the cited 2 tracts of parcels of land situate in Cedar Creek Hundred bounded by land sold to Thomas CAREY, George COVAN's land, land late of John DRAPER, land of John TRUITT, containing 144 & 1/2 acres. Signed: Nehemiah CARY, Elizabeth CARY. Wit: Thomas EVANS, Curtis SHOCKLEY. Elizabeth, wife of above Nehemiah CARY, being of full age was examined separate from her husband and did declare she became a part to the above of her own free will. Signed: Charles POLK.

O-14:449. Deed. This Indenture made 08 Nov 1790 between George GREER of Little Creek Hundred, Sussex cnty, DE, yeoman, of the one part & Jacob MERAIN of same, yeoman, of the other part. There is a tract of land situate in Little Creek Hundred, cnty afsd, part of which was granted by Patent dtd 05 Apr 1684 to George OLIPHANT & called George's Choice & also 4 acres out of a tract called Small Chance w/82 acres & 90 sq perches of land resurveyed from a tract called Moose's Lott which sd Resurvey w/the Patent & 4 acres afsd contains in the whole 133 acres & 10 sq perches of land. Sd 133 acres & 10 sq perches of land became the property of above George GREER part to these presents. Sd land bounded by a ditch, land of William MOORE's & land of Jonathan CATHELL. George GREER for the sum of £106 9s hath sold unto Jacob MERAIN all his right & title to above sd 133 acres & 10 sq perches of land. George GREER appoints Peter WHITE or Daniel RODNEY, merchants, or Richard GREEN, gent, his Attorney. Signed: George GREER, Eunice GREER. Wit: Wm COULTER, Edward WILLIAMS (mark).

O-14:450. Bill of Sale. Isaac BRADLEY Esq of Sussex cnty, DE for the sum of £173 2s 7p paid by John RICHARDS do grant & deliver unto sd John RICHARDS the following goods & chattels: one negro man called Boatle, one negro woman called Cloe, one negro woman called Bridge, three negro boys by names Jacob, Elluk & Bob, 4 horses, 4 cows and calves, 6 head of sheep, 20 hogs, 1 still, 1 set smiths tools, 5 beds, 2 walnut tables, 1 desk, 1 case of draws, 1 looking glass, 18 sitting chairs. But when debt above shall be satisfied then the above shall be entirely released unto sd Isaac BRADLEY. 13 Dec 1788. Signed: Isaac BRADLEY. Wit: Thomas LAWS, David RICHARDS.

O-14:451. Bond of Conveyance. Peter Fretwell WRIGHT of Lewes, Rehoboth Hundred, Sussex cnty, DE, Esq, is held & firmly bound unto John ORR of same in the sum of £540. 09 Feb 1789. Condition of sd Obligation is such that sd Peter

Fretwell WRIGHT shall make over & convey unto John ORR a good & sufficient Deed of Sale for that messuage & plantation & tract of land whereon sd Peter Fretwell WRIGHT now resides bounded on SE by the main road, on SW by lands of Phillips KOLLOCK & John RODNEY & NW by South Street on NE by lands of sd John ORR containing 25 acres. Signed: Peter F WRIGHT. Wit: D HALL, Richard HOWARD.

O-14:452. Bond. Edmond DICKERSON Jr of Sussex cnty, DE is firmly bound unto Edmond DICKERSON Sr in the sum of £500 dtd 16 Jun 1791. Edmond DICKERSON Sr by Indenture dtd herewith conveyed unto above bound Edmond DICKERSON Jr a parcel of land situate in Broadkiln Hundred containing 152 acres, condition of above Obligation is such that if above bound Edmond DICKERSON Jr do not sell above land any time during the life of sd Edmond DICKERSON Sr this Obligation shall be void. Signed: Edmond DICKERSON Jr. Wit: ? HAZZARD, W HARRISON.

O-14:452. Petition. Peter Fretwell WRIGHT Esq by conveyance dtd 09 Feb 1789 become bound unto John ORR of Sussex cnty, DE in penalty of £540 for the conveyance of a messuage & tract of land situate in Lewes, Rehoboth Hundred containing 25 acres & sd WRIGHT d: before execution of sd conveyance. Elizabeth WRIGHT & Fretwell WRIGHT, Exec's request an Order to execute a Deed for sd land to sd John ORR in discharge of sd Bond. Signed: Elizabeth WRIGHT, Fretwell WRIGHT. Petition granted.

O-14:452. Deed. Peter Fretwell WRIGHT Esq by Obligatory writing dtd 09 Feb 1789 bound himself unto John ORR in the penal sum of £540 with condition sd WRIGHT to convey sufficient Deed of Sale for all the messuage & plantation whereon sd WRIGHT then resided bounded on the SE by the main road & SW by lands of Phillips KOLLOCK & John RODNEY & on NW by ? Street & NE by lands of sd John ORR with condition sd Obligation to be void proved in Ct of Com Pleas 16 Jun 1791 & rec'd in Book O, No 14, folio 491. Sd Peter Fretwell after making the Obligation & before making conveyance d: having made his last will & testament dtd 07 Mar 1791 & therein appt Elizabeth WRIGHT & sd Fretwell WRIGHT, Execs. Sd Elizabeth & Fretwell WRIGHT as Execs of sd Peter Fretwell WRIGHT requested & rec'd Order of Ct of Com Pleas to execute a Deed to sd John ORR for the messuage & parcel of land afsd & not yet conveyed in discharge of sd Obligation. Elizabeth WRIGHT & Fretwell WRIGHT, Exec's afsd in consideration of the sum of £270 paid by sd John ORR to afsd Peter Fretwell WRIGHT during his lifetime do grant Deed of Sale to sd John ORR for afsd messuage & parcel of land containing 25 acres as above described. Signed: Elizabeth WRIGHT, Fretwell WRIGHT. Wit: D HALL, Kitty HALL.

O-14:454. This Indenture made 09 May 1791 between Rowland BEVINS & Sarah his wife of Sussex cnty, DE, of the one part & George MITCHELL, Robert HOUSTON, William MOOR, Rhoads SHANKLAND, John COLLINS & Daniel POLK, a majority of the Commissioners of Sussex cnty apptd by Act of General Assembly in Jan 1791 of the other part. Rowland BEVINS is seized of a parcel of land situate in Broadkiln Hundred on the S side of the road leading from Lewes to Northwest Fork surveyed & laid out for Richard PETTYJOHN or his widow Hannah containing 300 acres. Sd Rowland & Sarah his wife for the sum of £25 paid by the above Commissioners do sell unto sd Commissioners all that parcel of land bounded by land of Abraham HARRIS, Rowland BEVINS, Benj'm BUTLER & Joshua PEPPER, 50 acres of land bought by afsd Commissioners of Abraham HARRIS, containing 25 acres of land for the use of Sussex cnty agreeable to the Act of Assembly Untitled an Act for Removing the Seat of Justice from Lewes to More Central Part of Sussex cnty. Sd Rowland BEVINS & Sarah his wife appt John EVANS, Thomas LAWS or Seth GRIFFITH their Attorney. Signed: Rowland BEVINS (mark), Sarah BEVINS (mark). Wit: And' STANBURROUGH, John LAWS, Charles POLK. Sarah BEVINS was examined separate from her husband and did declare she signed the above Deed of her own free will. Signed: Charles POLK. 09 May 1791.

O-14:456. This Indenture made 09 May 1791 between Joshua PETTER & Elizabeth his wife, of Broadkiln Hundred, Sussex cnty, DE of the one part & George MITCHELL, Robert HOUSTON, William MOORE, Rhoads SHANKLAND, John COLLINS & Daniel POLK, being major part of Commissioners apptd by Act of General Assembly Jan 1791 untitled an Act for Removing the Seat of Justice from Lewes to More Central Part of Sussex cnty. Joshua PEPPER & Elizabeth his wife for the sum of £2 sold unto sd Commissions a parcel of land situate in Sussex cnty near the center of sd cnty in Broadkiln Hundred w/in ? miles of Ebenezer PETTYJOHN being part of a larger tract of land whereon sd Joshua PEPPER lives containing 1 acre bounded by land bought by sd Commissioners of Abraham HARRIS. Joshua PEPPER & Elizabeth his wife appt John EVANS, Thomas LAWS or Seth GRIFFITH their Attorney. Signed: Joshua PEPPER (mark), Elizabeth PEPPER (mark). Wit: John LAWS, Charles POLK, Adenijah STANBURROUGH. Elizabeth PEPPER was examined separate from her husband and did declare she signed the above of her own free will. Signed: Charles POLK. 09 May 1791.

O-14:457. This Indenture made 09 May 1791 between Abraham HARRIS & Director his wife of Broadkiln Hundred, Sussex cnty, DE of the one part & George MITCHELL, Robert HOUSTON, William MOORE, Rhoads SHANKLAND, John

COLLINS & Daniel POLK, being major part of Commissioners apptd by Act of General Assembly Jan 1791 untitled an Act for Removing the Seat of Justice from Lewes to More Central Part of Sussex cnty. Abraham HARRIS & Director his wife for the sum of £50 hath sold unto sd George MITCHELL, Robert HOUSTON, William MOORE, Rhoads SHANKLAND, John COLLINS & Daniel POLK a parcel of land situate 2 miles of Ebenezer PETTYJOHN's in Broadkiln, cnty afsd & in the center of sd cnty being part of a larger tract of land whereon the sd Abraham HARRIS now lives containing 188 acres bounded by land of Rowland BEVINS, Benjamin BUTLER & Joshua PEPPER, containing 50 acres of land. Abraham HARRIS & Director his wife appoint John EVANS, Thomas LAWS or Seth GRIFFITH their Attorney. Signed: Abraham HARRIS, Director HARRIS (mark). Wit: Trustin L POLK, Leven CONNOWAY, Charles POLK. Director HARRIS, wife of Abraham, was examined separate from her husband and did declare she signed the above of her own free will. Signed: Charles POLK. 09 May 1791.

O-14:459. Bond of Conveyance. John CLOWES, mariner, of Sussex cnty, DE is bound unto Mary PARRIMORE of sd cnty, widow, in the sum of £30 dtd 13 Apr 1781. Elnathan INKLY late of cnty afsd d: intestate seized of 217 acres which became the right of his 3 dtrs viz: Anna, Sarah & Mary. Anna & Sarah sold their parts of sd land, Mary d: intestate leaving issue one dtr who also d: intestate in her minority leaving no issue. Pariz CHIPMAN her father being next nearest kin to his dtr sold to the above bound John CLOWES Mary's part of the afsd land. John SPENCER Esq & Matthew PARIMORE assignees to the afsd Anne & Sarah had divided the whole between them agreeing that SPENCER should hold all on the SE side & PARIMORE all on the NW side. Condition of Bond is such that if John CLOWES by Deed of Sale confirms unto Mary PAREMORE all his right & title that afsd Mary INKLY had in sd land on NW side this Obligation to be void. Signed: John CLOWES. Wit: Isaac ALLEN, Noble TULL.

O-14:460. Petition. John CLOWES by his Bond dtd 15 Apr 1781 became bound unto Mary PARREMORE of Sussex cnty, DE in the sum of £30 w/condition that sd John CLOWES should make sufficient Deed confirming unto sd Mary PARREMORE a parcel of land situate in Broadkiln Hundred. The consideration money hath been fully paid. Mary CLOWES & Isaac CLOWES. Execs of John CLOWES, late of sd cnty petitioned & were granted an Order to execute sd lands to afsd Mary PARREMORE 16 Jun 1791. Signed: Mary CLOWES, Isaac CLOWES.

O-14:460. Power of Attorney. George MITCHELL, Robert HOUSTON, John

COLLINS, Rhoads SHANKLAND & William MOORE, Commissioners for building the Court House appoint William BELL to collect the several sums from respective subscribers to the building of the Court House. 21 Jun 1791. Signed: Rhoads SHANKLAND, George MITCHELL, William MOORE, Rob't HOUSTON, John COLLINS.

O-14:461. Deed. This Indenture made 06 May 1791 between Mary CLOWES & Isaac CLOWES, Exec's to the last will & testament of John CLOWES Esq, dec'd, of Sussex cnty, DE of the one part & Mary PAREMORE of the other part. Elnathan INKLY late of cnty afsd, dec'd, intestate seized of 230 acres of land in Broadkiln Hundred, cnty afsd, at the head of Long Bridge Branch on the N side adjoining lands then of Dav? ----. Sd Elnathan INKLEY left issue three dtrs viz: Anna, Mary & Sarah INKLY amongst whom the sd lands were divided equally. Sd Anna & Sarah sold their equal third parts which sd parts are now in the possession of the heirs of John SPENCER Esq, dec'd and of the heirs of Mathew PARIMORE, dec'd. Mary INKLEY md: Paris CHIPMAN by whom she had issue, one dtr, and she d: intestate having never disposed of her equal 1/3 part of the afsd land. The dtr of afsd Mary INKLY also dec'd intestate & w/o issue have never disposed of her equal 1/3 part of sd land. It is therefore assumed Mary INKLEY's equal 1/3 part of afsd tract of 233 acres was the lawful property of the afsd Parez CHIPMAN, her father being the next nearest of kin. Pariz CHIPMAN by his Deed of Sale dtd 26 Sep 1774 conveyed sd equal 1/3 part to sd John CLOWES Esq. Sd John SPENCER Esq & Matthew PARRIMORE assignees of afsd Anne & Sarah had divided the whole of the sd tract of land between them agreeing sd SPENCER should hold all on the SE side & PARIMORE all on the NW side which is now in the possession of sd Mary PARRIMORE. Sd John CLOWES Esq by his Bond dtd 30 Apr 1781 sold all his right & title sd Mary INKLY had to sd lands to Mary PARRIMORE on the NW side. Mary CLOWES & Isaac CLOWES Exec's of the afsd John CLOWES for the sum of £15 sold & conveyed unto sd Mary PAREMORE all the afsd lands lying on the NW side of the afsd Division. Signed: Mary CLOWES, Isaac CLOWES. Wit: Isaac DRAPER, William WITTEN.

O-14:462. Deed. 16 Jun 1791 Edmond DICKERSON Sr of Sussex cnty, DE of the one part for the sum of £150 hath sold unto Edmond DICKERSON Jr of same of the other part a parcel of land situate in Broadkiln Hundred beginning on E side of the head of Long Bridge Branch bounded by land of Richard PARREMORE, last corner of CHASE's land, containing 152 acres being part of lands to Edmond DICKERSON conveyed by several Deeds from Joseph CORD & Jane his wife, & from Thomas HAND, Admin of Samuel HAND, dec'd. Signed: Edmond DICKERSON. Wit: G HAZZARD, W HARRISON.

O-14:463. Deed. William ROBBINS & Aaron MARSHALL of Sussex cnty, DE, in Ct of Com Pleas recovered a judgement against Elizabeth MARSHALL, Admin'x of John MARSHALL, late of cnty afsd, pilot, dec'd, for the sum of £85 9s 6p together w/costs of suit upon a mortgage recorded by afsd John MARSHALL in is lifetime dtd 07 Feb 1788 whereby sd John MARSHALL did convey to William ROBINS & Aaron MARSHALL all that messuage & lot of land situate in Lewes whereon sd John MARSHALL then dwelt in length 200 feet & in breadth 60 bounded on the front by Lewes Creek, on the SE w/a lott of land formerly belonging to Jacob PHILLIPS Esq, dec'd now of Hannah NUNEZ, on SW w/Second St and NW w/lotts formerly belonging to John & Albutus JACOBS then in possession of John BUSTON now the property of John CRAIG, as by Deed of Mortgage recorded in Liber B, folio 310. 05 Aug 1789 the late Sheriff of Sussex cnty was ordered to levy sd debt & damages & have sd monies to Ct 04 Nov next to render to sd William ROBINS & Aaron MARSHALL. Sd Sheriff, Peter Fretwell WRIGHT, after due & public notice sold afsd lott of land at public sale to Aaron MARSHALL for the use of William ROBINS, for the sum of £90 be being the highest bidder. Sd Peter Fretwell WRIGHT was removed from office before he executed Deed of Conveyance to sd William ROBINS for sd land. Thomas EVANS, Sheriff, in consideration of the full sum of £90 paid to previous Sheriff WRIGHT & further consideration of 5s doth confirm unto sd William ROBINS the messuage & lott afore described. Signed: Thomas EVANS, Sheriff. Wit: Robert HOOD, Joshua HALL. 16 Jun 1791.

O-14:465. Bond of Conveyance. John EVANS Sr of Sussex cnty, DE stands bound unto John EVANS (LeaSide) in the penal sum of £20,000 to be paid unto John EVANS (Leaside) dtd 09 Aug 1780. Condition is such that if above bound John EVANS Sr doth make over to afsd John EVANS (Leaside) all his title of a tract of land called North Pealterton, also 50 acres called TimberLand formerly bought of Joshua EVANS, also 20 acres of land bought of John ORIONS called Atkins Lot, also a new survey on North Pealterton, also all the marsh and pasture ground below Jaquish HUTSONs only reserved a right for son William EVANS to turn in his own dry creatures as far as 6 or 8 head together w/the plantation where the afsd John EVANS (Leaside) now dwelleth then this Obligation to be void. Signed: John EVANS Sr. Wit: William CORD, Elijah EVANS.

O-14:466. Deed. This Indenture made 13 Jun 1791 between Thomas PARREMORE of Sussex cnty, DE, yeoman, of th one part & Peter DOLBEE, yeoman, of same of the other part. Matthew PARREMORE late of afsd cnty was possessed of a parcel of land containing 100 acres of Patent Land called Friendship & 17?6 he obtained a Proprietaries warrant of resurvey which was laid on the afsd 100 acres pattent & afsd Matthew PARREMORE making his last will & testament bequeathed the afsd lands to his son Ezekiel PARREMORE who 23 May last delivered to Tho's PASSEMORE a sufficient Deed of Conveyance for all the afsd lands. Thomas PARREMORE for the sum of £14 6s hath sold unto Peter DOLBEE 22 acres of land being part of the afsd pattent land & part of the survey viz 8 acres of pattent & 14 acres of the resurvey bounded by land called Wrights Choice situate in Broad Creek Hundred and in a Neck of land called Wimbojoceum. Signed: Thomas PARREMORE (mark). Wit: Jesse SAUNDERS, Joseph PARREMORE (mark).

O-14:467. Deed. This Indenture made 16 Jun 1791 between Thomas EVANS high Sheriff of Sussex cnty, DE of the one part & James BRATTEN & John MITCHELL of same, merchants, & Cyrus MITCHELL of Dorchester cnty, MD, gent, of the other part. There is a parcel of land situate in Little Creek Hundred originally granted by Patent w/additions thereunto added by Resurvey. Sd parcel of land was the right of Elijah WOOTTEN. Two writs issued by the Ct of Com Pleas dtd 09 Feb directed the Sheriff to levy against the estates of James TRUSHAM & Elijah WOOTEN late of Sussex cnty, yeomen, a debt of £300 which James BRATTON for the use of the Exec's of John MITCHELL had recovered against them as also £3 9s 1p. Sd Sheriff took in execution of sd writs two tracts of land, one called Hounds Ditch containing 200 acres of land, the other known as Calloways Neglect containing 70 acres the property of sd Elijah WOOTEN & that Isaac COOPER & Athanasius MARTIN assessed value of sd land to be insufficient to satisfy sd debts w/in 7 years whereupon sd Sheriff by Ct Order exposed sd lands to Public Sale & sold sd Elijah WOOTEN's land unto afsd James BRATTEN he being the highest bidder for the sum of £37 10s. Signed: Thomas EVANS, Sheriff. Wit: James P WILSON, Woodman STOCKLEY Jr.

O-14:468. Deed. Mary Magdeline HALL, Joseph HALL & David HALL, Admins of David HALL, late of Sussex cnty, DE, Esq, lately recovered against George WILTBANK, late of cnty afsd, a debt of £37 1s 6p as also 50s for costs & damages & writ dtd 04 Aug 1790 by Ct of Comm Pleas ordered same to be levied against the estate of George WILTBANK. Sheriff put the messuage & 1/4 part of a lot of ground to Public Sale by writ of sd Ct of Comm Pleas & same was purchased by Henry NIELL of cnty afsd, gent, for the sum of £41 10s on 24 Dec 1790 he being the highest bidder. Thomas EVANS, Sheriff, doth confirm unto Henry NEILL all that before mentioned messuage & 1/4 part of a lot of ground situate on Lewes Creek, adjoining the lot formerly belonging to the Rev Matthias HARRIS & the lot belonging to the heirs of Alexander WOLLESTON, dec'd. Signed: Thomas EVANS, Sheriff. Wit: Wm HARRISON, Nath'l MITCHELL.

O-14:469. Deed. This Indenture made 23 May 1791 between Ezekiel PARREMORE of Sussex cnty, DE, of the one part and Thomas PARREMORE of same of the other part. Matthew PARREMORE, late of the cnty, was seized of a tract of land & 29 Nov 1783 made his last will & testament & bequeathed to his son Thomas PARREMORE the use and property of his dwelling plantation & all land thereunto belonging to the whole w/a new Resurvey running from the old and the whole to be his right until Matthew's son, Ezekiel PARREMORE, arrives to the age of 21 and no longer. He then bequeathed to his son Ezekiel PARREMORE when he comes to age his afsd dwelling plantation w/100 acres of land called Friendship, also the new resurvey running from the old land to be his when he is 21 years of age & to be in the care of his Exec until he comes of age. By examination it is found that t he afsd 100 acres of land called Friendship is part of a tract containing by Patent 140 acres of land granted to John Niell SAUNDERS by his Lordships Patent dtd 27 Aug 1760 situate then in Worcester cnty, MD but not in Broad Creek Hundred, Sussex cnty, DE. John Neill SAUNDERS did about the 1769 convey same to Matthew PARREMORE 100 acres of & that 177? sd PARREMORE obtained a Proprietaries Warrant of Resurvey & he laid on an enlargement. After making the afsd will Matthew PARREMORE departed this life leaving his afsd son Thomas PARREMORE in possession thereof until his son Ezekiel PARREMORE came of 21 years of age. Ezekiel PARREMORE for the sum of £100 sells unto Thomas PARREMORE the afsd 100 acres of land called Friendship and likewise the Resurvey situate in Broad Creek Hundred on a neck of land called Wimbosocium. Ezekiel PARREMORE appoints Joseph MILLER, John Wise BATSON or John WOOLF his Attorney. Signed: Ezekiel PARREMORE (mark). Wit: Jesse SAUNDERS, Peter DOLBEE.

O-14:471. Deed. This Indenture made 01 Feb 1791 between Jacob HAZZARD of Sussex cnty, DE & Ann his wife, of the one part & Isaac DRAPER of same (son of Samuel DRAPER) of the other part. Joseph ELDRIDGE & Mary ELDRIDGE late of cnty afsd, dec'd, by virtue of their last will & testaments devised unto their two grandsons Thomas MOORE & Obadiah ELDRIDGE a messuage, tanyard, orchard & parcel of land situate in Lewes, Rehoboth Hundred, Sussex cnty, DE. May term 1778 of Ct of Com Pleas Thomas MOORE by Jacob MOORE Esq his Attorney & Obediah ELDRIDGE by Jabez FISHER his Guardian petitioning an amiable partition between them. By consideration of sd Ct & both parties Messrs Reece WOOLF, Anderson PARKER & Samuel PAYNTER were apptd to make division of the afsd estate which was done. By motion of Thomas MOORE by Jacob MOORE his Attorney the Partition was set aside. By consent of both parties & John RUSSELL, Rhoads SHANKLAND & Perry PRETTYMAN were apptd to make partition thereof. Thomas MOORE as his full share beginning at S side of the road from Lewes to Frames, corner of lot of Thomas FISHER, containing 7 acres. Sd Thomas MOORE by Indenture dtd 05 Nov 1778 sold sd land to Peter Fretwell WRIGHT as rec'd in Book M, No 12, folio 225. Sd Peter Fretwell WRIGHT by Indenture dtd 19 Jun 1788 sold the afsd unto w/in named Jacob HAZZARD by Indenture rec'd in Book O, No 14, folio 23. Jacob HAZZARD & Ann his wife for the sum of £109 have sold sd lands unto Isaac DRAPER together w/tanyard, tan vats, etc. Signed: Jacob HAZZARD, Ann HAZZARD. Wit: Peter ROBINSON, Hercules KOLLOCK. Ann HAZZARD, wife of Jacob, was examined separate from her husband and did declare she became a party thereto of her own free will. Signed: Peter ROBINSON.

O-14:472. Petition. 07 Jun 1791 William BELL Jr, admin of John BELL, late of Sussex cnty, DE, yeoman, dec'd, petitions whereas John BELL was seized of a tract of land situate in Broadkiln Hundred containing 140 acres & by his Bond dtd 15 Dec 1778 bound himself unto James REYNOLDS Sr in the sum of £770 to be paid unto sd James REYNOLDS w/condition that sd John BELL on recp't of £385 from sd James REYNOLDS sd BELL would convey a parcel of land situate in Broadkiln Hundred containing 140 acres of land joining lands of William REYNOLDS, Solomon DODD & lands in possession of James WOODS, then sd Bond to be void. Afsd James REYNOLDS by his Bond dtd 14 Oct 1784 bound himself unto Richard BLOXOM in the sum of £360 to be paid to Richard BLOXSOM w/condition that sd James REYNOLDS on recp't of £188 paid by Richard BLOXOM would make Deed of Sale for a tract of land in Broadkiln Hundred containing 100 acres adjoining lands formerly the property of William REYNOLDS, Solomon DODD & lands then in the possession of Richard ABBOT, the sd Bond then to be void. James BELL after making the Bond for the conveyance of the afsd 140 acres unto James REYNOLDS & before he executed any Deed d: Intestate whereof Admin of his estate was committed to Petitioner, William BELL Jr. The sum for which John BELL sold sd lands having been paid & sd James REYNOLDS after making Bond for the conveyance of 100 acres of land part of the 140 acres, unto sd Richard BLOXOM before he executed Deed d: Intestate. No Admin has been granted on the Estate of sd James REYNOLDS thereby enabling the estate to receive conveyance from Petitioner as Admin for John BELL for the 140 acres. Petitioner requests to make conveyance unto afsd Richard BLOXOM for the 100 acres of land in discharge of the afsd Bond. £3 hath been paid by Hannah BLOXOM for the additional 40 acres of the 140 acres. Sd Richard BLOXOM since d: Intestate leaving Hannah his widow and issue 5 children namely Elizabeth, William, his eldest surviving son, David, Fisher and Margaret BLOXOM to whom his right in sd 100 acres of land descended, 1/3 part thereof in 3 equal parts to be devised unto the afsd Hannah BLOXOM widow during the term of her natural life, 2/6 part of the remaining 2/3 unto the afsd William BLOXOOM the eldest surviving son, 1/6 part thereof unto Elizabeth BLOXOM, dtr of Intestate; 1/6 part thereof unto David BLOXOM son of the Intestate; 1/6 part thereof unto Fisher BLOXOM son of the Intestate; & the remaining part thereof unto Margaret BLOXOM dtr of the Intestate together w/the revisions of the 1/3 or Dower of the afsd Hannah the widow & relict of the Intestate after he deceased in like manner to be divided unto the afsd William, Elizabeth, David, Fisher & Margaret. Petitioner requests the Ct to issue an Order empowering him as Admin for John BELL to make sufficient Deed to Hannah BLOXOM, widow of Richard BLOXOM, dec'd, William, Elizabeth, David, Fisher & Margaret BLOXOM heirs of sd dec'd in discharge of sd Bonds. Signed: William BELL Jr, Admin. Indorsed on the back thereof 17 Jun 1791.

O-14:474. Deed. John BELL late of Broadkiln Hundred, Sussex cnty, DE, yeoman, dec'd, was seized of a tract of land situate in Broadkiln Hundred containing 140 acres called William's Tract & by his Bond dtd 15 Dec 1778 bound himself unto James REYNOLDS to convey unto James REYNOLDS sd 140 acres of land adjoining lands of William REYNOLDS, Solomon DODD & lands then in possession of James WOODS sd Bond to be void. Afsd James REYNOLDS by his Bond dtd 14 Oct 1784 bound himself to convey sufficient Deed for 100 acres of land adjoining lands of William REYNOLDS, Solomon DODD & lands then in possession of Richard ABBOTT, sd Obligation then to be void. John BELL after making sd Bond & before executing sufficient Deed d: Intestate whereupon Admin of his estate fell to William BELL party to these presents. Sd James REYNOLDS after making Bond to Richard BLOXOM & before executing sufficient Deed d: Intestate. There hath been no Admin on the estate of sd James REYNOLDS to receive conveyance from the Grantor, Admin for sd John BELL, to make conveyance to afsd Richard BLOXOM, his heirs, etc in discharge of sd Bonds. Whereas all consideration monies have been paid, whereas Richard BLOXOM hath since d: Intestate leaving Hannah his widow & 5 children namely Elizabeth, William his eldest surviving son, David, Fisher & Margaret BLOXOM to whom his estate descends: 1/3 unto the afsd Hannah BLOXOM, widow, during the term of her natural life; 2/6 of remaining 2/3 to William BLOXOM eldest surviving son; 1/6 unto Elizabeth BLOXOM dtr of Intestate; 1/6 unto David BLOXOM son of Intestate; 1/6 unto Fisher BLOXOM son of Intestate & remainder to Margaret BLOXOM dtr of Intestate together w/Revision of Dower right of Hannah BLOXOM, widow. Whereas Ct ordered sd William BELL, Admin of sd John BELL, to execute sufficient Deed to sd Hannah, Elizabeth, William, David, Fisher & Margaret BLOXOM heirs of sd Richard BLOXOM. William BELL do grant unto Hannah, William, Elizabeth, David, Fisher & Margaret BLOXOM all the afsd 100 acres of land being part of a larger tract situate in Broadkiln Hundred called William's Tract. 17 Jun 1791. Signed: William BELL Jr, Admin. Wit: Phillips KOLLOCK, Jno RUSSEL.

O-14:477. Deed. This Indenture made 10 May 1791 between Richard LITTLE of Lewes, Sussex cnty, DE, gent, & Sarah his wife of the one part & Hugh SMITH of same, millwright, of the other part. Thomas FENWICK late of Sussex cnty, dec'd, was seized of 12 acres in the town of Lewes between Market & South streets on one of the branches of Pigeon Creek, & by his last will & testament dtd 02 Mar 1778 devised the afsd land unto his son James FENWICK who by his Deed of Sale dtd 03 Jul 1722 conveyed same to Simon KOLLOCK Esq who being so seized by his Deed dtd 04 Mar 1729 sold afsd land unto John PRICE who beings so seized of afsd land by his writing Obligatory dtd 27 Sep 1737 contracted to sell afsd lands unto John SIMONTON who afterwards d: Intestate before he executed Deed for same. William TULL Admin of sd John PRICE by Order of Ct of Comm Pleas by Deed conveyed sd land to John SIMONTON who d: seized of afsd lands having first made his last will & testament dtd 29 May 1751 wherein he devised the house wherein he then lived & a small piece of land thereto adjoining called a garden unto his son John SIMONTON & devised the remainder of afsd 12 acres unto his 2 youngest dtrs Comfort & Elizabeth SIMONTON to be equally divided. John SIMONTON the younger & Comfort SIMONTON both d: Intestate & w/o issue leaving 4 sisters: Jennet the wife of Nathaniel BAILY, Sarah the wife of John SHANKLAND, Mary the wife of James DAVIDSON & afsd Elizabeth wife of Noble LEWIS to whom sd land descended. Nathaniel BAILY & Jennet his wife, John SHANKLAND & Sarah his wife, James DAVISON & Mary his wife by their several Deeds of Release conveyed all their right to the afsd lands unto John SIMONTON the younger & the afsd Comfort SIMONTON unto the afsd Noble LEWIS & Elizabeth his wife who being so seized by their Deed dtd 29 May 1773 sold afsd land unto Phillips KOLLOCK Esq who together w/Penelope his wife by their Deed dtd 24 Mar 1779 sold afsd land unto Uriah HAZZARD who together w/Sarah his wife by their Deed dtd 15 Jan 1791 sold afsd land for the quantity of 12 acres unto Richard LITTLE party to these presents. Richard LITTLE & Sarah his wife for the sum of £210 hath sold unto Hugh SMITH the afsd land containing 12 acres. Signed: Richard LITTLE, Sarah LITTLE. Wit: Jno WILTBANK, Isaac TURNER. Sarah LITTLE, wife of Richard, was examined separate from her husband and did declare she became a part to the above of her own free will. Signed: Jno WILTBANK.

O-14:479. Deed. This Indenture made 31 Dec 1778 between Richard BLOXOM of Broadkill Hundred, Sussex cnty, DE, yeoman, & Hannah his wife (late Hannah

AUBREY) of the one part & David TRAIN of Lewes, Sussex cnty, yeoman, of the other part. Hance BRUSTON late of cnty afsd, dec'd, was seized of a parcel of land situate on the banks of Lewes Creek in Lewes Hundred cnty afsd adjoining to the NE Lewes River, to the NW land formerly belonging to Stephen GREEN now the heirs of Wrixam LEWIS Esq, dec'd, to the SE lands formerly belonging to John WORWICK(?) late of sd cnty dec'd now in the possession of Jacob KOLLOCK Esq. Hance BRUXTON being so seized mortgaged same unto Jacob KOLLOCK Sr & Ryves HOLD Esq (the Trustees of the GLO) which not being paid the sd Mortgage the land & premises afsd were extended. By Order of Ct of Comm Pleas William SHANKLAND (then Sheriff of sd cnty) seized afsd land & exposed same to Public Sale & sold sd mortgaged land to Abigail, Elizabeth, Ann & Hannah AUBREY (which sd Hannah AUBREY is party to these presents) by Deed dtd 02 Feb 1746 rec'd in Liber G, No 7, folio 149. Sd Abigail md: Joseph SYMS & sd Elizabeth md: William HENRY which sd Joseph SYMS & sd Abigail his wife by their Deed dtd 05 Sep 175? & sd William HENRY & sd Elizabeth his wife by their Deed dtd 09 Aug 1759 & afsd Ann by her Deed dtd 31 Jan 1763 did sell afsd lands unto the afsd Jacob KOLLOCK Jr. Richard BLOXOM & Hannah his wife for the sum of £18 lawful money of PA sold unto David TRAIN the afsd land. Signed: Richard BLOXOM (mark), Hannah BLOXOM (mark). Wit: James DOUGHERTY, Jno RODNEY. Hannah BLOXOM, wife of afsd Richard, was examined separate from her husband and did declare she became a party to above of her own free will. Signed: Jno RODNEY.

O-14:481. Deed. This Indenture made 07 Jul 1780 between Moses LYNN of the twp of Fairfield, CT of the one part & John COLLINS of Sussex cnty, DE of the other part. Capt Aaron LYNN late of Somerset cnty, MD, dec'd, was seized of one tract of land called Wallbrook originally granted by the Lord Proprietor of MD to Edward FOWLER for the quantity of 260 acres & sd Aaron LYNN was also seized to one other tract of land called Aaron's Folly granted to him by the sd Lord Proprietor for the quantity of 150 acres & in like manner was seized of one other tract called Carters Lott containing 100 acres. Sd Aaron LYNN 14 Aug 1742 obtained a warrant to resurvey to afsd tracts called Wallbrook & Aaron's Folly to amend errors committed in the original survey w/liberty to add any vacant land contiguous to same by virtue of same was resurveyed & certificate thereof returned into the land office of MD & the whole included in one tract called Aaron's Chance which w/the surplus & vacant land contains the quantity of 1009 acres of land and being so seized d: Intestate by means whereof the same descended to the afsd Moses LYNN as Eldest son to sd Aaron. Sd Moses LYNN became seized of two tracts of land, one called Chance containing 12 acres & the other called Lott containing 9 acres by virtue of a Deed duly executed by Terrence BURK eldest representative & heir to

John BURK late of Somerset cnty, MD, dec'd, dtd 27 May 1780. Moses LYNN for the sum of £30,000 sold unto sd John COLLINS the afsd tracts of land called Wallbrook, Aaron's Folly, Carter's Lott, Aaron's Chance, Chance & Lott, containing in the whole 1030 acres of land situate in Little Creek, in Little Creek Hundred, Sussex cnty, DE & now leased by sd Moses to sundry tenants now occupying same whose leases or terms will expire 17 Dec next, including grist mill & saw mill. Sd Moses LYNN appoints Major Henry FISHER, the Honorable John CLOWES or Simon KOLLOCK Esq his Attorney. Signed: Moses LYNN. Wit: Seven VAUGHAN, Betty VAUGHAN.

O-14:483. Deed. This Indenture made 04 Nov 1780 between John COLLINS of Sussex cnty, DE of the one part & Phillips FORGUSSON of Baltimore town of the other part. Moses LYNN by Deed dtd 07 Jul 1780 conveyed unto sd John COLLINS the following tracts of land: viz: one tract called Wallbrook & one other called Aaron's Folly & one other called Carters Lott and also a resurvey adjoining sd land all situated in Sussex cnty, DE in Little Creek Hundred. John COLLINS for the sum of £350 hard cash pad by sd Phillips FORGUSSON hath sold us sd FORGUSSON the following tract of land viz: one tract called Aaron's Folly except such as may be covered by the water of Little Creek Mill containing 150 acres & one other tract of land adjoining the afsd called Wallbrook containing 260 acres except 20 & 1/2 acres which is to be laid off for the use of a grist mill on Little Creek & also one other tract called Carters Lott laid off for 92 acres & one other tract called Aaron's Chance, except 400 acres of sd tract which is to be laid off to the N side of sd tract and also such as may be covered by the water of Little Creek Mill Remainder of which supposed to be 100 acres all situated in Little Creek Hundred, Sussex cnty, DE. Sd John COLLINS appoints Henry FISHER, Honorable John CLOWES or Simon COLLOCK Esq as his Attorney. Signed: John COLLINS. Wit: Caleb BALDING, John CREIGHTON. Robert HOUSTON Esq 03 Aug 1791 confirmed the handwriting of Caleb BALDING & John CREIGHTON & of John COLLINS.

O-14:484. Bond of Conveyance. Thomas GAULT of Sussex cnty, DE is held & firmly bound unto Thomas INGRAM of same in the Just & full sum of £200 this 31 Aug 1782(?). Condition is such that if afsd Thomas GAULT shall convey by sufficient Deed to afsd Thomas INGRAM a tract of land known as Agreement laying in Sussex cnty on Vinses Creek containing 140 acres that bound by the penalty above to make all right & title that came to him by the death of his father, John GAULT and upon conveying sd title unto the afsd Thomas INGRAM this Obligation shall be void. Signed: Thomas GAULT. Wit: John W BATSON, Peter F WRIGHT. In compliance of an agreement entered into by Thomas INGRAM within mentioned to George MITCHELL of Sussex cnty, DE dtd 09 Mar 1790 by which agreement Thomas INGRAM stands bound unto George MITCHELL in the sum of £19 13s 11p w/Interest from date thereof & in case the above sum w/Interest was not paid one month from date of sd Agreement sd John INGRAM would for the securing payment of sd sum w/Interest assign unto sd George MITCHELL the within Bond of Conveyance. Sd John INGRAM has since purchased to the amount of £2 16s 6p & sd George MITCHELL has since rec'd an assignment of a Note from John W BATSON Esq dtd 10 Feb 1791 22s 6p on demand. In order to secure payment of the above sums at this time amounting to £24 2s 10p w/Interest for sd aggregate sum from this day until sd George MITCHELL, sd John INGRAM doth hereby assign unto sd George MITCHELL all his title to the w/in Bond of Conveyance. John INGRAM agrees w/George MITCHELL that if the whole of the aggregate sum w/Interest from date of this assignment is not paid w/in 6 months this assignment shall be good & gives George MITCHELL complete right of w/in Bond of Conveyance. Signed: Thomas INGRAM. 06 Jul 1791. Wit: Jehu EVANS, Robert EVANS. George MITCHELL of Sussex cnty, DE hereby acknowledges to have rec'd of Thomas INGRAM of same a Bond of Conveyance from Thomas GAULT to sd INGRAM wherein sd GAULT stands bound unto sd INGRAM in the penal sum of £280 conditioned for the conveying to the afsd Thomas INGRAM sufficient Deed all the sd Thomas GAULT's right to a tract of land called Agreement which came to him by the death of his father, which sd Thomas INGRAM doth covenant w/sd George MITCHELL to assign sd Bond of Conveyance to sd George MITCHELL for securing the payment of £19 13s 11p w/Interest. Signed: Thomas INGRAM. Wit: William BELL. 06 Jul 1791 Thomas INGRAM assigned the w/in mentioned Bond including his assignment of some other demands I have since obtained against him which includes all our former contracts. Signed: George MITCHELL.

O-14:485. Deed of Gift. Cornelius ROBINSON of Sussex cnty, DE have granted unto my son James ROBINSON one negro boy called Isaac. Oct 1785. Signed: Cornelius ROBINSON. Wit: Noah COLLINS, Isaac JOHNSON.

O-14:485. Deed of Release. This Indenture made 27 Jul 1791 between Benjamin ROBINSON of Sussex cnty, DE & Sarah his wife of the one part & Nanny MILBY of same, widow, of the other part. Perry BARKER late of Sussex cnty, dec'd, was seized of a tract of land & premises situate in Indian River Hundred in cnty afsd & d: Intestate leaving Ann Catherine his widow and issue 7 children to whom sd land & premises descended. Whereas Eli BARKER eldest son of sd dec'd Petitioned Orphans Ct 07 Nov 1787 to set off the widow's Dower & make partition of the remaining 2/3 among the children of the dec'd. Sd remaining 2/3 would not partition & valuation was set upon the remaining 2/3 & sd lands were adjudged to the sd Eli BARKER at the valuation he paying the rest of the heirs their respective share of sd valuation. Eli BARKER by Indenture dtd 19 Jan 17?8 conveyed unto Benjamin ROBINSON & Nanny MILBY the afsd remaining 2/3 of the lands afsd containing 139 1/2 acres. Benjamin ROBINSON & Sarah his wife for the sum of £61 sold unto Nanny MILBY afsd lands & premises. Signed: Benja' ROBINSON. Wit: Benj' BURTON Jr, Wm HARRISON. Sarah, wife of Benjamin ROBINSON was examined separate from her husband & did declare she became a party thereto of her own free will.

O-14:487. Commission. The DE State to Peter ROBINSON of Sussex cnty, Esq., Greetings. Whereas our President and General Assembly, did on 23 Jan last appt you, sd Peter ROBINSON, 4th Justice of the Ct of Comm Pleas & Orphans Ct of & for sd cnty of Sussex, agreeably to our Constitution or System of Government: Know ye therefore that in pursuance of sd appt we do by these presents commission you, sd Peter ROBINSON, the 4th Justice of sd Ct of Comm Pleas & Orphans Ct of & for sd cnty of Sussex, requiring you to do therein that which of right according to our Laws ought to be done & performed. In testimony whereof we have caused our Great Seal to be hereunto affixed. Witness his Excellency Joshua CLAYTON Esq our President and Commander in Chief at Newcastle, 05 Feb in the year of our Lord 1790 and in the 14th year of our Independency. Attest: Jas BOOTH, Sec'y.

O-14:487. Commission. The DE State to Peter ROBINSON of Sussex cnty, Esq., Greetings. Whereas our President and General Assembly, on 25 Oct in the present year 1790 did by joint Ballot elect & appt you, sd Peter ROBINSON, 3rd Justice of the Ct of Comm Pleas & Orphans Ct of & for sd cnty of Sussex, requiring you to do therein that which of right according to our Laws ought to be done & performed. In testimony whereof we have caused our Great Seal to be hereunto affixed. Witness his Excellency Joshua CLAYTON Esq our President and Commander in Chief at Newcastle, 08 Nov in the year of our Lord 1790 & of the Independence of the US, the 15th. Attest: Jas BOOTH, Sec'y.

O-14:488. Deed. 12 May 1791 James TWIFFORD of Little Creek Hundred, Sussex cnty, DE, yeoman, & Easter his wife, of the one part for the sum of £20 hath sold to William COULTER of same, yeoman, of the other part, all that parcel of land containing 32 acres part of a parcel containing 62 1/2 acres it being the Dower of Sarah BOOTHE, widow of George BOOTHE, dec'd & part of a larger tract of land situate in the Hundred & cnty afsd (and late the property of afsd George BOOTHE by virtue of a Deed from Dudson BACON dtd 25 --- 1781) called Coxes Discovery part of a larger tract of land whereof afsd George BOOTHE, dec'd, d: seized, containing 145 acres. Sd James TWIFFORD & Esther his wife appt Peter WHITE or Daniel RODNEY, merchants, or Richard GREEN, gent, as their Attorney to acknowledge this Deed for 32 acres. Signed: James TWIFORD (mark), Easther TWIFORD (mark). Wit: Charles POLK, Isaac COOPER. Esther TWIFFORD, wife of James, being of full age, was examined separate from her husband and did declare she became a part to this written Deed of her own free will. Signed: Charles POLK.

O-14:489. Deed. This Indenture made 13 Sep 1787 between Peter F WRIGHT Esq, High Sheriff of Sussex cnty, DE of the one part & Azariah BROOKFIELD of same of the other part. There are 2 tracts of land situate in Baltimore Hundred, cnty afsd, one of which is called Sandy Quarter situate on E side of Blackwater Branch bounded by Col John DAGWORTHY's line & COLLIN's old line containing 15 acres of land; the other called Chance devised by the last will & testament of Thomas COLLINS of cnty afsd to his son Levi COLLINS sd to contain 24 acres; both of which sd tracts became the property of Levi COLLINS afsd. Azariah BROOKFIELD recovered Judgement against sd Levi COLLINS for debt & damages, cost & charges in Ct of Comm Pleas. 09 May 1787 directed sd Sheriff to expose sd lands of Levi COLLINS to Public Sale & sd Sheriff for the sum of £15 sold same unto Azariah BROOKFIELD, he being the highest bidder. Signed: Peter F WRIGHT, Sheriff. Wit: Thomas EVANS, Jos MILLER.

O-14:491. Deed. This Indenture made 03 Aug 1791 between Thomas EVANS, Esq, High Sheriff of Sussex cnty, DE, of the one part & Thomas LAWS of same of the other part. By writ of Ct of Comm Pleas dtd 04 Aug 1790 Thomas EVANS, Sheriff, was ordered to levy against the estate of John JESSOP (in the hands of Unice JESSOP Admin'x of sd John JESSOP) late of the cnty, yeoman, dec'd, a debt of £37 17s 8p which Isaac BRADLEY recovered against him of £4 11s 8p damages was adjudged by sd Ct. Sd Sheriff was only able to collect £19 & a parcel of land situate in Northwest Fork Hundred, cnty afsd, which sd land remained unsold for want of buyers. Sd Sheriff put sd land to Public Sale & sold afsd lands for the sum of £34 unto Thomas LAWS, he being the highest bidder. Sd land situated in Northwest Ford Hundred being part of a tract of land called Partnership bounding to the E by land of ---- WRIGHT, to the S by land of Charles RICHARDS, to the N by lands of Jonathan ----, to the W by land of Daniel POLK sd to contain 30 acres. Signed: Thomas EVANS, Sheriff. Wit: Ezekiel BROWN, Kendle BATSON.

O-14:493. Petition. Joshua POLK some time before his death became bound to James BRATTON Jr for the conveyance of a tract of land situate in Nanticoke

Hundred, Sussex cnty, DE. That same Bond remains undischarged & remains against the estate of sd Joshua POLK, dec'd. Mary POLK, Exec'x of sd Joshua POLK petitions Ct to grant an order for her to convey to James BRATTON Jr the tract of land afsd in compliance w/sd Bond. Signed: Mary POLK, Exec' 03 May 1791. Indorsed on backside thereof 05 May 1791 read & Order made.

O-14:493. Deed. This Indenture made 23 Jul 1791 between Mary POLK, Exec'x of the estate of Joshua POLK, late of Sussex cnty, DE, dec'd, Esq of the one part & James BRATTON the younger of same of the other part. Joshua POLK 04 Nov 1789 was seized of two tracts of land in cnty afsd one of which contains 100 acres being that which sd Joshua POLK purchased by Deed from Josiah HURST called Stayton's Lott situate in Nanticoke Hundred, the other of which was conveyed to sd Joshua POLK by his father, James POLK, dec'd containing 100 acres adjoining lands now in the tenure of William OWENS. Joshua POLK 04 Nov 1789 by his writing Obligatory commonly called an Alienation Bond became bound unto James BRATTON the younger in the penal sum of £1000 with Condition that sd Joshua POLK would convey unto James BRATTON the younger the sd 2 tracts of land. Sd Joshua POLK d: having 1st made his last will & testament & apptd Mary POLK his Exec'x thereof. Mary POLK, Exec'x, petitioned Ct of Comm Pleas to make an Order enabling her to convey the afsd lands according to the Alienation Bond afsd which was granted. Mary POLK Exec's afsd in consideration of the further consideration of £3 doth grant & sell unto sd James BRATTON the younger all the 2 above tracts of land: Stayton's Lott bounded by the land of William HOUSTON. Signed: Mary POLK. Wit: John MARSH, Joshua POLK. Mary POLK appts David HALL or Joseph MILLER her Attorney. Signed: Mary POLK. Wit: John MARSH, Joshua POLK.

o-14:495. William STEEL, late of Sussex cnty, DE, dec'd, was seized of a tract of land situate in Broadkiln Hundred & made his last will & testament bequeathing to his wife Betty STEEL 1/3 part of sd lands & premises during her natural life. Betty STEEL by a Bond dtd 24 Nov 1783 become bound unto Prisgrove STEEL in the sum of £100 to be paid to sd Pisgrove STEEL w/condition that sd Betty STEEL should warrant unto sd Pisgrove STEEL her title to sd tract. William Cotman GUMM lately in Ct of Comm Pleas recovered a debt of £8 3s 2p & 44s 7p like money damages & costs by the default of sd Pisgrove STEEL & to be levied against the lands & tenements of sd Pisgrove STEEL in the hands of Elizabeth STEEL & Nehemiah READ. 04 Feb 1789 Thomas EVANS Esq was ordered by writ to levy sd debt & damages against the chattels & lands held by Elizabeth STEEL & Nehemiah READ there were of Pisgrove STEEL. Sheriff returned he had seized & taken in execution among other things a parcel of land containing 30 acres belonging (being the afsd Betty STEEL's 1/3 of the lands of the sd William STEEL) sd to be the property of sd Pisgrove STEEL which sd land & premises he had appraised & did say the profits & rents thereof were of insufficient yearly value to satisfy the debt & damages w/in 7 years & same remained in his hands. 06 May 1789 Ct of Comm Pleas ordered Thomas EVANS to put sd land to Public Sale & that same was purchased by George CORNWELL for Zechariah PETTYJOHN 08 Jul 1789 for the sum of £3 he being the highest bidder. Signed: Thomas EVANS, Sheriff. Wit: Nath'l MITCHELL, Kendle BATSON.

O-14:496. Bond of Conveyance. John POTTER Sr of Sussex cnty, DE, yeoman, is bound to John ADDISON, Jacob ADDISON & Jonathan ADDISON (sons & heirs to Jacob ADDISON, dec'd) in the sum of £270 1s 8p for the of which sum will & truly be paid. 27 Jun 1777. John POTTER Sr in right of his wife, Limor, as Admin to the estate of Jacob ADDISON, dec'd, hath rec'd £135 10p, the right & property of sd minors which money he hath expended for 70 acres of land adjoining the lands of sd minors & for their benefit & advantage. Sd land is situate on the S edge of Prime Hook Creek. Sd minors at the age of 21 may choose the afsd sum of £135 10p, the afsd 70 acres of land which must be left to their choice. Condition of this Obligation is such that John POTTER on 01 Jan next give possession of sd 70 acres & premises to the Guardian of the afsd minors for their use & by sufficient Deed w/a special Warrant therein from the heirs of Thomas GROVE, dec'd, & David STUART dec'd, convey unto the afsd John ADDISON, Jacob ADDISON & Jonathan ADDISON all & singular the above 70 acres of land together w/houses, etc. & that at the same time the afsd John & Jacob shall attain 21 years they shall choose to have the land conveyed refuse to take a Deed as afsd then John POTTER do pay to them the full & just sum of £135 10p (sd minors having had use of afsd land free of interest) & then this Obligation shall be void. Signed: John POTTER. Wit: John CLOWES, Samuel CLOWES. For the sum of £100 paid by Bevins MORRIS of Sussex cnty, yeoman, we do hereby assign the within Bond to him & release all our right & claim unto the w/in mentioned lands unto afsd Bevins MORRIS. 01 Feb 1789. Memorandum: we do except 4 acres of land Jacob ADDISON let Thos GROVES have on Cabin Point. Signed: Jacob ADDISON, Jonathan ADDISON. Wit: Jacob Stringer FINLEY, Samuel COLLINS. Bevins MORRIS giving John HAZZARD a conveyance Bond for 8 acres 22 Apr 1789. Wit: John HAZZARD, Jacob ADDISON, Jonathan ADDISON, Lot CLARK. Jacob Stringer FINLEY proved the assignment 03 Aug 1789.

O-14:498. Petition. Joseph HOUSTON & William WHITE are Admins of the estate of John POTTER of Sussex cnty, DE, dec'd. Sd John POTTER 27 Jun 1777 entered into a Written Obligation in the penal sum of £270 1s 8p to convey a tract of land to John ADDISON, Jacob ADDISON & Jonathan ADDISON of cnty afsd & sd John, Jacob & Jonathan ADDISON assigned same to Bibbins MORRIS which sd Bond is proved in Open Ct. Sd John POTTER d: before any conveyance was made. Petitioners therefore pray the Ct to make an Order directing sd Joseph HOUSTON & William WHITE to make a Deed of Conveyance to sd Bibbins MORRIS for the afsd tract of land, the consideration money being paid. Signed: Joseph HOUSTON, William WHITE. W/in Petition presented to Ct of Comm Pleas 03 Aug 1791 & granted. Signed: Nath'l MITCHELL, Proth'y.

O-14:499. Deed. This Indenture made 03 Aug 1791 between Joseph HOUSTON & William WHITE, Admins of the estate of John POTTER, late of Sussex cnty, DE, dec'd, of the one part & Bibbins MORRIS of same, yeoman, of the other part. There is a parcel of land situate in Broadkiln Hundred cnty afsd formerly the property of David STEWART late of cnty afsd. David STEWART by Deed of Sale conveyed same to afsd John POTTER Sr. Sd John POTTER by written Obligation dtd 27 Jun 1777 became bound unto John, Jacob & Jonathan ADDISON in the penal sum of £270 1s 8p w/Condition to convey sd tract of land to them & sd John, Jacob & Jonathan ADDISON did assign their claim of the above Obligation to afsd Bibbins MORRIS. Joseph HOUSTON & William WHITE petitioned Ct to make an order for them to make a Deed to sd Bibbins MORRIS for the afsd land in discharge of the afsd Obligation which Petition was granted. Joseph HOUSTON & William WHITE, Admins afsd, for the sum of £135 10p (paid to sd John POTTER by sd John, Jacob & John ADDISON) hath sold afsd lands unto sd Bibbins MORRIS. Signed: Joseph HOUSTON, William WHITE. Wit: John HAZZARD, Miers CLARK.

O-14:500. Deed. This Indenture made 11 Apr 179? between Thomas HARVEY Jr of the one part & Thomas WEST, carpenter, of the other part, both of Sussex cnty, DE. Thomas HARVEY Jr for the sum of £30 hath sold unto Thomas WEST all that part of a tract of land situate in Baltimore Hundred being part of a tract called Stockley's Adventure & being a piece of land that Avery MORGAN Deeded to Thomas HARVEY containing ? acres of land. Signed: Thomas HARVEY Jr. Wit: John WEST, Thomas HARVEY.

O-14:501. Deed. This Indenture made 06 Jul 1791 between Watson WHARTON Exec of the last will & testament of Harman WHARTON Sr, dec'd of Sussex cnty, DE of the one part & George MITCHELL of same, merchant, of the other part. Herman WHARTON Sr became bound unto Joseph DERRICKSON in the penal sum of £300 dtd 05 Jul 1771 conditioned for sd Herman WHARTON to confirm unto afsd Joseph DERRICKSON the quantity of 175 acres of land contained in 3 tracts of land known as Daniel's Luck containing

75 acres of land, Terripin Ridge containing 50 acres of land & Addition to Tarripin Ridge containing 50 acres of land. Joseph DERRICKSON 15 Jul 1789 all his right to the afsd land to George MITCHELL as rec'd in Liber O, No 14, folio 111. Watson WHARTON, Exec of Herman WHARTON Sr in consideration of the authority vested in him by the afsd Bond as Exec afsd & one of the heirs of afsd WHARTON as well as for the sum of 1s paid by sd George MITCHELL doth sell unto sd George MITCHELL all those 3 parcels of land afsd situate in Dagsbury Hundred called Daniel's Luck taken up by David WHARTON fthr of above Herman WHARTON containing 75 acres; one other tract situate afsd called Tarripin Ridge taken up by William MOORE & conveyed to afsd Herman WHARTON Sr containing 50 acres & one other tract called Addition taken up by afsd Herman WHARTON containing 50 acres. Watson WHARTON appoints Daniel RODNEY, Henry NEILL or Phillips KOLLOCK his Attorney. Signed: Watson WHARTON. Wit: John EVANS, Wm T BELL.

O-14:502. Articles of Agreement. This Agreement made 22 Mar 1791 between Mary AYDELOTT & Thomas HAZZARD of Sussex cnty,DE of the one part & Howard AYDELOTT & Mathias AYDELOTT of the other part. Mary AYDELOTT & Thomas HAZZARD agree w/sd George H AYDELOTT & Mathias AYDELOTT to give up all claim to the Estate of John AYDELOTT late, dec'd as Execs to sd Estate upon the following conditions: George Howard AYDELOTT & Mathias AYDELOTT do hereby Bind themselves in the sum of £500 to indemnify sd Mary AYDELOTT & Thomas HAZZARD from all debt & damages that may come against sd Mary AYDELOTT & Thomas HAZZARD concerning & further sd George Howard AYDELOTT & Mathias AYDELOTT hereby give up all the Personal Estate to Mary AYDELOTT that came into sd John AYDELOTT, dec'd, estate that is now quit claim of (together w/£20 cash & 100 lbs of salt port & 8 bushels corn & 2 bushels wheat that came to her the sd Mary AYDELOTT as follows: 1 bed & furniture, 1 spinning wheel, 1 trunk, 1 table, 1 iron pot, 1 kettle, 2 pare pot hooks, 1 iron tea kettle, 6 pewter plates, 1 small basin, two heifers that came of her cow, 1 set cups & saucers, 1 teapot, 2 chairs, 1 silver spoon; also to pay to Thomas HAZZARD the sum of £12 6s 3p for sd HAZZARD's account against sd Estate in consideration thereof sd Thomas HAZZARD & Mary AYDELOTT do hereby Bind themselves in the penal sum of £500 unto sd George Howard AYDELOTT & Mathias AYDELOTT & sd Thomas HAZZARD & Mary AYDELOTT Quit Claim any & all property that was the Estate of John AYDELOTT dec'd. Signed: Mary AYDELOTT (mark), Thomas HAZZARD, George H AYDELOTT, Mathias AYDELOTT. Wit: Phillip WHITE, John HAZZARD. Rec'd 22 Mar 1791 of George Howard & Mathias AYDELOTT the sum of £20. Signed: Mary AYDELOTT (mark). Wit: John HAZZARD.

18 Apr 1791 rec'd of George H AYDELOTT & Mathias AYDELOTT all the w/in articles mentioned & all estate I had when I md: or came by me into the estate of John AYDELOTT, dec'd. Signed: Mary AYDELOTT (mark), John HAZZARD.

O-14:503. Deed. This Indenture made 03 Aug 1791 between Bibbins MORRIS of Sussex cnty, DE, yeoman, of the one part & John HAZZARD of same, yeoman, of the other part. Bibbins MORRIS for the sum of £50 hath sold unto John HAZZARD a parcel of land & marsh situate in Broadkiln Hundred it being part of a tract of land the Admins of John POTTER Sr conveyed to Bibbins MORRIS bounded by marsh that Jonathan ADDISON sold to Bibbins MORRIS & Prime Hook Creek containing 8 acres. Signed: Bevins MORRIS. Wit: Joseph HOUSTON, Jacob Stringer TILNEY.

O-14:504. Deed. This Indenture made 26 Mar 1791 between Sarah DAUGHTERS, Elizabeth DAUGHTERS & Jemimah DAUGHTERS of Sussex cnty, DE of the one part & Noah COLLINS of same of the other part. There are 2 parcels of land lying in Baltimore Hundred, Sussex cnty one of which is known as Sandy Quarter on E side of Black Water Branch, Col John DAGWORTHY's land & COLLINS's old line containing 15 acres; the other tract called Chance & was devised by the last will & testament of Thomas COLLINS to his son Levy COLLINS containing 24 acres. Both parcels of land were the property of Thomas DAUGHTERS of cnty afsd by Deed of Conveyance from Simon KOLLOCK Esq. Thomas DAUGHTERS by his last will & testament dtd 10 Jan 1790 devised the afsd lands unto his mother Sarah DAUGHTERS during her natural life & at her decease to Elizabeth DAUGHTERS & Jemimah DAUGHTERS his 2 sisters. Sarah DAUGHTERS, Elizabeth DAUGHTERS & Jemimah DAUGHTERS for the sum of £40 hath sold unto Noah COLLINS the afsd lands. Sarah, Elizabeth & Jemimah DAUGHTERS appoint Phillips KOLLOCK, Joseph HALL or Wm BRUINGTON their Attorney. Signed: Sarah DAUGHTERS (mark), Elizabeth DAUGHTERS (mark), Jemima DARTER. Wit: Isaac COOPER, William LOCKWOOD, Wingate CANNON.

O-14:505. Deed. George BLACK of Sussex cnty, DE at Ct of Comm Pleas recovered against Andrew HOLEAGER, Exec of the estate of Ephraim HOLEAGER, late of sd cnty, dec'd, a debt of £3 12s 3p as 26s 10p for damages & costs. 08 Aug 1787 Ct of Comm Pleas directed Peter F WRIGHT, High Sheriff, to collect sd monies by 07 Nov next ensuing at which time sd Sheriff reported he had seized a parcel of land situate in Cedar Creek Hundred containing 100 acres, the property of sd Ephraim HOLEAGER which sd land was appraised as yearly income insufficient to satisfy sd debt & damages w/in 7 years. Sd Ct issued writ commanding sd Sheriff to expose sd lands to Public Sale & same was purchased by John RICHARDS 15 Jan 1788 for the sum of £30 10s, he being the highest bidder. Peter F WRIGHT, then Sheriff, was removed from Office before he executed Deed of Conveyance to sd John RICHARDS. Thomas EVANS, current High Sheriff of sd cnty hath confirmed unto sd John RICHARDS the afsd parcel of land & premises. Signed: Thomas EVANS, Sheriff. Wit: Charles POLK, Nath'l MITCHELL.

O-14:507. Deed. This Indenture made 03 Aug 1791 between Thomas EVANS, Esq, High Sheriff of Sussex cnty, DE of the one part & Clement JACKSON, Seth GRIFFITH, both of sd cnty & state of the other part. 04 Aug 1790 Ct of Comm Pleas directed Peter F WRIGHT, then Sheriff of sd cnty, to seize the goods & chattels of George PURVIS, late of sd cnty, yeoman, to discharge £170 judgement which William THARP recovered against sd PURVIS as well 44s 7p costs & damages at sd Ct 03 Aug 1785. Sd Sheriff so seized a messuage & parcel of land containing 2 acres situate on Nanticoke River in Northwest Fork Hundred which sd Ct ordered sold at Public Sale as John WILTBANK witnesseth. Sd Sheriff sold sd land to Clement JACKSON & Seth GRIFFITH for the sum of £7 18s, they being the highest bidders. Sd Peter F WRIGHT, Sheriff, was removed from office before executing a Deed for the land afsd. This Indenture witnesseth that Thomas EVANS Esq, High Sheriff of sd cnty, hath confirmed unto sd Clement JACKSON & Seth GRIFFITH afsd lot of ground situate on Nanticoke River in Northwest Fork Hundred being part of a tract called Luck bounded on the E by sd river, on the W by lands late of Peter HUBBARD, dec'd, in the possession of Jeremiah CANNON, on the S by lands of Levin LEWIS, containing 2 acres w/all the house, buildings, etc. Signed: Thomas EVANS, Sheriff. Wit: Rich' HAYS, Nath'l MITCHELL. Thomas FISHER appeared in Ct 03 Aug 1791 & made oath he saw one of the parties to the w/in Did pay £7 some shillings, the consideration money, to Peter F WRIGHT, Esq, Sheriff, or Robert JONES, sub Sheriff for him.

O-14:508. Deed. This Indenture made 02 Aug 1791 between John CRAIGE, blacksmith, Cornelius PAYNTOR & Ruth his wife, of Sussex cnty, DE of the one part & Benjamin RICHARDS of same, farmer, of the other part. John CRAIGE & Cornelius PAYNTOR & Ruth his wife for the sum of £9 7s 3p hath sold unto Benjamin RICHARDS a parcel of marsh situate in ? Neck bounded by marsh of Anderson PARKER containing 4 acres & 1/4 a moiety of 8 & 1/2 acres of marsh conveyed by Joseph PILES & John PILES to Edward CRAIGE & by a regular descent the title became vested John CRAIGE, Cornelius PAYNTOR & Ruth his wife. Signed: John CRAGE, Cornelius PAYNTER, Ruth PAYNTER. Wit: William PERRY, James P WILSON, Joseph WILSON, Thomas COLLINGS.

O-14:509. Deed. This Indenture made 10 Jun 1789 between Thomas DARTERS of Sussex cnty, DE, Admin of the estate of Asariah BROKFIELD, of the one part & Simon KOLLOCK Esq of the other part. There are two parcels of land situate in Baltimore Hundred, cnty afsd, the property of sd Asariah BROOKFIELD, one of which is called Sandy Quarter on the E side of Blackwater Branch near Col John DAGWORTHY'S line containing 15 acres of land; the other of which is the SE part of a tract called Chance devised by the last will & testament of Thomas COLLINS, late of cnty afsd, to his son Levi COLLINS of cnty afsd which part of the sd tract to contain 24 acres, both of which parcels of land became the property of the sd Levi COLLINS & were sold by Peter F WRIGHT Esq, late Sheriff, 09 May 1787 for the payment of a judgement afsd Azariah BROOKFIELD obtained against afsd Levi COLLINS which was done 13 Jul 1787 to the above Azariah BROOKFIELD he being the highest bidder. Peter F WRIGHT 10 Sep following gave Deed of Sale to sd Azariah BROOKFIELD. Thomas DARTERS by his Letters of Administration 05 May 1789 put to sale sd lands of Azariah BROOKFIELD in Baltimore Hundred sold sd lands for the sum of £12 unto afsd Simon KOLLOCK he being the highest bidder. Signed: Thomas DARTER. Wit: Edward HALL, George FRAME.

O-14:510. Deed. This Indenture made 27 Jul 1791 between Levi COLLINS & Mary COLLINS his wife of Sussex cnty, DE of the one part & Noah COLLINS of same of the other part. Levi COLLINS & Mary his wife for the sum of £30 hath sold unto Noah COLLINS part of a tract of land called Chance granted to Thomas COLLINS & Levi COLLINS by patent for 190 acres of land. Levi COLLINS 1795 Feb 13 Deeded sd land to afsd Noah COLLINS but there being a mistake found in the courses of sd Deed, a new Deed for part of sd tract being that part adjoining William POWDER's land containing 23 acres unto sd Noah COLLINS. Levi COLLINS & Mary COLLINS appoint Phillips KOLLOCK, Col David HALL or William LOCKWOOD their Attorney. Signed: Levi COLLINS, Mary COLLINS. Wit: Benj' HOLLAND, David GODWIN.

O-14:511. Deed. This Indenture made 02 Aug 1791 between Mary HITCH, William HITCH & Sally HITCH of Sussex cnty, DE of the one part & John May LAWS of same of the other part. Mary, William & Sally HITCH for the sum of £6 hath sold unto John May LAWS one acre of land part of a tract called Hitch Lott in Northwest Fork Hundred, cnty afsd bounded by a tract of land called Hale's Choice part of which sd land is now in the possession of the afsd Mary HITCH and Sally HITCH. Signed: Mary HITCH (mark), William HITCH (mark), Sally HITCH (mark). Wit: Thomas LAWS, David RICHARDS. Sd Mary, William & Sally HITCH appoint John W BATSON or David RODNEY their Attorney.

O-14:512. This Indenture made 13 Jun 1789 between Simon KOLLOCK Esq of Sussex cnty, DE of the one part & Thomas DARTERS of same of the other part. There are 2 parcels of land in Baltimore Hundred, Sussex cnty, one of which is called Sandy Quarter bounded by Col John DAGWORTHY's line & COLLINS' old line laid out for 15 acres; the other of which is called Chance & was devised by the last will & testament of Thomas COLLINS of cnty afsd to his son Levy COLLINS sd to contain 24 acres both of which sd parcels of land were formerly the property of Levi COLLINS of Baltimore Hundred & were sold by Peter F WRIGHT Esq, late sheriff of sd cnty by 09 May 1787 Ct writ for payment of debts of afsd Levi COLLINS to Azariah BROOKFIELD 09 Jul 1787. Sd Peter F WRIGHT confirmed same to afsd Azariah BROOKFIELD by Sheriff Deed 10 Sep 1787 Simon KOLLOCK 13 May 1789 purchased sd parcels of land of the above Thomas DARTERS who became Admin of the Estate of the afsd Azariah BROOKFIELD for the sum of £12 they being sold to discharge debts by order of 05 May 1789 Ct Order & Deed of Sale 10 Jun 1789 of Thomas DARTERS to Simon KOLLOCK. Simon KOLLOCK for the sum of £12 15s hath sold unto sd Thomas DARTERS the 2 parcels of land by the name of Sandy Quarter & by the name of Chance. Signed: Simon KOLLOCK. Wit: Edward HALL, George FRAME.

O-14:514. Deed. This Indenture made 17 May 1791 between Thomas HARNEY of the one part & Armwell LOCKWOOD of the other part both of Sussex cnty, DE. Thomas HARNEY for the sum of £?00 hath sold unto Armwell LOCKWOOD all that part of a tract of land called — Choice by patent dtd Nov 1696 also all that part of a tract of land called Puzle dtd 01 Jan 1749 also all the remaining part of a tract called Friendship purchased of William ---- by Deed dtd 25 Aug 1762 lying in Baltimore Hundred which sd Thomas HARNEY is now seized of in the whole of the remaining parts of sd tract of land of 268 acres except that part of each tract sold to Noah COLLINS). Signed: Thomas HARNEY. Wit: Thomas HARNEY Jr, Noah COLLINS.

O-14:514. Deed. This Indenture made 02 Aug 1791 between John AYDELOTT of Sussex cnty, DE of the one part & Benjamin HOLLAND of same of the other part. John AYDELOTT for the sum of £28 hath sold unto Benjamin HOLLAND the parcel of land called Cancor, it being a resurvey made by sd John AYDELOTT 13 Feb 1758 on a tract of land called Jacob's Strugle granted to Jacob GRAY which John AYDELOTT bought of Jacob GRAY bounded by land William HOLLAND specifies in his will to be a division between his two sons Benjamin & William HOLLAND containing 30 acres. John AYDELOTT appoints Phillips KOLLOCK, George HAZZARD or Peter WHITE his Attorney. Signed: John AYDELOTT (mark). Wit: Noah COLLINS, J Stephen HILL.

O-14:516. Deed. This Indenture made 04 Jun 1790 between Rhoads SHANKLAND of Lewes, Rehoboth Hundred, Sussex cnty, DE, surveyor, of the one part & Stephen BALEY of same, yeoman, of the other part. There is a parcel of land lying in cnty afsd on S side of Cold Spring Branch on the N side of the Cnty Road, land in the possession of Stephen BAILEY, the 4 acres belonging to the Meeting House of the ---, containing 50 acres. Rhoads SHANKLAND for the sum of £--- hath sold unto Stephen BAILEY the afsd land. Signed: Rhoads SHANKLAND. Wit: Hugh SMITH, Wm TUNNEL.

O-14:517. Deed. This Indenture made 14 Nov 1790 between Adonijah STANBURROUGH now or late of the city of Philadelphia, surveyor, of the one part & William MORRIS of Sussex cnty, DE, husbandman, of the other part. John YOUNG, merchant, of Philadelphia afsd by virtue of sundry conveyances declares himself seized of & sd Adonijah STANBURROUGH duly authorized as his Attorney to grant & sell the premises hereby intended to be sold by his Power dtd 06 Nov instant. For the sum of £60 12s 6p Adonijah STANBURROUGH hath sold unto William MORRIS a parcel of land situate in Broad Hill Hundred being part of a larger tract of land called Waterhole Savannah sd to be included in a Warrant to James REED which premises hereby granted bounded by land claimed by Foster DONOVAN the Elder, lands in possession of Thomas DUTTON, line of William MORRIS, containing 48 1/2 acres which premises are granted & accepted by the marks & survey made by Rhoads SHANKLAND. John YOUNG appoints Rhoads SHANKLAND or Joseph MORRIS to be his Attorney. Signed: Adon'ah STANBURROUGH, Atty in Fact for sd John YOUNG. Wit: Levi RUSSELL, Dennis MORRIS.

O-14:518. Deed. Thomas RALPH by Indenture dtd 08 Jan 1765 for a valuable sum granted unto William RELPH of Somerset Cnty, MD, Sussex cnty, DE sold unto William RALPH 2 tracts of land situate in Little --- Hundred; one tract is called Ralph's ---- & the other tract Ralph's Delight containing in the whole 66 acres. William RALPH d: seized of the 2 tracts of land & Admin of his Estate was committed unto Mary RALPH & sd Mary RALPH Petitioned Orphans Ct the personal estate of sd dec'd was not sufficient to discharged debts & asked Ct to grant an Order for sale of so much of the Real Estate to discharge the just Debts. Sd Ct so Ordered. 06 Oct 178? Mary RALPH by Public Sale sold the 2 parcels of land afsd unto ---- James ENGLISH, he being the highest bidder. Signed: Mary RALPH. Wit: Sylvester WEBB, W HARRISON.

O-14:518. Deed. This Indenture made 03 Aug 1791 between Thomas EVANS, High Sheriff of Sussex cnty, DE, of the one part & John GORDON, Treasurer of

DE, of the other part. An Execution directed Peter F WRIGHT late High Sheriff of cnty afsd for the goods & chattels of George POLK & Rhoads SHANKLAND he should cause to be made & a certain sum of money in sd Execution mentioned which DE State in Ct of Comm Pleas recovered against them & sd Peter F WRIGHT took in Execution 2 tracts of land situate in Nanticoke Hundred in Great Neck; the one tract called Polk's Privoledge being a MD survey containing 50 acres & the other tract known as Addition to Polk's Priviledge being a grant from the Proprietaries of PA, adjoining the lands of Charles POLK, Richard PASSWATERS & others. Sd Peter F WRIGHT caused a valuation of sd lands to be made & it was declared the incomes from same were insufficient to satisfy the debt & costs w/in 7 years. Whereupon Writ was made to Peter F WRIGHT, late Sheriff ordering the Public Sale of sd lands & 28 Oct 1789 sd WRIGHT sold sd lands unto John GORDON for the use of the DE State afsd. Thomas EVANS, now High Sheriff, being fully satisfied of the Proceedings of the sd Peter F WRIGHT, late Sheriff, dec'd, doth confirm unto John GORDON for the use of DE State afsd the afsd land & premises. Signed: Thomas EVANS, Sheriff. Wit: Ezekiel BROWN, W HARRISON.

O-14:519. Deed. This Indenture made 04 Aug 1791 between John GORDON, State Treasurer for DE of the one part & Charles POLK of Sussex cnty, DE, Esq, of the other part. 28 Oct 1789 purchased all the lands of George POLK at Public Sale being 2 tracts of land situate in Nanticoke Hundred on Great Neck; one tract called Polk's Privilege being a MD survey containing 50 acres of land; the other called Addition to Polk's Privilege being a grant from the Proprietary of PA, adjoining the lands of Charles POLK, Richard PASSWATERS & others. 20 May 1790 sd John GORDON set up the sd 2 tracts of land at Public Sale & sd Charles POLK purchased same. John GORDON for the sum of £150, well & truly paid for the use of DE state afsd, by sd Charles POLK hath sold unto sd Charles POLK the afsd lands. Signed: John GORDON. Wit: Robert BURTON, Wm HALL.

O-14:520. Deed of Sale. This Indenture made 04 Aug 1791 between James ENGLISH of Sussex cnty, DE of the one part & Mary RELPH of same of the other part. James ENGLISH for the sum of £28 hath sold unto Mary RELPH 2 parcels of land situate in Little Creek Hundred; one tract is called Ralph's Property containing 46 acres, the other tract called Ralph's Delight containing 20 acres; which sd lands were conveyed by Thomas RALPH unto William RALPH, dec'd by Indenture dtd 08 Jan 1765 & after death of sd William RALPH was sold by Mary RALPH, Admin of sd William RALPH, by order of Orphans Ct to James ENGLISH for the sum of £28. Sd 2 tracts of land hereby granted to sd Mary RALPH. Signed: James ENGLISH. Wit: Sylvester WEBB, W HARRISON.

O-14:521. Deed of Sale. This Indenture made 05 Aug 1791 between Jacob HAZZARD of Sussex cnty, DE, blacksmith, & Ann his wife, of the one part & Samuel ROWLAND of same, gentleman, of the other part. Jabez Maud FISHER late of sd cnty, dec'd, made his last will & testament dtd 13 Sep 1742 & thereby did devise unto his 3 sons Joshua, Edward & Fenwick FISHER all his lands & marsh w/in cnty afsd or elsewhere or the survivor of them. Edward & Fenwick FISHER by Deed dtd 06 May 1755 & sd Edward by another Deed dtd 08 Nov 1758 conveyed unto John FISHER a parcel of land called The Flatlands situate in Lewes, Rehoboth Hundred which sd parcel of land sd John FISHER by his last will & testament dtd 08 Feb 1776 did devise unto his son Jabez FISHER during his natural life & after his decease to sd Jabez FISHER's son Joshua FISHER & to the heirs of his body lawfully begotten. For want of such heirs to descend unto sd Joshua FISHER's next oldest brother Thomas FISHER & to the heirs of his body lawfully begotten. Joshua FISHER at a Ct of Comm Pleas suffered a common recovery for barring the entail on the land afsd as by several Deeds relating thereto may more fully appear. Joshua FISHER & Ann his wife by Indenture dtd 20 Feb last past sold unto above Jacob HAZZARD a parcel of land (part of the sd tract called The Flatlands) containing 46 1/2 acres. Jacob FISHER & Ann his wife, for the sum of 60 Spanish dollars paid by Samuel ROWLAND hath sold unto sd Samuel ROWLAND a parcel of land, part of the afsd 46 1/2 acres bounded by sd Samuel ROWLAND's line, WOOLF's line, Sarah ROWLAND's line & GORDON's line, containing 7 1/2 acres. Signed: Jacob HAZZARD, Ann HAZZARD. Wit: Simon HALL, W HARRISON. Ann HAZZARD, wife of Jacob, was examined separate from her husband & did declare she became a party thereto of her own free will. Signed: Jno WILTBANK.

O-14:522. Deed. This Indenture made 15 Dec 1790 between Capt Woolsey HATHAWAY of Doral cnty, Carolina of the one part & John AYDELOTT, bricklayer, of Sussex cnty, DE of the other part. Woolsey HATHAWAY for the sum of £80 hath sold unto John AYDELOTT a parcel of land containing 100 acres situate in Indian River Hundred, Sussex cnty, DE bounded by lands of William STEVENS, dec'd, bought by sd Woolsey HATHAWAY & sold by Ezekiel WEST, Admin of John HILL dec'd to Woolsey HATHAWAY by Deed dtd 05 May 1784. Signed: Woolsey HATHAWAY. Wit: John W BASTON, Benjamin AYDELOTT.

O-14:523. Deed. This Indenture made 01 Dec 1769 between John EVANS of Sussex cnty, DE of the one part & Benj'm BURTON, Thomas ROBINSON, Burton WAPLES, Reice WOOLFE, Anderson PARKER, John WILTBANK, Jacob KOLLOCK Jr, Wrixham LEWES, Parker ROBINSON & Daniel NUNEZ of Sussex cnty, gentlemen, of the other part. There is a parcel of land situate in

Angel's Neck being part of the tract that Thomas EVANS late of sd cnty, dec'd, possessed & being part of same land Thomas EVANS purchased of John POTTER by Deed dtd 27 Jul 1762 rec'd in Liber I, No 9, f 398. Sd Thomas EVANS having d; Intestate & sd lands not being sufficient to bear division amongst his several heirs, same was allotted unto afsd John EVANS, he being eldest son of afsd Thomas EVANS, after laying off the widow's 1/3. Part of sd land & marsh the afsd John EVANS hath sold unto the above Thomas ROBINSON & part thereof is butted on the edge of Rehoboth Bay, the widow's 1/3 & Hambleton CRAIG's line, containing 103 acres of land & marsh, including the widow's 1/3 containing 64 acres. John EVANS for the sum of £200 hath sold unto Benj'm BURTON, Thomas ROBINSON, Burton WAPLES, Reice WOOLFE, Anderson PARKER, John WILTBANK, Jacob KOLLOCK Jr, Wrixham LEWES, Parker ROBINSON & Daniel NUNEZ all the above land & marsh lying on the SE side of the division of the widow's 1/3 & W side of land sold to Thomas ROBINSON containing 39 acres & land & marsh laying to the NW side of the widow's 1/3 called Little Neck containing --- acres & all his right to the moiety of the afsd widow's 1/3 after her death & to the 1 moiety of other lands that may be recovered as part of the sd Intestate estate of the afsd tract of land lying on the NW side of afsd lines. Signed: John EVANS. Wit: Simon KOLLOCK, Phillips KOLLOCK.

O-14:525. Deed of Conveyance. This indenture made 18 Apr 1790 between James JONES of Sussex cnty, DE, planter, of the one part & Jehu WEST of same, yeoman. Isaac JONES late of cnty afsd was seized of a tract of land called Forrest Chance containing 100 acres of land situate formerly in --- Hundred, Worcester cnty, MD but now in Little Creek Hundred, Sussex cnty, DE. In pursuance of the Proprietaries warrant of survey dtd at Philadelphia 02 May 1776 granted to the afsd Isaac JONES on afsd tract called Forrest Chance but now called Content which resurvey was made 16 Sep 1776. Sd Isaac JONES made his last will & testament dtd 11 Dec 1784 & bequeathed the afsd tract of land called Forest Chance together with 1/2 the warrant land that he owned to his son James JONES. James JONES for the sum of £37 10s hath sold unto Jehu WEST all his right & title to 1/2 of the survey on Forrest Chance, now called Content). James JONES appoints William PERRY, Joseph MILLER or John WOOLF as his Attorney. Signed: James JONES. Wit: Jesse SAUNDERS, Peter DOLBEE.

O-14:526. Deed of Sale. Henry NEILL of Sussex cnty, DE lately in the Ct of Comm Pleas recovered Nicholas LITTLE, Exec of the estate of John LITTLE, dec'd, of cnty afsd, a certain debt of £487 19s 1/2p & 40s as damages & costs. Peter Fretwell WRIGHT, then High Sheriff, was ordered by sd Ct to collect sd monies & sd Sheriff returned that he had seized in execution sundry parcels of land situate in Lewes, Rehoboth, Indian River & Broadkiln Hundred, cnty afsd containing 2493 acres which sd land he had appraised & it was determined that sd lands issues & rents were insufficient to repay sd debt & damages w/in the space of 7 years. Sd Sheriff by order of the Ct put to Public Sale a certain parcel of land situate in Indian River Hundred containing 95 acres which sd land was purchased by Henry NEILL the plaintiff for the sum of £71 he being the highest bidder. Sd Peter Fretwell WRIGHT was discharged from office before he had executed a Deed of Conveyance securing sd land & premises to sd Henry NEILL. Thomas EVANS, High Sheriff of cnty afsd hath conveyed unto sd Henry NEILL the afsd land. Signed: Thomas EVANS, Sheriff. Wit: Wm PERRY, Nath'l MITCHELL.

O-14:527. Deed. This Indenture made 06 Aug 1791 between Hannah NUNEZ of Sussex cnty, DE of the one part & Henry NEILL of same of the other part. Daniel NUNEZ, late of sd cnty, dec'd, was seized of a parcel of land situate in Lewes, Rehoboth Hundred, cnty afsd, d: & by his last will & testament dtd 09 May 1772 appt'd his wife, Hannah NUNEZ, to be Exec'x. 12 Mar 1791 sd Hannah NUNEZ petitioned Orphan's Ct that the personal estate of sd Daniel NUNEZ was insufficient to discharge his just debts & asked Ct to grant her permission to sell as much of the Real Estate to be sufficient to discharge sd debts whereupon sd CT ordered Hannah NUNEZ to put to Public Sale a parcel of land situate in the town of Lewes adjoining the lots of John RODNEY & George PARKER, also a parcel of land situate in Lewes, Rehoboth Hundred adjoining the lands of Reece WOOLF, William GILL & others containing 130 acres. Afsd lands were purchased by Henry NEILL for the sum of £41 & the other afsd parcel of land for the sum of £53 4s, he being the highest bidder. Hannah NUNEZ for the sums above mentioned grants & sells unto Henry NEILL the afsd land. Signed: Hannah NUNEZ. Wit: John BENNET, W HARRISON.

O-14:528. Deed. This Indenture made 13 Jul 1791 between John SMITH of Cedar Creek Hundred, Sussex cnty, DE of the one part & William HARRISON of same, yeoman, of the second party & Henry SMITH of same, yeoman, of the third part. John SMITH for the docking & cutting of all estates & remainders in tail and in all that parcel of land situate in Cedar Creek Hundred in cnty afsd in Primehook Neck being part of a larger tract bounded by land of Robert WATTSON, containing 200 acres of land & marsh for the sum of 5s hath sold to William HARRISON. It is agreed upon by all 3 parties sd William HARRISON before the end of Aug next will permit sd Henry SMITH to recover. Signed: John SMITH, W HARRISON, Henry SMITH. Wit: William PERRY, Isaac CONNAWAY.

O-14:529. Deed. Daniel PALMER late of sd cnty was seized of a parcel of land situate on the W side of Delaware Bay in Sussex cnty, DE on the N side of Broadkiln Creek containing 405 acres of land & marsh being part of a larger tract originally granted at NY 20 Aug 1679 unto Thomas & Knight HOWARD for 600 acres of land & marsh called Howard's Choice. Sd Daniel PALMER d: after making his last will & testament devising sd land & premises unto Mary his wife who afterwards md: Charles DINGEE late of sd cnty. Mary being so seized d: Intestate leaving issue Joseph PALMER & Sarah PALMER & Daniel DINGEE to whom sd lands descended. Joseph PALMER oldest son of sd Mary DINGEE petitioned Orphans Ct 03 May 1744 asking sd Ct to appt 5 Freeholders to evaluate sd lands & make division thereof among the heirs of Mary DINGEE, dec'd. Joshua FISHER, Anderson PARKER, Jeremiah CLAYPOLE, John CLOWES & John PONDER made partition of sd lands & did allot unto Sarah, then the wife of John MILLARD of cnty afsd 100 acres off the N most part of the tract; and assigned unto Daniel a minor about 80 acres off the W most corner thereof adjoining lands of Eliza CORNWELL & 25 acres of marsh lying between that part allotted to sd Sarah & also 16 more acres adjoining the afsd 25 acres of marsh containing in the whole about 121 acres of land. Sd Sarah wife of the late, dec'd John MILLARD md: Andrew HEAVERLS by whom she had one son, Daniel HEAVERLO. Afsd Daniel DINGEE by Indenture dtd Feb 1768 sold the sd 121 acres unto the afsd Joseph PALMER who 07 Feb 177? sold unto afsd Andrew HEAVERLO 1 moiety of the 25 acres of marsh & of the afsd 16 acres adjoining thereto (being part conveyed by Daniel DINGEE to Joseph PALMER) the sd moiety sold to the sd Andrew HEAVERLS was off the S end of sd 16 acres of marsh & off W side of sd 25 acres containing 12 1/2 acres of marsh & 8 acres of land containing in the whole 20 1/2 acres of land & marsh. Andrew HEAVERLS & Sarah his wife were possessed of the sd 100 acres of land laid off & assigned to sd Sarah of her mother, Mary DINGEE's lands & also of the afsd 20 1/2 acres of land & marsh conveyed by the afsd Joseph PALMER unto the sd Andrew HEAVERLS. Andrew HEAVERLS & Sarah his wife by Indenture dtd 04, 8th mo, 1783 for divers good cause & consideration & because they were moving & for the parental love which they bear to the sd Daniel HAVERLS, their son, & further consideration of the sum of £5 gold & silver coins sold unto Daniel HEAVERLS all the above recited lands. Daniel HEAVERLS afterwards d: having first made his last will & testament wherein he appointed the afsd William MILLARD his Exec. After having fully administered the personal estate of Daniel HEAVERLS, it being insufficient to discharge the just debts of the estate, applied to Orphans Ct to sell the 121 1/2 acres & Ct so Ordered William MILLARD as Exec of the estate of Daniel HEAVERLS should expose sd lands to Public Sale. William MILLARD, Exec as afsd after duly published advertisement under the hand of Phillips KOLLOCK, Clerk sold sd lands & premises to Baptist LAY for the sum of £250 he being the highest bidder.

Signed: William MILLARD Esq. Wit: Dan'l RODNEY, Caleb RODNEY. 15 Sep 1791.

O-14:532. Letter of Attorney. Isaac KELLO of Rockingham cnty, Carolina, now being in Sussex cnty, DE have appointed my brother, John KELSO of Sussex cnty my lawful attorney to recover and receive from every person w/in DE of such sums of money as to be due or payable to me, either in my own right, as Guardian to the persons & estates of ---- HODGSON, John HODGSON & Joshua HODGSON. Signed: Isaac KELLO. Wit: Phillips KOLLOCK, George RICHARDS (mark).

O-14:532. Deed. This Indenture made 06 Sep 1791 between David RICHARDS of Sussex cnty, DE, Exec of the estate of John RICHARDS, late of same, dec'd of the one part & William RICHARDS of same, one of the surviving heirs of the afsd John RICHARDS, dec'd, of the other part. David RICHARDS, Exec, for the sum of £689 ?s hath sold unto William RICHARDS part of a tract of land called Poplar Peril Improved which was not heretofore given unto David by the afsd John RICHARDS dec'd, this land being part of a larger tract granted to afsd John RICHARDS dec'd by the Proprietary of MD by patent dtd 07 May 1762 and now in Sussex cnty in Northwest Fork Hundred; also one other tract called Parsimon Bottom which was granted by Proprietary of MD patent unto Thomas WILLIAM, son of Wm, dtd 10 Dec 1740 for 50 acres. Sd Thomas WILLIAMS son of Wm by deed dtd 12 Oc 1754 rec'd in Dorchester cnty, MD 07 Apr 1755 did sell unto afsd John RICHARDS dec'd; and also part of a tract called Bachelors Ridge granted by warrant of the Proprietary of PA unto James RICHARDS dec'd dtd Philadelphia ?? ?? 1776 bounded by a tract of land called Beach Grove. William RICHARDS being purchaser of the sd land S of division line & Elijah ADAMS being the purchaser (and one of the surviving heirs by right of his wife of the afsd John RICHARDS dec'd of the other part); and also a part of a tract of land called Beach Grove it being a resurvey on a tract called Long Ridge for the sd John RICHARDS dec'd containing in the whole 501 acres of land. Signed: David RICHARDS. Wit: Thomas LAWS, Charles POLK.

O-14:534. Deed of Sale. This Indenture made 15 Sep 1791 between Thomas FISHER of Sussex cnty, DE & Esther his wife of the one part & Isaac RIGGS of the same, yeoman, of the other part. There is a tract of land situate in Cedar Creek Hundred of which Thomas FISHER was seized a part of which he sold to his brother Jonathan FISHER to whom he gave a Bond dtd 15 Jan 1770 for the conveyance of same bounded by the 100 acres which sd Thomas FISHER conveyed to John R----, line of Joshua FISHER, containing 72 acres 59 sq perches including 152 perches of the dower of the afsd Jonathan FISHER which was laid out to her. Jonathan FISHER being seized of the 72 acres 59 perches together w/22 acres & 106 perches adjoining afterwards d: intestate leaving a widow & sundry children to whom the sd lands descended. Eldest son of sd Jonathan FISHER sold all right of sd lands to Isaac RIGGS for which he gave his Bond dtd 03 Jul 1790. Isaac RIGGS petitioned Orphans Ct to divide the 2/3 of the Real Estate of the sd Jonathan FISHER dec'd among his heirs, the widow's Dower 3rd being previously laid off. The 2/3 being found not fit for division were evaluated Isaac RIGGS being the assignee & same was confirmed unto him by the Ct. Thomas FISHER & Esther his wife for the sum of £20 19s sold unto sd Isaac RIGGS the above 72 acres 59 perches of land it being part of a survey situate in Cedar Creek Hundred on the W side of Bowman's Branch formerly laid off to Thomas PAYNTER for 200 acres. Signed: Thomas FISHER (mark), Ester FISHER (mark). 15 Sep 1791 Esther FISHER, wife of Thomas, was examined separate from her husband & declared she became a party to the above Deed of her own free will. Signed: Charles POLK.

O-14:535. Deed. This Indenture made 30 Aug 1791 between Abigail BELL of Sussex cnty, DE of the one part & George MITCHELL of same of the other part. Elizabeth CLAYTON formerly of NJ by last of DE was seized of a lot situate in the twp of Trenton in Hunterdon cnty, NJ & is part of a piece of ground originally containing 277 acres divided & mentioned in Lotts number 13 to 34 inclusive bounded by lott 16, lott 12, a five acres swamp & called Lot 17 & is the same as was sold by ---- MARTIN Esq formerly high sheriff of Hunterdon cnty as part of the estate of William TRENT, Admin to William CLAYTON by Deed dtd 02 Aug 1745 & rec'd Liber K, p3?? & also all that other lott situate in the twp of ?? bounded by lotts 21, 20 & 19, lot 10 containing 12 acres of land which last described lott is called Lot 18 & which was sold to William CLAYTON by Samuel BURGE by Deed dtd 2? Jun 1752; & also that lott situate in Trenton in Hunterdon cnty bounded by lott late of Gideon BICKERDIKE, King Street, lott late in the possession of Thomas CADWALADER, containing 35 perches of land which sd lott was sold by Thomas JANNEY to afsd William CLAYTON by Deed dtd 23 Dec 1751, & also all that other ground bounded by lott late of Robert BIEDFORD which was sold to afsd William CLAYTON by Elizabeth BILES, Asah LAMBERT, Thomas CADWALADER & Hanah his wife by Deed dtd 05 Apr 1761. Elizabeth CLAYTON d: having first made her last will & testament wherein she bequeathed 1/6 part of her real estate to Abigail BELL to be divided after the death of William son of Purnel CLAYTON. Abigail BELL for the sum of £?25 hath sold unto George MITCHELL the afsd lands. Signed: Abitail BELL Wit: John W BATSON, Kendle BATSON.

O-14:537. Deed. 08 Sep 1791 William RICHARDS & Tamson his wife of Sussex cnty, DE of the one part for the sum of £689 9s hath sold unto David RICHARDS of same of the other part all those parcels of land, part of a tract called Poplar Levil Improved which heretofore was not given unto David RICHARDS by John RICHARDS late of Sussex cnty, dec'd. Sd lands part of a large tract granted to John RICHARDS dec'd by the Proprietary of MD by patent dtd 07 May 1762 now in afsd Sussex cnty in Northwest Hundred & also one tract called Pissimon Bottom in Northwest Fork Hundred granted originally by patent unto Thomas WILLIAMS by the Proprietary of MD dtd 10 Dec 1740 for 50 acres. Thomas WILLIAMS, son of William, by his Deed dtd 12 Oct 1754 rec'd in Dorcester cnty, MD 07 Apr 1755 did sell unto Thomas RICHARDS dec'd. Sd land on S side of Beach Branch out of the NW fork of Nanticoke River, bounded by a parcel of land called Bachelors Ridge granted by warrant by Proprietary of PA unto James RICHARDS of Sussex cnty, dec'd, dtd 1776 bounded by a tract of land called Beachgrove. Elijah ADAMS one of the surviving heirs in right of his wife to the sd John RICHARDS dec'd became the purchaser of all of sd lands on N side of sd line. Also part of a tract called Beach Grove it being a resurvey for sd John RICHARDS, dec'd. In the whole of the afsd tracts & parcels of land being 501 acres William RICHARDS & Tamson his wife grant unto the sd David RICHARDS. William RICHARDS & Tamson his wife appoint John WILTBANK or ---- RODNEY of Lewes their Attorney. Signed: William RICHARDS, Tamson RICHARDS (mark). Wit: Thomas LAWS, Charles POLK. Tamsen RICHARDS, wife of William, was examined separate from her husband and did declare she became a party to the above of her own free will. Signed: Charles POLK.

O-14:539. Bond of Conveyance. William CANNON of Sussex cnty, DE, planter, is bound unto Jesse CANNON, son of Jesse CANNON, dec'd, in the sum of £500 to be paid to sd Jesse CANNON dtd 29 Sep 1791. Condition of sd obligation is such that if William CANNON on or before 29 Sep 1793 make over all his title of a certain tract of land being a resurvey to Cannon's Lott agreeable to the last will & testament of Jesse CANNON dec'd w/o delay this obligation to be void. Signed: William CANNON. Wit: Ralph ROBINSON, Jesse CLARKSON, Richard PERKINS.

O-14:539. Manumission. Hannah HOLLAND of Rehoboth Hundred, Sussex cnty, DE, widow, do by these presents for sundry good causes me thereunto moving set free & forever discharge from my service Cato my negro that has heretofore been my property now known by the name of Cato HOLLAND. Further I do warrant & defend the liberty of the sd negro Cato HOLLAND against any claim. 05 Oct 1791. Signed: Hannah HOLLAND. Wit: William HOLLAND, Eunice HOLLAND.

O-14:540. Mortgage. This Indenture made October 1791 between Baptist LAY of Sussex cnty, DE, ship wright, & Philena his wife of the one part and Samuel Rowland FISHER of the city of Philadelphia, merchant, of the other part. Baptist LAY by this Obligation dtd herewith stands bound unto Samuel Rowland FISHER in the sum of £200 gold or silver money of PA conditioned for the payment of £100 money as afsd on 01 Oct next the entire payment together w/interest for same. Baptist LAY & Philena his wife in consideration of afsd debt for the better securing the payment w/interest in discharge of sd Bond hath sold unto sd Samuel Rowland FISHER all that messuage, plantation & two tracts of land & marsh situate in cnty afsd on the N side of Broadkill Creek containing 120 1/2 acres which William MILLARD of Sussex cnty, Exec of the last will & testament of Daniel HEAVERLS late of cnty, yeoman, dec'd, by Order of Orphans Ct Jun last past 15 Sep last past rec'd, sold unto sd Baptist LAY in order to pay debts of sd HEAVERLS provided if Baptist LAY shall pay unto Samuel Rowland FISHER the afsd sum of £100 on day & time herein together w/interest for same, this Bond shall be void. Signed: Baptist LAY, Philena LAY. Wit: John WATTSON, Wm WALN. Philena LAY, wife of Baptist, was examined separate from her husband and did declare she became a party to the above of her own free will. Signed: John BARCLAY, Mayor of Philadelphia. 03 Oct 1791.

O-14:541. Incorporation. Incorporation of the Trustees of the Presbyterian Church Broad Creek wading place. Know all men by these presents that we the Subscribers Trustees elected and Chosen by the Society of the Presbyterian Church at Broad Creek wading place do hereby Certify that we have taken upon ourselves the name of the Trustees of Board Creek Congregation In Testimony whereof we have hereunto set our hands & seals this 15 Sep 1791. Signed: Leon HOUSTON, George BACON, Jonathan CATHELL, Henry EDGER, William VAUGHAN, Robt HOUSTON, John MITCHELL.

O-14:541. Bond of Conveyance. Benton COSTON of Sussex cnty, DE is held & firmly bound unto Joshua COSTON of same in the full sum of £600 to be paid to sd Joshua COSTON I bind myself dtd 24 Jan 1784. Benton COSTON Sr by his last will & testament devised unto above Benton COSTON all that tract of land whereon sd dec'd dwelt & whereon sd Joshua COSTON now dwells together w/all the other tracts of land contiguous thereunto that sd Benton COSTON dyed seized of in the Forrest of sd cnty. Whereas sd Benton COSTON hath now sold to sd Joshua COSTON all his title unto the first mentioned original tract & also the other tract devised to him by his father the sd Benton COSTON Sr. Condition of above Obligation is such that if above bound Benton COSTON shall at any time w/in the term of 7 years next ensuing when required by sd Joshua COSTON make over unto sd Joshua COSTON by sufficient Deed the above Obligations is to be void. Signed: Benton COSTON (mark). Wit: Benj'a MIFFLIN, John DOWNING.

O-14:541. Power of Attorney. William BLOXSOME of Accomack cnty, VA hath appointed Elias BAKER of Sussex cnty, DE my true & lawful Attorney to sue, levy, recover & receive all such sums of money, debts, goods & other demands whatsoever due unto me in any manner, ways or means by John ABBOTT of Sussex cnty, DE concerning all my right, title to that parcel of land in cnty afsd sold by me to sd John ABOTT, also granting unto my sd Attorney power & authority to make any Deed or Deed of Conveyance to execute to the sd John ABBOTT. 23 Dec 1786. Signed: William BLOXSOME (mark). Wit: Nath'l BEAVANS, Robert BLOXCOM (mark).

O-14:542. Bill of Sale. By the Award of John TENNANT, Thos ELLEGOOD & ---- SLAYTON, arbitrators, did find in favor of George CAMMERON against Alex'r MILLS of the Sloop John the sum of £93 15s to be paid 10 ?? 1793. Whereas Thomas ELLEGOOD of Sussex cnty, DE has become Security w/Alex'r MILLS for the payment of sd sum Alex'r MILLS doth make over unto sd Thomas ELLEGOOD the Sloop w/all her tackle & furniture in such manner that from this date to 10 Mar 1793 he shall have free privilege w/sd MILLS for the purpose of discharging sd debt & then at expiration of sd term if the sd MILLS or owners of sd Sloop not make payment to sd CAMMERON then shall sd ELLEGOOD hold possession of sd Sloop until debt by sd MILLS & partners is paid. It is further agreed no person shall sail the vessel w/o consent of all parties nor shall she leave the Chesapeake Bay w/o the like consent & that each party binds himself to use the utmost in the Power to procure Freights to keep sd vessel running until the sum for discharging sd debt. Signed: Alexander MILLS. Wit: William SAFFORD, James GREENLESS.

O-14:543. Deed of Sale. This Indenture made 04 Aug 1791 between Richard HOWARD, pilot, & Comfort his wife of Sussex cnty, DE of the one part & James Patriot WILSON of same of the other part. Richard HOWARD & Comfort his wife for the sum of £21 hath sold unto sd James WILSON all that parcel of land containing 2 lots situate in Lewes on the SW side of the Meeting House & bounded by HALL's line. Signed: Richard HOWARD, Comfort HOWARD (mark). Wit: Andrew WILLEY, Leah PULLET (mark).

O-14:543. Deed. Gilbelsher PARKER late of Rehoboth Hundred, Sussex cnty, DE, Esq, dec'd, (grndfthr of John SHANKLAND) was seized of a parcel of land, part of a larger tract, situate in hundred & cnty afsd called Sundyal by virtue of

Deed from William ---- of cnty afsd dtd 10 Nov 1735 rec'd in Liber G No 6 f 140, which parcel of land, part of the larger tract, is contained by land late of James HOLLAND, dec'd, on SW side of Daniel FLING's Swamp, containing 70 acres of land. Jacob KOLLOCK Esq dec'd, afsd Gilbelsher PARKER obtained a Warrant of Resurvey to the Sundyal tract by virtue of which sd Gilbelsher PARKER added to the 70 acres another 8 acres situate on the SW side of the above described land. Gilbelsher PARKER made his last will & testament dtd 18 Oct 1779 wherein among other things he devised unto his son in law David SHANKLAND the use of all his land & estate during his natural life & immediately after he did give & devised afsd land & improvements unto his grndsn John SHANKLAND. John SHANKLAND & Sarah his wife being about to remove to Back Settlement for the sum of £100 hath sold sd lands unto their father, David SHANKLAND. John SHANKLAND & Sarah his wife appoint Peter WHITE or John RUSSELL of Lewes their Attorney. Signed: John SHANKLAND, Sarah SHANKLAND. Wit: Jno WILTBANK, Jno RUSSELL. Sarah SHANKLAND, wife of John, was examined separate from her husband and did declare she became a party thereto of her own free will. Signed: Jno WILTBANK.

O-14:545. Deed of Sale. William CLARK late of Sussex cnty, DE, tanner, dec'd, was seized of lands & tenements in Broadkiln Hundred & d: Intestate, unmarried, w/o issue, whereby sd lands descended to his 2 sisters: Elizabeth the wife of Charles McLIN & Jane ROWLAND, which sd lands were by Order of Orphans Ct divided between sd Charles McLIN & Elizabeth his wife & the afsd Jane ROWLAND. Whereas sd Jane ROWLAND is dec'd leaving issue James ROWLAND, Elen FRAME, Sarah ROWLAND, William ROWLAND & John ROWLAND to whom her moiety of sd lands descended, which sd moiety was by Order of Orphans Ct divided among the heirs afsd, amongst the several allotments laid off unto sd William FRAME & Elon his wife the quantity of 18 acres & unto sd Sarah 18 acres. Sarah ROWLAND d: intestate, unmarried, w/o issue, whereby sd land descended to the afsd Elon FRAME, James ROWLAND, William ROWLAND & John ROWLAND which sd James, William & John ROWLAND by instrument dtd 11 Oct instant did empower the afsd William FRAME to dispose of & convey their several rights unto the afsd lands. William FRAME & Elon FRAME for the sum of £36 hath sold unto John STAFFORD all the above mentioned lands which sd William CLARK, Jane ROWLAND & Sarah ROWLAND at the time of their death or which sd William & Elon his wife, James ROWLAND, William ROWLAND & John ROWLAND had claim or title to. 12 Oct 1791. Signed: William FRAME, Elon FRAME (mark). Wit: Stephen COSTON, W HARRISON. 13 Oct 1791. Elon FRAME, wife of William, was examined separate from her husband & did declare she became a party thereto of her own free will. Signed: Jno WILTBANK.

O-14:547. Deed. 06 May 1791 George MESSECK, yeoman, of Sussex cnty, DE of the one part for the sum of £75 hath sold unto Morgan WILLIAMS, yeoman, of same, of the other part a parcel of land situate in Cedar Creek Hundred, being part of a larger tract which formerly belonged to William COLLINS , containing 79 acres. George MESSECK appoints Ahab CLENDANIEL as his Attorney. Signed: George MESSECK. Wit: Custis SHOCKLEY, J P BROWN.

O-14:548. Deed. This Indenture made 09 Nov 1791 between Jacob TOWNSEND of Sussex cnty, DE, yeoman, of the one part & Curtis SHOCKLEY of same, yeoman, of the other part. There is a parcel of land situate in cnty afsd being in Forest Creek taken up & surveyed for Solomon TOWNSEND, father to the afsd Jacob TOWNSEND who devised same unto Jacob TOWNSEND afsd being the easternmost part thereof bounded by land of Obadiah ELDRIDGE, containing 78 acres. Jacob TOWNSEND for the sum of £5 hath sold unto Curtis SHOCKLEY the afsd 78 acres. Signed: Jacob TOWNSEND. Wit: Thos GRAY, Ahab CLENDANIEL (mark).

O-14:548. Deed. This Indenture made 09 Nov 1791 between Nicholas ABBOTT of Sussex cnty, DE yeoman, of the one part & Curtis SHOCKLEY of the same of the other part. There is a parcel of land situate in Sussex cnty, DE bounded by lands of Curtis SHOCKLEY & lands of Laurence RILEY, land late of Ahab CLENDANIEL, containing 53 1/2 acres. Nicholas ABBOTT for the sum of £3 2s 6p hath sold unto Curtis SHOCKLEY the afsd 53 1/2 acres. Signed: Nicholas ABBOTT (mark). Wit: Thos GRAY, Morgan WILLIAMS (mark).

O-14:549. Deed of Sale. This Indenture made 09 Nov 1791 between Elias BAKER of Sussex cnty, DE of the one part & Curtis SHOCKLEY of same, yeoman, of the other part. There is a parcel of land situate in cnty afsd being in the forest of Cedar Creek Hundred called Thompson's Ridge taken up & surveyed for David SMITH & by sundry conveyances reverted to William BLOXSOME of Accomack cnty, VA. Sd William BLOXSOME by his POA dtd 23 Dec 1786 authorized afsd Elias BAKER his Attorney to convey & make over the afsd tract or parcel of land unto John ABBOTT of Sussex cnty, DE & John ABBOTT by his Writing Obligatory dtd 01 Mar 1785 Obligated himself & his heirs to convey & make over afsd tract of land & premises unto sd Curtis SHOCKLEY, sd land bounded by lands of Ahab CLENDANIEL, containing 81 1/4 acres of land by survey 20 Jan 1775. Elias BAKER by POA of afsd William BLOXSOME for the sum of £150 hath sold unto sd Curtis SHOCKLEY the afsd 81 1/4 acres of land. Signed: Elias BAKER. Wit: Thos GRAY, Ahab CLENDANIEL (mark).

O-14:550. Deed of Sale. 13 Oct 1791 John SHARP Sr of Sussex cnty, DE, yeoman, of the one part for the sum of 5s & for divers other considerations me thereunto moving have released unto Jacob SHARP of same, yeoman, of the other part, all my right & claim unto two tracts of land, the one tract made by John SHARP from Isaac DRAPER bounded by a tract surveyed to John CORD, ---- CLOWES & JONES's 40 acres & John FOWLER's, containing 252 acres of land; the other being part of a tract granted to John FOWLER containing 95 acres it being the whole of sd parcel excepting 9 1/2 acres which Job SHARP purchased of sd John SHARP Sr set out of sd tract last mentioned the contents of sd tract therefore is 85 1/4 acres. John SHARP Sr appts Thomas GRAY as his Attorney. Signed: John SHARP. Wit: Zachariah REYNOLDS (mark), Selby SHARP (mark)

O-14:551. Deed of Conveyance. This Indenture made 01 Feb 1791 between West JONES of Sussex cnty, DE of the one part & Jehu WEST of same, yeoman, of the other part. Isaac JONES late of sd cnty, yeoman, was seized of certain tracts of land & did on 11 Dec 1784 make his last will & testament in manner & form following: The first I give & bequeath unto my son James JONES 100 acres of land called Forrest Chance where he now lives & 1/2 the warrant land that I own to be laid off as may be most convenient for both plantations; I give & bequeath unto my beloved wife, Elizabeth JONES, 90 1/2 acres where I now live w/my houses, plantation & 1/2 my warrant land during her life & widowhood & then the 90 /12 acres & 1/2 my warrant land to my son West JONES after my wife's marriage or decease. Whereas it is found the afsd 90 1/2 acres is part of a tract of land called Hap Hazzard containing 300 acres & sd Isaac JONES in his lifetime obtained a Deed of Conveyance for the sd 90 1/2 acres being part of the afsd tract called Hap Hazzard from William BEVINS Exec of William BEVINS, dec'd, which sd Deed is rec'd in Liber B, f ?. Sd land was a resurvey made on a tract of land called Forrest Chance first containing 100 acres by virtue of a Warrant of Resurvey dtd Philadelphia 02 May 177? granted unto Isaac JONES then living in Little Creek Hundred & resurveyed for sd Isaac JONES 16 Sep 1776 now called Content all of which lands are situate in ? Creek Hundred. Now West JONES for the sum of £80 sells unto Jehu WEST all his right & claim to the afsd 90 1/2 acres of land called Hap Hazzard & likewise the 1/2 of the warrant land called Content at the marriage or decease of sd Elizabeth JONES. Signed: West JONES (mark). Wit: Wingate HALL, Wingate CANNON, Philip WINGATE.

O-14:553. Deed. This Indenture made 09 Nov 1791 between Ahab CLENDANIEL of Sussex cnty, DE, yeoman, of the one part & Curtis SHOCKLEY of same, farmer, of the other part. There is a tract of land situate in Broadkiln Hundred, cnty afsd, surveyed for Caleb BURIER & by sundry conveyances reverted to afsd Ahab CLENDANIEL who by his Obligation dtd 30 Jan 1789 did Obligate himself to confirm unto Curtis SHOCKLEY 105 1/2 acres of the above land laid out for 142 1/2 acres. Ahab CLENDANIEL for the sum of £100 hath sold & confirmed unto Curtis SHOCKLEY the afsd 142 1/2 acres of land excepting 30 acres of sd land on the NE end thereof & also 7 acres more on S side thereof. Signed: Ahab CLENDANIEL (mark). Thos GRAY, Richard SHOCKLEY (mark).

O-14:554. Deed of Sale. This Indenture made 09 Nov 1791 between Curtis SHOCKLEY of Sussex cnty, DE, farmer, of the one part & Luke CLENDANIEL a minor son of Luke CLENDANIEL, late of same, dec'd of the other part. There is a parcel of land being part of a larger tract of land granted to ---- SMITH called Thompson's Ridge & by sundry conveyances became the property of afsd Curtis SHOCKLEY who by his writing Obligatory dtd 06 Apr 1786 Obligated himself to convey part of the part of the tract afsd to afsd Luke CLENDANIEL, dec'd, who devised same unto Luke CLENDANIEL afsd laid out for 5 1/4 acres of land. Curtis SHOCKLEY for the sum of £25 hath sold unto Luke CLENDANIEL a minor the afsd 5 1/4 acres. Signed: Curtis SHOCKLEY. Wit: Thos GRAY, Ahab CLENDANIEL (mark).

O-14:554. Deed of Sale. This Indenture made 09 Nov 1791 between William COLLINS of Sussex cnty, DE, yeoman, of the one part & James HALL of same, farmer, of the other part. There is a tract of land situate in cnty afsd being part of a larger tract granted to George PERKINS 16 Sep 1748 for 200 acres of land being in ?? Creek Hundred adjoining a tract belonging to Job SMITH called Strife & by sundry conveyances became the property of the afsd William COLLINS who by his writing Obligatory dtd 04 Jan 1784 did obligate himself to convey his claim to afsd land called Oak Hall unto the afsd James HALL sd land being bounded by a tract called Thompson's Ridge, Nathan SPENCER's land, George MESSICK's land, COLLINS's outfield, Job SMITH's patent line called Strife, William COLLIN's land & his brother Frederick COLLINS' land, containing 150 acres of land. William COLLINS for the sum of £200 hath sold unto James HALL the afsd 150 acres of land. Signed: William COLLINS. Wit: Phoebe SPENCER, Morgan WILLIAMS (mark).

O-14:555. Deed. This Indenture made 09 Nov 1791 between Mary ABBOTT, Admin of John ABBOTT late of Sussex cnty, DE, dec'd, of the one part & Curtis SHOCKLEY of same, farmer, of the other part. 01 Mar 1785 John ABBOTT by his writing Obligatory obligated himself to make over unto Curtis SHOCKLEY 123 acres of land situate in Broadkiln Hundred granted by Proprietaries Warrant to Dormand LOFLEY dtd 28 Oct 1746 who by his last will & testament devised afsd land & premises to his dtr Sarah LOFFLEY who md: John CLENDANIEL who by their writing Obligatory dtd 24 Jul 17?? obligated themselves to convey afsd land unto Caleb CURRIER. Caleb CURRIER 30 Nov 1752 assigned the afsd Obligation transfer all his right, title to sd land to Abraham WYNKOOP, merchant, who 13 Dec 175? assigned his right, title of sd land to William BENNETT of Sussex cnty his assignment on sd Obligation dtd 16 Aug 1760 assigned his claim to sd 123 acres of land to the afsd John ABBOT, late of Sussex cnty. For the sum of £50 already paid unto the afsd John ABBOTT in his lifetime Mary ABBOTT hath sold afsd 123 acres to Curtis SHOCKLEY. Signed: Mary ABBOTT (mark). Wit: Thos GRAY, Morgan WILLIAMS (mark).

O-14:556. Deed. This Indenture made 13 Oct 1791 between John SHARP Sr of Sussex cnty, DE, yeoman, of the one part & Selby SHARP of same, yeoman, of the other part. John SHARP Sr for the sum of 5s & for divers other good causes conveys unto Selby SHARP two tracts of land, one called the Fork Tract granted to John LOFFLAND & conveyed by to sd John SHARP Sr containing 30 acres of land & the other tract being 1 moiety or half part of a larger tract granted to William TOWNSEND & by sundry conveyances became the property of John SHARP containing 100 acres of land. John SHARP appts Thomas GRAY as his Attorney. Signed: John SHARP. Wit: Zechariah REYNOLDS (mark), Jacob SHARP (mark).

O-14:557. Bond of Conveyance. Joseph DRAPER of Sussex cnty, DE is firmly bound unto Charles DRAPER of same in the sum of £400 to be paid to sd Charles DRAPER. 04 Mar 1784. Condition of sd Obligation is such that if Joseph DRAPER conveys a tract of land in Slatter Neck the land lying on the WE side of by a sufficient Deed the above Obligation to be void. Signed: Joseph DRAPER. Wit: William HINDS, William DAVIS.

O-14:558. Petition. Joseph DRAPER was seized of a tract of land situate in Slaughter Neck, Sussex cnty, DE & by his Bond dtd 01 Mar 17?4 bound himself to Charles DRAPER of cnty afsd, yeoman, in the sum of £400 that if sd Joseph DRAPER made a sufficient Deed for the lands laid off for him by Orphans Ct as his Share of lands of ---- HINDS dec'd containing 51 acres then sd Obligation to be void. Joseph DRAPER d: w/o having made conveyance. Elizabeth DRAPER, Admin of Joseph DRAPER dec'd requests Ct to grant an Order to Petitioner to make sufficient Deed to Charles DRAPER. Signed: Elizabeth DRAPER. Ct so Orders. 09 Nov 1791.

O-14:558. Deed of Sale. There is a tract of land situate in Slaughter Neck,

Sussex cnty, DE known as Hinds' Onion Field being part of a larger tract now in the possession of Thomas HINDS Jr & Charles DRAPER so seized thereof thereafter d: having made no will or testament. Joseph DRAPER one of the heirs petitioned Orphans Ct to make division of sd lands which were granted & sd Ct devised sd Joseph DRAPER should hold his part of sd land which was 51 acres. Joseph DRAPER by his Bond dtd 01 Mar 1784 bound himself to Charles DRAPER for the sum of £400 w/condition should Joseph DRAPER make sufficient Deed for the above mentioned 51 acres to Charles DRAPER sd Bond to be void. Joseph DRAPER d: w/o having made such Deed. Elizabeth DRAPER, Admin of sd Joseph DRAPER, petitioned sd Ct for order to make sufficient Deed unto Charles DRAPER & sd Ct so Ordered. Elizabeth DRAPER confirms unto Charles DRAPER that parcel of land called Onion Field bounded by William HICKMAN's land & Slaughter Creek containing 119 acres of land. Signed: Elizabeth DRAPER. Wit: Thos FISHER, Rich'd HAYES.

O-14:560. Deed of Sale. This Indenture made 09 Nov 1791 between Judah CLENDANIEL, Exec of the last will & testament of Luke CLENDANIEL late of Sussex cnty, DE, yeoman, dec'd of the one part & Obadiah ELDRIDGE of same, farmer, of the other part. Luke CLENDANIEL in Apr 1786 obligated himself in writing to convey unto Obadiah ELDRIDGE 20 acres of land situate in the forrest of Cedar Creek Hundred, cnty afsd, being part of a larger tract which formerly belonged to Solomon TOWNSEND who by his devise intended to be the property of his son Solomon TOWNSEND Jr but sd Solomon TOWNSEND Jr selling sd land to Luke CLENDANIEL & before any Deed was made sd Solomon TOWNSEND Jr d: therefore afsd Solomon TOWNSEND the elder devised sd land & premises to sd Luke CLENDANIEL. Sd lands bounded by tract of land conveyed from Luke TOWNSEND to afsd Obadiah ELDRIDGE laid out for 20 acres. For the sum of £25 already paid to Luke CLENDANIEL by sd Obadiah ELDRIDGE, Judah CLENDANIEL confirms unto sd Obadiah ELDRDIGE afsd 20 acres. Signed: Judah CLENDANIEL (mark). Wit: Thos GRAY, Ahab CLENDANIEL (mark). Ack: 09 Nov 1791.

O-14:560. Deed of Sale. This Indenture made 1791 between George MESSICK of Sussex cnty, DE, taylor, of the one part & Curtis SHOCKLEY of same, yeoman, of the other part. There is a parcel of land situate in the forest of Cedar Creek Hundred part of a larger tract called Oak Hall surveyed for George PERKINS & by sundry conveyances became the property of Frederick COLLINS late of cnty afsd. Frederick COLLINS by his POA dtd 11 Nov 1784 authorized afsd George MESICK to convey afsd parcel of land unto William BLOXOM by his writing Obligatory dtd 18 Mar 1783 which sd William BLOXOM by his assignment dtd 20 Mar following transferred of sd Obligation containing 12 acres of land & premises unto Curtis SHOCKLEY & also sd Frederick COLLINS by his writing Obligatory dtd 19 Aug 1783 did obligate himself to convey to David GOTT all the remained of the afsd tract called Oak Hall remaining unsold which sd David GOTT by his assignment transferred 20 Mar 1786 unto Samuel IRELAND who on 23 Feb 1788 did assign his title to sd land & premises unto Curtis SHOCKLEY. Sd tract bounded by dividend of Morgan WILLIAMS, land of Nathan SPENCER's, Thompson's Ridge, corner of ABBOTTs & Solomon TOWNSEND's land, Charles TOWNSEND's land & land laid off to Anthony HEAVELO, containing 72 1/2 acres. George MESICK appts Ahab CLENDANIEL his Attorney. Signed: George MESSICK. Wit: Margain WILLIAMS (mark), T BROWN. Ack: 09 Nov 1791.

O-14:562. Deed. 07 Nov 1791 Philip MARVEL Sr of Sussex cnty, DE, yeoman, of the one part for the sum of £60 doth sell unto Thomas MARVEL son of Philip of the same, yeoman, of the other part all that parcel of land being part of a tract surveyed for Joseph INGLISH formerly of cnty afsd situate in the forest of Broadkiln Hundred which sd land Joseph INGLISH sold to James RICHARDSON & sd land was sold by Sheriff's vendue to William STEEL & William STEEL by his Deed of Sale dtd 24 ?? 1776 conveyed afsd land to Cornelius BEAVANS & Cornelius BEAVENS by his Deed of Sale dtd 11 Oct 1784 conveyed same to Philip MARVEL. Sd land laid off for 100 acres. Signed: Philip MARVEL (mark). Wit: John MORRIS, Sommerset D COSTON. Ack: 09 Nov 1791.

O-14:562. Deed. 22 Jul 1791 Anthony HEAVELO Sr of Sussex cnty, DE, farmer, of the one part, for the sum of £50 hath sold unto Jonathan HEAVELO of same of the other part, all that parcel of land lying on the W side of Delaware Bay in Broadkiln Hundred formerly the property of Daniel CARLISLE & wife & Thomas CARLISLE & wife & sold by them to Nicholas GREEN & wife for the use of Jabez Maud FISHER by Deed dtd 0? Feb 1719. After death of afsd Jabez Maud FISHER marsh & meadow descended unto his son Edward FISHER & afterwards sold by him unto above sd Anthony HEAVELO. Sd land bounded by mouth of Samuel WILTBANK's ditch & Dyers Gut containing 61 1/2 acres of marsh or meadow land. Anthony HEAVELO appts William PERRY his Attorney. Signed: Anthony HEAVELO Sr. Wit: Anthony HEAVELO Jr, Sarah McCAY (mark). Ack: 09 Nov 1791.

O-14:563. Deed of Sale. This Indenture made 09 Nov 1791 between Obadiah ELDRIDGE of Sussex cnty, DE of the one part & Curtis SHOCKLEY of same, yeoman, of the other part. There is a small parcel of land being part of a larger tract situate in the forest of Cedar Creek Hundred, cnty afsd, which formerly belonged to Solomon TOWNSEND who by his devise gave same to his son Luke TOWNSEND by Deed unto afsd Obadiah ELDRIDGE dtd 04 Aug 1783. Sd Obadiah ELDRIDGE by his writing Obligatory dtd 06 Apr 1786 Obligated himself to convey 12 acres of the above land on the S most corner unto sd Curtis SHOCKLEY. Sd land bounded by Home Line of sd ELDRIDGE's tract near sd SHOCKLEY's fence. Obadiah ELDRIDGE for the sum of £25 hath sold unto Curtis SHOCKLEY afsd 12 acres of land & premises. Signed: Obadiah ELDRIDGE. Wit: Thos GRAY, Ahab CLENDANIEL (mark). Ack: 09 Nov 1791.

O-14:564. Deed. This Indenture made 18 Oct 1791 between Robert HOUSTON, Rhoads SHANKLAND, George MITCHELL, William MOORE & John COLLINS of Sussex cnty, DE, Commissioners apptd by General Assembly of DE for removing the Seat of Justice from Lewes to more central part of Sussex cnty & for other purposes, of the one part & Joshua HALL of Lewes, blacksmith, of the other part. Sd Commissioners in pursuance of afsd Act sold by Public Vendue unto Joshua HALL as the highest bidder for the sum of £55 the old Prison or Jail standing in Lewes. Signed: Robert HOUSTON, Rhoads SHANKLAND, Geo MITCHELL, Wm MOORE, John COLLINS. Wit: Kendle BATSON, Nath'l MITCHELL, W T BELL. Ack: 10 Nov 1791.

O-14:564. Deed of Sale. 22 Mar 1791 William HARRIS of Lewes, Sussex cnty, DE, house carpenter & joiner, & Winefred his wife of the one part for the sum of £20 hath sold unto Jehu EVANS of same, gent, of the other part, all that parcel of land late the property of Charles PERRY late of Sussex cnty, dec'd formerly being in Dorchester cnty, MD on the N side of the NE branch of Nanticoke River on the E side of Turtle Creek but since by settlement of Territory between the Proprietary of MD & Proprietary of PA and cntys on Delaware become part of Sussex cnty at present situate in NorthWest Fork Hundred, cnty afsd, laid out according to Certificate of Survey returned to land office at city of St Mary's dtd 27 Apr 1782 & '83, for 250 acres of land called Cypress Swamp. Signed: William HARRIS, Winefred HARRIS. Wit: Charles JOHNSON, Albertus BRUCE. Winefred HARRIS, wife of William, was examined separate from her husband and did declare she became a party thereto of her own free will. Signed: Charles POLK. William HARRIS appts William HARRISON of Lewes his Attorney. Ack: 10 Nov 1791.

O-14:566. Deed of Sale. 09 Nov 1791 Jaquish HUDSON of Sussex cnty, DE, farmer, & Mary is wife of the one part for the sum of £210 hath sold unto Riley AKE, blacksmith, of same of the other part, a tract of land called Hopkin's Discovery lying on the S side of Indian River near the head of Black Water

Creek. Josiah HOPKINS & John HOPKINS obtained a right to the above named tract of land containing 360 acres of land. John HOPKINS father of Ezekiel HOPKINS was seized of sd tract & d: w/o making his son Ezekiel, being his eldest son & heir at law. Ezekile HOPKINS by Deed made over his title in above sd land to John EVANS (Cedar Neck). John EVANS by Deed conveyed sd land unto Jaquish HUDSON who has now sold all the sd tract of land called Hopkin's Discovery that is not already sold off or taken away by elder surveys estimated to be 170 acres of land unto the afsd Riley AKE. Jaquish HUDSON & Mary his wife appt William LOCKWOOD or John AYDELOTT, bricklayer, our Attorney. Signed: Jaquish HUDSON (mark), Mary HUDSON (mark). Wit: LIttleton TOWNSEND, Eli EVANS. Ack: 10 Nov 1791.

O-14:567. Deed of Sale. This Indenture made 09 Nov 1791 between Stephen COSTON of Broadkiln Hundred, Sussex cnty, DE, yeoman, of the one part & William MARVEL of same, yeoman, of the other part. There is a parcel of land containing 128 acres being part of a larger tract formerly surveyed & laid out for John MORRIS of Sussex cnty lying in Broadkiln Hundred near Green Branch in the forest thereof & the same which Robert Watson McCALLEY by Indenture dtd 24 Feb 1776 sold to Mitchell SCOTT. Mitchell SCOTT by Deed of Sale dtd 04 Nov 1784 conveyed same to Joshua COSTON. Joshua COSTON by his Deed of Sale dtd 06 Sep 1786 sold his right to Stephen COSTON. Stephen COSTON for the sum of £140 hath sold unto William MARVEL all that parcel of land afsd containing 128 acres being part of a larger tract as afsd. Signed: Stephen COSTON. Wit: John MORRIS, Thomas MARVEL. Ack: 10 Nov 1791.

O-14:568. Deed of Sale. This Indenture made 18 Oct 1791 between George MITCHELL, William MOORE, Robert HOUSTON, John COLLINS & Rhoads SHANKLAND, Commissioners appt'd by Act of General Assembly of DE for removing the seat of Justice from Lewes to a more central part of Sussex cnty on behalf of the cnty of Sussex of the one part & Thomas M HAM of same of the other part. The Commissioners afsd for the sum of £85 hath sold unto Thomas M HAM the old Court House of Sussex cnty situate in the town of Lewes sold at Public Sale, sd HAM being the highest bidder. Signed: George MITCHELL, Wm MOORE, Robt HOUSTON, John COLLINS, Rhoads SHANKLAND. Wit: Nath'l MITCHELL, Nath'l HICKMAN, W J BELL. Rec: 10 Nov 1791.

O-14:568. Deed of Conveyance. This Indenture made 07 Nov 1791 between Thomas PARREMORE of Sussex cnty, DE, planter, of the one part & Jonathan BETTS Sr of the other part. Mathew PARAMORE late of cnty afsd, dec'd, was seized of a tract of land called Friendship & in 1776 obtained a proprietaries warrant of resurvey of afsd tract of land & in his last will bequeathed the afsd tract of land together w/the resurvey made thereon to his son Ezekiel PARREMORE who 23 May 1791 signed unto the afsd Thomas PARREMORE a good & sufficient Deed. Thomas PARAMORE for the sum of 72s 5p hath sold unto Jonathan BETTS Sr 100 acres of land being part of the afsd tract, 17 acres of patent & 83 acres of resurvey situate in Broad Creek Hundred in Winbrosorcom Neck laid off for 100 acres. Signed: Thomas PARAMORE (mark). Wit: Jesse SAUNDERS, Nathan SAUNDERS.

O-14:569. Deed of Sale. DE state lately at a Ct of Comm Pleas held at Lewes in Sussex cnty recovered against George & Levin BACON a debt of £97 as £4 17s 8p adjudged for damages & costs, to be levied against the goods & chattels of sd George & Levin BACON. 09 Feb 1791 sd Ct ordered Thomas EVANS, High Sheriff of sd cnty, to seize sd goods & chattels to render payment & sd Sheriff seized a tract of land situate in Little Creek Hundred containing 75 acres of land sd to be the property of Levin BACON sd land bounded on the W by Little Creek Branch, on the E by a tract of land called Leavel Ground belonging to John BACON which sd land was appraised as insufficient to satisfy the debt & damages w/in 7 years. 04 May 1791 sd Ct ordered Public Sale of sd land. 08 Jul sd Sheriff sold sd land at Public Sale to John BACON for the sum of £45 10s, he being the highest bidder. Thomas LAWS, current High Sheriff of Sussex cnty, DE confirms unto John BACON all that mentioned tract of land & premises. Signed: Thomas LAWS, Sheriff. Wit: Jonathan CATHELL, Jno. BOYCE. 11 Aug 1791 rec'd of John BACON the sum of £35 12s 2p in full of the debt & suit DE state against George & Levin BACON. Signed: Richard LITTLE. Ack: 10 Nov 1791.

O-14:570. Deed. 08 Nov 1791 Jonathan HEARN & Rhodah HEARN his wife of Sussex cnty, DE, of the one part for the sum of £80 hath sold unto William ELZEY of same of the other part, all that tract of land called Parrismores Misfortune situate in Little Creek Hundred E from the main road that leads from Spring Hill to Broad Creek Bridge bounded by land called Ralphs Delight containing 50 acres. Signed: Jonathan HEARN, Rhoda HEARN. Wit: Kendle BATSON, Nath'l MITCHELL. 08 Nov 1791 Rhodah HEARN, wife of Jonathan, was examined separate from her husband & did declare she became a party thereto of her own free will. Signed: Charles POLK. Jonathan HEARN appts Kendle BATSON to be his Attorney. Signed: Jonathan HEARN. Wit: Sommerset D COSTON, G HAZZARD. Ack: 10 Nov 1791

O-14:571. Deed. 09 Mar 1791 John JONES Esq of Sussex cnty, DE of the one part for the sum of £60 & for the natural love & affection he hath unto Dagworthy

JONES of same, of the other part, & for the better maintenance of him the sd Dagworthy JONES hath sold unto Dagworthy JONES one equal undivided fourth part of all that tract of land by a Resurvey to be found in Worcester but not Sussex cnty, called Unity Grove, it being the place where John JONES now lives, containing 1768 acres & also one equal undivided fourth of a tract of land in same cnty called Lebanon containing 2170 acres being the same premises John MIFFLIN by Indenture dtd 12 Feb 1772 in the records of Worcester cnty in Liber I, folio 30,31,32 granted to Joseph MIFFLIN & which sd Joseph MIFFLIN by Indenture dtd 12 Aug 1785 enrolled among the records of Sussex cnty in Liber N, No 13, folio 321 granted to afsd John JONES. John JONES appts David HALL or James P WILSON his Attorney. Signed: John JONES. Wit: David MURRAY, Thomas STEVENS (mark), Severn JONES. Ack: 10 Nov 1791.

O-14:572. Deed of Sale. This Indenture made 21 Jun 1791 between George MITCHELL, Robert HOUSTON, William MOORE, John COLLINS & Rhoads SHANKLAND being Commissioners apptd by Act of Gen Assbly of DE to removing seat of Justice from Lewes to more central part of Sussex cnty of the one part & Nath'l MITCHELL of Sussex cnty, DE of the other part. Sd Commissioners for the sum of £30 13s had sold unto Nath'l MITCHELL two lotts, viz: No 16 situate in George Town containing 27 sq perches, also No 14 situate in town afsd containing 2? sq perches. Afsd Commissioners appt John W BATSON, George MITCHELL or Rhoads SHANKLAND their Attorney. Signed: George MITCHELL, Robt HOUSTON, Willm MOORE, John COLLINS, Rhoads SHANKLAND. Wit: Peter PARKER, William HARRIS, Kendle BATSON. Ack: 11 Nov 1791. Jno WILTBANK.

O-14:573. Deed of Sale. This Indenture made 11 Nov 1791 between George MITCHELL, William MOORE, Robert HOUSTON, John COLLINS & Rhoads SHANKLAND, Commissioners apptd by DE Gnrl Assbly to relocate Seat of Justice from Lewes to more central part of Sussex cnty, DE, of the one part & William TEAGE of Sussex cnty, DE of the other part. Sd Commissioners for the sum of £2 5s hath sold unto sd William TEAGE a lott of ground No 94 situate in George Town containing 27 sq perches. Sd Commissioners appt John W BATSON or Rhoads SHANKLAND as their Attorney. Signed: Geo MITCHELL, John COLLINS, Rhoads SHANKLAND. Wit: H HAZZARD, K BATSON. Ack: 11 Nov 1791 Nath'l MITCHELL, Proth'y.

O-14:573. Deed. This Indenture made 13 Sep 1791 between George MITCHELL, Robert HOUSTON, William MOORE, John COLLINS & Rhoads SHANKLAND Commissioners apptd by DE Gnrl Assbly to relocate Seat of

Justice from Lewes to more central part of Sussex cnty, DE, of the one part & Thomas MARVEL son of Philip for the use of his son Abraham Harris MARVEL when of age of sd cnty & state of the other part. Sd Commissioners for the sum of 4s hath sold unto Thomas MARVEL Lott No 42 situate in George Town at corner of Bedford Street & Strawberry Alley containing 2? sq perches. Sd Commissioners appt Thomas LAWS or Seth GRIFFEN or Robert JONES as their Attorney. Signed: Geo MITCHELL, John COLLINS, Rhoads SHANKLAND. Wit: K BATSON, G HAZZARD. Ack: 11 Nov 1791.

O-14:574. Deed. 11 Nov 1791 George MESSICK of Sussex cnty, DE, yeoman, & Mary his wife of the one part for the sum of £50 10s hath sold unto Job INGRAM of same, yeoman, of the other part, all that tract of land situate in Broadkiln Hundred, a 100 acre MD patent to Obediah MESSICK, dec'd, on E side of Gravelly Branch near to Collingers Mill, & a division line between Eli SHORT & Isaac INGRAM's land, Dobson's Beaver Dam Branch. Signed: George MESSICK, Mary MESSICK (mark). Wit: D HALL, Nathaniel WRIGHT. 11 Nov 1791 Mary MESSICK, wife of George, was examined separate from her husband and did declare she signed above of her own free will. Signed: Peter ROBINSON.

O-14:575. Deed. 21 Feb 1791. Samuel HANDY & Elizabeth his wife of Sussex cnty, DE for the sum of £41 12s 6p sold to Joshua O'BEER yeoman of same, part of a tract of land situate in N W Fork Hundred, it being part of a tract called Little Worth beginning at the SE side of the County Road containing 27 & 3/4 acres of land. Samuel HANDY & Elizabeth his wife appt William PERRY or Rhoads SHANKLAND as their Attorney. Signed: Samuel HANDY, Elizabeth HANDY. Wit: John HOOPER, John HANDY, Perry O'BEER. Elizabeth HANDY, wife of Samuel, was examined separate from her husband and acknowledged she signed the w/in Deed of her own free will. Charles POLK. Ack: 11 Nov 1791.

O-14:576. Deed of Sale. 11 Nov 1791. Job INGRAM & Mary his wife, yeoman of Sussex cnty, for the sum of £190 sold to Richard HUDSON, yeoman, of same, two tracts of land situate in Broadkiln Hundred, one tract called Long Delay containing 100 acres of land; the other beginning near Collin's Mill Pond along Collin's Resurvey, along the intersection of the division line between Eli SHORT & Isaac INGRAM in the middle of Gravelly Branch until it intersects the main run of Dobson's Beaver Dam Branch, intersects the line of Obediah MESSICK's patent land, containing 178 acres of land w/all improvements to sd tracts. Signed: Job INGRAM, Mary INGRAM. Wit: D HALL, Nunez DEPUTY. Mary INGRAM, wife of Job, was examined separate from her husband & did declare she signed the above of her own free will. Signed: Peter ROBINSON. Ack: 11 Nov 1791.

O-14:577. Deed of Sale. Jonathan CLIFTON, late of Sussex cnty, DE, possessed sundry tracts of land situate in North West Fork Hundred made his will dtd 18 Mar 1788 appointing his son, Nathan CLIFTON as Exec, who afterwards d: Intestate w/o fully administering the estate of afsd Jonathan CLIFTON. LOA were granted 09 Dec last past to Henry CLIFTON who petitioned Orphans Ct the personal estate of dec'd was not sufficient to discharge just debts & obtained an Order to sell sd real estate of Jonathan CLIFTON at public sale for that purpose. 11 Jun 1790 Henry CLIFTON sold at public sale one tract of land called Cliftons Chance containing 50 acres, one other tract of land called Good Luck containing 16 acres, one other tract called Clifton Security containing 34 acres, one other tract called Cliftons Support containing 57 acres, one other tract called Venture containing 41 acres & one other tract called White Marsh containing 50 acres to Peter RUST of cnty afsd for the sum of £90, he being the highest bidder. Signed: Henry CLIFTON. Wit: John W BATSON, Elijah FREENY, Isaak WARTON (mark). Ack: 11 Nov 1791.

)-14:577. Mortgage. 17 Dec 1791. William COLEMAN, yeoman, of Sussex cnty, DE, silver smith, for the sum of £60 granted unto Elon HAZZARD, widow, of same, all that tract of land containing 83 acres formerly of Peter HARMONSON, dec'd & Joshua FISHER of cnty afsd & also a tract of land sold by Peter F WRIGHT, dec'd, to sd William COLEMAN for 8 & 3/4 acres, sd parcels of land situate in Lewes, Rehoboth Hundred, cnty afsd w/all buildings & improvements provided that is sd William COLEMAN shall pay unto sd Elon HAZZARD the sd sum of £60 w/interest at the rate of 6% per annum on 01 Jan 1794 w/o delay this Indenture shall be void. Signed: William COLEMAN. Wit: James NEWBOLD, Prissilla PAYNTER.

O-14:578. Deed of Sale. Robert WHITE, late of Lewes, Rehoboth Hundred, Sussex cnty, DE was seized of a parcel of Marsh containing 11 acres being part of a larger tract containing 100 acres, situate in Hundred afsd of the S side of Coolspring Creek called Greenfield originally granted by patent dtd 02 second month 1687 unto Francis CORNWELL, d: after making his will wherein he apptd Ann WHITE, his widow, as Exec'x. Ann WHITE on 05 Nov 1791 put sd lands to public sale & same was purchased by Reice WOOLF of same, yeoman, for the sum of 30s per acres, he being the highest bidder. Ann WHITE for the sum of £16 10s hath sold unto Reice WOOLF the afsd 11 acres w/all improvements. Signed: Ann WHITE. Wit: Jno WILTBANK, Kendle BATSON. Ack: 23 Nov 1791.

O-14:579. Deed of Sail. 15 Nov 1791. Reice WOOLF of Lewes, Rehoboth Hundred, Sussex cnty, DE, yeoman, & Mary his wife for the sum of £16 10s sold unto Ann WHITE a parcel of Marsh containing 11 acres being part of a larger tract containing 100 acres situate in hundred & cnty afsd on SE side of Coolspring Creek known by the name of Greenfield, originally granted by patent dtd 02 of second month 1687 unto Francis CORNWELL. Afsd 11 acres being the same which sd Ann WHITE as Exec'x of her late husband Robert WHITE, dec'd, by Deed dtd one day before the date of these presents to the afsd Reice WOOLF. Reice WOOLF & Mary his wife appt John WILTBANK or Phillips KOLLOCK their Attorney. Signed: Reice WOOLF, Mary WOOLF. Wit: Jno WILTBANK, Kendle BATSON. Mary WOOLF, wife of Reice, was examined separate from her husband and did acknowledge she became a party thereto of her own free will. Signed: Jno WILTBANK. Ack: 23 Nov 1791.

)-14:580. Deed of Sale. John MILLER, late of Sussex cnty, DE, was seized of a parcel of land situate in Cedar Creek Hundred called Swilby's & afterwards d: leaving several children to whom sd tract descended. Robert MILLER, oldest son of afsd petitioned Orphans Ct to partition sd land & evaluation was set at 30s per acre, there being the quantity of 154 acres amounting to the sum of £231 7s 6p. Robert MILLER by Indenture dtd 09 Mar 1785 sold unto Betty MILLER a parcel of land, part of the afsd tract called Twilleys, near Rachel TURNER's fence, bounded by land of Branston LOFTLAND, laid off for 32 acres w/all improvements. 04 Feb 1789 Betty MILLER bound herself unto Littleton TOWNSEND of sd cnty in the sum of £5 w/condition sd Betty MILLER to provide sufficient Deed unto Littleton TOWNSEND for the 32 acres & improvements sd Bond to be void. Afsd Littleton TOWNSEND d: before such conveyance was made & by his will dtd 15 Feb 1791 bequeathed his entire estate to his 4 children to be equally divided & apptd Richard HAYS Esq his Exec. Betty MILLER for the sum of £23 paid by Richard HAYS hath sold the afsd 32 acres unto Richard HAYS for the proper use & benefit of Elizabeth TOWNSEND, William TOWNSEND, Littleton TOWNSEND & Comfort TOWNSEND, heirs of the afsd Littleton TOWNSEND, dec'd. Signed: Betty MILLER. Wit: ---- WILSON, W HARRISON. Betty MILLER appts Phillips KOLLOCK or William HARRISON her Attorney. Ack: 23 Nov 1791.

O-14:581. Deed of Sale. 16 Nov 1791. Samuel BUTLER of Sussex cnty, DE, silver smith, for the sum of £50 had sold unto Joshua COSTON of same, a parcel of land situate in Broadkiln Hundred laid off for 19 acres of land, it being part of a tract called His or Hern. Signed: Samuel BUTLER. Wit: H BATSON, Rhoads SHANKLAND.

O-14:582. Petition. Elizabeth SKIDMORE, Admin'x of the estate of Benton

COSTON, dec'd, late of Sussex cnty, DE, son of the Petitioner Elizabeth SCIDMORE states Benton COSTON bound himself in the sum of £600 to Joshua COSTON dtd 24 Jan 1784 for the conveyance of all that tract of land on which Benton COSTON dwelt in his lifetime & by his will devised to the afsd Benton COSTON all the other tract of land contiguous that Benton COSTON Sr d: seized of. Benton COSTON is since d: & no conveyance of afsd land was made. Petitioner requests an Order to execute such Deed in discharge of sd Bond. Signed: Elizabeth SKIDMORE. Granted 19 Nov 1791. Signed: Nath'l MITCHELL, Proth'y.

0-14:582. Deed of Sale. 23 Nov 1791. Elizabeth SKIDMORE, Admin'x of the estate of Benton COSTON Jr, late of Sussex cnty, DE of the one part & Joshua COSTON of same of the other part. Benton COSTON Jr 24 Jan 1785 was seized of a tract of land situate in Broadkiln Hundred, it being the land Benton COSTON Sr devised to afsd Benton COSTON Jr & also other tracts of land contiguous. 24 Jan 1784 Benton COSTON Jr by his Alienation Bond bound himself to Joshua COSTON in the penal sum of £?00 w/Condition sd Benton COSTON Jr should convey sufficient Deed to Joshua COSTON for the afsd lands. Benton COSTON Jr d: before making such conveyance. Elizabeth SKIDMORE, Admin'x of his estate obtained Order of the Court to make sd conveyance to discharge afsd Bond. Elizabeth SKIDMORE for the further sum of £5 confirms & conveys unto Joshua COSTON the afsd lands w/all improvements. Signed: Elizabeth SKIDMORE. Wit: K BATSON, Edwd POLK. Ack: 23 Nov 1791.

O-14:583. Deed of Sale. 07 Nov 1791. Ann WHITE, Admin'x of the estate of Robert WHITE late of Sussex cnty, DE, dec'd, to John WILTBANK Esq. There is a parcel of land in Lewes, Rehoboth Hundred, Sussex cnty, DE being part of a larger tract containing 87 & 1/4 acres formerly sold by Jacob WALKER to Jacob WHITE & devised by same to Robert WHITE. Robert WHITE by his will dtd 28 Jan 1789 directed sd parcel lying on SE side of the County Road from Lewes to Indian River adjoining the lands of Paul WHITE & John WILTBANK to be sold. Ann WHITE, Admin'x, for the sum of £14 2s 9p sold same to John WILTBANK the sd land & improvements containing 6 & 1/4 acres after the deduction for the road. Signed: Ann WHITE. Wit: Lewis HARGIVE, John HALL. Ack: 23 Nov 1791.

O-14:583. Deed of Sale. 23 Nov 1791. Ruth SHAVER, Admin'x of the estate of Levin SHAVER, late of Sussex cnty, DE, dec'd, to John SHAVER of same. Levin SHAVER d: seized of a parcel of land situate in Cedar Creek Hundred called Halls That Or Nothing & Administration of his estate was committed to afsd Ruth SHAVER who petitioned Orphans Ct the personal estate was insufficient to discharge his just debts & was granted an Order to sell at public sale as much of his real estate as was sufficient to pay the debts by virtue of which 04 Jul 1789 Ruth SHAVER, Admin'x, put to sale a part of the afsd tract bounded on the SE side of the County Road & SW side of the whole tract containing ?3 & 1/2 acres of land and same was purchased by John SHAVER for the sum of £70, he being the highest bidder. Signed: Ruth SHAVER. Wit: H BATSON, Edw'd POLK. Ack: 23 Nov 1791.

O-14:584. Petition. James READ, Admin of the estate of his father, James READ Sr, dec'd, of Sussex cnty, DE, sheweth the afsd James READ Sr on 23 Jan 1773 bound himself for £50 unto Thomas DUTTON of same, to convey unto sd Thomas DUTTON a sufficient special warrantee Deed to all his title to a tract of land situate in Broadkiln Hundred adjoining lands now in the possession of sd Thomas DUTTON, Edward STEPHENSON, Benjamin MIFFLIN, Foster DONAVAN w/all improvements containing 135 acres of land & sd Thomas DUTTON requests his Deed to the Condition afsd & James READ requests permission to comply. Signed: James READ. 24 Nov 1791. Petition granted. Rec 23 Nov 1791.

)-14:584. Deed of Sale. 24 Nov 1791. The late James READ Sr, of Sussex cnty, DE, dec'd, in his lifetime was seized of a tract of land situate in Broadkiln Hundred adjoining lands of Thomas DUTTON, Edward STEVENSON, Benjamin MIFFLIN & Foster DONAVAN containing 135 acres of land & 23 Jan 1773 by his Alienation Bond bound himself unto Thomas DUTTON in the penal sum of £50 w/Condition James READ Sr upon reasonable request would convey by sufficient Deed title to afsd land. James READ Jr, Admin of the estate of afsd James READ Sr, petitioned for & was granted an Order of Orphans Ct to makes such Deed in discharge of afsd Bond. James READ Jr for the sum of £50 paid by Thomas DUTTON to James READ Sr hath sold & does convey to sd Thomas DUTTON the afsd land which is bounded by lands of Jesse DUTTON & Foster DONAVAN containing 135 acres of land w/all improvements. Signed: James READ. Wit: A STANBURROUGH, Kendle BATSON. Ack: 23 Nov 1791.

O-14:585. Deed of Sale. 19 Mar 1790. Zachariah PETTIJON, yeoman, & Youfama his wife, of Sussex cnty, DE for the sum of £11 hath sold unto Joshua COSTON of same, yeoman, two parcels of land lying in Broadkiln Hundred, of sd parcels was surveyed for John SMITH & became the property of Benton COSTON, dec'd & sd Benton COSTON, dec'd, gave afsd tract of land unto his son, Benton COSTON, also dec'd; the other parcel was formerly by first mentioned Benton COSTON, dec'd, being in the Behuve swamp; w/all improvements to both sd parcels. Zachariah PETTIJON & Youfama his wife, appt Thomas Hercules KOLLOCK their Attorney. Signed: Zachariah PETTYJOHN, Youfamey PETTYJOHN (mark). Wit: William DICKERSON, Job PRIDE (mark). Youfama PETTIJOHN, wife of Zachariah, was examined separate from her husband acknowledged she became a party to same of her own free will. Signed: Peter F WRIGHT. Ack: 23 Nov 1791.

O-14:586. Bond. Solomon TOWNSEND Sr of Sussex cnty, DE, is firmly bound unto Louder TATMAN of same in the penal sum of £120 current money of PA to which payment I do hereby bind himself 09 Mar 1769. Condition of sd Obligation is such if sd TOWNSEND Sr make over to sd TATMAN the tract of land then above contract to be void, if he doth not the above sum remains in full force of law. Signed: Solomon TOWNSEND (mark). Wit: Reynsear WILLIAMS, Alex DRAPER Jr. Thomas LAWS to the hand writing of Alexander DRAPER.

O-14:586. Deed of Sale. 25 Jan 17??. Isaac SMITH of Lewes, Rehoboth Hundred, Sussex cnty, DE, yeoman & Mary his wife, to Meritta HAZZARD of Broadkiln Hundred, Sussex cnty, DE, spinster. There is a small parcel of land situate on the W side of Delaware Bay in White Oak Neck containing 100 acres being part of a larger tract of 400 acres called Swan Hill granted by Patent unto John STREET which sd STREET conveyed unto William CLARK & sd CLARK conveyed unto Thomas FISHER & sd FISHER by his last will & testament dtd 17 Nov 1713 devised to his son Joshua FISHER & sd FISHER by his Deed dtd 07 Jul 1744 conveyed same to Grisham MOTT & sd MOTT by his Deed dtd 06 Jul 1750 conveyed 100 acres & premises unto Solomon KNOX & sd KNOX w/Comfort his wife conveyed to the above Isaac SMITH by Deed of Sale dtd 27 Aug 1774 rec'd in Liber L, No 11, folio 433. Sd land bounded by land sold by Joshua FISHER to Gersham MOTT on the NW side, containing 100 acres. Isaac SMITH & Mary his wife for the sum of £225 lawful money of PA hath sold unto Meritte HAZZARD the afsd 100 acres of land & premises. Signed: Isaac SMITH, Mary SMITH. Wit: John WILTBANK, Hester BURTON, Dan DINGEE. 25 Jan 17?? Mary SMITH, wife of Isaac, was examined separate from her husband and declared she became a party to the w/in of her own free will. Signed: John WILTBANK.

O-14:588. Deed of Gift. Elizabeth PRETTYMAN of Sussex cnty DE, widow, for the sum of 5s & the natural affection which she bears to Agnes COFFIN, wife of Nehemiah COFFIN; Ebby PEPPER, wife of Eli PEPPER; & Hester WARREN hath granted unto sd Agnes COFFIN, Ebby PEPPER & Hester WARREN 8 heads of horned cattle, 3 beds & furniture, 1 horse, 12 head of sheep, £15 each in one place & £10 in another place, 7 hogs & 7 ? the personal estate in my possession, articles should be remaining after the death of the sd Elizabeth PRETTYMAN &

Joseph WHARTON, they to have the same during their natural lives. 10 Feb 1792. Signed: Elizabeth PRETTYMAN (mark). Wit: ---- RUPEL, Wm HARRIS.

O-14:588. Deed. 08 Feb 1792. Nehemiah REED of Sussex cnty, DE & Issabell his wife to Mary REED of same. 02 Dec 1752 William SHANKLAND sold to Joshua COLLINS a tract of land sd to contain 300 acres called Collins Folly by virtue of a warrant dtd 09 Jun 1743 which sd COLLINS 05 Feb 1753 conveyed to Isaac BRITTINGHAM of Worcester cnty, MD rec: Liber H, No 7, folio 347 which sd BRITTINGHAM 01 Apr 176? sold to Edward STEPHENSON who by Deed w/Margaret his wife dtd 07 May 1778 conveyed same to Nehemiah REED. For the sum of £145 Nehemiah REED & Isabella his wife, hath sold unto Mary REED all that parcel of land sd to be part of the afsd tract bounded by lands of Zachariah REED & Jesse DUTTON, John COLLINS, Broadkiln LANDING, Thomas DUTTON & James READ & Joshua COLLINS containing 100 acres of land w/all improvements. Signed: Nehemiah REED, Isabella REED (mark). Wit: Peter ROBINSON, J HAZZARD. 08 Feb 1792 Isabella REED, wife of Nehemiah, was examined separate from her husband & did declare she became a party to w/in Deed of her own free will. Signed: Peter ROBINSON. Ack: 08 Feb 1792 Nath'l MITCHELL, Proth'y.

O-14:589. Deed. 10 Jan 1792. Charles ROBINS of Sussex cnty, DE, carpenter, one of the surviving issue of Levi ROBBINS late of same, yeoman, dec'd, to Nathaniel HICKMAN of same, yeoman. Levi ROBBINS in his lifetime was seized of two parcels of land situate in Broadkiln Hundred & he d: Intestate leaving a widow, Phebe (late the wife of Nathaniel HICKMAN) & 6 children. The personal estate of Levi ROBBINS proving insufficient to discharge his sd debts an Order of the Orphans Ct was granted for the sale of 30 acres of land, part of one of the sd parcels of land & was sold accordingly to Hap HAZZARD where sd Hap now dwells. Afsd Phebe by Order of Orphans Ct had her 1/3 of Dower & in both tract of land laid off containing 60 acres of the one tract above & 42 acres of the other, being in the whole for her sd Dower 102 & 3/4 acres w/improvements to be held by sd Phoebe during her natural life. Eldest sons of afsd Levi ROBBINS d: Intestate & w/o issue. Charles ROBINS for the sum of £18 had sold unto Nathaniel HICKMAN his claim to the afsd 102 & 3/4 acres w/improvements. Charles ROBINS appts Jacob HAZARD or John WARRINGTON, yeoman, his Attorney. Signed: Charles ROBINS. Wit: Saml PAYNTOR Jr, Wm PAYNTER. Ack: 08 Jan 1792.

O-14:591. Deed of Sale. 01 Feb 1792. Job READ, Admin of the estate of Joshua TURNER late of Sussex cnty, DE & Admin of Mary TURNER former Admin of sd Joshua, now also dec'd, to Edmond READ of same. There is a parcel of land situate in Cedar Creek Hundred on the N side of Sowbridge Branch containing 100 acres which sd Joshua TURNER, dec'd, was seized of in his lifetime & being so seized 20 Dec 1751 by Alienation Bond bound himself to convey sd 100 acres unto Benjamin CLIFTON & sd CLIFTON by endorsement on sd Bond dtd Nov 1772 assigned sd Bond unto Levin HICKMAN & sd Levin HICKMAN by indorsement on sd Bond dtd 28 Dec 1791 assigned his interest in sd bond to the afsd Edmond READ. Joshua TURNER dying Intestate before making conveyance Job READ petitioned Ct of Comm Pleas to make Order empowering him to sign Deed of Conveyance to sd Edmond READ for sd 100 acres of land in discharge of the Bond afsd, same being duly approved & money for sd land being fully paid, sd Ct granted same. Job READ for the sum of £12 10s paid to Joshua TURNER in his lifetime, had sold unto Edmund READ the afsd 100 acres w/improvements. Job READ & Abigail REED his wife, hath sold unto Edmund READ the whole of the described parcels containing 22 acres. Signed: Job READ (mark), Abigail READ (mark). Wit: Lazarus TURNER, Elias JONES. Abigail REED, wife of Job REED, was examined separate from her husband, by me, one of the Justices of the Ct of Comm Pleas & did say she became a party to the same of her own free will. 08 Feb 1792. Peter ROBINSON. Ack: 08 Feb 1792.

O-14:592. Deed of Sale. Thomas LAWS, High Sheriff of Sussex cnty, DE to Joseph MELSON. There is a tract of land late situate in Somerset cnty, MD but now in Broad Creek Hundred, Sussex cnty, DE originally granted by Proprietary of MD Patent dtd 05 Apr 1710 unto Alexander ADAMS for 234 acres of land called ?? & sd ADAMS by his last will & testament conveyed sd tract unto his son Samuel ADAMS who by his last will & testament dtd 01 Sep 17?? conveyed sd tract unto his sons Samuel ADAMS & John Wittingham ADAMS jointly & by the decease of sd Samuel ADAMS became the property wholly of John Wittingham ADAMS & sd John Wittingham ADAMS by his Deed of Sale sold 33 acres unto Joseph CANNON Sr lying on the eastern most side of sd tract as by Patent recorded in the records of MD afsd & Deed of Sale among the records of Sussex cnty, DE. Joseph MELSON, gentleman, of Sussex cnty in 1700 by consideration of the Justices of the Sussex cnty Supreme Ct recovered a judgement against sd John Wittingham ADAMS for the sum of £100 w/costs. Sheriff took in execution of Order of sd Ct a parcel of land situate in Broad Creek Hundred containing 200 acres late the estate of sd John Wittingham ADAMS & exposed same to Public Sale & sold sd land & premises to Joseph MELSON of Broad Creek Hundred he being the highest bidder. The Sheriffalty of Thomas EVANS, Esq, expired before Deed for same was executed. Thomas LAWS, Sheriff of Sussex cnty, for the sum of 10s hath granted & conveyed unto sd Joseph MELSON 200 acres of land being the residue of sd 234 acres of land.

Signed: Thomas LAWS, Sheriff. Wit: John EVANS, Stephen STYER.

O-14:594. Bond. 20 Dec 1751. Joshua TURNER of Sussex cnty, DE is firmly bound unto Benjamin CLIFEN of same in the sum of £25 current money of PA to be paid unto sd CLIFEN. Condition of sd Bond is such that if Joshua TURNER convey sufficient Deed of Sale for a tract of land situate in Prime Hook Hundred containing 100 acres it being part of a tract that Joshua TURNER now lives on this Obligation to be void. Signed: Joshua TURNER (mark). Wit: John JOHNSON, Robert CLIFEN (mark). I hereby assigned my claim & interest of this Bond unto Levin HICKMAN for value received. 04 Mar 1776. Signed: Benjamin CLIFEN (mark). Wit: Isaac WUTTSON, Elias WATTSON. John S CAMPBELL, Verter DEPUTY, James BURTILL, Levin FARRINGTON. I hereby assign all my title & claim of the w/in Bond unto Edmund REED for value received. 28 Dec 1791. Signed: Levin HICKMAN. Wit: Joshua REED, Caleb NUTTER. Sylvester DEPUTY. Ack: 08 Feb 1792.

O-14:595. Petition. Job REED, Admin of the estate of Joshua TURNER, late of Sussex cnty, DE, dec'd for former Admin Mary TURNER, also now dec'd, to Ct of Comm Pleas. Joshua TURNER was seized of a tract of land situate in Cedar Creek Hundred & 20 Dec 1751 entered an Alienation Bond obliging himself to convey 100 acres of sd tract to Benjamin CLIFTON. Benjamin CLIFTON by his indorsement on sd Bond dtd Nov 1772 assigned sd Bond unto Levin HICKMAN. Sd HICKMAN by indorsement on sd Bond dtd 28 Dec 1791 assigned sd Bond unto Edmund READ & no conveyance had been made for sd 100 acres by Joshua TURNER or Mary TURNER former Admin now also dec'd. Consideration fee for sd Alienation Bond has been paid & recited endorsements have been proved in Ct & Rec. Petitioner requests an order empowering Petitioner to deliver Deed of Conveyance of sd 100 acres to afsd Edmund READ. Order so granted 08 Feb 1792. Signed: Job REED (mark).

O-14:595. Deed. 13 Dec 1791. William WELCH of Sussex cnty, DE, yeoman, to Thomas CAREY Sr, farmer. John WELCH late of Dorcester, MD, dec'd, was seized of a tract of land in Sussex cnty called John Welches Bear Scull, alias Welches Chance, situate in Cedar Creek Hundred being the lands John WELCH and Daniel FORMER lived but now where Joseph GRIFFITH & William WELCH live. John WELCH d: Intestate leaving no Issue & land descended to sons & dtrs of Daniel WELCH, brother of John WELCH to wit: John WELCH, Jacob WELCH, Daniel WELCH, Sarah WELCH now Sarah WHITE & Ebenezer WELCH. Afsd land still undivided amongst afsd heirs. Jacob WELCH, John WHITE & Sarah his wife,

& Ebenezer WELCH for the sum of £9 sold unto Thomas CARY 3/5 part of afsd land that was 3 shares of Jacob WELCH & John WHITE & Ebenezer WELCH. Sd CARY afterwards sold it to John WELCH & Daniel WELCH, brothers, land still undivided, & Daniel WELCH sold his part unto Joseph GRIFFITH & Thomas CARY did convey all right to land Daniel WELCH sold to sd GRIFFITH leaving the other 1/2 of the land which was 3/5 of 280 acres leaving the other half which belonged to John WELCH but sd John WELCH d: before other half was conveyed to him which was 1/5 & 1/2 of 3/5. William WELCH son to sd John WELCH, dec'd, was Admin of the estate of John WELCH. Thomas CARY was Bound to make over afsd land unto John WELCH & sd William WELCH as Admin & hath conveyed unto sd William WELCH being Admin of John WELCH. Signed: Thomas CARY. Wit: James P WILSON, John WELCH. Ack: 08 Feb 1792.

O-14:596. Deed of Sale. 26 Jul 1791. John WILLIAMS & Molly his wife for the sum of £80 hath sold unto Isaac FISHER all that parcel of land situate in Sussex cnty, DE but formerly in Worcester, MD containing 100 acres & improvements. Signed: John WILLIAMS (mark), Molley WILLIAMS (mark). Wit: William SWAIN, Richard DURHAM. Molly Williams, wife of John, was examined separate from her husband & did say she became a party to same of her own free will. 08 Feb 1792. Signed: Charles POLK.

O-14:597. Deed of Sale. 08 Feb 1792. William POLK of Sussex cnty, DE, house joyner, for the sum of £462 10s hath sold unto Trustin Laws POLK of same, planter, all that parcel of land on the E most side of division line made by Daniel POLK between Trustin Laws POLK & William POLK Jr that William POLK Esq gave him called Callaways, reference being made to will of William POLK Esq, dec'd, containing 377 acres, 7 acres of land excepted to be laid off by the side of County road beginning on the land of Joseph RICARDS, situate in North West Fork Hundred, & improvements. Signed: William POLK. Wit: Nath'l MITCHELL, Hales SPICER.

O-14:598. Deed of Sale. 08 Feb 1792. Charles ROBINS of Sussex cnty, DE, house carpenter to Stephen BALEY of same. There is a parcel of land situate in Broadkill Hundred which Levi ROBINS, father of Charles, d: Intestate seized of. Order of Orphans Ct divided sd land amongst the several heirs of sd Levi ROBINS which sd land was of sd Charles ROBINS as his share of his father's land bounded by Mary CORD's part & containing 45 acres. Charles ROBINS for the sum of £67 10s hath sold unto Stephen BALEY the afsd land & improvements. Signed: Charles B ROBINS. Wit: Joshua COSTON, Benjamin READY.

O-14:598. Deed Poll. Thomas LAWS Esq, High Sheriff of Sussex cnty, DE, to John McGEE. 25 Oct 1786 Writ issued by Ct of sd cnty directed Peter Fretwell WRIGHT, Esq, then High Sheriff of cnty afsd, to seize the real estate of John LITTLE late of Sussex cnty, dec'd in the hands of Nicholas LITTLE, Exec of sd John LITTLE, & cause to be made a debt of £2000 which Samuel FISHER, Exec of the estate of Joshua FISHER in same Ct had recovered also £29 ?s ?p which sd Thomas & Samuel Rowland FISHER were adjudged for costs & damages. 25 Oct 1790 Ct ordered sd Peter Fretwell WRIGHT, then High Sheriff, to execute Public Sale of sd lands & 08 Feb 1791 sold a parcel of land situate in Indian River Hundred bounded by land of John TOWNEY's, now HARRIS's fence & land of Anderson PARKER's heirs containing 68 acres which sd land was purchased by John McGEE for the sum of £39 he being the highest bidder. Sd Peter Fretwell WRIGHT was removed from office before any Deed was executed. Thomas LAWS, High Sheriff confirms unto John McGEE all the before mentioned parcel of land & improvements. Signed: Thomas LAWS, Sheriff. Wit: W HARRISON, Nath'l MITCHELL. Ack: 08 Feb 1792.

O-14:599. Deed. 08 Feb 1792. Gilliss SMITH & Marshall SMITH of Sussex cnty, DE to Woodman STOCKLEY, the elder, & George WALTON Jr of same. Cornelius STOCKLEY late of cnty afsd was seized of lands & tenements situate in Indian River Hundred but d: Intestate leaving 4 children: Mary who md: John BLACK, Woodman STOCKLEY, Cornelius STOCKLEY & Frances STOCKLEY who md: Marshall SMITH to which sd lands descended. Cornelius STOCKLEY obtained an Orphans Ct order to make partition of sd lands & sd Frances STOCKLEY that part of sd lands running along line of Cornelius STOCKLEY's part of sd lands until it intersects David HAZZARD's line laid out for 166 acres. Sd Frances then md: Marshall SMITH by whom she had one dtr, Frances SMITH, to whom sd land descended after the death of her father. Sd Frances d: Intestate, unmarried & w/o issue whereby sd lands were devised unto her brothers & sisters of the 1/2 blood: Gilliss SMITH, William Marshall SMITH, Polly & Judith SMITH. Sd Marshall SMITH relinquished his right & title to the afsd allotment of land whereupon w/the consent of his fthr, sd Marshall SMITH 20 Jan last obtained an Order of Orphans Ct to make partition of afsd allotment among the heirs of sd Frances SMITH the younger & evaluation of sd land was made & same was adjudged to Gillis SMITH he paying the others their respective share of the valuation. Gilliss SMITH & Marshall SMITH for the sum of £166 hath sold unto Woodman STOCKLEY & George WALTON all the afsd allotment containing 166 acres w/improvements. Signed: Marshall SMITH, Gilliss SMITH (mark). Wit: Isaac BENSON, George FRAME.

O-14:600. Deed of Release. Sarah HAVELO & Daniel HAVELO of Sussex cnty, DE, widow & son of Andrew HAVELO late of cnty afsd now dec'd for the sum of 5s and divers other good causes & because we are moving forever Quit Claim unto William ROBINS all their right & interest they might have to a parcel of land situate in Broad Kill Forest w/in the lines of a Patent granted Abraham INGRAM called Bare Garden containing about 25 acres, sd land is part of a tract conveyed by Deed of Sale from John CLOWES to Andrew HAVELO for the whole of Bare Garden being 50 acres. Signed: Sarah HEAVERLO, David HEAVERLO. Wit: William CORD, Lydia MILLARD.

O-14:601. Lease. 05 Feb 1792. Smith WINGATE of Sussex cnty, DE, yeoman for the sum of 5s sells unto Kendle BATSON of same, one tract of land called Long Acre & 87 acres of land called White Oak Swamp w/appurtenances for sd Kendle BATSON from day next unto the full end term of one whole year paying unto sd Smith WINGATE the yearly rent of one pepper corn at the expiration of sd term. Signed: Smith WINGATE, Kendle BATSON. Wit: W HARRISON. H WILSON. Ack: 08 Feb 1792.

O-14:601. Deed of Sale. 22 Jun 1790. Luke WATSON of Cedar Creek, Slaughter Neck Hundred, Sussex cnty, DE & Mary his wife for the sum of £20 hath sold unto Elizabeth LOTFLAND of same, spinster, all that parcel of land situate in Slaughter Neck in Cedar Creek, Slaughter Neck Hundred being part of a larger tract formerly belonging to Robert MILLER bounded on SE by land of Baker JOHNSON, on SW by lands of Branson LOFTLAND, on NW by lands of ---- & on NE by lands of Jacob HICKMAN containing 30 acres w/all improvements. Signed: Luke WATSON Jr, Mary WATSON. Wit: Avory DRAPER, Joseph STOCKLEY. 22 Jun 1790 Mary WATSON, wife of Luke, was examined separate from her husband & did declare she signed above Deed of Sale of her own free will. Signed: Charles POLK. Luke WATSON appts Sylvester WEBB his Attorney. 09 Jul 1791. Signed: Luke WATSON Jr. Ack: 09 Feb 1792.

O-14:601. Deed of Sale. Thomas LAWS Esq, High Sheriff of Sussex cnty, DE to Jane OWENS. Mary CLOWES & Isaac CLOWES, Exec's of the estate of John CLOWES Esq late of sd cnty, dec'd. obtained an Order for Thomas EVANS Esq, then High Sheriff of sd cnty, to attach James MAXWELL, late of cnty afsd, gentleman, sd Sheriff attached 1/3 part of a tract of land containing 130 acres of land situate in Nanticoke Hundred, then in the possession of William OWENS, now dec'd. Mary & Isaac CLOWES, Exec's afsd, obtained Judgement & Condemnation of the land & Ct ordered sd Sheriff to expose same to Public Sale. 10 Oct last past sd Sheriff sold same to Jane OWENS of cnty afsd, widow, for the sum of £8 1s, she being the highest bidder. Thomas EVANS was removed from Office of Sheriff before he executed Deed of Sale. Thomas LAWS Esq, High Sheriff, hath conveyed unto Jane OWENS for the sum of 5s and monies already paid, all that tract of land called Conclusion, formerly of James MAXWELL. Signed: Thomas LAWS, Sheriff. Wit: ---- RUSSELL, James POLLOCK. 10 Oct 1791 rec'd of Jane OWENS £8 1s for absolute purchase of lands w/in mentioned: Signed: Thomas EVANS, late Sheriff. Ack: 09 Feb 1792.

O-14:602. Deed. 10 Nov 1789. Levin ELLIS of Sussex cnty, DE to Isaac MOORE of same. Levin ELLIS by Deed of Sale dtd 08 Mar 1786 had due unto him 45 acres of land part of a tract originally surveyed to Thomas WALLER called Round Savannah situate n Somerset cnty, MD but no in Sussex cnty, DE described in two Deeds of Sale to John ---- ..... Thomas WALLER one dtd 08 Feb 1759 the other dtd May 1761 which remain on Somerset cnty records. Levin ELLIS for the sum of £187 10s hath sold unto Isaac MOORE all that part of sd tract called Round Savannah laid off for 45 acres w/all improvements. Levin ELLIS appts David HALL, Isaac COOPER, Capt William MOORE or W ??his Attorney. Signed: Levin ELLIS (mark). Wit: William MOORE, John DASHIELL, Thomas PHIPPEN. Ack: 09 Feb 1792.

O-14:604. Deed of Sale. 13 Sep 1791. George MITCHELL, Robert HOUSTON, William MOORE, John COLLINS & Rhoads SHANKLAND Esqs, of Sussex cnty, DE, Commissioners apptd by DE Assembly for removing Seat of Justice from Lewes to a more central part of sd cnty, to John WILLIS of same. Afsd Commissioners for the sum of £8 17s 6p hath sold unto John WILLIS all that parcel of land number 18 situate in George Town bounded by Strawberry Alley, Cherry Alley , lot number 17 & lot number 3 laid out for 7200 sq ft. Signed: George MITCHELL, Robt HOUSTON, John COLLINS, Rhoads SHANKLAND. Wit: Elisha DICKERSON, Kendle BATSON. Ack: 09 Feb 1792.

O-14:605. Deed of Sale. 11 Nov 1791. George MITCHELL, William MOORE, Robert HOUSTON, John COLLINS & Rhoads SHANKLAND, Esqs, of Sussex cnty, DE, Commissioners apptd by DE Assembly for removing the Seat of Justice from Lewes to a more central part of sd cnty to John WILLIS of same. Sd Commissioners for the sum of £1 1s hath sold unto John WILLIS a lot of ground, number 98, situate in George Town at the corner of Front St & Strawberry Alley, bounded by South Alley & lot number 97 containing 27 sq perches. Signed: George MITCHELL, Jno COLLINS. Wit: H HAZZARD, K BATSON. Rhoads SHANKLAND Ack: 09 Feb 1792.

O-14:606. Deed of Sale. 11 Nov 1791. George MITCHELL, William MOORE, Robert HOUSTON, John COLLINS & Rhoads SHANKLAND, Esqs, of Sussex cnty, DE, Commissioners apptd by DE Assembly for removing the Seat of Justice from Lewes to a more central part of sd cnty to John WILLIS of same. Sd Commissioners for the sum of £2 10s hath sold unto John WILLIS all that parcel of land, lot number 96, situate in George Town bounded by South Alley, Market St, lot number 95, containing 27 sq perches. Signed: George MITCHELL, John COLLINS, Rhoads SHANKLAND. Wit: G HAZZARD, K BATSON. Ack: 09 Feb 1792.

O-14:606. Deed of Sale. 08 Feb 1792. George MITCHELL, William MOORE, Robert HOUSTON, John COLLINS & Rhoads SHANKLAND, Esqs, of Sussex cnty, DE, Commissioners apptd by DE Assembly for removing the Seat of Justice from Lewes to a more central part of sd cnty to Joseph MELSON of same. Sd Commissioners for the sum of £?7 5s hath sold unto Joseph MELSON all those two lots of ground, numbers 37 & 38, situate in George Town bounded by number 35 on Front St, Strawberry Alley, lot number 36 & Love Lane containing 54 sq perches of land. Signed: Geo MITCHELL, Robt HOUSTON, Rhoads SHANKLAND. Wit: John RUSSEL, K BATSON. Ack: 09 Feb 1792. John W BATSON.

o-14:607. Deed of Sale. 09 Feb 1792. George MITCHELL, William MOORE, Robert HOUSTON, John COLLINS & Rhoads SHANKLAND, Esqs, of Sussex cnty, DE, Commissioners apptd by DE Assembly for removing the Seat of Justice from Lewes to a more central part of sd cnty to Abraham HARRIS Jr of same. Sd Commissioners for the sum of £17 5s hath sold unto Abraham HARRIS Jr a lott of ground, number 94, situate in George Town bounded by Bedford St, Strawberry Alley & the Square containing 20 sq perches. Sd Commissioners appt John W BATSON or Thomas LAWS their Attorney. Signed: Geo MITCHELL, Robt HOUSTON, Rhoads SHANKLAND. Wit: Joseph MELSON, John INGRAM. Ack: 09 Feb 1792.

O-14:608. Deed. 13 Oct 1791. John JONES (son of M Lamney) of Worcester cnty, MD for the sum of £310 current money of MD hath sold unto James FASSETT of same 1/2 or moiety of a tract of land called Pattey's Folly situate formerly in Worcester cnty, MD but Sussex cnty, DE near the head of the Sound formerly granted to Richard PATTY for 200 acres of land which sd 1/2 or moiety containing 100 acres by many mutations & conveyances became the estate of Solomon RODGERS by a conveyance from sd Solomon to M Lamney JONES father of sd John JONES who willed it to his son. John JONES appts John W

BATSON or William PERRY his Attorney. Signed: John JONES. Wit: Jacob ROGERS, Joseph ROGERS, Jesse GRAY. Ack: 09 Feb 1792.

O-14:608. Deed. 10 Nov 1791. Levin ELLIS of Sussex cnty, DE for the sum of £150 hath sold unto Isaac HITCH of same all that part of a parcel of land situate in cnty afsd called Rough Savannah which is bounded by John McDOWEL's land containing 5 acres w/all appurtenances. Levin ELLIS appts Charles MOORE, Robert JONES, Isaac COOPER or James ENGLISH his Attorney. Signed: Levin ELLIS (mark). Wit: John DASHULL, Levin BACAN, Samuel SCROGIN. Ack: 09 Feb 1792.

O-14:609. Deed. 06 Dec 1791. John CRAIG, black smith, Cornelius PAYNTER, ship carpenter, & Ruth his wife, for the sum of £9 11s 3p hath sold unto Benjamin RICKETS of same, yeoman, all that parcel of marsh formerly sold by Joseph & John PILES to Edward CRAIG for 8 1/2 acres from whom by regular descents & conveyances became the right of the afsd John CRAIG, Cornelius PAYNTER & Ruth his wife, beginning at a corner of Anderson PARKER's marsh, w/all appurtenances. John CRAIG, Cornelius PAYNTER & Ruth PAYNTER appt Phillips KOLLOCK or Nathaniel MITCHELL their Attorney. Signed: John CRAIG, Cornelius PAYNTER, Ruth PAYNTER. Wit: Jno WILTBANK, Joseph PRETTYMAN (mark). Ruth PAYNTER, wife of Cornelius, was examined separate from her husband & did assert she became a party to this Deed of her own free will. Signed: Jno WILTBANK. Ack: 09 Feb 1792.

O-14:610. Deed. 04 May 1791. James WALLER of Sussex cnty, DE by his two rights of land; one right a Deed of Sail dtd 17 June 1760, the other right being part of a Resurvey made from the afsd Deed & conveyed 1776 had dew unto him 143 acres, part of a tract originally surveyed for ________ called Round Savannah then situated in Somerset cnty, MD but now in Sussex cnty, DE described in 2 wrights of land, on a Deed of Sail from Isaac JONES to William WALLER dtd 04 Apr 1760 the other surveyed in Sussex cnty by afsd James WALLER in 1776 in manner afsd, one recorded in Somerset cnty & the other in Sussex cnty. James WALLER for the sum of £72 hath sold unto Isaac MOORE all that part of the tract of land called Round Savannah beginning at the corner of a plantation formerly of Levin ELLIS but now deeded to Isaac MOORE containing 143 acres of land w/all appurtenances. James WALLER appts David HALL, Isaac COOPER, Capt Wm MOORE or George BACON his Atty. Signed: James WALLER. Wit: William MOORE, John DASHULL, Thomas PHIPPENS. Ack: 09 Feb 1792.

O-14:611. Deed of Sale. 21 Jan 1792. Daniel POLK Esq & Margaret his wife of

Sussex cnty, DE to Willice CLARKSON of same, farmer. In consideration of a tract of land situate in cnty afsd lately the property of Willice CLARKSON which afsd tract of land afsd Willice CLARKSON hath conveyed unto sd Daniel POLK Esq, receipt whereof Daniel POLK & Margt his wife hereby acknowledge, hath granted & sold unto sd Willice CLARKSON a tract of land called Roses Hazzard situate in Sussex cnty in North West Fork Hundred whereon Isaac MELVIN now lives, containing 120 acres & premises. Daniel POLK & Marg't his wife appt John WHEELBANK or Phillips KOLLOCK their Attorney. Signed: Daniel POLK. Margaret N POLK. Wit: Henry SMITH, Charles POLK. Margaret Nutter POLK, wife of Daniel POLK, was examined private from her husband and did declare she became a party to w/in Deed of her own free will. Signed: Charles POLK. Ack: 09 Feb 1792.

O-14:612. Deed. 27 Jul 1791. John HANDY & Mary his wife, of Sussex cnty, DE for the sum of £60 hath sold unto Samuel HANDY of same, yeoman, all that part of a tract of land called Handy's Chance situate in North West Fork Hundred on the NW side of a line between Samuel HANDY & John HANDY bounded by a tract of land called Millers Mistake & John TENNENT's land; & also all that part of afsd tract on the NW side of afsd division line containing 16 12/ acres of and & all that part of Handys Chance that is so laid off contained 75 1/2 acres. John HANDY & Mary his wife appt William PERY or Rhoads SHANKLAND as their Attorney. Signed: John HANDY, Mary HANDY (mark). Wit: John TENENT, Benjamin WILLIAMS (mark). Mary HANDY, wife of John, was examined separate from her husband and acknowledged she did sign the Deed afsd of her own free will. Signed: Charles POLK. Ack: 09 Feb 1792.

O-14:613. Deed. 07 Dec 1791. Elijah HEARN of Worcester cnty, MD for the sum of £100 hath sold unto Zepheniah MADDUX of Sussex cnty, DE all that parcel of land called Kings Folley situate in Sussex cnty containing 100 acres. Elijah HEARN appts John W BATSON or Sam'l HALL his Attorney. Signed: Elijah HEARN. Wit: Sam
l HEARN, Hezekiah MADDUX. Ack: 09 Feb 1792.

O-14:614. Part of a Bond of Conveyance. Ebenezer CARY from Smith FRAME. Singular the premises thereunto belonging or in any wise appertaining by a good & sufficient Deed & General Warrantee to him Ebenezer CARY his heirs, assigns, forever then the above obligations to be null & void & of none effect to be & remain in full ____ in law. Signed: Smith FRAME. Wit: Simon KOLLOCK, Peter DOLBEE. Simon KOLLOCK 09 Feb 1792 did prove the execution of the w/in Bond (& also that he wrote same) in due form. Ack: 09 Feb 1792.

O-14:614. Deed of Sale. 05 Feb 1792. Robinson SAVAGE & Mary his wife of Sussex cnty, DE to Dennis MORRIS of same. There is a parcel of land situate in Broadkiln Hundred part of which is included w/in a survey made in pursuance of a Warrant granted to Andrew FULLERTON & part of sd tract is included w/in a Patent granted to John RICHARDSON containing in the whole 234 & 3/4 acres which sd 2 parcels of land sd Andrew FULLERTON by Deed of sale dtd 01 ? 1760 conveyed to Edmond STEVENSON & Sd Edward STEPHENSON by Deed dtd 23 ? 1779 conveyed sd 2 parcels to Robinson SAVAGE father of above Robinson SAVAGE & who be his will devised sd 2 parcels of land to his son, the above Robinson SAVAGE, which 2 parcels of land are bounded by lands formerly of Hugh STEPHENSON but now of Robert HOOD, containing & surveyed for 234 & 3/4 acres. Robinson SAVAGE & Mary his wife for the sum of £175 hath sold unto Dennis MORRIS the afsd 234 & 3/4 acres & appurtenances. Signed: Robinson SAVAGE, Mary SAVAGE (mark). Wit: William PERRY, Thos LAWS. Mary SAVAGE, wife of Robinson, was examined separate from her husband & did declare she signed the w/in Deed of her own free will. Signed: Peterson ROBINSON. Ack: 09 Feb 1792.

O-14:615. Bond. 04 Mar 1790. Pirnal NEWBOULD of Sussex cnty, DE is firmly bound unto Clouds Brought WARRING of same in the sum of £500 gold or silver this date. Condition of the Obligation is such that if Pirnal NEWBOULD conveys by lawful Deed of Sail unto Clouds Brougt WARRING ___ w/improvements whereon Mathew CREIGHTON lives all the land w/o the lines of Willey THOMAS, _______ LAVERTY lines & Mathew MERIN's line & line of survey of Thomas NEWBOULDT the quantity of acres not known to be of none effect. Signed: Purnel NEWBOLD. wit: Jas NEWBOLD, Thomas TRUITT. Ack: 09 Feb 1792.

O-14:615. Deed. 09 Dec 1791. Sarah NEWBOLD of Sussex cnty DE for divers causes & her thereunto moving in the sum of £12 hath sold unto Mathew MARINE of same the land that sd Sarah NEWBOLD by the death of her father, John NEWBOLD who d: Intestate sd parcel of land being 1/3 of a tract of land her father d: possessed of the other 2/3 having been sold unto Clouds Brougt WARRING by his brother Pirnal NEWBOLD sometime previous to Purnal NEWBOLD's death which piece of land situate in Nanticoke Hundred on the Main County Road that leads John Town to Broad Creek one part thereof (of the whole tract) lying on the NE side of sd road & the other part SW side of sd road it lying nearly 1/2 way between Charles POLK Esq's bridge & Winder CROCKETT's Mill adjoining land belong to Clouds ________ the heirs of Thomas LAVERTY, Mathew MARINE & lands formerly belonging to Thomas NEWBOLD now William NEWBOLD's which Thomas TRUITT now _______ w/all buildings & improvements contained in afsd land. Sarah NEWBOLD appoints Richard HAYES or ____ her Attorney. Signed: Sarah NEWBOLD. Wit: Robert SHANKLAND, Elisha EVANS. Ack: 09 Feb 1792.

O-14:616. Deed. 19 Mar 1790. David LINCH & Hannah his wife of Worcester cnty, MD, planter, for the sum of £50 hath sold unto Stephen STYER of Sussex cnty, DE all that parcel of land situate in Baltimore Hundred, Sussex cnty, called Linches Choice originally granted by the Proprietary of MD & Patent of sd rec: 1789 unto David LINCH containing 100 acres situate back in the woods from the seaboard side on the N side of a road from St Martins Bridge about 3 miles from sd bridge whereof sd David LINCH by the MD rec: will of Abraham LINCH became lawfully seized. David LINCH & Hannah his wife appt Daniel RODNEY or Samuel PAYNTER their Attorney. Signed: David LINCH, Hannah LINCH (mark). Wit: George ROBINSON (mark), Eli COLLINS (mark). Ack: 09 Feb 1792.

O-14:617. Deed. 21 Dec 1791. Robert WILLIAMS of Talbot cnty, MD for the sum of £357 7s 8p current money of DE hath sold unto John ROBINSON of Sussex cnty, DE all the following tracts or parts of tracts of land, to wit: part of a tract of land called Wales, part of a tract of land called Adam's Delight, part of a tract called Hog Quarter also part of a resurvey made on the two latter, containing 246 acres of land all which parts of tracts of land being in Sussex cnty, DE on the branches of Marshy Hope & on the main road that leads from Marshy Hope Bridge to Johns Town and hereby authorizes Jehu EVANS or Rhodes SHANKLAND as his Attorney. Signed: Robert WILLIAMS. Wit: James POLLOCK, Philip HUGHS. Ack: 10 Feb 1792.

O-14:618. Deed. 21 Dec 1791. Robert WILLIAMS of Talbot cnty, MD for the sum of £242 12s 3p current money of DE had sold unto Michael TODD of Caroline cnty afsd at those parts of tracts of land lying in Sussex cnty, De on the branches of Marshy Hope & main road the leadeth from Marshy Hope Bridge to John's Town called Wales & Hog Quarter & Adams Delight & also all part of a Resurvey made on the 2 latter that is bounded by a tract called Ramble, containing 160 acres of land. Robert WILLIAMS appts John EVANS or Rhodes SHANKLAND as his Attorney. Signed: Robert WILLIAMS. Wit: James POLLOCK, Phillip HUGHES. Ack: 10 Feb 1792.

O-14:619. Deed. 26 Jul 1791. Richard DURHAM of Sussex cnty, DE, carpenter, to John WILLIAMS of same, yeoman. There is a tract of land in Nanticoke Hundred in the forest, adjoining Richard DURHAM containing 154 acres of land about 60 acres of land being of same tract of land whereon sd Richard DURHAM now lives & the NW end of sd land was by Deed of Sale dtd 04 Sep 1738 from Joseph SHANKLAND conveyed to William ORR & the other part adjoining the 60 acres toward the NW containing about 90 acres is bounded on the SW by Green Branch & on the NE by Little ____ Branch was surveyed by virtue of Proprietor's Warrant to Wm ORR & by his Deed dtd 08 May 1751 the 2 afsd tracts to Jonathan DICKERSON & sd Jonathan DICKERSON by his Deed dtd 06 May 1772 for the consideration of £77 10s convey & make over the afsd 154 acres unto Richard DURHAM. Richard DURHAM for the sum of £100 hath sold the afsd 154 acres to John WILLIAMS. Signed: Richard DURHAM, Betty DURHAM (mark). Wit: William SWAIN, Isaac FISHER. Betsy DURHAM, wife of Richard, was examined separate from her husband & did declare she became a part to the same of her own free will. 08 Feb 1792. Signed: Nath'l MITCHELL, Proth'y.

O-14:620. Deed. 06 Mar 1792. Stephen COSTON, Somersit D COSTON & Mathias COSTON of Sussex cnty, DE for the sum of £45 hath sold unto Joshua COSTON of same, 2 tracts of land situate in Broadkiln Hundred, one of which sd tracts was taken up by John SMITH & the other by Benton COSTON the elder, dec'd which sd land adjoins the head of a branch called Green Branch binding on the Bee Hive Swamp it being the same tract which the afsd Benton COSTON the elder devised to his son Benton COSTON the younger who has since ______ to contain 250 acres of land w/all hereditements. Stephen COSTON, Somerset D COSTON & Mathias COSTON appt Abraham HARRIS Jr or Kendle _______ their Attorney. Signed: Stephen COSTON, Somerset D COSTON, Mathias COSTON. Wit: Thomas FISHER, Wm DICKERSON. Ack? 07 Mar 1792.

O-14:621. Manumission. Daniel RODNEY of Lewes in Sussex cnty, DE in consideration of 08 years service of my Negro woman slave called Lydia & for divers other good purposes do set free the afsd Lydia from her slavery after she has served me the term of 08 years or to the year 1800 whom I desire may be called Lydia RICHARD & granting unto the sd Lydia RICHARD after the time above mentioned a full & absolute clearance & discharge from her slavery afsd w/full liberty to make contracts & receive wages w/o giving unto me any account thereof & generally be untitled to same privileges & liberty as other free born Negroes are allowed. 12 Mar 1792. Signed: Dan'l RODNEY. Wit: Caleb RODNEY, Mary LEVICK.

O-14:621. 06 Mar 1792. Petition. Solomon TOWNSEND for leave of Ct to convey lands to Louder TATMAN. To the Ct of Comm Pleas for Sussex cnty, DE held at George Town. Jacob TOWNSEND Exec of the last will & testament of

Solomon TOWNSEND late of cnty afsd, dec'd. Solomon TOWNSEND 09 Mar 1769 by his written Obligation obligated himself, his heirs & Executors to make over unto Louder TATMAN of cnty afsd a parcel of land situate in the cnty afsd called Woolfs Den. Afsd Lowder TATMAN has since dec'd, Petitioner therefore as Exec of the afsd Solomon TOWNSEND requests Order to convey the afsd parcel of land to the heirs of Lowder TATMAN according to the sd Obligation. Signed: Jacob TOWNSEND. 06 Mar 1792 Ct so granted. Signed: Nath'l MITCHELL, Proth'y.

O-14:621. Deed. 06 Mar 1792. Solomon TOWNSEND of Sussex cnty, DE, planter, Exec of the estate of Solomon TOWNSEND late of cnty afsd to Nehemiah TATMAN, Joshua TATMAN & Sylvester TATMAN, yeomen, heirs of Lowder TATMAN, yeoman, of cnty afsd, dec'd. Solomon TOWNSEND in his lifetime 09 Mar 1769 Obligated himself to make over a Deed unto Lowder TATMAN one tract of land called Woolf Den situate in Nanticoke Hundred adjoining on the SE side of land belonging to Alexander ARGO Sr & on the E side of Alexander ARGO Jr's land & also Elizabeth TATMAN's land, also on the E side of WALTON'S Land per Deed dtd 06 Feb 17?? from James WALKER to afsd Solomon TOWNSEND which sd tract was granted to Robert ARGO containing 200 acres by Surveyer's Certificate. Jacob TOWNSEND petitioned Ct of Comm Pleas for leave to execute a Deed for afsd land agreeable to the Obligation which was granted. For the sum of £60 already paid to afsd Solomon TOWNSEND sd Jacob TOWNSEND doth make deed to Nehemiah, Joshua & Sylvester TATMAN the afsd 200 acres of land. Signed: Jacob TOWNSEND. Wit: G HAZZARD, Nath'l MITCHELL. Ack: 06 Mar 1792.

O-14:622. Deed of Sale. Thomas LAWS Esq Sheriff of Sussex cnty, DE to John WILTBANK Esq. There is a lott of land situate in Lewes, cnty afsd fronting Lewes Creek bounded on the SW side of Ships Carpenters St. Andrew HIGGINS late of same, pilot, dec'd about 1755 obtained consent of the Justices of sd cnty to build a dwelling house & make other improvements to sd lott on the Liberty so given him who then d: Intestate. The representatives of sd HIGGINS sold afsd lott & improvements to Thomas WILLIS, cordwainer, who lived thereon until his death & at the time of his death being indebted to Joseph BAILEY, pilot in a considerable sum. William HARRIS & Winefred his wife, late Winefred BAILEY, Admins of Joseph BAILEY, dec'd, by consideration of the Ct of Comm Pleas recovered Judgement for the debt against William DELANEY, Admin of afsd Thomas WILLIS. Thomas EVANS, then Sheriff, was ordered by sd Ct to expose afsd lott to Public Sale & same was purchased by Levin OAKEY for the sum of £15 he being the highest bidder. Levin OAKEY lived on same for 2 years

& built an addition to the dwelling & sundry other buildings & improvements & sold same to John WILTBANK Esq for the sum of £40. Thomas EVANS was removed from office of Sheriff his term having expired before making over a Deed for same. Thomas LAWS, High Sheriff of cnty afsd, hath conveyed Deed for same to John WILTBANK 07 mAR 1792. Signed: Thomas LAWS, Sheriff. Wit: ---- RUSSELL, James WILLEY. Ack: 07 Mar 1792.

O-14:623. Bond of Conveyance. William SALMON, blacksmith, & James SALMON, planter, of Worcester cnty, MD are firmly bound unto Benjamin SALMON of same in the sum of £120 current money of MD 23 Mar 1772. Condition of sd Obligation is such that if William & James SALMON convey a parcel of 100 cres of land, it being part of a tract called Seven Lotts situate in cnty & province afsd on the W side of Dry Branch to Benjamin SALMON sd Obligation to be void. Signed: Wm SALMON, James SALMON. Wit: John EVANS, Nehemiah EDGE. Ack: 08 Mar 1792.

O-14:624. Petition for Order. 05 Mar 1792. Solomon WILLEY, Exec of James SALMON, late of Sussex cnty, DE, dec'd. James SALMON in his lifetime was seized of a parcel of land situate near the road from Dagsbury to the head of Indian River in Dagsbury Hundred called Seven Lotts containing 100 acres which was granted by Patent dtd 28 May 1756 from the Proprietary of MD to William SALMON. William SALMON by Deed dtd 22 ?? 1767 sold afsd tract to James SALMON & sd James SALMON by Bond Obligatory dtd 23 Mar 1772 bound himself to Benjamin SALMON of Worcester cnty, MD, planter, in the sum of £120 to be paid to sd Benjamin SALMON w/Condition if James SALMON should convey title of sd land to Benjamin SALMON sd Bond to be void. Sd James SALMON by his last will & testament did constitute Solomon WILLEY Exec of his estate. Petitioner requests an Order to make good & sufficient Deed to afsd lands unto Benjamin SALMON. Signed: Solomon WILLEY. Read & granted 07 Mar 1792. Nath'l MITCHELL, Proth'y.

O-14:625. Deed Poll. Solomon WILLEY, Exec of James SALMON, yeoman, late of Worcester cnty, MD, dec'd, to Benjamin SALMON. James SALMON in his lifetime was seized of a tract of land called Seven Lotts granted 28 May 1756 unto William SALMON by Patent from the Proprietary of MD for 150 acres in Dagsbury Hundred on the cnty road leading from Dagsbury to the head of Indian River near Dry Branch. William SALMON by Deed of Sale dtd 22 Oct 1767 conveyed his right to afsd land to James SALMON. James SALMON by his Bond Obligatory dtd 03 Mar 1772 bound himself to Benjamin SALMON in the sum of £120 w/Condition if James SALMON made sufficient Deed unto Benjamin

SALMON for afsd land sd Bond to be void. James SALMON after making sd Bond & before making sufficient Deed died leaving Solomon WILLEY his sole Exec. Solomon WILLY petitioned & received an Order to make sufficient Deed for 100 acres to Benjamin SALMON to satisfy sd Bond. Solomon WILLEY doth convey unto Benjamin SALMOND the afsd 100 acres. Signed: Solomon WILLEY. Wit: John EVANS, John W BATSON. Ack: 07 Mar 1792.

O-14:626. Deed. 17 Feb 1792. David STOCKLEY of Sussex cnty, DE to John STOCKLEY of same, shipwright. There is a parcel of land situate in Indian River Hundred, Sussex cnty, DE which by sundry conveyances became the property of George and ?? by Deed of Sale dtd 03 Feb 1779 conveyed same to Prettyman STOCKLEY late of afsd cnty, dec'd, which sd parcel of land bounded by MARRINER's land, land of John STOCKLEY, Burton Mill Pond & Ivy Branch containing 170 acres. Prettyman STOCKLEY d: Intestate leaving 7 children: David, Nathaniel, Comfort, Jeremiah, Nancy, Betsy & Prettyman STOCKLEY to whom sd land descended. David STOCKLEY for the sum of £20 hath sold unto John STOCKLEY his right unto the land afsd being 1 equal 4th part thereof. David STOCKLEY appts Peter ROBINSON or Phillips KOLLOCK his Attorney. Signed: David STOCKLEY. Wit: John BENNETT, W HARRISON. Ack: 07 Mar 1792.

O-14:627. Deed. 08 Mar 1792. Joseph SALMON of Sussex cnty, DE, yeoman, to Smothers WATSON of same, yeoman. Joseph SALMON for the sum of £100 hath sold unto Smothers WATSON part of a parcel of land called Seven Lotts situate in Dagsbury Hundred, Sussex cnty, DE on the County Road leading from Dagsbury to the head of Indian River near Dry Branch being the E most part of sd tract bounded by land of Benjamin SALMON, laid out for 100 acres. Joseph SALMON doth sell unto Smothers WATSON one other small parcel of land called Barnets Choice laid out for 5 3/4 acres which sd Joseph SALMON holds by virtue of a Bond Obligatory from William SALMON to Solomon WILLEY dtd 19 Feb 1779 which sd 5 3/4 acres adjoins to Seven Lotts & also Joseph SALMON doth sell unto Smothers WATSON one other small parcel adjoining afsd land called Last Chance taken up by warrant under the Proprietary of PA containing 16 acres. Signed: Joseph SALMON. Wit: Solomon WILLEY, Robert BOYCE. Ack: 07 Mar 1792.

O-14:628. Deed. 07 Mar 1792. Stephen COSTON of Sussex cnty, DE to John MARTIN of same. Stephen COSTON for the sum of £80 hath sold unto John MARTIN a parcel of land situate in Broadkiln Hundred lying on the S side of Green Branch adjoining lands of Joshua COSTON on the E, a savannah on the SE called Warter Hole Savana, it being part of a larger tract called ??, containing 108 acres of land & improvements. Signed: Stephen COSTON. Wit: Edwd DAWSON, Kendle BATSON. Ack: 07 Mar 1792.

O-14:628. Deed. 06 Mar 1792. Benjamin SALMON, of Sussex cnty, DE, planter, to Joseph SALMON of same, yeoman. Benjamin SALMON for the sum of £50 hath sold unto Joseph SALMON (son of late James SALMON) one parcel of land being part of a tract called Seven Lotts situate in Dagsbury Hundred on the County Road from Dagsbury to the head of Indian River near Dry Branch, containing 50 acres. Signed: Benjamin SAMON. Wit: Solomon WILLEY, Robert BOYCE. Ack: 07 Mar 1792.

O-14:629. Deed. 16 Nov 1791. George MITCHELL, William MOORE, Robert HOUSTON, John COLLINS & Rhoads SHANKLAND, Commissioners by Act of DE General Assembly to removing the Seat of Justice of Sussex cnty, DE, to a more central part of sd cnty on behalf of sd cnty to Robert PRETTYMAN of cnty & state afsd. Afsd Commissioners for the sum of £3 15s hath sold to Robert PRETTYMAN 2 lots of ground number 99 & 91 hundred situate in George Town bounded by Front St, Pine Street & Strawberry Alley containing 2 lots or 54 sq perches. Sd Commissioners appt John W BATSON or Charles POLK their Attorney. Signed: George MITCHELL, Rob't HOUSTON, Rhoads SHANKLAND. Wit: Stephen COSTON, K BATSON, James P WILSON. Ack: 07 Mar 1792.

O-14:630. Deed. 02 Feb 1792. Solomon WILLEY of Sussex cnty, DE to Joseph SALMON of same. Solomon WILLEY for the sum of £5 hath sold unto Joseph SALMON all that parcel of land called Last Chance surveyed for 23 acres of land. Solomon WILLEY appts Thomas CONNOR his Atty. Signed: Solomon WILLEY. Wit: Phillip WINGATE, Scarburrough PEPPER. Ack: 07 Mar 1792.

O-14:631. Bond of Conveyance. 12 Mar 1788. John CARLISLE, yeoman, of Sussex cnty, DE is firmly bound unto William HINDS of same in the sum of £250. Condition of sd Bond is such that if John CARLISLE shall convey by sufficient Deed to a tract of land being in Cedar Creek Neck whereon sd John CARLISLE now dwells adjoining lands of Thomas ASBURN & afsd William HINDS the above Obligation shall be void. Signed: John C CARLISLE (mark). Wit: Isaac BEAUCHAMP, James JOHNSTON. Ack: 08 Mar 1792.

O-14:631. Petition. Elizabeth CARLISLE, Admin of the estate of John CARLISLE, late of Sussex cnty, DE, dec'd, to convey lands to William HINDS. John CARLISLE sold unto William HINDS a parcel of land situate in Cedar Creek Hundred containing 83 1/2 acres of land for the sum of £180 & became bound unto William HINDS in the sum of £250 to convey sufficient Deed for same to sd HINDS. John CARLISLE thereafter died w/o having executed sufficient Deed according to sd Bond. Petitioner requests Order to convey same as Obligated. Signed: Elizabeth CARLISLE (mark). Read & granted 08 Mar 1792. Nath'l MITCHELL, Proth'y.

O-14:632. Deed of Sale. Elizabeth CARLISLE, Admin of the estate of John CARLISLE, late of Sussex cnty, DE, dec'd, to William HINDS of same. There is a parcel of land situate in Cedar Creek Hundred, cnty afsd which by sundry conveyances became the property of Jonathan MANLOVE who conveyed same to William McCAY which sd William McCAY & Patience his wife by Deed dtd 21 Sep 1772 conveyed unto John CARLISLE which sd one moiety of afsd tract is butted by Robert TWILLEY's land, on the N side of Beaver Dam Branch, by OSBURN's land, a division line between John CARLISLE & Thomas OSBURN & William HINDS' land containing 83 1/2 acres of land. John CARLISLE by Bond Obligator dtd 05 Mar 1788 became bound unto William HINDS in the sum of £250 w/Condition John CARLISLE should convey sufficient Deed for sd land to William HINDS. John CARLISLE d: Intestate before executing sufficient Deed. Admin of his estate was granted to Elizabeth CARLISLE who petitioned Ct of Comm Pleas for order to convey same to discharge afsd Bond which petition was granted. Elizabeth CARLISLE hath granted unto sd William HINDS all that afsd parcel of land w/in mentioned. Signed: Elizabeth CARLISLE (mark). Wit: Thomas FISHER, Isaac BEAUCHAMP. Ack: 08 Mar 1792.

O-14:632. Deed of Sale. 28 Dec 1791. George RILEY & Thomas RILEY & Elizabeth his wife of Sussex cnty, DE for the sum of £120 hath sold unto John WILSON of same a parcel of land late the property of Thomas RILEY, fthr of the afsd George & Thomas RILEY situate in Slaughter Neck containing 102 acres of land, part of a larger tract called Codes Quarter bounded by lands of the heirs of Stephen TOWNSEND late of Sussex cnty, dec'd now in the possession of John YOUNG, lands now in the possession of John HAYES, lands of John Simpson CAMPBELL Esq, lands late the property of Purnell BENNETT dec'd now belonging to the heirs of sd BENNETT & in the possession of Sylvester WEBB, Beaver Dam Branch & lands of Joseph STOCKLEY. George RILEY & Thomas RILEY & Elizabeth his wife appt John W BATSON or Charles POLK their Attorney. Signed: George RILEY, Thomas RILEY, Elizabeth RILEY (mark). Wit: M DAVIS, Sarah DAVIS, Kendle BATSON. Elizabeth RILEY, wife of Thomas, was examined separate from her husband & did declare she became a party thereto of her own free will. Signed: Jno WILTBANK. Ack: 09 Mar 1792.

O-14:633. Bond. 07 Aug 1781. Jesse WINDSOR of Sussex cnty, DE is firmly bound unto Philip Thomas WINDSOR of same in the penal sum of £180. Condition of sd Obligation is such that if Jesse WINDSOR makes over sufficient Deed to a parcel of land called Mill Lot w/improvements to Philip Thomas WINDSOR sd Obligation shall be void. Signed: Jesse WINDSOR. Wit: Nancy ROBINSON (mark), Robt ROBINSON. Philip Thomas WINDSOR assigns unto John MARTIN all his right & title to w/in Bond 28 Jul 178?. Signed: Philip Thomas WINDSOR. Wit: Festis Hales SPICER, John SPICER. John MARTIN of Sussex cnty, DE, blacksmith, assigns unto John WILLIS all right & title to w/in Bond 17 Nov 1791. Signed: John MARTIN. Wit: John BENSON, John WILLIS Jr. Ack: 07 Mar 1792.

O-14:634. Return & Plot on Division of Robert WHITE's Lands. Robert WHITE, late of Sussex cnty, DE by his last will & testament dtd 08 Jan 1789 directed that William PERRY Esq, Hap HAZZARD & Jacob HAZZARD, gentlemen, to sell such of his land as needed to pay his just debts, lay off to his widow her dower therein U divide the residue of his lands to his 4 children equally; laying off to his 2 sons 20 acres each more than to his dtrs. 1. We have laid off to Ann WHITE, widow of dec'd, her full 1/3 part of all lands, 130 & 1/4 acres bounded by Land in the possession of Walter HUDSON, lands formerly possessed by John CRAIG, w/improvements & premises. 2. We surveyed & laid off to Robert Craig WHITE, minor son, 112 & 1/4 acres. 3. To Jacob WHITE, the other minor son, 113 acres. 4. To Esther, dtr of Testator 98 acres w/improvements. 5. To Elizabeth the younger dtr of the Testator 88 acres. 20 Mar 1792. Signed: William PERRY, Hap HAZZARD, Jacob HAZZARD.

Map of the lands of Robert WHITE & the divisions made by the above.

O-14:635. Deed of Sale. 30 Apr 1792. Henry NEILL of Sussex cnty, DE & Mary his wife, to Hannah NUNEZ of same. Hannah NUNEZ, Exec of the estate of Daniel NUNEZ, late of sd cnty, dec'd, 12 Mar 1791 petitioned Orphans Ct the personal estate of dec'd was not sufficient to pay his just debts. Ct granted Order to Hannah NUNEZ to expose to Public Sale a lot situate in Lewes adjoining the lots of John RODNEY & George PARKER, also a parcel of land situate in Lewes, Rehoboth Hundred containing 130 acres adjoining the lands of William ----, GILL's [D:104-5] heirs, Riece WOOLF and others. 13 Apr 1791 Hannah NUNEZ sold the above lands to Henry NEILL he being the highest bidder. 06 Aug 1791 Hannah NUNEZ by Indenture granted same to Henry NEILL. Henry NEILL & Mary his wife for the sum of £94 4s hath sold to Hannah all the afsd lot and parcel of land & premises. Signed: Henry NEILL, Mary NEILL. Wit: Magdalene PERRY,

Wm HARRISON. 30 Apr 1792 Mary NEILL, wife of Henry, was examined separate from her husband & did declare she became a party thereto of her own free will. Signed: Jno WILTBANK. Ack: 09 May 1792.

O-14:636. Deed of Sale. 12 Nov 1791. John KING late of Sussex cnty, DE but now of Washington cnty, PA, and Margaret KING his wife to Thomas STOCKLEY of the town & cnty of Washington in PA. Hugh KING of Sussex cnty, DE, dec'd, had a quantity of land on which the family did reside, sd land adjoining Mill Creek on the W & bounded by land late of CLOWES' heirs, Hap HAZZARD & others known as the property of the heirs of sd dec'd of which John KING is one & William PERRY, James MARTIN & Parker ROBINSON laid off part of sd tract as apptd by the widow now dec'd & William MATHEWS and John Seldron DORMAN did assist w/the division. John KING did purchase a lot of land containing 17 3/4 acres from William LEWKER & Catharine his wife of Sussex cnty. John KING & Margaret his wife for the sum of £105 hath sold unto Thomas STOCKLEY the afsd lands & premises. Signed: John KING, Margaret KING. Wit: Tho SCOTT, A FULTON. Margaret KING, wife of John, was examined apart from her husband & ack same of her own free will. Signed: Alex'r ADDISON. David REDICK, PA Proth'y certifies Alexander ADDISON. Signed: David REDICK. Thomas MIFFLIN, Govn'r of PA as to David REDIC & Alexander ADDISON. 14 May 1792. Signed: James TRIMBLE, Dept'y Sheriff.

O-14:637: Deed of Sale. 14 Mar 1792. Joshua COSTON of Broadkiln Hundred, Sussex cnty, DE yeoman, & Rebecca his wife to Peter Parker HARRIS of same, yeoman. There is a parcel of land situate in hundred & cnty afsd on S side of Green Branch on S side of a tract of land formerly in occupation of John MORRIS, bounded by Beehive Swamp, the line of John MORRIS' land & S side of the road leading to Somerset cnty, containing 216 acres of land which sd land was surveyed by virtue of a Commissioners Warrant from Jacob TAYLOR surveyor general dtd at Philadelphia 11d 4th m 1717 for John SMITH late of Sussex cnty, dec'd who being so seized thereof by his last will & testament devised same to Mary his wife who afterwards md: Andrew PENNIS which sd Andrew PENNIS & Mary his wife by Deed of Sale dtd 15 Dec 1727 sold to Andrew WHITE. Andrew WHITE by Deed of Sale dtd 08 Aug 1745 sold to Samuel SAMPLES who by Deed of Sale dtd 01 Feb 1747 sold same to Job INGRAM who by Deed of Sale dtd 01 May 1753 sold same to Benton COSTON. 29 Mar 1758 Benton COSTON obtained a Warrant from the Proprietary of PA & Cntys on DE for the purpose of securing a piece of vacant land contiguous to the afsd tract of land & 07 May 1759 had surveyed to him by William SHANKLAND deputy surveyor of Sussex cnty all that parcel of land in the line of Hugh VIRDIN's land, line of COSTON's land afsd containing 4 1/4 acres called Come

By Chance. Benton COSTON being so seized of the above two parcels of land d: having first made his last will & testament dtd 10 Jun 1777 where he devised unto his son Benton COSTON the younger the two afsd parcels w/all improvements. Benton COSTON the younger by his Bond Obligatory dtd 24 Jan 1784 bound himself unto Joshua COSTON in the sum of £600 w/condition sd Benton COSTON should make over a Deed to the afsd two parcels of land unto Joshua COSTON. Benton COSTON after making the Bond & before he made any Deed for same d: Intestate whereof Admin of his estate fell unto Elizabeth SKIDMAN late Elizabeth COSTON his mthr. Joshua COSTON procured the Execution of above Bond & obtained an Order empowered afsd Elizabeth SKIDMAN to execute sufficient Deed for the two afsd parcels of land which sd Elizabeth executed sd Deed 23 Nov 1791. Joshua COSTON for better securing the title of the 2 parcels of land procured from Stephen COSTON, Somerset Dickerson COSTON & Mathias COSTON, the surviving heirs of afsd Benton COSTON a Deed of Bargain & sale for all their right if any they had. Joshua COSTON by virtue of Deed of Sale dtd 16 Nov 1791 from Samuel BUTLER is seized of one other small parcel of land situate in the hundred & cnty afsd contiguous to the afsd 2 parcels, being part of a larger tract called This Or None containing 19 acres of land. Joshua COSTON & Rebecca his wife for the sum of £170 hath sold unto Peter Parker HARRIS the 3 afsd parcels of land containing in the whole 275 1/4 acres of land w/all improvements & premises. Joshua COSTON & Rebecca his wife appt Abraham HARRIS Jr, or Thomas MARVEL Jr, gentlemen, as their Attorney. Signed: Joshua COSTON, Rebecca COSTON (mark). Wit: Jno RUSSEL, Wm RUSSEL. Rebecca COSTON, wife of Joshua, was examined separate from her husband and acknowledged she became a party thereto of her own free will 04 Mar 1792. Signed: Jno WILTBANK. Ack: 09 May 1792.

O-14:640. Deed of Sale. 30 Apr 1792. Hannah NUNEZ of Sussex cnty, DE to George PARKER of same. There is a lot situate in Lewes on Second Street adjoining the lots of ground now in possession of John RODNEY on the NW side of a lot of ground devised by Samuel ?? to his dtr Hannah the wife of George PARKER containing in front on Second St 60 ft running W from Second St 200 ft which sd lot was by John RHOADS late of Sussex cnty, dec'd, by Deed of Sale dtd 08 May 1768 conveyed unto Daniel NUNEZ, late of Sussex cnty, dec'd. Daniel NUNEZ's last will & testament dtd 09 May 1772 apptd Hannah NUNEZ his sole Exec who petitioned Orphans Ct the personal estate was insufficient to discharge dec'd's just debts asking for an Order to make sale of so much of the real estate as sufficient to discharge sd debts which petition was granted. Thus Ordered Hannah NUNEZ sold the afsd lot of ground at Public Sale to Henry NEILL of the town of Lewes for the sum of £41 he being the highest bidder. Hannah NUNEZ by Deed of Sale dtd 03 Aug 1791 conveyed same unto sd

Henry NEILL which sd lot of ground Henry NEILL & his wife by Indenture granted unto sd Hannah NUNEZ. Hannah NUNEZ for the sum of £? 10s had sold unto George PARKER the above described lot of ground. Hannah NUNEZ appts Henry NEILL or Phillips KOLLOCK her Attorney. Signed: Hannah NUNEZ. Wit: Hap HAZZARD, Phillips KOLLOCK. Ack: 09 May 1792.

)-14:641. Deed of Sale. 01 Dec 1791. Isaac TURNER of Lewes, Sussex cnty, DE, house carpenter, to George PARKER of same, merchant. Cornelius KOLLOCK late of cnty afsd Esq dec'd was seized of a parcel of land commonly called a savannah situate in town & cnty afsd bounded on the NE by 3rd St, on the SE by South St, on the SW by 4th St and to the NW by the lot devised by Samuel PAYNTER late of sd cnty, dec'd, to his dtr, Hannah, now the wife of George PARKER. Cornelius KOLLOCK being so seized made his last will & testament devising part of his real & personal estate to certain persons named in the will & did devise all the rest of his real & personal estate to his 4 children: Royal KOLLOCK, Lemuel KOLLOCK, William KOLLOCK & Mary NEILL & his grnddtr Hester GRIFFITH now Hester LITTLE wife of Nicholas LITTLE of cnty afsd, to be equally divided between them of which the above mentioned lot is a part. Royal KOLLOCK, Lemuel KOLLOCK, by Royal KOLLOCK his Atty, William KOLLOCK & Leah his wife & afsd Nicholas LITTLE & Hester his wife by their Indenture dtd 01 Jan 1785 sold same unto Henry NEILL all their undivided & equal 4/5 part to sd described lot whereby the premises vested in sd Henry NEILL & Mary his wife 4 parts out of 5 in his own right and the other 1/5 to sd Henry & Mary his wife in right of the sd Mary & who by their Indenture dtd 07 Jun 1791 sold afsd lot w/improvements unto Isaac TURNER. Isaac TURNER by Indenture dtd 05 Nov 1791 sold one moiety or half part of afsd lot front 4th St unto Evan McHAM. Isaac TURNER for the sum of £22 10s hath sold unto George PARKER all that one moiety of the above lot w/all improvements. Signed: Isaac TURNER. Wit: Jno RUSSEL, D HALL.

O-14:642. Deed of Sale. 09 May 1792. John STUART of Broadkiln Hundred, Sussex cnty, DE, yeoman, & Sarah his wife, Jonathan STEWARD of same & Margaret his wife to John RUSSEL of Lewes, Sussex cnty, DE, scrivener. There is a parcel of land situate in the forest of Broadkiln Hundred containing 100 acres being part of a larger tract containing 250 acres originally granted by Proprietaries Warrant dtd at Philadelphia 09 Jun ??43 unto William BOUCHER who be Deed of Sale dtd 08 Sup 1762 sold the larger tract together w/other lands unto John CLOWES Jr who by his Deed of Sale dtd 24 Feb 1776 sold afsd 100 acres, part of the larger tract, to John STUART, sd parcel bounded by lands of John DAY. John

STUART & Sarah his wife, Jonathan STUART & Margaret his wife for the sum of £130 hath sold unto John RUSSEL the afsd 100 acres of land w/improvements. Signed: John STUART, Sarah STUART (mark), Jonathan STUART, Margaret STUART (mark). Wit: William COLEMAN, Job JEFFERSON. Sarah, the wife of John STUART & Margaret the wife of Jonathan STUART were examined separate from their husbands and did declare they became a party to the above of their own free will. Jno WILTBANK 09 May 1792.

O-14:643. Deed. 17 Mar 1792. Jesse GRIFFITH of Sussex cnty, DE, yeoman, & Mary his wife to the heirs of Absolam WILLEY of same, dec'd, represented by Margaret WILLEY widow & Admin of dec'd. Jesse GRIFFITH & Mary his wife became lawfully seized to a tract of land called Croney's Folley situate in Nanticoke Hundred & granted by Patent of the Proprietary of MD dtd 20 Dec 1741 unto James CRANEY for 194 acres of land then in Dorcester, now in Sussex cnty & being so seized sold sd land (except 20 acres & 47 perches) to Absolam WILLEY & obliged himself & his wife Mary to convey same to Absolam WILLEY for a valuable consideration. Jesse GRIFFITH & Mary his wife for the sum of £175 12s hath sold & conveyed all the above tract of land called Croney's Folley excepting 20 acres & 47 perches, adjoining the land of Joseph GRIFFITH Sr, containing 175 acres & 97 perches w/all improvements unto the heirs of sd Absolam WILLEY, to wit: James WILLEY, John WILLEY, Nancy WILLEY, Magdalane WILLEY, Absalom WILLEY, Boyde WILLEY, Margaret WILLEY, Mary WILLEY, Levin WILLEY & William Polk WILLEY, sons & dtrs of sd Absalom WILLEY dec'd, subject to the widow's dower to be laid off & remaining 2/3 to be divided among the heirs of sd dec'd by Order of Orphans Ct or otherwise disposed of. Jesse GRIFFITH & Mary his wife appt Joseph MILLER, William PERRY, John W BATSON, Phillips KOLLOCK or James WILSON their Attorney. Signed: Jesse GRIFFITH, Mary GRIFFITH. With: William JOHNSON, Charles POLK. 17 Mar 1792 Mary, wife of Jesse GRIFFITH, was examined separate from her husband & did declare she became a party to same of her own free will. Signed: Charles POLK. Ack: 09 May 1792.

O-14:644. Deed. 19 Oct 1790. Joshua WRIGHT of Cedar Creek Hundred, Sussex cnty, DE, yeoman & Priscilla his wife to Richard HAYS of same, yeoman. There is a tract of land situate in Cedar Creek Hundred bounded by land of William JOHNSON, Bowman's Branch & land of Henry HUDSON containing 152 acres & 13 sq perches being part of a larger tract surveyed for John CLIFTON which sd 152 acres & 31 perches of land by sundry transmutations become the property of William WILLEY who w/his wife on 18 Sep 1789 conveyed same unto Joshua WRIGHT by Deed rec'd in Libra O-14:152. Joshua WRIGHT & Priscilla for the sum of £200 10s hath sold unto

Richard HAYS the afsd 152 acres & 31 sq perches. Joshua WRIGHT & Priscilla his wife appt Thomas EVANS High Sheriff or William HARRISON of Lewes town their Attorney. Signed: Joshua WRIGHT (mark), Priscilla WRIGHT (mark). Wit: William JOHNSON Jr, Manlove HAYS. 21 Jan 1792 Priscilla WRIGHT, wife of Joshua, was examined separate from her husband and did declare she became a party to same of her own free will. Signed: Charles POLK. Ack: 09 May 1792.

O-14:645. Deed of Sale. 03 May 1792. Jacob JONES of Kent cnty, DE, gentleman to Hannah HOSSMAN of Sussex cnty, DE. Penelope Holt JONES late of Sussex afsd, dec'd, was seized of 2 lots of ground situate in the town of Lewes one of which sd lots is bounded by 2nd St, 3rd St, Mulberry St & lot belonging to Hester Nunez McHAM; & the other lot being contiguous to the former bound by 3rd St, 4th St, Mulberry St & one other lot belonging to Hester Nunez McHAM. Penelope Holt JONES d: seized of afsd 2 lots having made her last will & testament dtd 20 Jun 1786 devising unto Jacob JONES all her estate real & personal. Jacob JONES for the sum of £155 hath sold unto Hannah HOSSMAN the 2 afsd lots of land w/improvements. Jacob JONES appts Peter ROBINSON or Phillips KOLLOCK as his Attorney. Signed: Jacob JONES. Wit: Nicholas RIDGELEY, Rhoads SHANKLAND. Ack: 09 May 1792.

O-14:646. Release of Dower. Elizabeth SKIDMORRE of Broadkiln Hundred, Sussex cnty, DE, widow, (late Elizabeth COSTON formerly the widow & relict of Benton COSTON the elder, late of cnty afsd, yeoman, dec'd), for the sum of £100 & divers other good causes & Elizabeth SKIDMORE thereunto moving, hath sold unto Peter Parker HARRIS of same, yeoman, all her Right of Dower unto 2 tracts of land situate in Broadkiln Hundred on the S side of Green Branch containing 256 & 1/4 acres of land described in a Deed of Sale from Joshua COSTON & Rebecca his wife unto Peter Parker HARRIS dtd 14 Mar 1792 being same lands which Benton COSTTON, late husband of sd Elizabeth SKIDMORE by his last will & testament devised unto his son Benton COSTON the younger, now dec'd. Elizabeth SKIDMORE appts Abraham HARRIS Jr or Thomas MARVEL Jr, gentlemen, as her Attorney. Signed: Elizabeth SKIDMORE (mark). Wit: Abraham HARRIS, Jonathan DODD (mark). Ack: 09 May 1792.

O-14:647. Deed of Sale. 10 May 1792. George MITCHELL, William MOORE, Robert HOUSTON, John COLLINS & Rhoads SHANKLAND, Esqs, Commissioners apptd by Act of General Assembly of DE to Remove the Seat of Justice of Lewes in a more central part of Sussex cnty, to Peter Parker HARRIS of Sussex cnty. The Commissioners afsd for the sum of £20 2 s hath sold unto

Peter Parker HARRIS lot Number 5 situate in George Town bounded by Bedford St & Strawberry Alleyn & lot Number 6 containing 27 sq perches of land. Sd Commissioners appt John W BATSON or Thomas LAWS Esq their Attorney. Signed: George MITCHELL, Will MOORE, John COLLINS, Rhoads SHANKLAND. Wit: Jehu EVANS, Stephen STYER. Ack: 10 May 1792.

O-14:648. Deed. 04 Feb 1792. James BRATTEN & John MITCHELL of Broad Creek Hundred, Sussex cnty, DE & Cyrus MITCHELL of MD, Exec'rs of John MITCHELL, dec'd to Alexander SMITH. John MITCHELL late of Broad Creek Hundred, dec'd was seized amongst diverse other parcels of land, of a messuage & lott of in hundred afsd on the N side of Broad Creek & by his will dtd 20 Dec 1787 apptd sd James BRATTEN, John MITCHELL & Cyrus MITCHELL his Exec'rs. Sd Exec'rs petitioned Orphans Ct in 1791 that the personal estate was insufficient to discharge debts of the dec'd & requesting an Order to sell such lands as necessary to discharge the debts which request was granted. Sd Exec'rs in due course sold the afsd lot to Alexander SMITH for the sum of £200 he being the highest bidder. Signed: James BRATTEN, John MITCHELL, Cyrus MITCHELL. Wit: John POLK, Phillips SCROGIN. Ack: 10 May 1892.

O-14:648. Deed. James BRATTEN & John MITCHELL of Broad Creek Hundred, Sussex cnty, DE & Cyrus MITCHELL of Dorset cnty, MD, Exec'rs of John MITCHELL, dec'd to John MITCHELL late of Broad Creek Hundred, dec'd was seized in sundry tracts of land to wit 1201 acres of land being part of a larger tract called Sands butted in part by land of John CREIGHTON, dec'd & land devised by John MITCHELL to Anne WINSOR, containing 1201 acres exclusive of several lots heretofore sold & hereafter to be conveyed by James BRATTEN, John MITCHELL & Cyrus MITCHELL: to Isaac MOORE Number 2, to Robert EWART Number 3, to Jonathan CATHELL Number 5, to John BACON Number 6, to Alexander SMITH Number 7, to Robert HOUSTON Number 8 being the Meeting House Lot & also two lots, Number 1 & 4, heretofore sold to George MITCHELL & now hereby conveyed to George MITCHELL & George CORBIN w/a saw mill & all improvements; one other tract called Now or Never situate in Little Creek Hundred containing 4 !/2 acres; one other containing 63 acres w/grist mill; one other called Snow Hill containing 100 acres together w/the Resurvey adjoining containing 386 acres & 55 perches vis 117 acres and 120 perches patented & 268 acres & 95 perches vacancy w/allowance of 6%; also one other parcel of land being part of the before mentioned tract called The Indian Lands. John MITCHELL being so seized made his last will & testament dtd 09 Jan 1788 & appointed James BRATTEN, John & Cyrus MITCHELL Execs. Sd Execs petitioned Orphans Ct dec'd personal estate was not sufficient to discharges his just debts & Ct granted an order to sell dec'd's lands at Public Sale. Sd Exec's sold sd lands unto George MITCHELL & George CORBIN for the sum of £2980 5s they being the highest bidders. 19 Sep 1791. The Execs' of John MITCHELL's estate w/in mentioned empower John W BATSON or Thomas LAWS their Attorney. Signed: James BRATTEN, John MITCHELL, Cyrus MITCHELL. Wit: Nath'l MITCHELL, W T BELL. Ack: 10 May 1792.

O-14:650. Deed of Sale. 09 May 1792. Philip CONNAWAY of Sussex cnty, DE to Bagwell BALEY of same. Philip CONNEWAY for the sum of £100 hath sold unto Bagwell BALEY a tract of land situate in Nanticoke Hundred bound on the E by land of James DOUGLASS, on the W by lands of John SWAIN, on the N by lands of Philip CONNEWAY & on the S by lands of E SPICER containing 100 acres of land w/all improvements. Signed: Philip CONNEWAY. Wit: Kendle BATSON, Isaac WILSON. Ack: 09 May 1792.

O-14:651. Deed. 07 Jan 1792. Saxagotha LAWS of Sussex cnty, DE, farmer, to John ROBBERSON of same, farmer. Saxagotha LAWS for the sum of £172 10s hath sold until John ROBBERSON all that part of a tract called David Hope & The Prevention situate lying in North West Fork Hundred bounded by David POLKE's plantation, Marten's Hundred & land of Dutton LAWS w/all improvements. Saxagotha LAWS appts John WHEELBANK or Phillips KOLLOCK his Attorney. Signed: Saxagotha LAWS. Wit: Daniel POLK, Trustin L POLK. Ack: 09 May 1792.

O-14:652. Deed of Sale. 10 May 1792. John HICKMAN of Sussex cnty, DE, yeoman, from Thomas WILLSON & Peirce his wife of same. Thomas WILSON & Peirce his wife for the sum of £500 hath sold unto John HICKMAN part of a tract of 107 acres of land that ---- WILLSON sold & conveyed to William WILSON & sd William WILSON in his will bequeathed unto his 2 sons the sd Thomas WILSON the elder son & John WILLSON the younger to be equally divided lying in Cedar Creek Hundred bounded by CARPENTER's land & land of John YOUNG & Joshua BENNETT's land containing 53 1/2 acres. Signed: Thomas WILLSON, Peirce WILLSON (mark). Wit: William RICHARDS, Rhoads SHANKLAND. 10 May 1792 Peirce WILLSON, wife of Thomas, was examined separate from her husband and did declare she became a party thereunto of her own free will. Signed: Jno WILTBANK. Ack: 10 May 1792.

O-14:652. Deed of Sale. 10 May 1792. George PRETTYMAN of Sussex cnty, DE & Martha his wife, late Martha READ to Samuel LINGO of same. Alan READ was seized of a tract of land situate in Indian River Hundred bounded by land of sd LINGO containing 20 acres of land. Allen READ d: Intestate and Admin of his estate was granted unto Martha READ, present wife of George PRETTYMAN. Martha READ petitioned Orphans Ct the personal estate of Allen READ was not sufficient to discharge his just debts & Ct granted her an Order to sell at Public Sale as much real estate as to discharge sd debts excepting 80 acres secured by Bond to Alexander READ. Martha READ exposed afsd land to Public Sale and same was purchased by Samuel LINGO for the sum of £17, he being the highest bidder. Signed: George PRETTYMAN (mark), Martha PRETTYMAN (mark). Wit: Francis WRIGHT, Wm HARRISON. Ack: 11 May 1792.

O-14:653. Deed. 28 Feb 1792. Hester MOORE & Phillips KOLLOCK of Sussex cnty, DE, Exec's of the estate of Jacob KOLLOCK Esq, of same, dec'd to Samuel PAYNTER of same. Jacob KOLLOCK was seized of a parcel of land & marsh called the Marsh Pasture situate 1 mile SE of Lewes on the SW side of Lewes Creek containing 43 3/4 acres & 32 perches which in his will he desired to be sold. Exec's sole the afsd land & marsh at Public Sale to Samuel PAYNTER, he being the highest bidder. Hester MOORE & Phillips KOLLOCK for the sum of £76 18s 3p convey unto Samuel PAYNTER the afsd land. Signed: Hester MOORE, Phillips KOLLOCK. Wit: Saml PAYNTER Jr, John BENNETT, John CRAIG. Ack: 10 May 1792.

O-14:654. Deed of Sale. 29 Oct 1790. Ezekiel WILLIAMS & Elizabeth his wife of Sussex cnty, DE for £40 hath sold unto Thomas TAYLOR of same a parcel of land situate in Baltimore Hundred containing 16 & 1/2 acres. Signed: Ezekiel WILLIAMS, Elizabeth WILLIAMS (mark). Wit: Comfort DELANEY (mark), John EVANS. Elizabeth WILLIAMS, wife of Ezekiel, was examined separate from her husband & did declare she became a part thereunto of her own free will. Signed: Peter F WRIGHT. Ack: 10 May 1792.

O-14:655. Deed of Sale. 30 Jan 1792. John CRAIG of Sussex cnty, DE, blacksmith, the only surviving son of John CRAIG, dec'd, who d: Intestate, to Cornelius PAYNTER of same, shipwright who md: Ruthy CRAIG sister to sd John CRAIGE, party to this deed. George CHAMBERS of Sussex cnty be Deed dtd 06 May 1730 sold unto Robert CRAIGE of cnty afsd a parcel of land being part of 500 acres originally granted by Patent to Mitchell CHAMBERS called Orkney as appears in Liber F, No 5, f:377 & 378. Robert CRAIG by his will dtd 10 Jan 1763 bequeathed unto his son John CRAIGE all his land & plantation situate on the N side of the County Road whereon sd Robert CRAIGE lived w/all improvements & sd Robert CRAIGE also bequeathed unto his grndsn Robert CRAIGE son of his son Alexander CRAIGE then dec'd all the land sd Robert CRAIG on the S side of the County Road which sd

Robert CRAIGE purchased of George CHAMBERS & what Robert CRAIGE had taken up by Warrant of Resurvey being the land where the sd John CRAIGE then dwelt, till his afsd grndsn Robert arrived of age, he sd John CRAIGE taking off of sd plantation for sd Robert as well taking care of sd Testator while he lived. By Deaths the afsd land & improvements bequeathed to Robert CRAIGE afsd grndsn Robert fell to sd John CRAIGE who held the sd Plantation and d: Intestate leaving issue 2 children, Ruthy & John, the oldest son being dec'd. Petition was made to Orphans Ct to have afsd plantation equally divided among the heirs of sd John CRAIG dec'd & same was granted, there being 250 of land whereon the improvements been made, & 26 acres of land which was then in contention w/Anderson PARKER. Sd land was divided as follows: 27 Dec 1786 Cornelius PAYNTER who md: Ruth CRAIGE should have 92 acres clear of Dispute whereon the buildings had been erected, John CRAIGE should have 168 acres of land unimproved clear of Dispute. John CRAIGE for the sum of £130 hath sold unto Cornelius PAYNTER the afsd 168 acres of land together w/all improvements. Signed: John CRAIGE. Wit: Meretta PAYNTER, Samuel PAYNTER Jr. Ack: 10 May 1792.

O-14:656. Deed of Sale. 05 May 1792. John HICKMAN & Betsey his wife of Sussex cnty, DE for the sum of £220 hath sold unto Thomas WILSON of same, gentleman, all that tract of land situate in Cedar Creek Hundred whereas John SMITH by his will bequeathed afsd land & marsh unto his children: David, Nutter, John, Sarah, Mager, Comfort & Betsy & they dying w/o issue the same became subject to Division by Order of Ct dtd 17?7 & Thomas SMITH one of the surviving brothers by his Indenture dtd 1773 conveyed same to John HICKMAN. Sd land & marsh is situate in Slaughter Neck on the N side of Barnwells Branch & called Notters Farms bounded by Thomas PRISE's line & Indian Branch, land Nehemiah DAVIS & John SMITH, dec'd, by Obligation dtd 21 Aug 1751, containing 176 acres of land together w/all improvements. Signed: John HICKMAN, Betty HICKMAN (mark). Wit: William RICHARDS, Rhoads SHANKLAND. 10 May 1792 Betty HICKMAN, wife of John, was examined separate from her husband & did declare she signed the w/in Deed of her own free will. Signed: Jno WILTBANK. Ack: 11 May 1792.

O-14:657. 06 Jun 1791. Charles LANGRELL of city of New York for the sum of £54 hath sold unto John HANDY of Sussex cnty, DE, joyner, all that parcel of land called Charles Lott containing 108 acres of land in Fork Hundred beginning near Turkey Branch, joining a tract called Lucky Chance w/all improvements. Charles LANGRALL appts John WHEELBANK or Phillips KOLLOCK his Attorney. Signed: Charles LANGRALL. Wit: Henry SMITH, Humphriess BROWN. Ack: 10 May 1792.

O-14:658. Deed of Gift. Jean MULLINEX of Sussex cnty, DE for the natural love she hath unto Israel MULLINIX hath granted unto afsd Israel MULLINIX all that messuage & tenement known as Israel Fansey beginning on line with Joseph TRUITT's land containing 100 acres of land. Jean MULLINEX appts John POLK Sr her Attorney. Signed: Jean MULLINEX (mark) 07 May 1792. Wit: John POLK, Sarah POLK.

O-14:658. Deed of Sale. 30 Apr 1792. Joshua HALL of Lewes, Sussex cnty, DE, blacksmith, & Comfort his wife to Henry NEILL of same, merchant. There is a lott of ground situate in the town of Lewes containing 130 ft front & 100 ft back which Fenwick STRETCHER late of cnty afsd, dec'd, by Indenture dtd 12 Sep 1743 conveyed to Elizabeth GODDARD who after md: James BROOKS. James BROOKS & Elizabeth his wife by Deed of Mortgage dtd 18 Jan 1773 mortgaged the afsd lott to the GLO for the sum of £12. Trustees of the GLO caused Judgement entered at Ct of Comm Pleas whereupon Peter ROBINSON then High Sheriff of afsd cnty was ordered to seize sd lott & expose it to Public Sale & sd Sheriff sold same to John RODNEY Esq for the use of Joshua HALL for the sum of £20 he being the highest bidder. Joshua HALL & Comfort his wife for the sum of £7 10s hath sold unto Henry NEILL the lot afsd beginning at the corner of South St & King St then w/King St to that part of sd lott sold to John CRAIG then unto Adam HALL's land thence to South St being 86 ft in front and 100 ft back. Joshua HALL & Comfort his wife appt Phillips KOLLOCK or Nathaniel MITCHELL their Attorney. Signed: Joshua HALL, Comfort HALL. Wit: Jno WILTBANK. W HARRISON. 30 Apr 1792 Comfort HALL, wife of Joshua, was examined separate from her husband & did declare she became a party thereto of her own free will. Signed: Jno WILTBANK. Ack: 10 May 1792.

O-14:659. Deed of Sale. 09 May 1792. Luke BURTON of Sussex cnty, DE, & Elizabeth his wife for the sum of £90 hath sold unto Benjamin McILVAIN of same all that parcel of land situate in Indian River Hundred being at a corner of Loves Branch, corner of William ALLEN's land, Woodman STOCKLEY's line & the division line between lands of William BURTON & Benjamin McILVAIN, containing 64 1/2 acres being part of a tract of land called Rustic together w/all improvements. Signed: Luke BURTON, Betty BURTON. Wit: Jno WILTBANK, Nath'l MITCHELL. 09 May 1792 Elizabeth BURTON, wife of Luke, was examined separate from her husband & did declare she became a party thereto of her own free will. Jno WILTBANK. Ack: 09 May 1792.

O-14:660. Deed of Sale. 24 Apr 1792. Cornelius PAYNTER & Ruthy his wife, late Ruth CRAIGE, of Sussex cnty, DE, shipwright, to Samuel PAYNTER Jr of Broadkiln, Sussex cnty, merchant. James RUSSEL & Phebe his wife by Deed of Sale dtd 26 Jul 1749 conveyed unto John DAUGHERTY a tract of land & marsh situate on the S side of Broadkiln Creek containing 120 acres of land & marsh being part of one equal 3rd part of a larger tract formerly called Phillip SEYMEY's Land containing in the whole 420 acres which sd land by sundry conveyances & gifts became the proper of John SMITH, fthr of sd Phebe, & sd John SMITH in his will devised sd land to his 4 dtrs one of which being ---- the surviving 3 dtrs conformable to their fthr's will divided sd land & marsh between them & mutually released to each other. The afsd 120 acres of land is the residue of the one equal 3rd part being to Phebe, the wife of James RUSSELL & sd Phebe having heretofore conveyed part of her dividend vis 21 acres unto John CLOWES by Deed rec'd in Liber H, No 7, f 231. John DAUGHERTY by Deed of Sale dtd 07 Aug 1750 sold unto William HAZZARD of Worcester cnty, MD, blacksmith, for the sum of £115 the sd 120 acres of land & marsh & sd Deed rec'd in Liber H, No 7, f 273. William HAZZARD being so seized of afsd & other lands d: Intestate leaving issue six children (Ann is since dec'd) namely Molly, Arcada, Meretta, Anne, William & Sally (alias Sarah). Molly md: John CRAIG & had issue, Ruthy wife of Cornelius PAYNTER, & John CRAIG & after the death of John CRAIGE the elder she md: Isaac SMITH Esq & afterwards d: Intestate leaving issue by sd Isaac 3 children: Sally, Jacob & William SMITH. Whereas 2 of the children of sd William HAZZARD the elder d: Intestate & leaving no issue, William HAZZARD the younger & Sally HAZZARD. Whereupon the lands of William HAZZARD the elder by Order of Orphans Ct divided amongst the surviving 4 children of William HAZZARD the elder & their issue as will appear by the return of Rhodes SHANKLAND, John HOLLAND, Robert JONES, Reice WOOLF & Miers CLARKE who made division thereof. 40 acres of land & marsh, part of the afsd 120 acres purchased by William HAZZARD the elder ... John DAUGHERTY afsd were in the sd division of land laid off to the heirs of Molly or Mary SMITH late the wife of John CRAIG & late Molly HAZZARD & there being 5 children: Ruthy CRAIG now Ruthy PAYNTER), John CRAIG, Sally, Jacob and William SMITH being heirs of sd Molly hold the afsd 40 acres of land & marsh together in common. Petition was made by Cornelius PAYNTER & Ruth his wife to Orphans Ct for division of the sd 40 acres of land amongst the 5 heirs of sd Molly upon which sd Ct ordered Rhoads SHANKLAND, John HOLLAND, Reice WOOF, Robert JONES & Miers CLARKE to assess sd land for division & they returned the 40 acres would not admit of partition amongst the 5 heirs. Cornelius PAYNTER being the oldest heir by virtue of Ruthy his wife accepted the land at valuation & became payable to the other heirs. Cornelius PAYNTER & Ruthy his wife for the sum of £60 hath sold unto

Samuel PAYNTER Jr the afsd 40 acres of land & marsh being part of the sd William HAZZARD the elder's land which was allotted the heirs of the sd Molly bounded by Broadkiln Creek, land of John S DORMAN & land allotted to Samuel PAYNTER Sr & Meritta his wife containing 40 acres. Signed: Cornelius PAYNTER, Ruth PAYNTER. Wit: William PAYNTER, Mary OLIVER (mark). Ruthy PAYNTER, wife of Cornelius, was examined separate from her husband & did declare she became a party to same of her own free will. Signed: Jno WILTBANK. Ack: 10 May 1792.

O-14:662. Deed of Sale. 28 Feb 1792. Samuel PAYNTER of Sussex cnty, DE, house carpenter, & Amaritta his wife for the sum of £50 14s 2p silver monies hath sold unto Peter WHITE of Lewes, cnty afsd, merchant all that parcel of land & marsh w/improvements whereof Jacob ----LOCK dec'd was seized & which were sold & bidden off by Samuel PAYNTER at Public Vendue, he being the highest bidder. Sd lands & marsh situate near Lewes on the SW side of Lewes Town Creek bounded by lands of the heirs of ---- HALL dec'd & Pothook Creek containing 28 3/4 acres & 26 perches of land & marsh. Samuel PAYNTER appts Samuel PAYNTER Jr his Attorney. Signed: Samuel PAYNTER, Merritta PAYNTER. Wit: Jno WILTBANK, John CRAIG, Sam'l PAYNTER Jr. Amaritta PAYNTER, wife of Samuel, was examined separate from her husband & did acknowledge she became a party thereto of her own free will. Signed: Jno WILTBANK. Ack: 10 May 1792.

O-14:663. Deed of Sale. 12 Apr 1792. John RODNEY of Lewes Town, Sussex cnty, DE, merchant, to William HALL of same, blacksmith. There is a parcel of land near Lewes Town containing 20 acres called The Cedars which Jane CORD, widow of Joseph CORD, conveyed to John RODNEY by Indenture dtd 04 Dec 1787. John RODNEY for the sum of £10 hath sold unto William HALL 2 acres, part of afsd parcel of land to be laid off on the N end of sd lands being 8 perches wide & 41 perches long from Sandy Land to a pond of water, w/all improvements. John RODNEY appts Jno WILTTBANK, Thos McHAM Jr, Phillips KOLLOCK or David HALL his Attorney. Signed: Jno RODNEY, Wit: Jno WILTBANK, Thos McHAM. Ruth RODNEY, wife of John, was examined separate from her husband & acknowledged her voluntary consent to the sale of the afsd 2 acres of land. 30 Apr 1792. Signed: Ruth RODNEY. Before: Jno WILTBANK. Ack: 10 May 1792.

O-14:663. Deed. Philip KENSEY of Philadelphia, Atty & assignee of Hinchman TALLIMAN, late of NJ to Job INGRAM of Sussex cnty, DE, gentleman. A tract of land of 544 acres called What You Pleas surveyed for Thomas COLLIER 24 Feb 1759 situate in Sussex cnty, DE was by Patent dtd Oct 1756 granted to Ashier MOTT & he d: seized thereof having first granted the same in Mortgage to

Keziah & Joseph TALLMAN, Execs of James TALLMAN, dec'd, which Mortgage of the Premises was vested in sd Hinchman TALLMAN & he being indebted to sd Philip KINSEY by Instrument dtd 12 Mar 1772 assigned to sd Philip KENSEY w/full power to sell & convey the premises. Philip KENSEY for the sum of £20 hath sold to Job INGRAM all that afsd parcel of land called What You Please situate in Dagsbury Hundred on the W side of Shoals Branch containing 544 acres of land w/improvements. Philip KENSEY appts Simon KOLLOCK or David HALL as his Atty. 01 May 1792 Signed: Philip KENSEY. Wit: Benjamin BURTON, James BARNET. Ack: 10 May 1792.

O-14:664. Bond of Conveyance. George CONWELL & Unice his wife are firmly bound unto Richard ABOTT of Accomack cnty, VA in the just sum of £600 lawful money of DE 30 Jun 1782. There is a tract of land in DE bounded by lands of John BELL, Purnal JOB, & Job PARRIMORE containing 114 acres which sd tract was formerly the property of John SPENCER Esq, dec'd, who devised same unto Unice CONWELL as one of the children & heirs of sd John SPENCER which by her marriage w/George CONWELL became the property of sd George CONWELL. Condition of sd Obligation is such that if George CONWELL &/or Unice his wife make sufficient Deed containing a claws of General Warrantee for 100 aces of the tract afsd together w/improvements (sd George & Unice reserving the other 14 acres of the use of their Mill & contiguous to same) ... the thirds in sd tract of the late widow of sd John SPENCER dec'd as laid off to her by Order of former Ct ... at their expense, above Obligation to be void. Signed: George CONWELL, Eunice CONWELL. Wit: Benja MIFFLIN, John TAM. Ack: 10 May 1792.

O-14:664. Bond. William BURTONS of Worcester cnty, MD is firmly bound unto Sarah BURTON of same in the penal sum of £250 current money of MD. 20 Aug 1770. Condition of above Obligation is such that if William BURTON shall, after Sarah BURTON shall be 21 years old & after she doth relinquish all her right unto all her lands or estate she has in Sussex cnty, DE & make over all that parcel of land called Exchange & marsh adjoining this Obligation shell be void. Signed: William BURTON. Wit: William TUNNELL, Rhoda HALL (mark). Ack: 11 May 1792.

O-14:665. Deed of Release. Elisha RICKARDS of Sussex cnty, DE for the sum of 5s doth release unto William RICKARDS of same all that parcel of land situate in Indian River Hundred which my fthr Jones RICKARDS late of same cnty, dec'd, d: seized of & which by his last will & testament devised to my brthr William Rickards RICKARDS & if he dies w/o heirs then to me the sd Elisha RICKARDS together w/all improvements. 10 May 1792 Signed: Elisha RICKARDS (mark).

Wit: William PERRY, Clouds Brought WARREN. Ack: 11 May 1792.

O-14:665. Deed of Sale. 05 May 1792. Joshua HALL of Lewes, Sussex cnty, DE, blacksmith, & Comfort his wife for the sum of £3 hath sold unto John RUSSEL of same, scrivener, all that parcel of land situate on the S side of the town of Lewes beginning at the N corner of a lot belonging to John RUSSEL that Ruth RUSSEL now dwells, then Fourth St, a corner of part of the same lot now sold to Henry NEILL, the line of land belonging to John HALL late of cnty afsd, blacksmith, dec'd, containing 5280 sq feet of ground w/improvements. Joshua HALL & Comfort his wife appt Phillips KOLLOCK or Thomas LAWS as their Attorney. Signed: Joshua HALL, Comfort HALL. Wit: Jno WILTBANK, Wm RUSSEL. Comfort HALL, wife of Joshua, was examined separate from her husband & did acknowledge she became a party to the w/in Deed of her own free will. 05 May 1792. Jno WILTBANK. Ack: 09 May 1792.

O-14:666. Deed of Sale. 18 Jan 1792. Burton WAPLES of Indian River Hundred, Sussex cnty, DE & Comfort his wife, Anderson PARKER of Lewes, Rehoboth Hundred, cnty afsd; & John WILTBANK of Lewes, cnty afsd & Mary his wife to Peter ROBINSON of Indian River Hundred afsd. Thomas EVANS, late of Angola & Indian River Hundred, dec'd, by virtue of an Indenture of Sale from John POTTER dtd 27 Jun 1762 rec: Liber I, No 9, f?? was seized of a parcel of land situate in Angola Neck in Indian River Hundred binding upon Lewes Creek containing 424 acres of land & marsh. He afterwards d: Intestate leaving Susannah his widow & 5 children: John his eldest son, Angelita, Thomas, Elizabeth & Isaiah EVANS to whom the afsd lands descended. Angelita md: John Tunnell GARRETT & by their Deed dtd 01 Dec 1769 released their claim unto John EVANS whereof John EVANS became untitled to 1 moiety or 1/2 of the tract of land & premises afsd. John EVANS obtained an Order of Orphans Ct apptg 5 freeholders to make partition among the heirs, who laid off unto Susannah the widow all that part .... during the term of her natural life. Sd freeholders returned to Ct that the remainder would not admit of division among the heirs w/o spoiling the whole. John EVANS obtained an order of sd Ct apptg 3 freeholders to estimate the value of the 2/3 parts of sd estate. John EVANS eldest son of the Intestate accepted th sd 2/3 parts of the land & premises at the Valuation & being so seized of the remaining 2/3 first sold unto Thomas & Peter ROBINSON, merchants, 245 acres of land & marsh situate on the SE sid of sd tract by Deed dtd 01 Dec 1769. & conveyed the residue w/all his right in Reversion to the 1 moiety or the afsd widow's thirds after her dec & also to the 1 moiety or equal q/w of all other lands that might be Recovered as part of the Intestate's estate. unto Benjamin BURTON, Thomas ROBINSON, Burton WAPLES, Reice WOOLF, Anderson PARKER, John WILTBANK, Jacob

KOLLOCK Jr, Wrixsom LAWS, Parker ROBINSON & David NUNEZ of Sussex cnty, gentlemen, as joint tenants to be used as a Glebe for the Churches of St Peters at Lewes & St Georges at Indian River. The Congregations of afsd Churches resolved it would be most advantageous that the Glebe should be sold & same was exposed to Public Sale Sat, 27 Aug 1791 on which day sd lands were sold to Peter ROBINSON for the sum of £200 & also subject to a Rent of £9 per annum unto Susannah DAVIS, late Susannah EVANS, late the widow of afsd Thomas EVANS, dec'd during her natural life agreeable to a Lease taken for her thirds, sd Peter ROBINSON being the highest bidder. This Indenture witnesseth sd Burton WAPLES & Comfort his wife, Anderson PARKER & John WILTBANK & Mary his wife being the Surviving grantees from the afsd John EVANS for the sum of £200 & payment of the annuity of £9 per annum hath sold unto Peter ROBINSON all that part of the lands & premises afsd containing 190 acres of land & marsh. Signed: Burton WAPLES, Comfort WAPLES, Anderson PARKER, Jno WILTBANK, Mary WILTBANK. Wit: Jno RUSSEL, Wm RUSSEL. Comfort WAPLES, wife of Burton, & Mary WILTBANK, wife of John, were examined separate from their husbands & did declare they became parties thereto of their own free will. Ack: 11 May 1792.

O-14:668. Deed of Sale. 21 Jun 1792. Richard DURHAM, Admin of the estate of George DURHAM late of Sussex cnty, DE & Rachel STEWART of same to William PEERY. There is a parcel of land situate in Broadkiln Hundred containing 85 1/2 acres of land being part of a larger tract called Mill Plantation, which sd 85 1/2 acres was seized of in his lifetime & sd George DURHAM d: Intestate & his personal estate insufficient to discharge his just debts Richard DURHAM petitioned Orphans Ct for Order to sell as much of the land as would discharge sd debts which was granted whereupon Richard DURHAM put sd land to Public Sale & sold it unto William PEERY for the sum of 25s 6p per acre, he being the highest bidder. Whereas there is one other parcel of land situate in hundred & cnty afsd adjoining the afsd 85 1/2 acres & being part of the afsd larger tract called Mill Plantation containing 50 acres which sundry conveyances became the right of Rachel STEWARD which sd 2 parcels of land being now reduced into one tract are included w/in the following boundaries: beginning on the E side of Hollands Mill Pond along the line of William PEERY containing 140 acres. This Indenture witnesseth sd Richard DURHAM, Admin, for the sum of £109 & sd Rachel STEWART for the sum of £5 hereby hath sold unto William PEERY the afsd lands. Signed: Richard DURHAM, Rachel STEWART. Wit: Thomas COULTER, Phillips KOLLOCK. Ack: 20 Jun 1792.

O-14:669. Deed of Sale. Abraham GUM late of Sussex cnty, DE possessed a tract of land situate in Broadkiln Hundred containing 50 acres it being part of a larger tract late the property of Abraham GUM, dec'd, father to the above sd Abraham GUM as laid off by 5 Freeholders apptd by Orphans Ct. John HAZZARD, Admin of Jacob GUM, dec'd, obtained a writ of Attachment from Ct of Comm Pleat at George Town against Abraham GUM whereupon the Justices of sd Ct made an Order for the Sheriff of the cnty to seize & expose to sale the above mentioned land & convey same to the buyer. Sd Sheriff sold the afsd tract unto John HAZZARD for the sum of £23 6p he being the highest bidder. Thomas LAWS, High Sheriff of Sussex cnty, DE, do sell unto afsd John HAZZARD all the afsd tract of land bounded by land of Hannah GUM & John BERGMENT's land containing 50 acres w/improvements. Signed: Thomas LAWS, Sheriff. Wit: Kendle BATSON, Joseph STOCKLEY. Ack: 20 Jun 1792.

O-14:670. Deed of Sale. 13 Jun 1792. Thomas LAWS, Esq, High Sheriff of Sussex cnty, DE to Andrew SIMPLER of same. There is a tract of land situate in Broadkiln Hundred containing 114 acres being part of a larger which sd 114 acres of land stands on the S side of a beaver dam. Whereas also there is a parcel of marsh being in hundred & cnty afsd containing 25 acres being part of a larger tract of land & marsh which was granted to John HALL which sd 25 acres bounded by Samuel HEAVELO's line. Nathan BEDFORD late of afsd cnty, dec'd, was seized of sd 2 parcels of land & being indebted to Leven MILBY of cnty afsd the sd Leven obtained a judgment against sd Nathaniel BRADFORD in Ct of Comm Pleas by which sd Ct Order Peter F WRIGHT then High Sheriff returned rents & profits from sd land was not sufficient to satisfy sd Judgement w/in 7 years whereupon Ct ordered sd 2 parcels of land to be sold at Public Sale. Peter F WRIGHT sold sd lands & marsh 01 May 1786 for the sum of £132 unto Andrew SIMPLER he being the highest bidder. Thomas LAWS, present High Sheriff of Sussex cnty for the sum of £132 paid to sd Peter F WRIGHT by sd Andrew SIMPLER doth convey unto sd SIMPLER afsd 2 parcels of land & marsh w/improvements. Signed: Thos LAWS, Sheriff. Wit: James POLLOCK, Kendle BATSON. Ack: 21 Jun 1792.

O-14:671. Deed of Sale. 29 May 1792. Hester MOORE of Sussex cnty, DE, widow, gentlewoman, for the sum of £12 10s had sold unto William HALL of same, blacksmith, all that piece of marsh containing 4 acres situate on Lewes Creek being part of an island called Kollock's Island formerly the property of Jacob KOLLOCK dec'd & sold pursuant to his will at Public Sale & purchased by Hap HAZZARD who conveyed it back to sd Hester MOORE. Sd land bounded by Copes Chimney. Hester MOORE appts David HALL Esq her Attorney. Signed: Hester MOORE. Wit: James P WILSON, W HARRISON.

O-14:672. Deed of Sale. Edmund ANDROSS Esq, late Lt Govn'r of Province of NY by Patent granted unto James WILLS late of Sussex cnty, DE a parcel of land situate by a beaver dam out of Loves Creek in Rehoboth Hundred called Sun Dials containing 400 acres which sd parcel of land by sundry conveyances became the property of William ORR late of cnty afsd, dec'd, by whose death sd parcel of land descended to his only son William ORR which sd William ORR sold same unto James HOLLAND & Gilbert PARKER about 120 acres part of the afsd 400 acres of land. William ORR by Deed of Sale dtd 08 Aug 1754 sold unto Jacob KOLLOCK, Esq all the residue of the afsd 400 acres which sd land is on Loves Creek near the Mill Tail bounded by Gilbetcher PARKER's land, SW side of Daniel FLINGS's swamp, the valley of 46 acres formerly belonging to James HOLLAND, dec'd, containing 289 acres. Jacob KOLLOCK made his last will & testament dtd 14 Jun 1771 & empowered his Execs to make sale of all his real estate w/in Sussex cnty by virtue of which Phillips KOLLOCK & Hester MOORE 15 May 1792 expose to Public Sale the afsd 289 acres, also all the Warrant land thereunto adjoining surveyed by Warrant dtd Philadelphia 06 May 1715 granted to Edward PARKER, guardian of sd William ORR, surveyed by William SHANKLAND containing 150 acres , all of which lands w/improvements were purchased by Woolsey BURTON & David BURTON for the sum of £1031, they being the highest bidders. Signed: Phillips KOLLOCK, Hester MOORE. Wit: D HALL, Woodman STOCKLEY Jr.

O-14:673. Deed of Sale. 23 May 1792. Mary PILES of Philadelphia, PA, widow, for the sum of £12 hath sold unto Adam HALL of Lewes, Sussex cnty, DE, taylor. all that parcel of land situate on the S side of Lewes binding upon SE side of South St being part of a larger piece whereof John HALL, late of cnty afsd d: Intestate sized of containing 2 acres lying between the part allotted to heirs of Lydia HARMONSON, late Lydia HALL, one of the dtrs of afsd John HALL & the line of a parcel of land of Simon EDWARDS, w/all improvements. Signed: Mary PILES. Wit: Daniel RODNEY, George PARKER. Ack: 20 Jun 1792.

O-14:674. Bill of Sale. Elizabeth HOLLAND of Sussex cnty, DE, seamster, for the sum of £50 hath sold unto John JACOBS of same one negro woman named Hagra together w/3 small children named: Lelah, Grace & Abigail together w/all their bedding & clothes this 30 Jul 1792. Signed: Elizabeth HOLLAND. Wit: Britingham HILL (mark).

O-14:674. Deposition. Oct 1791. William STEPHENSON for Peter JUMP's being heir to John JUMP. Lincoln cnty, KY: William STEPHENSON came into Ct & made oath that Peter JUMP is heir at large to John JUMP, dec'd, late of

Sussex cnty, DE which is ordered to be certified. Signed: John REED. Lincoln cnty, KY: I do hereby certify that the above is a true transcript from the records in my office. In testimony whereof I have hereunto set my hand and affixed the seal of the sd cnty this 20 Oct 1791. Signed: Willis GREEN.

O-14:674. Power of Attorney. I, Peter JUMP of Lincoln cnty, KY for divers good cause appt Robert BROWN of same place my Attorney to sue for, collect & received every sum of money which are due to me as heir to John JUMP late of Sussex cnty, DE, dec'd, or in any of the United States. 12 Oct 1791 Signed: Peter JUMP (mark).

- Fini -

INDEX

TRACTS OF LAND (continued)

www.ingramcontent.com/pod-product-compliance
Lightning Source LLC
Chambersburg PA
CBHW061717270326
41928CB00011B/2010

* 9 7 8 1 6 8 0 3 4 6 0 1 5 *